THE LETTERS OF
John Keats

1814–1821

VOLUME ONE

1814–1818

HAYDON'S LIFE-MASK OF KEATS

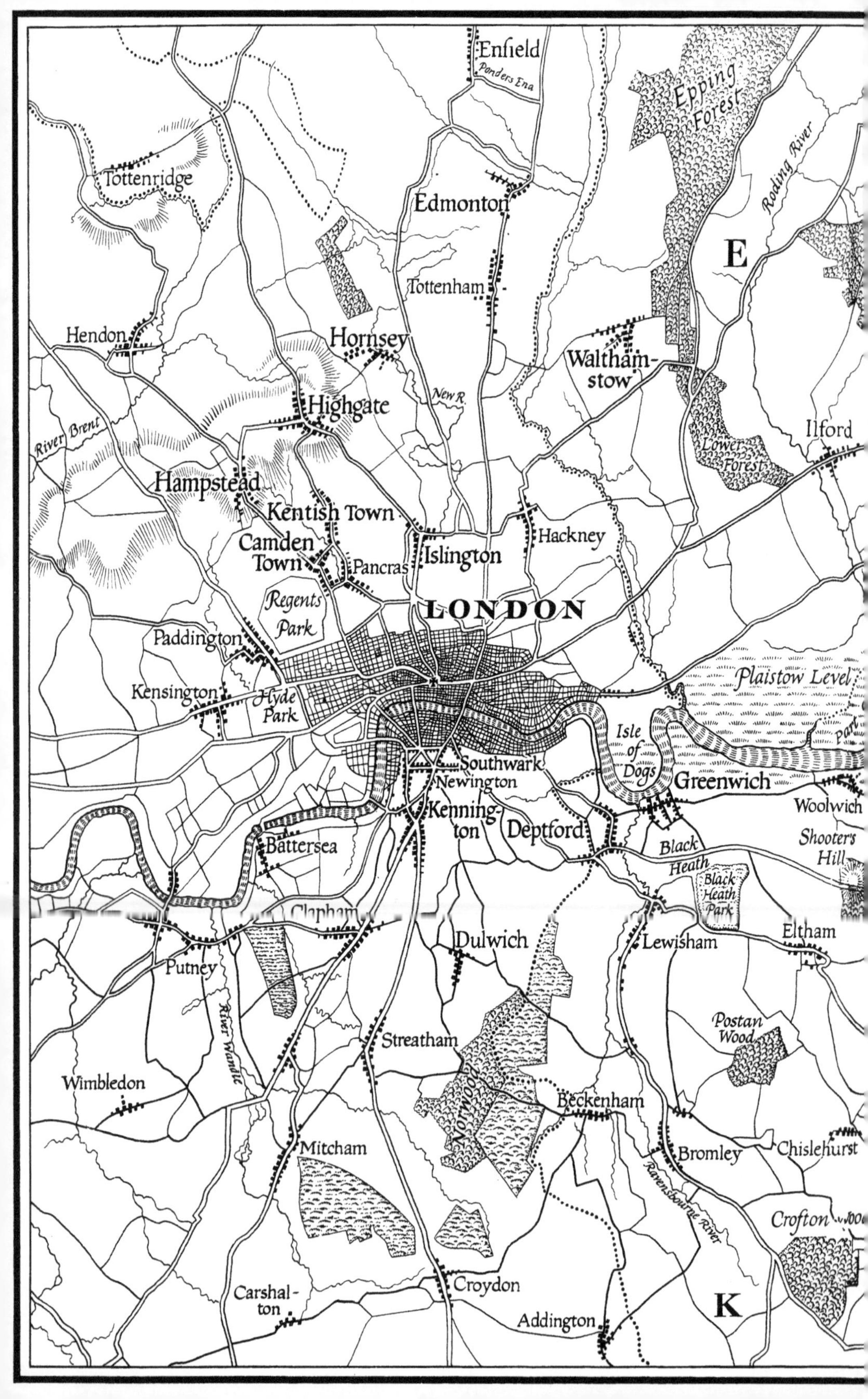
Enfield
Ponders End
Epping Forest
Roding River
Tottenridge
Edmonton
E
Tottenham
Hendon
Hornsey
Waltham-
stow
New R.
Highgate
River Brent
Ilford
Lower Forest
Hampstead
Kentish Town
Hackney
Camden
Town
Pancras
Islington
LONDON
Regents
Park
Paddington
Plaistow Level
Kensington
Hyde
Park
Isle
of
Dogs
Southwark
Newington
Greenwich
Kenning-
ton
Deptford
Woolwich
Battersea
Black
Heath
Shooter's
Hill
Black
Heath
Park
Clapham
Dulwich
Lewisham
Eltham
Putney
River Wandle
Postan
Wood
Streatham
Wimbledon
Norwood
Beckenham
Bromley
Chislehurst
Mitcham
Ravensbourne River
Crofton
Carshal-
ton
Croydon
K
Addington

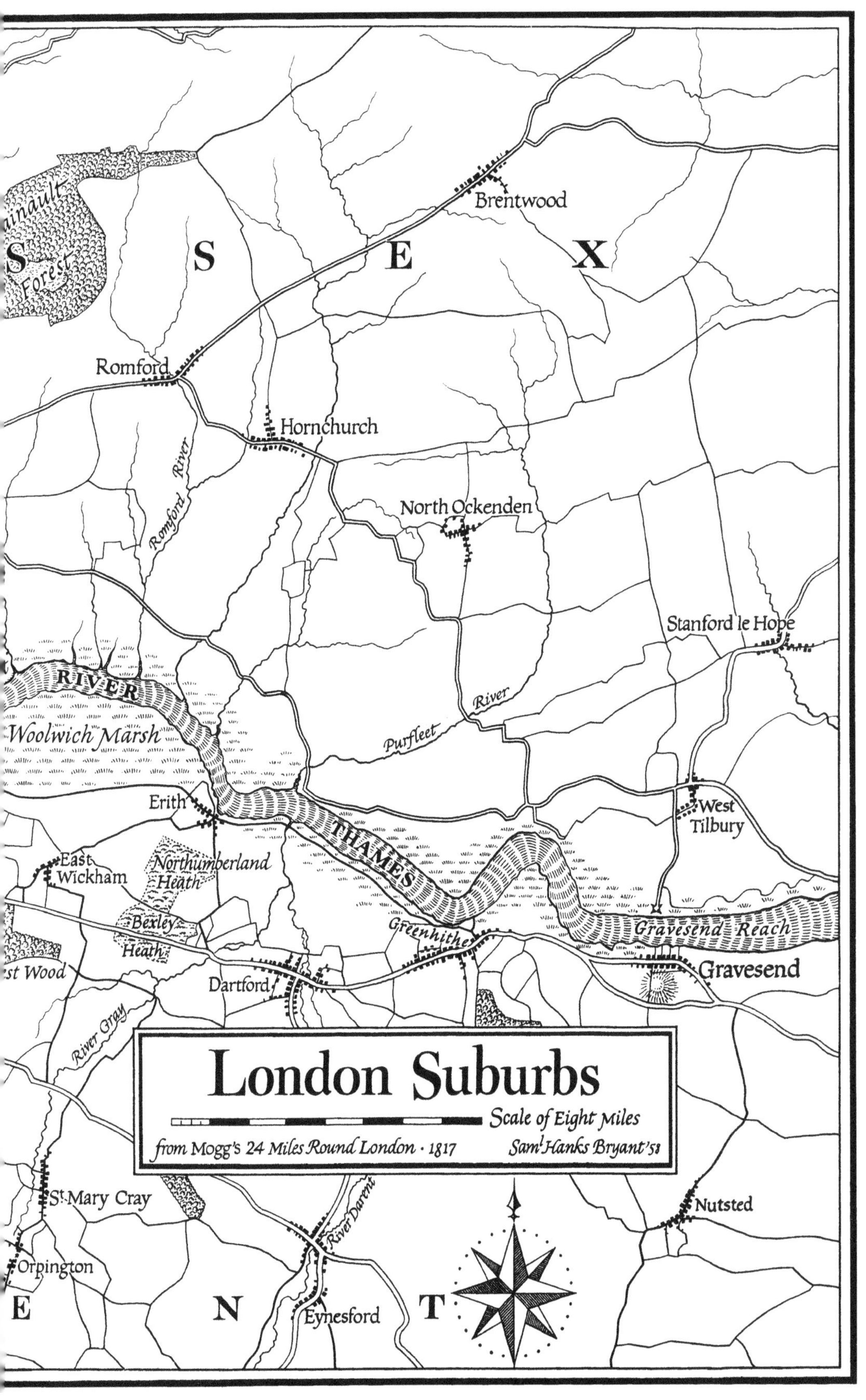
London Suburbs
Scale of Eight Miles
from Mogg's 24 Miles Round London · 1817
Saml Hanks Bryant '58
S
S
E
X
Forest
Brentwood
Romford
Hornchurch
Romford River
North Ockenden
Stanford le Hope
RIVER
Woolwich Marsh
Purfleet River
Erith
THAMES
West Tilbury
East Wickham
Northumberland Heath
Bexley Heath
Greenhithe
Gravesend Reach
Gravesend
Dartford
River Gray
River Darent
St Mary Cray
Nutsted
Orpington
E
N
T
Eynesford

THE LETTERS OF

John Keats

1814–1821

EDITED BY

Hyder Edward Rollins

VOLUME ONE

CAMBRIDGE
AT THE UNIVERSITY PRESS
1958

CAMBRIDGE UNIVERSITY PRESS
Cambridge, New York, Melbourne, Madrid, Cape Town,
Singapore, São Paulo, Delhi, Tokyo, Mexico City

Cambridge University Press
The Edinburgh Building, Cambridge CB2 8RU, UK

Published in the United States of America by Cambridge University Press, New York

www.cambridge.org
Information on this title: www.cambridge.org/9781107608207

First published 1958
First paperback edition 2011

A catalogue record for this publication is available from the British Library

ISBN 978-1-107-60820-7 Paperback

PREFACE

So much information has turned up in recent years about the dating and arrangement of Keats's letters as to make a new edition almost imperative. Several letters and papers, too, not included in the English editions of his correspondence are available, as are a number of new texts.

For permission to print the letters I am indebted to Messrs. Adam and Charles Black, Mr. Richard B. Holman, Houghton, Mifflin, and Company, the Oxford University Press, Charles Scribner's Sons, and the officials of the Berg Collection of the New York Public Library, the British Museum, the Dedham (Massachusetts) Historical Society, the Houghton Library of Harvard University, the Haverford College Library, the Indiana University Library, the Keats Museum of the Hampstead Public Library, the Keats-Shelley House at Rome, the Maine Historical Society, the Massachusetts Historical Society, the Pierpont Morgan Library, the National Library of Scotland, the Historical Society of Pennsylvania, the Princeton University Library, the University of Texas Library, the Victoria and Albert Museum, the University of Virginia Library, the Wisbech Museum of Cambridgeshire, and the Yale University Library. The following individuals have also kindly permitted me to print letters owned by them: Mr. Seymour Adelman, Mr. Archibald S. Alexander, Mr. Roger Barrett, Miss Joanna Hutchinson, Mr. Carl H. Pforzheimer, Jr., Dr. Dallas Pratt, Mr. Robert H. Taylor.

Many phrases and references in Keats's letters elude satisfactory explanation, but my notes and illustrations contain much new material. In the proper places below, my indebtedness for some of it is explicitly recorded, but here I must express my deepest gratitude for aid of one kind or another to a number of my old students, particularly to Professor Herschel Baker, Professor W. J. Bate, Dr. William H. Bond, Dr. Marie Louise Edel, Professor David B. Green, Professor Leonidas M. Jones, Professor Cecil Y. Lang, Professor Willard B. Pope, Professor Edgar F. Shannon, Jr., Miss Mabel A. E. Steele, Professor Jack C. Stillinger, and Professor Carl R. Woodring. Three of these deserve more special mention. Miss Steele, the gracious custodian of the Harvard Keats Collection, has been of constant assistance throughout my work. Mr. Stillinger not only contributed a large number of annotations but gave invaluable aid in the proofreading. Mr. Pope, who knows more about Keats and his circle than anyone else, read the manuscript with meticulous care, explained certain passages that had evaded me, and saved me from many mistakes. After all this expert help from a group of men and women who gladly learned, and who have gladly (and successfully) taught their old instructor, I am embarrassed to realize that whatever errors or mistakes of judgment may be found in my edition are entirely my own.

With a bow to the past as well as the present, I may remark that no worth-while edition of Keats's letters (or of his poems) could be made had it not been for the collecting zeal of Fred Holland Day, Harry Buxton Forman, Maurice Buxton Forman, Louis A. Holman, Mr. Arthur A. Houghton, Jr., Mr. William A. Jackson, and Amy Lowell.

January 1, 1958 H. E. R.

CONTENTS

VOLUME ONE

INTRODUCTION

LETTERS AND PAPERS

1814–1818

CONTENTS

CONTENTS

CONTENTS

VOLUME TWO

LETTERS AND PAPERS

1819–1821

CONTENTS

CONTENTS

CONTENTS

CONTENTS

CONTENTS

LIST OF ILLUSTRATIONS

VOLUME ONE

INTRODUCTION

INTRODUCTION

Keats's Letters and Their Editors

Keats's reputation as a letter-writer has had its ups and downs. James Freeman Clarke, a well-known Boston and Louisville divine, was permitted to see some of the letters in the hands of George Keats, and as long ago as 1836, in printing parts of two, he enthusiastically declared:

> These have not hitherto been published, but it appears to us, from the specimens which we have seen of them, that they are of a higher order of composition than his poems. There is in them a depth and grasp of thought; a logical accuracy of expression; a fulness of intellectual power, and an earnest struggling after truth, which remind us of the prose of Burns. They are only letters, not regular treatises, yet they touch upon the deepest veins of thought, and ascend the highest heaven of contemplation. . . . We feel a little proud that we, in this western valley, are the first to publish specimens of these writings.[1]

It is a pity that heavy theological and philosophical articles kept other Keats letters from illuminating the transcendental *Western Messenger*, and a dozen years passed before R. M. Milnes included about eighty, wholly or partly, in his biography (1848). "The journal-letters to his [Keats's] brother and sister in America," he said,[2] "are the best records of his outer existence. . . . They are full of a genial life . . . and, when it is remembered how carelessly they are written, how little the writer ever dreamt of their being redeemed from the far West or exposed to any other eyes than those of the most familiar affection, they become a mirror in which the individual character is shown with indisputable truth, and from which the fairest judgment of his very self can be drawn."

[1] *Western Messenger*, Louisville, June, 1836 (I, 773). In December, 1834, George Keats had "indulged" John Howard Payne "with a glance at the private correspondence" of the poet. Three years later, in the *Ladies' Companion*, New York, August, 1837 (VII, 185–187), Payne printed from No. 159 a long prose extract and the poems "Fame like a wayward girl" and "As Hermes once" and also two sentences and the poem "'Tis the witching time" from No. 120.

[2] I, 245 f. For full details about various editions see J. R. MacGillivray, *Keats: A Bibliography and Reference Guide* (Toronto, 1949). Three years after that book appeared Maurice Buxton Forman's fourth edition, *The Letters of John Keats* (Oxford University Press), was published.

Milnes's collection—a new edition appeared in 1867—was unique for thirty years. Unluckily, no attempt was made to improve upon it until 1883, though five years earlier Harry Buxton Forman published a small volume, *Letters of John Keats to Fanny Brawne* (1878), that created a sensation in Great Britain and America. Sir Charles W. Dilke, who had made vain efforts to prevent the publication, while holding back (and apparently destroying) an undisclosed number of the originals,[3] bitterly denounced "the *owners* of these letters" (Fanny Brawne Lindon's children), and declared that "if their publication . . . is the greatest impeachment of a woman's sense of womanly delicacy to be found in the history of literature, Mr. Forman's extraordinary preface is no less notable as a sign of the degradation to which the bookmaker has sunk." [4] A New Yorker, Richard Henry Stoddard, echoed that judgment, demolishing the Lindons, Keats, Forman, and "this most objectionable book." [5] Simultaneously Swinburne, of all persons, was lambasting both the editor and the poet: "While admitting that neither his [Keats's] love-letters, nor the last piteous outcries of his wailing and shrieking agony, would ever have been made public by merciful or respectful editors, we must also admit that, if they ought never to have been published, it is no less certain that they ought never to have been written; that a manful kind of man or even a manly sort of boy, in his love-making or in his suffering, will not howl and snivel after such a lamentable fashion." [6] Matthew Arnold, too, had joined in the hunt (1880). The letters to Fanny Brawne, he pontificated, "ought never to have been published." They show "the abandonment of all reticence and all dignity." Keats writes like "a surgeon's apprentice." He writes "the sort of love-letter of a surgeon's apprentice which one might hear read out in a breach of promise case, or in the Divorce Court." He was a "sensuous man of a badly bred and badly trained sort." [7]

At least one member of the poet's family welcomed the edition.

[3] On September 6, 1890 (*HLB*, IV [1950], 248), he told Fred Holland Day that he had returned to Herbert Lindon "all but one (or possibly two)," but on February 12, 1878 (*More Letters*, p. 101), he wrote to Fanny Keats de Llanos, "A Mr Forman has published, very much against my wish, those of the letters which he has (not those which I have)."

[4] *Athenaeum*, February 16, 1878, p. 218.

[5] *Appleton's Journal*, IV (1878), 379–382.

[6] *Complete Works*, ed. Gosse and Wise, XIV (1926), 297.

[7] *Essays in Criticism, Second Series* (1893), pp. 102–104.

His niece, Emma Keats (Mrs. Philip) Speed, wrote to Señora Llanos from Louisville (April 7, 1878) that, although the family had not consented to Forman's enterprise, she herself did not regret the appearance of the letters: not one of them "fails to increase our respect and admiration" for her uncle, who seemed "to have detected the unlovely qualities of the woman, although he was immovably constant to the last." [8] But the tirades of critics soon made her change her mind. To the same correspondent, October 28, she remarked: "Uncle John's letters were very very sad, but I think ought never to have been published. . . . [Fanny Brawne] was not the least fitted to have been the companion of John Keats with his ardent sensitive nature." [9]

Undaunted by what on May 9, 1878, he described to Señora Llanos as "the vulgar outcry of pressmen here or in America," Forman continued to amass Keatsiana. Two years later (May 18, 1880) he told her that he had personally approached Sir Charles Dilke and had enlisted his aid: "We have agreed to sink our differences of opinion about certain questions affecting your brother, and he has very liberally conceded to me all his materials that are available for the edition of Keats's Works which I am preparing." For the edition (Reeves and Turner, 1883) it was presumably Dilke who allowed him to include two further letters to Fanny Brawne, bringing the total to thirty-nine, where it has remained. Again most of the reviewers fulminated at his impiety, the *Edinburgh Review*, July, 1885,[1] solemnly stigmatizing it as "an act of sacrilege to the memory of Keats," an "act of desecration." With one hundred fifty-seven "miscellaneous letters" of Keats, Forman's 1883 volumes contained an impressive number, one hundred ninety-six.

Meanwhile, in 1878 *Letters of John Keats to Fanny Brawne* had been published in New York by Scribner, Armstrong, and Company, and in 1883 its thirty-seven letters plus seventy-seven to other correspondents reappeared there as volume I of *The Letters and Poems of John Keats* (Dodd, Mead, and Company) edited by John Gilmer Speed. Speed had access to what remained of his grandfather George Keats's manuscripts, but his editorial work was perfunctory, indeed negligible.

[8] *More Letters*, p. 103.

[9] Unpublished letters herein quoted are, if no source is mentioned, in the Harvard Keats Collection.

[1] CLXII, 36.

When thirty-five of the love letters were sold at a London auction on March 2, 1885, realizing £543 17*s*., a mere fraction of their sales-value today, Keats lovers everywhere were, or pretended to be, greatly aroused, and slurs at Fanny Brawne became more common than ever. But as a dozen are now accessible only in Forman's printed texts, students are grateful to him for having copied and published them when he had the opportunity.[2]

Despite the hostile critics, in 1889 and then in 1895 Forman issued through Reeves and Turner new editions of all the letters he could find, both excellent for their dates. The next editor, Sidney Colvin[3] (Macmillan and Company, 1891), adopted Arnold's point of view. He described Keats's letters to his relatives and friends as "among the most beautiful in our language," but as for those to Fanny Brawne, "in this, which I hope may become the standard edition of his correspondence, they shall find no place." They gave the reader, he insisted, an unhappy "sense of eavesdropping, of being admitted into petty private matters with which he has no concern," and hence were still excluded from his reissues (with additions) of 1918 and of 1921, 1925, and 1928. In his biography of Keats (1920) Colvin heaped praise on the other letters: "Their struggling, careless tissue is threaded with such strands of genius and fresh human wisdom that one often wonders whether they are not legacies of this rare young spirit equally precious with the poems themselves."

But in general the nineteenth-century critics were hostile. Many were shocked, even appalled, as they read. Coventry Patmore, for example, who in 1847 had copied a few of Keats's letters for the use of Milnes, finding them terrible and nightmarish, after reading one of Forman's editions in 1888 could "find nothing . . . that deserves a much better name than 'lust,' " and detected "artifice and cold self-consciousness in his most rhapsodical out-pourings."[4] The height of Victorian vituperation was reached by Sir William Watson, who in reviewing Forman's 1889 and then Colvin's 1891 editions, flayed Keats and denied merit to all the letters. "They distinctly

[2] Twenty-five of the autograph letters have been located, and two others are available in facsimile reproductions.

[3] "Their publication," he had remarked in 1887 (*Keats*, New York, p. vi), "must be regretted by all who hold that human respect and delicacy are due to the dead no less than to the living, and to genius no less than to obscurity."

[4] MBF, pp. vii f.

lower one's estimate of Keats as a man— . . . they are emphatically a disservice and an injury to his fame. They bring out in strong light a poor and vulgar side of his nature."[5] The letters are not "pleasant reading."[6] Keats "blurts out everything," he is "the most monotonous reading imaginable," he writes "flat trivialities," he is "jocose without being in the least witty or amusing," he has "an incontinent gushiness which is neither manly nor properly boy-like, but simply hobbledehoyish. And Cockney vulgarity, unfortunately, is never far distant." Compared to Charlotte Brontë's letters Keats's are "the veriest infantine prattle and babble."[7]

To pass by selections in so-called complete editions like Horace E. Scudder's (Boston and New York, 1899) and Nathan Haskell Dole's (London and Boston, 1906), Forman's most important edition of Keats was issued by Gowans and Gray, Glasgow, 1900–1901. In volumes IV and V he brought together two hundred seventeen letters or parts of letters. On this 1901 collection was based the work of his son, Maurice Buxton Forman, whose first Oxford University Press edition (1931) contained two hundred thirty-one letters, his second (1935) two hundred forty-one, his third (1947) and fourth (1952) two hundred forty-four.[8]

In the twentieth century the pendulum of criticism swung in Keats's favor. Whereas the American scholar, Arlo Bates, had in 1896 called the publication of the letters to Fanny Brawne "an outrage incomparably greater than any attack made upon the poet in his lifetime by hostile reviewers,"[9] one finds Mr. J. H. Preston describing them as "comparable with the finest ever written,"[1] and Mr. Robert Lynd echoing that they "now seem to many of us to be among the most beautiful love-letters ever written."[2] Indeed nobody today, so far as I am aware, is distressed by the love letters, unpleasant as some of them undoubtedly

[5] *National Review*, August, 1890 (XV, 768).

[6] These comments are from his *Excursions in Criticism* (1893), pp. 37–45.

[7] Barclay Dunham assured New York readers in 1901 that the Fanny Brawne letters are "wonderful," "gems," for which "it is unnecessary to make any apologies," but he was praising wares that he and George Broughton were publishing.

[8] Such at least are the figures he himself gives, but one of his letters (No. 238 in his last edition) is a forgery.

[9] *Poems by John Keats* (Boston), p. xvii. Mention should also be made of John Drinkwater, who in *A Book for Bookmen* (1926), p. 215, remarked, "Nothing . . . can ever justify the publication of Keats's love letters to Fanny Brawne."

[1] *The Story of Hampstead* (1948), p. 35.

[2] *Books and Writers* (1952), p. 39.

are; for without them only a half-Keats could be visualized. Instead, all the letters are greatly admired. In 1922 Henry Ellershaw asserted that "For the understanding of the man the letters are more important almost than the poetry, for in them he speaks out as he expresses his hopes, his fears, his aspirations." [3] It is certainly true, as Sir B. Ifor Evans declares, that Keats's "verse is always several stages behind the letters and the letters are the truest criticism of the verse." [4] Praise could scarcely be higher than that bestowed by Mr. T. S. Eliot, who in *The Use of Poetry and the Use of Criticism* (1933) "descants" upon "the general brilliance and profundity of the observations scattered through Keats's letters," and characterizes them as "models of correspondence," a "revelation of a charming personality," "certainly the most notable and the most important ever written by any English poet." A writer in *The Times Literary Supplement*, January 29, 1954, approvingly remarks: "Mr. Auden has suggested that the day may come when Keats's letters—which he sees as Shakespearian in their vigour—will be more widely read and admired than his poetry itself." For the striking change in critical opinion from Patmore and Arnold to Eliot and Auden both the Formans are largely responsible. Their editions abound in good material, and will never be completely superseded.

In addition to many letters from Keats's relatives and friends, the present work includes seven letters or other documents signed or written by Keats that appear in no English edition, and new texts of seven other letters by him (Nos. 62, 64, 127, 232, 235, 237, 239). Furthermore, all the letters known only in Woodhouse's transcripts (Nos. 16, 18, 22, 31, 36, 44, 47, 49, 58, 59, 68, 74, 76, 79, 80, 96, 108, 110, 175, 193) and in Jeffrey's transcripts (Nos. 45, 52, 56, 61, 93, 102, and part of 159) are here printed for the first time exactly as Woodhouse and Jeffrey copied them. This edition, then, will be found to have comparatively little resemblance to any of its predecessors, for not only are most of the texts based upon an independent transcription of the originals, but about half the notes are new, and about sixty of the letters have been redated and rearranged.

No edition of Keats's letters, however, may justifiably be called "complete," for many have not survived or are hidden from

[3] *Keats* (Oxford), p. 202. [4] *Poems of John Keats* (1950), pp. xv f.

the public. In 1934[5] L. A. Holman and J. H. Birss published a brief list of letters here and there referred to but then unknown, and to it a few additions were made by M. B. Forman in his 1935 edition.[6] The following composite list, also no doubt incomplete, cites the volume and page where references will be found to letters written by Keats but apparently not preserved. Actually, too, many of the letters preserved only in transcripts (all of those by Jeffrey and eight by Brown) have "lost" omissions, though I have not listed every one of them below.

1816

To George Keats — August — (I, 109)

Keats wrote "three words" on the lost cover enclosing No. 5

1817

To George Keats — Spring — (I, 141)

On May 10, 1817, Keats referred to "my Letters to him," but only one letter to George (No. 21) is now known between August, 1816, and this date. Again in October (I, 169) he mentions "a Letter I wrote to George in the spring," and he may have referred to the letter which Brown (*KC*, II, 56) says he wrote "some time before May 1817 . . . to one of his brothers"

To J. H. Reynolds — September — (I, 151)

Only part of No. 31 is known

To George Keats — *c.* 10 September — (I, 155)

To Charles Cripps — *c.* 22 November — (I, 184)

1818

To Benjamin Bailey — *c.* 3 January

A. E. Newton's sale catalog (New York, 1941), Part II, item 523, lists a letter of Bailey's, January 3, 1818, in which he says, "I wrote Keats just last night." Presumably Keats replied immediately, since in No. 55 he refers only to a letter that Bailey wrote on January 11[7]

To George and Tom Keats — 31 January — (I, 222)

[5] *NQ*, January 6, 1934, p. 7.

[6] 2nd ed., pp. xiii f.

[7] The same catalog, however, item 521, enumerates "a stamped addressed envelope reading 'Miss B. [*sic*] Barrett 50 Wimpole St,' apparently in Keats, [*sic*] writing"!

1818

To George Keats	*c.* 14 March	(I, 246)

Keats says that he "forgot to tell George" about going to the Teignmouth theater

To George Keats	*c.* 17 March	(I, 247)

George replied on March 18 to a letter telling him about Tom's illness

To George Keats	*c.* 27 April	(I, 274, 283)
To Benjamin Bailey	27 April	(I, 275)
To William Wordsworth	27 June	(I, 302 f., 306)
To Tom Keats	25–27 June	(I, 298)

Only part of No. 91 has been printed

To George Keats	*c.* 1 July	(I, 308)

Keats mentions two letters, one of them No. 92

To C. W. Dilke (?)	*c.* 2 July	(I, 317)

Possibly Keats had sent him a letter with a copy of "Meg Merrilies"

To Richard Abbey	25 August	(I, 365)
To Fanny Brawne	?September	(II, 132)

Or in "the very first week I knew you"—whenever that was (see I, 66f.)

To Mrs. C. W. Dilke	20 September	(I, 369)
To Charles Brown	?November	

Brown told Fanny Brawne on December 17, 1829 (Keats Museum) that in his proposed biography he wished to include a letter from Keats, now unknown but presumably sent to him, which was "written when he dispaired of Tom's recovery"

To "P. Fenbank"	*c.* 11 November	(II, 17)
To C. C. Clarke	*c.* 2 December	

See his *Recollections of Writers* (1878), p. 157

To Richard Woodhouse	*c.* 2 December	(I, 409)

Woodhouse is replying to a note (possibly written by Brown) that informed him of Tom Keats's death

To William Haslam	18 December	(II, 12)
To Charles Brown	28 December	(II, 18)

1819

To Richard Abbey	February	(II, 39, 59 f.)
To Mrs. James Wylie	19 February	(II, 63)
To William Haslam	February	(II, 66)

Keats had written "some Letters" to him

To William Haslam	*c.* 22 March	(II, 82)

Evidently Keats replied to the letter announcing the death of Haslam's father

To B. R. Haydon	*c.* 10 April	(II, 53)
To Many Friends	12 May	(II, 110)
To Fanny Brawne	29 June	(II, 122)

Not sent, and probably destroyed

To Holt (? or Holland)	6 July	(II, 228 f.)
To George Keats	July	(II, 184, 211 f.)

This may also be the letter mentioned at II, 128, though MBF identifies it with No. 173 to Fanny Keats

To Richard Abbey	7 July	(II, 131)
To J. H. Reynolds	11 July	(II, 128)

Part of No. 175 is missing

To William Haslam	July	(II, 124, 148)
To Benjamin Bailey	14 August	(II, 139)

Part of No. 181 is missing

To Richard Abbey	August	(II, 148)

"Some correspondence . . . with M[r] Abbey," which may have been the "many teasing letters of business" mentioned on August 16 (II, 140)

To James Rice	24 August	(II, 146)
To A Friend	31 August	(II, 153)

Keats mailed "a third Letter to a friend of mine—who . . . has neither answerd right or left"—possibly Haslam

To Fry	?September	(II, 185)
To Charles Brown	*c.* 12 September	(II, 173, 180)
To Charles Brown	*c.* 16 September	(II, 173, 180)
To Charles Brown	*c.* 16 September	(II, 215)

The "short note" as from "Nathan Benjamin"

1819

To Charles Brown	22 September	(II, 176)

Part of No. 195 is missing

To Charles Brown	23 September	(II, 181)

Part of No. 197 is missing

To Joseph Severn	*c.* 11 October	(Sharp, p. 40)
To William Haslam	2 November	(II, 226)

Only a fragment of No. 206 is known

To Mrs. James Wylie	?1819	(*KC*, II, 29)
To the George Keatses	?1819	

Quoted in the New York *World*, June 25, 1877, and at II, 215 n.

To the George Keatses ?1819

Quoted in *Harper's New Monthly Magazine*, LV (1877), 361, and at I, 225 n.

To Mrs. James Wylie	?1819	(II, 283 n.)

The signature and postscript heretofore printed at the end of No. 253 belong to some lost letter

To the George Keatses ?1819

John Jeffrey on March 8, 1844, sent to the Rev. W. L. Breckinridge, of Louisville, a signature cut from a presumably lost letter of Keats to be forwarded to the Albany, New York, autograph collector, the Rev. W. B. Sprague

1820

To George Keats	March	(II, 284)

Written by Brown "as from me"

To Barry Cornwall	*c.* 1 March	(II, 267 f.)
To George Keats	Spring	

Writing to Fanny Keats in February, 1824 (*More Letters*, pp. 16, 18), George says, "The last time I heard from you was thro' our dear John"—evidently some time after George had left London on January 28, 1820, but no such letter is known

To Charles Brown	15 May	(II, 289)

No. 260 and others (like Nos. 266, 288) are printed only in part

To Fanny Brawne May (II, 290)

Keats says that "I shall be selfish enough to send" a letter that he wrote "yesterday." MacGillivray thinks that it was No. 271, but see the notes

To B. R. Haydon 14 July (II, 308)

Obviously Keats sent back a reply by Haydon's bearer. It was either No. 283 or a lost letter

To J. A. Hessey *c.* 14 July (II, 318)

"Crumpled" by Keats and probably destroyed

To Richard Abbey 20 August (II, 330 f.)

To Charles Brown *c.* 20 August (II, 329)

This letter may well have been No. 284 or No. 288, in which Brown deleted Keats's request

To John Aitken *c.* 26 August (II, 324)

Keats must surely have replied to No. 286

To Charles Brown 28 September (II, 350)

"Which I did not send and am in doubt if he ever will see it"

?To Fanny Brawne 30 September (II, 346)

To C. W. Dilke 30 September (II, 346)

On September 30 Keats told Brown (II, 344), "I have many more Letters to write," but none seems to be known

To ——? 1 or 2 December (II, 360)

Keats says, "I shall write to x x x to-morrow, or next day." Whether he did write that letter and another "to x x x x x in the middle of next week" is not known

As for other missing letters, Brown informed Fanny Brawne in December, 1829, that he was about to write a life of Keats, incorporating "passages from letters to me, and to his brothers,—which last are in my possession";[8] but of those to George and Tom Keats that have been published Brown could have had only Nos. 5, 21, 69, and possibly 48 and 98, not Nos. 97 and 101, which Haydon attached to his journal, or Nos. 45, 52, 56, 61, 64, 91, 93, 95, 137, 158, 199, which George Keats kept in Louisville. Again, Leigh

[8] The letter is in the Keats Museum.

Hunt in 1846[9] told Milnes that Keats and "I were so much together during the whole time of our intimacy, that I hardly received above three or four letters from him in all." Of these "three or four" only two have yet been printed, although an anonymous writer in the *Cornhill Magazine*, May, 1892,[1] said, "Of Keats's letters to Hunt I have several." Other friends and acquaintances of Keats, like Peter De Wint, William Hilton, the Mathews, Hazlitt, Kirkman, Archer, are still unrepresented in the correspondence. There is a possibility that some day they will be represented, and it is certain that at least one of Keats's unpublished letters is hidden in a safe-deposit box in a Southern city. Unfortunately for his biographers, too, his practise was every so often to make "a general conflagration of all old Letters and Memorandums."[2] Before he left England he seems to have destroyed all the letters he could find—all that Brown had not secreted—and hence his correspondence remains largely one-sided. If by some miracle every letter that Keats wrote had been preserved, biographers would have practically a day-by-day chronicle of his life in 1816–1820.

Readers will notice in the letters a certain stiffness, showing that Keats did not wear his heart on his sleeve. While Taylor and Woodhouse always call each other "Dear Dick" and "Dear John," and while Keats apparently called Mathew "Felton," Rice "Jem" or "Jemmy," Reynolds "John" or "Jack" (and the Wylie brothers "Henry" and "Charles"), except for Clarke he invariably salutes correspondents who were not relatives by their surnames, and so they saluted him. The conclusions are equally formal. On the basis of "Your affectionate friend" and the like, he felt closer to Reynolds, Haydon, Bailey (for a time), and Brown than to his other friends. Rice, whom he admired profoundly, Clarke, Woodhouse, Dilke, Richards, Taylor, and the rest do not get "affection," whereas Mrs. Brawne, Mrs. Wylie, and for a short period the Reynolds girls (and once Hunt) do. Only to his brothers and sister did he sometimes sign his name "John," though he also uses "J—K—" or "John Keats." To others he nearly always pens his full name. Oddly enough, just one of the letters to Fanny Brawne is signed "J.," all the rest "John Keats," "Keats," "J. Keats," or "J. K."

[9] *KC*, II, 170.
[1] See I, 78.
[2] See II, 112.

His addresses, too, are somewhat stylized. In every case he takes pains to add "Esquire" to the names of the tradesman Abbey and of Hessey, Hunt, Monkhouse, Shelley, Elmes, and Horace Smith. Taylor, Woodhouse, Dilke, and Severn, too, are usually "Esquires," but his brothers, Clarke, Haslam, Reynolds, and nine times out of ten Bailey are "Mr.," while in half a dozen addresses "Haydon" has no title prefixed or added.

The Plan of This Edition

The Texts. In the texts of all the letters the spelling, capitalization, and punctuation of the originals are reproduced as exactly as possible, with a few slight exceptions designed for readability and typographical unobtrusiveness. Thus dots or dashes under superior letters or figures are omitted; flourishes, lines, or braces attached to addresses, signatures, or dates are ignored; and postscripts, wherever written, are printed at the end of the letters. "I" = "j" and "u" = "v" are everywhere modernized to "j" and "v." Three asterisks (***) warn that the beginning or end of a document is missing.

Where a possibility of real confusion exists, misspellings are corrected by letters inserted in square brackets ([ ]). Such brackets enclose all other editorial insertions, like words necessary for the sense and omitted by oversight. When a reading is doubtful, it is commented on in a note. Curly braces ({ }) indicate letters or words inserted to fill gaps caused by holes, tears, frayed edges, and the like. Those enclosing three dots ({. . .}) call attention to gaps, the extent of which is mentioned in a footnote, and which the editor did not attempt to fill conjecturally. Canceled letters or words that result from the writers' corrections of misspellings, repetitions, and so on are not noted, nor are changes by which one word is written over another (for example, when "who" becomes "what"). But whenever the canceled readings appear to be of interest or significance, they are, if decipherable, printed in shaped brackets (⟨ ⟩) or recorded in footnotes. So much for general editorial practises. But since the texts are taken from different sources, various other problems have had to be faced.

Autograph letters, if available, are followed. Those of Keats himself are ordinarily written in a good, clear hand, yet it is often impossible to tell whether a light punctuation mark made by him is intended for a comma, a period, or a dash, and I have arbitrarily settled that matter on the basis of what I suppose to have been his intention. Again, all his "k's" look like capitals, and I have printed "k" sometimes as a small, at other times as a capital, letter. He also has two totally different ways of making an "S," one unmistakably a capital, the other at times clearly a capital, at others apparently lower case, though one cannot be sure about what he intended. Actually no two persons would in every instance agree on these "S's" and "K's." Frequently, too, he runs words together, like "tobe," and just as frequently leaves a space in a word, like "a bout," but these thoughtless aberrations I have ignored.

Keats penned his sentences rapidly and spontaneously, not carefully and artfully. "It will be impossible for me to keep any order or method in what I write: that will come first which is uppermost in my Mind," he confessed to George (I, 392). Again, "If I scribble long letters I must play my vagaries. . . . I must play my draughts as I please" (I, 279). He dashed off sentences, ignoring unity and coherence, and seldom rereading what he had written. Hence the frequent misspellings, the substitution of an incorrect for a correct word, the queer punctuation, the occasional grammatical slips.

He had the greatest difficulty in writing (and one supposes in pronouncing) "r," and so on page after page there are such misspellings as "affod," "depeciate," "expession," "gieved," "peach," "poof," "procue," "shot," "surpised," "sping," "thead," "thee," "witten," "wost." In the poem at II, 56, "three" appears four times as "thee," and four other times it was first written without an "r." The lines at II, 86, have "thee" and "pince" (twice). Such misspellings, which might mislead readers, have been corrected with a bracketed "r."

On the other hand, "evey," "arbitary," and especially "you" (for "your") occur so many times as to denote Keats's own spelling and pronunciation, and have been retained unemended. Brackets are also omitted in words which we today should call misspelled but which are readily intelligible, among them

accomodate	colums
apropo	desendants
arive	elipsis
autum	hethen
avantage	infalibly
bord	ocured
cobler	oprobrium

refered	vermil
remembring	warf
solitry	wether
tresury	wondring.

And, of course, proper nouns are kept as he wrote them—he pronounced "Chister," "Enmoor," and perhaps "Kirkudbright" as spelled—and errors that resemble those of typewriting, as "firends" and "perpaps," are left unchanged, but are usually commented on. In his reading Keats had seen old forms or spellings like "avantage," "to" for "too," and "of" for "off." Consciously or unconsciously he took them over, and I have not corrected them. Nearly anyone can ferret out his meaning (certainly his young sister could) when he writes "where" for "were," "in" for "am," "&" for "&c," but to prevent such readings from being considered misprints I have called attention to them in the notes.

In his letters as in his verse he loved to interchange parts of speech. When he wrote "All civiled countries" (II, 193), "The enquires about you" (II, 231), "Notwithstand the part" (I, 396 f.), "Notwithstand your Happiness" (I, 403) he was using old words that somewhere or other he had seen or that he had blithely invented, and I have left them alone. Various other coinages, like "intermiten," "titterly," "couthly" appear in his sentences, along with occasional dialectic or colloquial forms like "ope" meaning "hope," and "as," "ax," "of," "years" for "has," "ask," "have," and "ears."

Richard Woodhouse's Transcripts. The above-mentioned editorial methods are likewise applied to the letters of Keats's contemporaries—George and Tom Keats, Brown, Haydon, Severn, and the rest—that I have included. But Woodhouse's transcripts of Keats's autographs merit special attention. He copied fifty-seven in a letter-book and a manuscript volume of Keats's poems,[1] and twenty of these are the only texts known. Woodhouse was an admirable scholar and a painstaking copyist whose transcripts are, in the main, reliable. He *could* have copied with almost literal exactness

[1] In the letter-book, Nos. 16, 18, 22, 27, 28, 30, 34, 36, 38, 41 (part), 43, 44, 47, 49, 54, 55, 57, 58, 59 (and part of it a second time), 60, 62, 65, 67, 68, 71, 72, 74, 76, 77, 78, 79, 80, 83, 86, 88, 96, 99, 108, 110, 118, 122, 128, 133, 163, 175, 181, 183 (part), 185, 188 (part), 190, 193, 211 (twice), 212, 228, 263, 279; in his manuscript of poems, Nos. 31 and 74. Both manuscripts are at Harvard.

if he had thought such work desirable. Instead he felt free silently to correct misspellings, to supply or omit punctuation, to change a capital to a small letter or *vice versa.* He was overfond of contractions like "sh^{d}" and "w^{d}." But in regard to what seemed to him important he was meticulous.

Some of the transcripts are entirely in his hand, others in his clerk's, or secretary's, a few partly by him, partly by the clerk. But always Woodhouse carefully verified the copy with the original letter. The clerk had difficulty in reading some of Keats's words. So in No. 22 he copied "Joy" (twice) and "Full," which Woodhouse corrected to "ivy" and "ink." Again in No. 44 he put down "too many errands," which Woodhouse changed to "two penny errands," and he left a blank (I, 190) for a word after "the Woman said to the." If Keats actually did have something after "the," both the clerk and Woodhouse failed to decipher it, though someone later penciled in an unreadable word. Similar spaces were left at I, 133, but Woodhouse in pencil supplied "Laurel" and "Prunus." At II, 156, however, he was stumped by "withe axe," and so he omitted it, leaving a space in the sentence. "Consequitive" (I, 185), "couthly" (I, 220), and "merely" (I, 322), too, he marked "(so)," the last because it should have been "nearly." Emendations by Woodhouse that nearly all the editions have accepted will be found at I, 130, 166, 188, 242, and elsewhere.

Several times he attached interesting notes to his copies (as at I, 326, 388), and ordinarily he gave information about postmarks, or supplied missing dates. That he transcribed only parts of the verses Keats put into certain letters is understandable: already these poems were in his manuscript anthologies, and he believed it sufficient to add a reference to the page numbers of the manuscripts. Up to the present moment Woodhouse's texts have been printed with extremely numerous changes, misreadings, and "improvements." I have tried to print them as exactly as Keats's autographs. Since they are copies, naturally I have not furnished them with made-up addresses and postmarks.

Brown's Texts. Nine letters of Keats were transcribed by Charles Brown. Of these (Nos. 195, 197, 260, 266, 284, 288, 302, 306, 310) only one (No. 302) is at present known in autograph. Brown made no special effort at literal accuracy. He misread "best" as "last," "my lungs or stomach" as "my stomach, or lungs," "you" as "your," and above all took pains to conceal the identity of the persons mentioned. Hence he substitutes crosses for names, or disguises them by pronouns, and omits whole sentences. But within his limits he was a good transcriber, who seldom did much damage to what Keats wrote. His changes resemble those of most Victorian editors.

John Jeffrey's Texts. In 1845 Jeffrey volunteered to copy for Milnes the autograph letters brought into his possession by his marriage to George Keats's widow, and unsuspectingly Milnes accepted them as accurate. But the Kentucky businessman felt no obligation to make literal, complete copies. He was, I imagine, bored by the task, and he considered many of Keats's details too personal or trivial or dull to copy in full. Accordingly, he changed words or phrases that he disliked or did not understand or could not decipher; he reversed the order of certain sentences, reformed spelling, punctuation, grammar. Worse yet, with no warning he omitted words, sentences, paragraphs, at times whole pages. An extreme example is the journal letter No. 199, which runs to about thirty-four printed pages, but which he reduced to three. If the autograph of No. 199 had disappeared in 1845, here is how (undated) that extraordinary epistle would look:

(No Date)

Dear George.

I spent yesterday with Dilke, who is entirely swallowed up in his boy, T'is really lamentable to what a pitch he carries a sort of parental mania. He said a word or two about the Isle of Wight, which is a pet hobby horse of his, but he soon deviated to his boy, "I am sitting at the window expecting my boy from school." Dilke had some friends to Dinner I forget who—but there were two old ladies among them; Brown was there' they had known him from a child. Brown is very pleasant with old ladies, & on that day it seems behaved so well; that they became hand & glove together, & a little complimentary, Brown was obliged to depart early, he bid them good bye, & passed into the passage, his back was no sooner turned than the old ladies began to praise him to the skies. When Brown had reached the street door & was just going, Dilke threw up the window & called "Brown! Brown! they say you look younger than ever you did!" Brown went on, & had just turned the corner into the other street, when Dilke appeared at the back window crying; "Brown! Brown! By God! they say you're handsome—!" x x x — I must tell you a good thing Reynolds *did*, it was the best thing he ever *said*. He was taking leave of the party he delayed; well good bye, still he dallied, we joked him & even said be off, at which he put the tails of his coat between his legs & sneaked off as much like a Spaniel as could be; He went with flying colours. He has been taking french lessons at the cheap rate of two & sixpence a fag, he observed to Brown, "Gad the man sells his lessons so cheap he must have stolen them." You have heard of Hook the Farce writer. Horace Smith was asked if he was acquainted with Hook. Oh yes Hook & I are very intimate. There is wit for you, to put John Bunyan's Emblems out of countenance— Tuesday—You see I add a sheet daily to my packet. From the time you left us our friends say I have altered so completely, I am not the same person: I daresay you have altered also. Mine is not the same hand I clenched at Hammond. We are like the relic garments of a Saint, the same & not the same; for the careful monks patch it, & patch it, till there is not a thread of the original in it, & still they show it for ⟨the⟩ St Anthony's shirt. This is the reason why men who have been bosom friends on being separated for a number of years, afterwards meet coldly neither of them know why. Some think I have lost that poetic fire & ardour they say I once had; the fact is I perhaps have, but instead of that I hope, I shall substitute a more thoughtful & quiet power. I am more contented to read & think, but seldom haunted with ambitious thoughts. I am scarcely content to write the best verse for the fever they leave behind. I want to compose without this fever. I hope I shall one day You cannot imagine how well I can live alone; I told the servant today to say I was not at home to any one that called, I am not sure how I should endure loneliness, & bad weather at the same time; it is beautiful weather now. I walk for an hour every day before dinner; Now for a word to your wife. My dear sister I must quarrel with you for sending me such a shabby sheet of paper, but, that it was in some degree made up, by the very beautiful impression of the Seal. I have all the Examiners ready for you, I will pack them up when the business with Mr Abbey comes to a conclusion. I have dealt out your best wishes like a pack of cards, but being always given to cheat I have turned up Ace. You see I am making game of you. I see you are not happy in America, Your observations on the Musquitoes are beautiful & really poetic. Are you quizzing me or Miss W. when you talk of promenading—As for *pun* making I wish it were as profitable as pin-making. there is but little business of that sort going on now. we struck for wages like the Manchester Weavers, but to no purpose, for we are all out of employ; I am more lucky than some, you see, as I have an opportunity of exporting a few, getting into a little foreign trade, which is a comfortable thing. I wish you could get change for a pun in silver currency. I would three & a half any night to get into Drury pit. but they will not ring. no more will notes you will say, but notes are a different thing tho' they make together a pun-note as people say. If you would prefer a joke just hatched I have two for you, The first I played off at Brown. the second I played on myself; Brown when he left me "Keats my good fellow" (staggering on his left heel, & fetching an irregular pirouette with his right) "Keats" says he (⟨still in the same posture⟩, depressing his left eye brow & elevating his right one, tho' by the way, at the moment I did not know which was the right one) "Keats" (says he still in the same posture, but both his hands in his waistcoat pockets, & putting out his stomack "Keats My gooood fellow" (says he interlarding his exclamation with certain ventriloquial parenthesis) No! this is all a lie, he was as sober as a judge, when a judge happens to be sober, & said if any letters come for me, do not forward them, but open them & give me the marrow of them in a few words. At the time when I wrote my first to him, no letters had arrived, I thought I would invent one, & as I had not time to manufacture a long one, I dubbed off a short one, & that was the reason of the joke succeeding beyond my expectations, Brown let his house to a Mr Benjamin a Jew. Now the water which furnishes the house is in a tank, sided with a composition of lime, & the lime impregnates the water unpleasantly; taking advantage of this circumstance, I pretended that Mr Benjamin had written the following short note, Sir, by drinking your damned tank water, I have got the gravel, what reparation can you make to me & my family? (Nathan Benjamin). By a fortunate hit I pitched upon his right Hebrew name, his right pronomen; Brown in consequence it appears wrote to the surprised Mr Benjamin, the following; Sir I cannot offer you any remuneration for your gravel, until it shall have formed itself into a stone, when I will cut you with pleasure. C. Brown— This of Brown's Mr Benjamin has answered, insisting on an explanation of the singular circumstance. Brown says when I read your letter & his following I roared, & in came Mr Snook, who on reading them seemed ready to burst the hoops of his fat sides— Now for the one I played on myself. I must first give you the scene & the dramatis personae. There is an old Major & his young girl wife living in the next apartment to mine; his bedroom door opens at an angle with my sitting room door; Yesterday I was reading as demurely as a parish Clerk, when I heard a rap at the door. I opened it, no one was to be seen. I listened & heard some one in the Majors room, Not content with this I went up stairs & down, at last I sat down again to read, not quite so demurely, when there came a loud rap, I rose determined to find out who it was; I looked out, the staircases were all silent, this must be the Major's wife, said I, at all events I will find out; so I rapped at the Mjors door & went in to the utter surprise & confusion of the lady who was there; After an explanation which it is impossible to describe, I made my retreat from her convinced of my mistake, she is a silly body & is really alarmed at it— I have discovered that a little girl is the rapper, as I was the *rappee* I should have made her sneeze. If the lady tells I shall put a very grave & moral face on the matter with the old Major, & make his little boy a present of a humming top.

Your Brother

(Signed) John Keats.

Jeffrey informed Milnes that he had copied "nearly all the letters," though he was "rather disappointed" with them, and found "almost all miserably illegible & badly dated." The "nearly all" amounted to fifteen, of which six (Nos. 45, 52, 56, 61, 93, 102) and a small part of a seventh (No. 159) are otherwise unknown.[2] One regrets that he did not copy all, for at least two that he must have owned in 1845 have survived only in brief, partial summaries.[3] Some of the six letters for which Jeffrey is the only source are likely to turn up sooner or later, and, if they do, they will undoubtedly show the same kind of maltreatment that he gave to Nos. 64 and 199. In the meantime I have followed his texts almost as he wrote them, even when they are glaringly incorrect, enumerating in footnotes my few changes. Since they are transcripts I have printed the signatures and addresses as he gave them.

The Formans' and Colvin's Texts. As the first real collector and annotator of Keats's letters, Harry Buxton Forman deserves, and has everywhere received, great credit, and several of the letters to Fanny Brawne, as I have said, are now known only through his texts. In his 1883 edition, which I have sometimes been obliged to follow, he says that his editing involved "the correction of a few obvious clerical errors, and such amendment of punctuation as is invariably required by letters not written for the press." Similarly his rival editor, Colvin, explained in 1891, "I have not thought it worth while to preserve mere slips of the pen or tricks of spelling." Neither Forman nor Colvin admired, or tried to make, diplomatic texts, but they did not, except for sometimes misreading words (like all other editors) distort what Keats wrote. It is probably true, so far as the "general reader" is concerned, that the H. B. Forman–Colvin texts are the best. Those of Maurice Buxton Forman give, with a few exceptions, exactly what Keats wrote.

A. Forbes Sieveking's Texts. Sieveking first published Nos. 81, 84, 164, 166 in 1893. The autographs of Nos. 84 and 164 are all that I have seen, and a comparison of them with his printed texts proves that he transcribes accurately.

[2] The others are Nos. 48, 64, 95, 100, 120, 137, 199, 215. All the Jeffrey transcripts are at Harvard. Jeffrey often puts between sentences very wide spaces, which I have generally ignored. Nor have I kept words that he runs together, like "donot" and "tomeet."

[3] See the notes at I, 225, II, 215.

Other Texts. Seven letters (Nos. 54, 91, 149, 206, 237, 291, and part of No. 218) are available only in printed texts that are not altogether trustworthy, but until, or unless, the originals turn up, they will have to serve.

Footnotes. In the first note to each document I have given the present location of the autograph or specified the transcript or other source followed, occasionally indicating by whom it was discovered and first printed and, here and there, naming a former owner. As for explanatory notes—with the exception of such things as "misprints," obvious quotations from Shakespeare and the Bible, or information derived from the *Examiner*, other familiar magazines, the *New English Dictionary*, *The Complete Peerage*, and the *Dictionary of National Biography*—I have made an effort to credit those which did not originate with me,[4] particularly those later than 1947, to their first propounders. I have not always distinguished, since even the 1952 edition distinguishes irregularly, the notes of the two Formans, but a number of annotations contributed by Louis A. Holman, of Boston, to earlier editions are now assigned to him. Personal names are identified only at their first appearance, and can then be followed by means of the Index. Many well-known persons, many familiar books and quotations, are identified in order to be recorded in the Index; for Keats's reading, or "learning," is a matter of considerable interest and importance. But his critical ideas and his indebtedness to Shakespeare, Milton, Wordsworth, and Hazlitt are subjects too large to be dealt with adequately here. In the notes, as in the biographical sketches, I have dropped all titles like "Mr." and "Miss," considering such references as "Lowell" mere abbreviations. In references to books the place of publication is given only when it is not London.

Biographical Sketches. The sketches, which make no claims to originality or completeness, are for the most part condensed from those I printed in *The Keats Circle* (1948), but I have made numerous corrections and additions, and have referred to sources of further information. Except for Richard Abbey, who played a

[4] Various notes on the letters by me will be found in *KC;* the *Journal of English and Germanic Philology*, XLVII (1948), 139–145; *HLB*, IV (1950), 239–253, 374–391, VII (1953), 172–187, VIII (1954), 241–246; *K-SJ*, II (1953), 19–34; University of Virginia *Studies in Bibliography*, IX (1957), 179–195.

big role in the lives of the Keats children, correspondents to whom only one letter of Keats is addressed are, when necessary, identified briefly in notes to the individual letters.

Cross-References. To save space and to avoid "see above," "see below," all cross-references, except when documents are referred to by their numbers, are given in the form "I, 50," "see I, 50," "see II, 130," "at I, 250," which means volume I, volume II, and the appropriate pages.

Abbreviated Names and Titles

In the footnotes and generally elsewhere the following abbreviations of names or titles are used:

Adami. Marie Adami, *Fanny Keats*, 1937.

Apperson. G. L. Apperson, *English Proverbs*, 1929.

Blunden. Edmund Blunden, "Keats's Letters, 1931; Marginalia," *Studies in English Literature*, Tokyo Imperial University, October, 1931, XI, 475–507.

Bodurtha and Pope. *Life of John Keats By Charles Armitage Brown*, ed. Dorothy H. Bodurtha and Willard B. Pope, 1937.

Brown's Journal. Charles Brown, "Walks in the North," *Plymouth and Devonport Weekly Journal*, October 1, 8, 15, 22, 1840. See I, 419–442.

Bushnell. Nelson S. Bushnell, *A Walk after John Keats*, New York, 1936.

Colvin. (Sir) Sidney Colvin, *Letters of John Keats to His Family and Friends*, 1891.

Colvin, 1920. Sir Sidney Colvin, *John Keats: His Life and Poetry, His Friends, Critics, and After-Fame*, New York, 1920.

De Selincourt. *The Poems of John Keats*, ed. Ernest De Selincourt, 5th ed., 1926.

DNB. Dictionary of National Biography.

Edgcumbe. *Letters of Fanny Brawne to Fanny Keats*, ed. Fred Edgcumbe, New York, 1937.

Finney. Claude Lee Finney, *The Evolution of Keats's Poetry*, 2 vols., Harvard University Press, 1936.

Garrod. *The Poetical Works of John Keats*, ed. H. W. Garrod, Oxford, 1939.

Gittings. Robert Gittings, *John Keats: The Living Year*, Harvard University Press, 1954.

GM. Gentleman's Magazine.

Hale-White. Sir William Hale-White, *Keats as Doctor and Patient*, 1938.

Hampstead Keats. *The Poetical Works and Other Writings of John Keats*, ed. Harry Buxton Forman, revised by Maurice Buxton Forman (Hampstead Edition), 8 vols., New York, 1938, 1939.

Haydon, F. W. *Benjamin Robert Haydon: Correspondence and Table-Talk*. With a Memoir by his son, Frederic Wordsworth Haydon, 2 vols., 1876.

Hazlitt, *Works*. *The Complete Works of William Hazlitt*, ed. P. P. Howe, 21 vols., 1930–1934.

HBF, 1878. *Letters of John Keats to Fanny Brawne*, ed. Harry Buxton Forman, 1878.

HBF, 1883. *The Poetical Works and Other Writings of John Keats*, ed. Harry Buxton Forman, 4 vols., 1883. (Other editions in 1889 and [5 vols.] in 1900, 1901.)

HBF, 1895. *The Letters of John Keats*, ed. Harry Buxton Forman, 1895.

Hewlett. Dorothy Hewlett, *A Life of John Keats*, 2nd ed., 1949.

HLB. *Harvard Library Bulletin*.

Holman. Louis Arthur Holman, Notes and Other Keatsiana in the Harvard Keats Collection.

Howe. P. P. Howe, *The Life of William Hazlitt*, new ed., 1947.

KC. *The Keats Circle: Letters and Papers*, ed. Hyder E. Rollins, 2 vols., Harvard University Press, 1948.

K–SJ. *Keats-Shelley Journal*.

K–SMB. *Keats-Shelley Memorial Bulletin Rome*.

Lowell. Amy Lowell, *John Keats*, 2 vols., Boston and New York, 1925.

MBF. *The Letters of John Keats*, ed. Maurice Buxton Forman, 4th ed., 1952. (Earlier editions in 1931, 1935, 1947.)

Milnes. Richard Monckton Milnes, *Life, Letters, and Literary Remains, of John Keats*, 2 vols., 1848.

MLN. *Modern Language Notes*.

More Letters. *More Letters and Poems of the Keats Circle*, ed. Hyder E. Rollins, Harvard University Press, 1955.

NED. *A New English Dictionary on Historical Principles*, 10 vols., Oxford, 1888–1928.

NQ. *Notes and Queries*.

Olney. Clarke Olney, *Benjamin Robert Haydon*, Athens, Georgia, 1952.

Papers. *The Papers of a Critic. Selected from the Writings of the Late Charles Wentworth Dilke*, 2 vols., 1875.

Partridge. Eric Partridge, *A Dictionary of Slang and Unconventional English*, 3rd ed., 1949.

Penrose. *The Autobiography and Memoirs of Benjamin Robert Haydon*, ed. A. P. D. Penrose, 1927.

PMLA. Publications of the Modern Language Association of America.

Richardson. Joanna Richardson, *Fanny Brawne, A Biography*, 1952.

Sharp. William Sharp, *The Life and Letters of Joseph Severn*, 1892.

TLS. The [London] *Times Literary Supplement.*

Williamson. *The Keats Letters, Papers, and Other Relics Forming the Dilke Bequest in the Hampstead Public Library*, ed. George C. Williamson, 1914.

Woodruff. Bertram L. Woodruff, "Keats and Hazlitt: A Study of the Development of Keats," Harvard University dissertation, 1956.

Milton is quoted from F. A. Patterson, *The Student's Milton*, New York, 1933; Shakespeare, from W. A. Neilson's edition, Boston and New York, 1906 (which is closer to Keats's quotations than many recent texts); Wordsworth, from Thomas Hutchinson's Oxford Edition of his *Poetical Works*, 1913.

Events in the Life of Keats[1]

1795

October	31	Born at the Swan and Hoop Livery Stables, 24 Moorfields Pavement Row (see Pope, *TLS*, December 22, 1932, p. 977,[2] and *K-SJ*, II [1953], 112)
December	18	Baptized at St. Botolph's, Bishopsgate

1797

February	28	George Keats born

1799

November	18	Tom Keats born

1799 (?)

The Keats family move to Craven Street, City Road (Ernest Raymond, *Two Gentlemen of Rome* [1952], p. 14)

1801

April	28	Edward Keats born
September	24	George, Tom, and Edward Keats baptized at St. Leonard's, Shoreditch; Edward dies before February 1, 1805 (Pope)

1803

June	3	Fanny (Frances Mary) Keats born; baptized at St. Botolph's, Bishopsgate, June 17 (Pope)

1803–1811

With George Keats attends Clarke's school at Enfield; Tom goes and remains there later (Hewlett, pp. 21, 31; Kirk, Hampstead Keats, I, lxxviii–lxxx)

1804

April	16	His father, Thomas, dies, and is buried, April 23, at St. Stephen's, Coleman Street (Pope)

[1] This "calendar" of Keats's doings and whereabouts has been made as detailed as possible. Many of its dates, to be sure, are conjectural or controversial, but, if so, they are discussed in the notes to the separate letters or in the Introduction.

[2] Cited below only as "Pope."

1804

June 27 — His mother, Frances, marries William Rawlings at St. George's, Hanover Square (Pope). The Keats children live with their grandparents, John and Alice Jennings, at Ponders End (Adami, p. 18)

1805

February 1 — John Jennings signs his will (Hewlett, p. 375)

March 8 — John Jennings dies and is buried, March 14, at St. Stephen's, Coleman Street (Pope). The family move to Edmonton (Colvin, 1920, p. 9; Lowell, I, 27 f.)

1809

January — His uncle, Captain Midgley John Jennings, Royal Marines, dies (Rollins, *HLB*, IV [1950], 384)

1810

March 20 — His mother buried at St. Stephen's, Coleman Street (Pope)

July — Mrs. Jennings appoints guardians for the Keats children (Colvin, 1920, p. 15; Adami, p. 30)

1811

Summer — Leaves Enfield school and is apprenticed to Hammond, a surgeon of Edmonton (Colvin, 1920, p. 16)

1813

November 4 — His great-aunt, Mary Sweetingburgh, dies (Hewlett, p. 23)

1814

Writes "Imitation of Spenser" (sometimes dated as early as 1812), "To Lord Byron," "Fill for me a brimming bowl," "On Death"

December 19 — His grandmother, Mrs. Jennings, buried at St. Stephen's, Coleman Street (aged 78) (Pope)

1815

February 2 — Writes a sonnet to Leigh Hunt [3]

[3] For the date on which Hunt left the prison see the *Examiner*, February 5, p. 51.

February		Writes "To Hope" and "Ode to Apollo" ("In thy western halls")
October	1	Enters Guy's Hospital this Sunday as a student; lodges with three other students in St. Thomas's Street and then (in the same house) with Henry Stephens, George Mackereth, and one Frankish (*KC*, II, 207; Rollins, *HLB*, IV [1950], 388)
	29	Guy's returns six guineas to him, "he becoming a dresser" (Hewlett, p. 35)
November		Writes an epistle to G. F. Mathew (No. 2)

1815

Writes "To Some Ladies," "On Receiving a Curious Shell," and other poems

1816

February	14	Writes "Hadst thou liv'd in days of old"
March	3	Entered at Guy's as dresser to the surgeons "12 Mo. £1.1." (Hewlett, p. 36)
Spring	(?)	Meets Severn (Lowell, I, 105 f.; *KC*, I, cxxix)
May	5	"O Solitude," his first published verses, appears in the *Examiner*
June		Writes "To one who has been long in city pent"
	13	The three Keats brothers authorize their guardian Abbey to pay Joseph Burch £3 15*s*. from Alice Jennings' estate (No. 3)
	29	Writes a sonnet to C. J. Wells
July	25	Passes examination at Apothecaries' Hall; becomes eligible to practise as apothecary, physician, surgeon (Lowell, I, 154)
August		Takes Tom to Margate (*KC*, I, 3); writes an epistle to George (No. 5)

1816

Month	Day	Event
September		Writes an epistle to C. C. Clarke (No. 6); leaves Margate and takes lodgings before October 9 (No. 7) with his brothers at 8 Dean Street, Southwark
October		Writes the Chapman's Homer sonnet; meets Hunt, Haydon, Reynolds (I, 114 n.; *KC*, I, 4–6); Mathew's "To a Poetical Friend" appears in the *European Magazine*
November	1	Sees Clarke, who promises to spend the evening of December 17 with him (I, 121)
	2	Has an engagement because of which he declined an invitation from Severn (No. 9)
	3	First visit (for breakfast) to Haydon's studio (No. 8)
	9	Plans to burn some of his "worst" verses and to visit Hunt with Clarke (I, 113)
	18	Writes a sonnet "To My Brothers"; he and his brothers have moved to 76 Cheapside (No. 11)
	19	Spends the evening with Haydon (No. 11)
	20	Writes the "Great Spirits" sonnet (I, 117 ff.)
November–December		Writes "Sleep and Poetry" (Lowell, I, 216; Finney, I, 134)
December		Listed as a certified apothecary in the *London Medical Repository* (VI, 345)
	1	His Chapman's Homer sonnet appears in Hunt's *Examiner* article on "Young Poets" (Keats, Shelley, Reynolds); calls on Hunt with Clarke (Hewlett, pp. 65 f.)
	c. 14, 15	Meets Reynolds at Haydon's; visits Thomas Richards at night and stays all the next day (I, 121)
	17	His life mask made by Haydon before this date. Reynolds, Severn, Clarke spend the evening with him (I, 121)

	18	Finishes "I stood tiptoe" (Garrod, p. lxxvi). ?Calls on Clarke (I, 121)
	22	Writes a sonnet on "Vulgar Superstition" (Lowell, I, 233 f.; Finney, I, 158)
	30	He and Hunt write sonnets on "The Grasshopper and Cricket" (Garrod, p. 49)
December		Writes "To Kosciusko," "Happy is England," "Nymph of the downward smile"

1817

January	20	Dines at Horace Smith's with Haydon, Hunt, and Shelley (Haydon's unpublished Journal)
	31	Writes "After dark vapours"
February	5	With Reynolds has supper with Hunt and Shelley (F. L. Jones, *Mary Shelley's Journal* [Norman, Oklahoma, 1947], p. 76)
	12	With George Keats has tea and supper with Mrs. Shelley at the Hunts' (the same, p. 77)
	15	Calls on Mrs. Shelley and the Hunts (the same, p. 77)
	16	"To Kosciusko" printed in the *Examiner*. At a dinner party Hunt shows some of Keats's verse to the Shelleys, Godwin, Basil Montagu, and Hazlitt (Howe, p. 208)
	23	"After dark vapours" printed in the *Examiner*
	27	Writes "This pleasant tale is like a little copse"
March	1 or 2	Sees the Elgin Marbles with Haydon (and Reynolds?) and writes the Elgin Marbles sonnets (Lowell, I, 275; Finney, I, 184)
	3	His *Poems* published by C. and J. Ollier (Lowell, I, 269 f.); with Clarke and Reynolds visits Haydon at night (I, 122)
	9	Reynolds reviews his *Poems*, printing the Elgin Marbles sonnets, in the *Champion*. The sonnets also appear in the

1817

Examiner. About this time has an engagement at night with Reynolds and Haydon (I, 125)

March 16 "This pleasant tale" printed in the *Examiner*

25 With his brothers has moved by this date to Benjamin Bentley's house, 1 Well Walk, Hampstead (No. 19). Slightly before this date meets Taylor, who is impressed by his unconventional dress (Blunden, *Keats's Publisher* [1936], p. 41)

26 With Hunt to the Novellos'; Clarke also there. Has written a sonnet on Hunt's *Rimini* (I, 126 f.)

April 7 Takes a walk with Haydon (Hewlett, p. 382)

c. 13 Taylor and Hessey decide to publish his future books (Olive Taylor, *London Mercury*, XII [1925], 258). Writes to the publishers from Reynolds' house (No. 20)

14 Goes to Southampton (I, 128 f.)

15 Crosses to the Isle of Wight and sleeps at Newport (I, 129, 132)

16 Visits Shanklin but lodges at Carisbrooke (I, 130 f.)

17 Writes a sonnet "On the Sea" (I, 132)

18 Plans to begin *Endymion* (I, 134)

c. 24 Moves to Margate (I, 138, 142), and Tom joins him. Has begun *Endymion* (I, 139)

May Mathew reviews his *Poems* in the *European Magazine*

11 Has written a little of *Endymion*, Book I (I, 142, 145)

16 Gets a £20 loan from Taylor and Hessey; goes to Canterbury with Tom (I, 146 f.); visits Bo-Peep, near Hastings, alone at the end of May or the beginning of June and meets Isabella Jones (Sharp, p. 30; Gittings, p. 59)

June	1	Hunt reviews his *Poems* in the *Examiner*
	10	Back at Well Walk; calls at Reynolds' home; asks Taylor and Hessey for £30 (No. 28)
July	6, 13	Hunt continues the *Examiner* review of his *Poems*
August	17	"On the Sea" published in the *Champion*
	c. 21	Visits Reynolds, who is ill; has finished *Endymion*, Book II (No. 29)
August	(?)	"One Sunday" he visits Clarke and reads to him and Severn extracts from *Endymion*, Books I, II (Clarke, *Recollections of Writers* [1878], p. 141)
September	*c.* 1	Dines at the Reynoldses' (I, 149)
	c. 3	Goes to Oxford to visit Bailey (I, 149, 153 f.). George and Tom are in Paris (I, 154 f.)
	5	Completes *Endymion*, III.1–41 (Garrod, p. lxxxvi)
	15–20	Has "regularly a Boat on the Isis" (I, 162)
	20	Writes *Endymion*, III.766–806 (I, 166; *KC*, I, 7); has been reading Katherine Philips and *The Round Table* (I, 163–166)
	21	"The poetry of earth" appears in the *Examiner*
	26	Finishes *Endymion*, Book III (Garrod, p. lxxxvi); about this time looks up Cripps for Haydon (I, 167)
October		*Blackwood's* first article on the Cockney School published; the *Monthly Repository* prints his and Hunt's sonnets on "The Grasshopper and Cricket"
	2	Visits Stratford-on-Avon with Bailey (I, 323 n.; Colvin, 1920, p. 150)
	5	Returns to Hampstead (I, 168)
	6	Calls on the Reynoldses, Hunt, Haydon, and sees Shelley (I, 168)

1817

October 7 He and Reynolds spend the day at Brown's (I, 169)

8 The Keats brothers dine with Brown (I, 171)

c. 10–24 Is confined at Hampstead; is taking mercury (I, 171 f.)

25 Visits Rice at night (I, 172)

27 Rice spends the day with him; Tom unwell (I, 172)

29 In town and calls on the Reynoldses. Plans to finish *Endymion* in three weeks (I, 172, 176)

31 Sends Jane Reynolds "O Sorrow" (No. 40)

November 2 or 3 With Rice at Reynolds' (I, 181)

5, 12, or 19 Asks the Dilkes to send him *Sibylline Leaves* (No. 42)

18 Calls with Hunt and the journalist Walter Coulson on the Shelleys at 19 Mabledon Place, London (*Mary Shelley's Journal*, p. 86)

20 or 21 Meets Christie, Rice, Martin at the Reynoldses' (I, 187)

22 Goes to Burford Bridge (I, 187); plans to go with Reynolds to Oxford at Christmas; is reading Shakespeare's *Poems* (I, 188 f.)

28 Finishes the first draft of *Endymion* (Finney, I, 234)

December *c.* 5 Returns to Hampstead

14 Dines with Haydon after George and Tom Keats leave for Teignmouth (I, 192)

15 Sees Kean at Drury Lane (I, 191)

c. 16 Goes with Haydon to meet Wordsworth at Monkhouse's (T. O. Mabbott, *NQ*, May 10, 1941, pp. 328 f.)

c. 17 Dines with Horace Smith, Thomas Hill, and others, who "talked of Kean" (I, 192 f.)

18 Sees Kean at Drury Lane (I, 191); Godwin, Lamb, and Talfourd there (Godwin's Journal)

19 Spends the evening with Wells (I, 192)

20 Goes to the Royal Academy exhibition; spends the evening with Dilke (I, 192)

21 His review of Kean appears in the *Champion;* spends another evening with Dilke (I, 192)

24 Spends the day with Reynolds (I, 193)

25 Godwin notes in his Journal, "Meet Keats"

26 Goes with Brown and Dilke to the Drury Lane pantomime (I, 193)

28 Attends Haydon's "immortal dinner" with Lamb, Ritchie, Wordsworth, and others (I, 194, 197 f.)

29 Calls on but misses Haydon (I, 194)

31 Breaks his January 4 engagement with Haydon; meets Wordsworth on Hampstead Heath (I, 194 f.)

December Writes "In drear-nighted December" (Finney, I, 235)

1818

January 1 or 2 Goes to Covent Garden and talks to Bob Harris (I, 199)

3 Calls on the Wordsworths and Sara Hutchinson at Monkhouse's (I, 197). About this time goes to a ball at Redhall's (I, 200 f., II, 13)

4 His reviews of *Retribution* and *Harlequin Gulliver* published in the *Champion.* Wells and Severn dine with him (I, 196 f.)

5 Calls on Solomon Sawrey (I, 196); dines with Wordsworth and Monkhouse, sups with Wells (I, 197, 202;);

1818

has lately seen "a great deal" of Rice (I, 197); has seen Fanny Keats twice and dined with Haslam (I, 198 f.)

January *c.* 6 Begins to correct the manuscript of *Endymion* (I, 196, 201)

7 Expects "Loveless" (I, 200)

10 Is attending "a sort of a Club every Saturday evening"; is raising subscriptions for Cripps (I, 202 f.)

11, 12 In the City at John Taylor's (I, 204)

12 Goes with Wells to Drury Lane and a private theater (I, 205 f., 215 f.). About this time Haydon invites him to dine "every Sunday at *three*" (I, 204)

15 Was "called away" (I, 206)

16 Writes "To Mrs. Reynolds's Cat"

c. 16, 17 To dances at Dilke's and the London Coffeehouse (I, 206)

18 Has Haslam for breakfast; dines with Hazlitt, Haslam, Bewick at Haydon's; sees Hunt (I, 206, 214); has revised *Endymion*, Book I (I, 206)

c. 19 Dines with Brown (I, 214)

20 Takes *Endymion*, Book I, to the publishers (I, 206 f., 212). Goes to Hazlitt's lecture just as it ends, and sees Wells, Bewick, the Landseers, and others (I, 214)

21 At Hunt's writes lines on a lock of Milton's hair. About this time calls on Haydon to discuss a drawing for *Endymion* (I, 207 f., 210, 213)

22 Writes a sonnet on rereading *King Lear* (I, 212, 214 f.), which "one January evening" he reads to Severn (Sharp, p. 31)

23 Begins to prepare *Endymion*, Book II, for the press. Tom's blood spitting continues. Has seen "a good deal of Wordsworth" (I, 212). Spends the evening working at Dilke's (I, 215)

27 Hears Hazlitt's lecture (I, 212)

30 Rewrites a passage in *Endymion*, Book I (I, 218)

31 Writes "O blush not so" and "Hence, Burgundy"; copies "When I have fears" (I, 219–222)

February — Supposedly begins to write "Isabella" (Lowell, I, 596; Finney, I, 371)

3 Copies "No! those days are gone away" and "Souls of poets dead and gone" (I, 225). Hears Hazlitt's lecture (I, 227, 237)

4 Calls on Reynolds and they "trudge together" perhaps to Novello's (I, 225). Writes "Time's sea hath been" and a sonnet "To the Nile" in competition with Hunt and Shelley (I, 227 f.)

5 Has "employ in the affair of Cripps"; writes a sonnet to Spenser; sees *Fazio* at Covent Garden (I, 226 f.)

6 Sees Reynolds; sends *Endymion*, Book II, to the publishers (I, 226)

8 Writes "Blue! 'Tis the life of heaven"

10 Hears Hazlitt's lecture. About this time Crabb Robinson calls (I, 227)

11 Dines at Hunt's with the Shelleys, Peacock, Hogg, Jane Clairmont (R. Glynn Grylls, *Claire Clairmont* [1939], p. 87)

c. 14 Copies extracts from Smith's "Nehemiah Muggs"; sees a printed sheet of *Endymion* (I, 227–230); has been writing "many songs & Sonnets" (I, 228)

17 Attends Hazlitt's lecture (I, 237)

18 Visits Reynolds, who is ill (I, 236)

19 Cancels an engagement with Horace Smith; writes "What the Thrush Said" (I, 233 f.)

1818

February	21	Before this day has visited the British Gallery exhibition (I, 235 f.). Is reading Voltaire and Gibbon (I, 237)
	24	Perhaps attends Hazlitt's lecture (I, 237)
	c. 27	Finishes the fair copy of *Endymion*, Book III, and begins Book IV; is reading proofs of the earlier books (I, 238 f.)
March	*c.* 3	Sees Peter Moore at Drury Lane (I, 282)
	4	Leaves London in a tempest (*KC*, I, 12 f.)
	6	Reaches Exeter
	6 or 7	Joins Tom Keats at Teignmouth; George returns to London. Rain for six days (I, 245 f., 249)
	10	About this time is insulted at the Teignmouth theater (I, 245 f.)
	13	Writes "Four seasons fill." Tom has a hemorrhage (I, 243 f.)
	14	Finishes copying *Endymion*, Book IV (I, 246)
	18	George sends him £20 and pays his bills (I, 248)
	19	Writes and dates the original preface to *Endymion* (Garrod, pp. lxxxviii f.)
	21	Sends the publishers the remainder of the *Endymion* copy and the preface (I, 253). Writes "For there's Bishop's teign" and "Where be ye going" (I, 249 ff.)
	23	Goes to Dawlish Fair (I, 256)
	24	Writes "Over the hills" (I, 256 f.)
	25	Writes a poetical epistle to Reynolds (No. 74)
April	9	Hears that Reynolds and the publishers have rejected his preface (I, 266)

	10	Sends Reynolds the second preface; copies a letter of Nelson's (I, 269)
	18–20	Rice apparently visits him at Teignmouth; writes "To J. R." (Lowell, I, 615–618)
	23	Is invited to a party at Ollier's (I, 227)
	24	Receives an advance copy of *Endymion* and lists errata (I, 270–273)
	27	Has finished "Isabella" (I, 274). *Endymion* published about this day; two other issues with new errata slips shortly after
May	1	Writes "Mother of Hermes" (I, 278)
	4 or 5	With Tom (and Sarah Jeffrey: see I, 283, II, 112 n.) leaves Teignmouth, stopping at Honiton and Bridport, reaching Hampstead before May 11
	9	His "Hymn to Pan" published in the *Yellow Dwarf*
	11	Dines at Haydon's (Hewlett, p. 383)
	18	Has been "very much engaged with his Friends" (I, 286)
	19	*Endymion* registered for publication (MBF, p. xxx)
	24	Dines with Hazlitt, Barnes, Wilkie at Haydon's (I, 288)
	26	Calls on Taylor and the Reynoldses (I, 288)
	c. 28	George Keats marries Georgiana Wylie (I, 290)
	30	Bailey reviews *Endymion* in an Oxford paper (second part on June 6) (I, 292 n.)
May		*Blackwood's* slurs at him
June		The *British Critic* demolishes his *Poems*
	4	"John K. in account with Abbey Cock. C°" is credited with £500, to which interest of £8 6*s.* 1*d.* is added

1818

on December 31 (William Dilke's notes, 1833, Keats Museum [see II, 49 n.])

June	6	The doctor says he "mustn't go out" (I, 291)
	7, 14	John Scott (?) reviews *Endymion* in the *Champion*
	10	With "a little indisposition" is "not at home" (probably at Taylor's) (I, 293)
	c. 18	Monkhouse calls during his absence from home (I, 297). The George Keatses entertain him, Reynolds, and perhaps Taylor at night (*KC*, I, 30)
	19–21	Has "been hard run these three" days (I, 295). Gets £30 from Abbey on the 19th, £140 on the 20th (I, 295 n.)
	22	With Brown and the George Keatses starts for Liverpool, seeing Henry Stephens at Redbourne (I, 295; *KC*, II, 212)
	23	Arrives at Liverpool in the late afternoon (Lowell, II, 13)
	24	He and Brown go to Lancaster by coach (I, 298 n.)
	25	They walk to Burton and Endmoor (I, 298 n.)
	26	They walk to Kendal, Bowness, Ambleside (I, 298 f., 302)
	27	They walk through Rydal, leaving a note for Wordsworth, and from Grasmere to Wythburn (I, 302 f.; Bushnell, p. 301). He writes "Give me your patience" (I, 303 f.)
	28	They walk to Keswick, Derwent Water, Lodore. He writes "Sweet, sweet is the greeting" (I, 304)
	29	They climb Skiddaw and walk to Ireby (I, 306 f.)
	30	They walk to Wigton and Carlisle (I, 307 f.)
July	1	By coach through Gretna Green to Dumfries (Bushnell, p. 301). He writes "On Visiting the Tomb of Burns" (I, 308 f.)

2 They walk to Lincluden and Dalbeattie (I, 311 n.; Bushnell, p. 301)

3 They walk through Auchencairn to Kirkcudbright. He writes "Old Meg she was a gipsy" and "There was a naughty boy" (I, 311–315, 317 f.)

4 They walk through Gatehouse-of-Fleet perhaps to Creetown (Bushnell, p. 282)

5 They walk via Newton-Stewart to Glenluce (I, 318 n.)

6 They walk and ride the mail coach through Stranraer to Portpatrick and sail to Donaghadee (I, 319)

7 They walk to Belfast (I, 321)

8 They walk back to Donaghadee, and sail to Portpatrick (I, 321)

9 They walk through Stranraer to Ballantrae (I, 328 n.)

10 They walk to Girvan. He writes "Ah! ken ye what" and "To Ailsa Rock" (I, 327–330)

11 They walk via Kirkoswald and Maybole to Ayr; he writes lines in Burns's cottage (I, 323 f., 330 ff.)

12 They walk to —— (possibly Kilmarnock) (Bushnell, p. 301)

13 They walk through Kingswells to Glasgow (I, 331 f.)

14–16 They walk to —— (possibly Dumbarton and Tarbet) (Bushnell, p. 301)

17 They walk through Cairndow to Inverary. He writes "All gentle folks who owe" and "Of late two dainties" (I, 334–337)

18 They walk to Cladich (Bushnell, p. 302)

19 They walk via Port-in-Sherrich to Ford (Bushnell, p. 302)

20 They walk to Kilmelfort (Bushnell, p. 302)

1818

July	21	They walk to Oban (I, 339)
	22	They go by ferry through Kerrera and on to Glen More (Bushnell, p. 302). He copies "There is a joy in footing slow" (I, 344 f.)
	23	They walk to —— (possibly Bunessan) (Bushnell, p. 302)
	24	They go by boat to Iona, Staffa, and then perhaps to Salen (Bushnell, p. 302). He writes "Not Aladdin magian" (I, 349 ff.)
	25	They go by ferry perhaps to Oban (Bushnell, p. 302)
	26–29	They perhaps stay at Oban (I, 351; Bushnell, p. 302)
	30, 31	They walk to —— (possibly Portnacroish and Ballachulish) (Bushnell, p. 302)
August	1	They apparently go to Fort William (Bushnell, p. 302)
	2	They climb Ben Nevis (I, 352 ff.), to which he writes a sonnet (I, 357 f.)
	3	They go to Letterfinlay (I, 352). He writes "Upon my life, Sir Nevis" (I, 354–357)
	4, 5	They walk to —— (possibly Fort Augustus and Foyers) (Bushnell, p. 302)
	6	They walk to Inverness (I, 357)
	7, 8	At Inverness and by coach to Beauly and Cromarty (Bushnell, p. 302). He sails for London (I, 364). Abbey mails him a draft for £30 on the 8th (I, 365 n.)
	18	Reaches London and Well Walk, Hampstead. Tom is very ill (I, 364). Possibly shortly after meets Fanny Brawne
	19	Has a bad sore throat and a toothache (I, 364 f.)
	25	Still has "a little Indisposition" (I, 366)

September	1	Calls on Abbey and possibly on the Reynoldses (I, 366). *Blackwood's* August issue with the fourth Cockney School tirade appears about this time
	14	Dines at Hessey's with Hazlitt, Woodhouse, and others, and spends the night there (Blunden, *Keats's Publisher* [1936], p. 56)
	c. 19	Calls on the Reynoldses and meets Jane Cox (I, 370 f., 394 ff.)
	c. 21	Has copied out "Isabella." Translates a sonnet of Ronsard's. Is confined to the house with a sore throat (I, 371)
	c. 27	Croker's attack on *Endymion* appears in the *Quarterly Review* (*KC*, I, 44)
October	3, 8	J. S. and R. B. defend him in the *Morning Chronicle* (I, 373 f., 393)
	6	Reynolds' defense of *Endymion* appears in *Alfred, West of England Journal* (I, 393)
	9	Tom is "weaker every day" (I, 375)
	12	The *Examiner* reprints Reynolds' defense of him (I, 393)
	13	Reynolds calls and borrows the manuscript of "Isabella" (I, 376; *KC*, I, 43 f.)
	14	Reynolds urges him to publish "Isabella" (I, 376, 393). He writes "A Prophecy." Tom much worse (I, 391, 398, 400)
	15	Calls on Mrs. Millar and sees Henry Wylie (I, 392 f., 400)
	16	Calls on Dilke; plans to write a prose tale (I, 401); has lately called on Haydon, Hunt, Rice, Hessey (I, 400)
	18	Charles and Henry Wylie dine with him and Tom (I, 401)
	c. 19	Calls on Abbey (I, 378, 385)
	22	Walks with Hazlitt and dines with the Wylies at Mrs. Millar's (I, 401 f.). Calls on Hessey at night (*KC*, I, 53)

1818

October	23	Calls on Hunt and meets Charles Ollier (I, 402)
	24	Meets the Hastings lady, Mrs. Isabella Jones (I, 402 f.)
	25	Reynolds calls (I, 402)
	27	Calls on Abbey and gets £20 in cash (I, 386)
	31	Haslam calls (I, 405)
November	5	Has seen Abbey three times recently (I, 406)
	9	"P. Fenbank" sends him a sonnet and £25 (II, 16 f.)
	24	Shortly before this date calls on Rice (I, 406)
November		Hunt's "sickening" (II, 7) *Literary Pocket-Book* prints "The Human Seasons" and "To Ailsa Rock"
November (?)–April, 1819		Is writing "Hyperion" (De Selincourt, p. 484)
December	1	Tom Keats dies. Accepts Brown's invitation to live in Wentworth Place (II, 4 f.)
	5	Attends the Jack Randall–Ned Turner prize fight at Crawley Hunt, Sussex (Clarke, *Recollections of Writers* [1878], p. 145; Lowell, II, 121)
	7	Tom Keats buried at St. Stephen's, Coleman Street (Pope)
	9	Calls on Abbey and gets £20 in cash (William Dilke's notes, Keats Museum)
	c. 10	With Mrs. Dilke calls on Fanny Keats (II, 6)
	12	About this time goes with Brown to Payne's *Brutus* (II, 8); meets Caroline Robinson at the Brawnes' (II, 13 f.)

13 With Haslam calls on Fanny Keats; spends the night with Haslam (II, 6)

14 Calls on Mrs. Wylie, Mrs. Millar, Hazlitt (II, 6, 8), and Mrs. Reynolds (I, 411)

15 Haydon calls (II, 6). Perhaps on this day goes with Brown and Hunt to the Novellos' (II, 8, 11)

16 Mr. Lewis calls (II, 6)

17 At home while Brown and his nephews go sight-seeing; Bentley brings him a basket of books; goes on a little with "Hyperion" (II, 11 f.)

18 Visits the Dilkes (MBF, p. 268). Declines to meet the Misses Porter (I, 412)

20 Cancels engagement with Haydon and dines with Haslam (I, 413 f., II, 14)

21 Calls on Fanny Keats, dines with Haydon (I, 413 f., II, 14)

22 Mr. Lewis calls in the morning (II, 15). Absent when Haydon's servant calls, but offers to lend Haydon money (I, 415). Confined at Hampstead with a sore throat (II, 15)

c. 23 Brown goes to Chichester (II, 15). About this time goes shooting with Dilke (II, 18)

24 Plans to go to Chichester on the 30th (II, 18); asks Taylor for £30 (I, 417)

25 Dines with Mrs. Brawne; has an "understanding" with Fanny Brawne (I, 411; Edgcumbe, pp. 55 f.)

27 Dines with Haydon; sees Ritchie's letter and some "Pre-Raphaelite" engravings (II, 16, 19)

28 Sore throat makes him postpone his trip to Chichester (I, 417, II, 18); stays in for several days (II, 3)

1819

January	1	Dines with the Dilkes at Mrs. Brawne's (II, 20)
	2	?Haydon calls (II, 4). Dilke spends the evening with him. His throat better; copies "Ever let the fancy roam," "Bards of Passion," and "I had a dove" (II, 21–27)
	3	Kirkman calls in the morning. Archer has called twice lately. Dines with Mancur at the Dilkes', has tea with Mrs. Dilke (II, 27 f., 30)
	4	?Is out this morning (II, 30)
	5	?Goes to town (II, 30)
	7	Haydon asks him for a loan (II, 31)
	c. 10–12	?Goes to the bank "some thrice" (II, 32)
	18	Calls on Abbey and gets £20 in cash (II, 33 n.)
	18 or 19	Goes to Chichester, where he writes "St. Agnes" and attends two card parties (II, 33 n., 58 f.)
	23	Walks with Brown to the Snooks' at Bedhampton (II, 35)
	24	With Brown calls on Mr. Burton and Mr. Butler (II, 35)
	25	Goes to the dedication of Way's chapel at Stansted (II, 35, 62 f.)
	26	Brown returns to Wentworth Place (II, 35)
February	1 or 2	Returns to Wentworth Place with a sore throat (II, 37; Rollins, *HLB*, VIII [1954], 244 f.)
	13	To town for the first time "these three weeks," seeing Woodhouse, Mrs. Hazlitt, and others (II, 59)
	13–17	Writes "The Eve of St. Mark" (II, 62; Finney, I, xv)
	17	Tries to call on Mrs. Wylie and Haslam (II, 63, 66). Goes to Woodhouse's coffeehouse (II, 64). ?Sees Abbey (II, 39). ?Mrs. Jones gives him a pheasant (II, 65)

	18	Has had "several interviews" with Abbey (II, 39). With Brown and Mrs. Brawne to tea at the Dilkes' (II, 66)
	19	Calls on Mr. Lewis (II, 63). Goes to Miss Millar's birthday dance (II, 8, 45, 60)
	20	Dines with others at the Dilkes' (II, 65)
	22	?Haydon calls at noon (II, 41)
	24–26	In town, staying with Taylor (II, 41 f., 60). Calls on Mrs. Wylie on the 24th (II, 63 n.). ?Writes "Bright Star" and "To Fanny" ("Physician Nature") (Colvin, 1920, p. 335)
	26	Returns to Wentworth Place (II, 41 f.)
March	1	Visits the British Museum with Severn (II, 68). Gets £6 from Abbey (William Dilke's notes, Keats Museum). Severn and Cawthorn dine with him, and he, Brown, and Cawthorn go to the theater (II, 67 f.)
	8	Has been "about every three days" to Abbey's and the lawyer's (II, 42)
	10	Haydon again asks him for money (II, 44)
	11	Goes to town (II, 71)
	12	Has been reading Hazlitt on Gifford (II, 71), Moore, Beaumont and Fletcher (II, 73)
	13	Walks "past westend" (II, 74). Entertains the Davenports and others (II, 76)
	14	Dinner with Haslam canceled because of the elder Haslam's illness (II, 74). Dines with the Davenports and wastes the afternoon (II, 77)
	15	Does "nothing," but gets £60 from Abbey (II, 77 n.)
	16	Calls on Abbey. Taylor and Hilton dine with him; walks with them to Camden Town (II, 77 f.)

1819

March	17	In bed till 10 A.M.; reads Beaumont and Fletcher, and goes to Mrs. Bentley's (II, 78)
	18	Gets a black eye in playing cricket (II, 78)
	19	Is indolent after sleeping till 11 A.M. (II, 78). Copies "Why did I laugh tonight" (II, 81)
	20	Calls on Haslam (II, 79)
	24	Goes to "the other end of the Town" from Cheapside (II, 47)
	25	Calls on Fanny Keats in Pancras Lane, and gets £10 from Abbey (II, 47 n.)
	29	His miniature by Severn to be exhibited at the Royal Academy (II, 48)
	31	Coaches Fanny Keats for her confirmation (II, 49 ff.)
April	1	Goes to town (II, 49)
	2, 3	Gets £106 7*s.* 7*d.* from Abbey (II, 49 n.)
	4	Dines with the Wylie brothers at Mrs. Brawne's (II, 52, 82)
	c. 10	Hunt and Davenport dine with him and Brown (II, 83)
	11	Informs Haydon that he can't make a loan (II, 53 ff.). Walks with Coleridge and Joseph Green (II, 88 f.). About this date has a claret feast for Dilke, Reynolds, Martin, and others (II, 90)
	12	Goes with Hunt to Leicester's gallery (II, 83). Dines with the Dilkes in Westminster (II, 51 f.)
	13	Goes to a rout at Sawrey's (II, 51, 82). Shortly after this time he lends Haydon £30 (II, 55 n., 206)
	14	Calls on Taylor (II, 82)

15 Collects old letters left at Mrs. Bentley's (II, 82). Writes "When they were come unto the Faery's court" (II, 85–88)

16 Writes "He is to weet a melancholy Carle" and copies "As Hermes once"; reads the Amena letters of Wells to Tom (II, 89 ff.)

17 ?Sees Barker's panorama (II, 95). Goes with Rice, Reynolds, Martin to Covent Garden (II, 94)

18 Spends the day with Woodhouse at Taylor's (II, 94 f.)

19 Calls on Mrs. Wylie. Taylor, Woodhouse, Reynolds dine with him and Brown; they play cards all night (II, 93)

20 Is not "worth a sixpence" (II, 93)

21 Writes a review of Reynolds' *Peter Bell;* writes "La Belle Dame" and "Happy, happy glowing fire." Has been reading Robertson and Voltaire (II, 93–100)

25 The Wylie brothers dine with him and Brown (II, 93). His review of Reynolds appears in the *Examiner*

30 Copies sonnets on Fame, Sleep, and "If by dull rhymes" and the "Ode to Psyche" (II, 104–108)

April Sends Woodhouse the manuscript of "Hyperion," which he refuses to complete (Lowell, II, 226)

May 1 The Dilkes dine with him and Brown (II, 56). Writes "Two or Three Posies" (II, 56 f.)

3 Calls on Fanny Keats (II, 57)

12 Hears from George Keats and calls on Mrs. Wylie (II, 109)

23 Is obliged to stay at home (II, 110)

27 Calls on Fanny Keats and finds Mrs. Abbey cordial (II, 111, 117 f.)

c. 29 Returns all borrowed books (II, 111, 114). Burns old letters (II, 112)

1819

May	31	Thinks of living near Teignmouth or going as a surgeon on an Indiaman (II, 112 ff.)
May		Writes the odes on a Grecian Urn, a Nightingale, Melancholy, and Indolence
June	8	Rice calls and invites him to go to the Isle of Wight (II, 115, 117)
	9	Gives up the ideas of Devonshire and the Indiaman (II, 115, 117)
	13	Sees Monkhouse (II, 120)
	14	Goes to town with Brown; postpones visit to Fanny Keats; sends the Nightingale ode to Elmes (II, 118 ff.)
	15	Is "engaged" and "much in want of Money" (II, 119 f.)
	16	Postpones a visit to Fanny Keats, calls on Abbey, learns that Mrs. Midgley Jennings is filing a bill in Chancery against the Keats family (II, 121)
	17	Asks Haydon and others to return loans; is "fully employed" (II, 119 f., 122)
	27	On the Portsmouth coach with Rice in a violent storm (II, 125)
	28	Crosses to the Isle of Wight and settles at Shanklin (II, 122–126)
	29	Writes (but does not send the letter) to Fanny Brawne (II, 122)
July	1	Sends his first letter to Fanny Brawne from Shanklin (II, 122)
	8	Has every day been writing verse (II, 127)
	11	Completes the first act of *Otho* and "Lamia," Part I (II, 128)
	15	Has been for two or three days in an irritable state of health; has "three or four stories half done" (II, 129 f.)

	16	Looks "about the country" (II, 130)
	22	About this date Brown arrives at Shanklin (II, 132)
	24	Rice, Brown, Martin, and he have been playing cards night and morning (II, 132)
	25	Rice and Martin leave Shanklin. He is employed all day in writing an abstract poem (II, 132)
July		The Nightingale ode published in Elmes's *Annals* (II, 118 n.)
August	*c.* 1, 2	Alone at Shanklin while Brown gads over the country (II, 138)
	12	He and Brown move from Shanklin to Winchester, nearly having an accident while crossing from Cowes (II, 137 f., 142, 147)
	12–September 4	His and Brown's mail goes astray (II, 153 f.)
	14	Has completed Act IV of *Otho* and is working on "The Fall of Hyperion"; "Lamia" half finished (II, 139)
	23	Asks Taylor for money; has finished *Otho* (II, 143 f.)
	31	Repeats his request to Taylor for a loan (II, 154)
September	5	Gets £30 from Hessey and £30 or £40 from Haslam (II, 154); has finished "Lamia," is revising "St. Agnes," and is studying Italian (II, 157)
	c. 7	Brown goes to Chichester (II, 159, 186)
	10	A letter from George Keats hurries him on the night coach to London (II, 160, 184)
	11	Arrives in London. Talks with Woodhouse and Hessey (II, 162)
	11 or 14	Goes to the theater and sees Hodgkinson (?) (II, 192)
	12	Breakfasts with Woodhouse, and they talk for six hours (II, 162–165). Dines with the Wylies at Mrs. Millar's (II, 186, 206)

1819

September 13 Sees Fanny Keats (II, 160, 187), Rice, Martin (II, 187). Watches Henry Hunt's triumphal entry into London (II, 194). Has tea with Abbey (II, 184, 192)

14 ?Sees Haslam (II, 187)

15 Returns to Winchester (II, 169, 186). About this time plays a joke on Brown at Bedhampton and Benjamin at Wentworth Place (II, 215 f.)

17 Writes "Pensive they sit," and takes his daily walk (II, 188, 209)

18 Has been reading Burton's *Anatomy* (II, 191 f.)

19 Composes "To Autumn" (II, 167, 170 f.)

20 Copies "The Eve of St. Mark" (II, 201–204). Says his friendship with Haydon is at an end (II, 205 f.)

21 Has given up "The Fall of Hyperion" (II, 167) but sends Woodhouse passages from it (II, 171 f.). Begins a sonnet in French (II, 172). Is reading Ariosto (II, 212)

22 Will persist in not publishing "Isabella" (II, 174); decides to be a journalist in Westminster (II, 174, 177)

24 Hears from Brown in Chichester (II, 212 f.)

c. 25 Visits Rice (II, 175)

October *c.* 1 Brown rejoins him in Winchester (II, 218)

c. 8 Returns with Brown to London (II, 218)

10 Visits Fanny Brawne in Hampstead (II, 222); writes "The day is gone" (?) (Finney, II, 723)

11 Sees Mrs. Dilke in the morning (II, 223)

c. 11–14 In lodgings at 25 College Street, Westminster (II, 222 n.). On one of these days Severn calls and protests his giving up "Hyperion" (Sharp, pp. 40 f.)

c. 15–17	Visits the Brawnes (II, 222 n.)
18–20	Gives up his lodgings; stays with the Dilkes (II, 222 n.)
20	Visits Fanny Brawne (II, 224)
21	Probably back with Brown at Wentworth Place (II, 222 n.)
c. 22	Sends *Otho* to Drury Lane (II, 229)
24	?Severn calls on this Sunday and finds him "well neither in mind nor in body" (Sharp, p. 41)
c. 29	Calls on Mrs. Wylie (II, 229)
November 2	Asks Haslam for a loan of £30 (II, 226)
5	In a lecture, which he missed, Hazlitt quotes him (II, 230)
c. 8	Calls on Dilke at the Navy Pay Office (II, 230)
11	Gets some money, the first in ten months, from Abbey (II, 230)
12	Gets an invitation from Severn to see "The Cave of Despair" (II, 230). Calls on Abbey (II, 229)
15	Dines with Hilton and Woodhouse at Taylor's (Taylor to his brother James, November 15 [Keats Museum])
16	Goes to the City (II, 232), and has gone "frequently" (II, 233)
17	Has determined to publish nothing he has yet written; is reading Holinshed's *Chronicles* and thinking of writing on the Earl of Leicester's history (II, 234 f.)
18	Calls on Fanny Keats (II, 233)
November	Writes "King Stephen" and "I cry your mercy" (?). Is writing "The Cap and Bells" and "remodelling" "Hyperion" (*KC*, II, 72)
December 20	*Otho* is accepted by Drury Lane for the next season (II, 237)

1819

December	21	Hears some schoolboys "Speechify" (at Westminster School?); has been to Abbey's "lately" (II, 237 f.)
	22	Has been and continues "rather unwell" (II, 238)
	25	Dines with the Dilkes (II, 237)

1820

January		?The Grecian Urn ode is published in Elmes's *Annals*
	9	Dines with George Keats, just arrived in London, at Mrs. Millar's with Mrs. Wylie, Charles Wylie, and Lacon (II, 240)
	10	George Keats takes Mrs. Wylie to the theater (II, 242)
	11	Goes with George to a hop at the Dilkes' (II, 241, 244)
	12	Dines with George at Taylor's (II, 240). George then goes to Haslam's, where he stays two days (II, 242 f.)
	13	Is about to send *Otho* to Covent Garden (II, 241)
	15	Entertains Charles Wylie (II, 243, 245)
	16	Has a pleasant party for George and their old set (II, 243, 245)
	22	Dines with Brown, Reynolds, Rice, Taylor, and probably Thomas Richards and George at the Dilkes' (MBF, *TLS*, December 6, 1941, p. 624)
	28	George leaves for Liverpool at 6 A.M. (II, 247)
	29	George reaches Liverpool at 6 P.M. and sails for America about February 1 (II, 248)
February	3	Returns from London on the stage-coach "this bitter day" at 11 P.M., has a severe hemorrhage, and is attended by George Rodd (II, 251, 280 n.; *KC*, II, 73 f.)
	5	Mr. Davenport invites him to supper (II, 252)

	6	Mrs. Reynolds and the Wylie brothers call (II, 252). Gives Brown £40 (Brown to Dilke, May 2, 1826 [Keats Museum])
	7	Has a slight fever and is on a starvation diet. Mrs. Wylie calls (II, 253)
	9	Takes a walk in the garden (II, 255)
	13	Reynolds calls (II, 260). About this time offers to break his engagement to Fanny Brawne (II, 259)
	27	Barry Cornwall has sent him two books. Will soon proceed with "The Cap and Bells" (II, 267 f.)
	c. 28	Fanny Brawne sends him a ring (II, 270)
March	6	Has "violent palpitations at the heart" (II, 273 f.)
	8	Dr. Bree calls and "gives very favourable hopes" (II, 274)
	10	Is now "out of danger" (II, 274 f.)
	12, 13	Much better, he is revising "Lamia" (II, 276)
	14	Dines with Taylor (Blunden, *London Mercury*, IV [1921], 141)
	20	Has had several attacks of heart palpitation (II, 280)
	24	?Charles Wylie calls (II, 282)
	25	Attends private view of Haydon's "Christ's Entry" (II, 284 n.)
April		His *Endymion* praised in the *London Magazine*. ?Writes "The house of mourning" (R. F. Rashbrook, *NQ*, November 13, 1948, pp. 498 f.)
	12	Has been to town once or twice (II, 285)
	20	Henry Wylie calls (II, 287)
	21	Plans to go to Scotland with Brown (II, 287)

1820

April	27	Taylor and Hessey receive the manuscript of the *Lamia* volume (Blunden, *London Mercury*, IV [1921], 141)
May	2	Goes to town; has given up the idea of going to Scotland (II, 288)
	4	Moves his belongings to 2 Wesleyan Place, Kentish Town, paying in advance a week's rent, as Brown rents Wentworth Place (Bodurtha and Pope, p. 113)
	6	Borrows £50 from Brown (Brown to Dilke, May 2, 1826 [Keats Museum]); moves to 2 Wesleyan Place (II, 288 n.); sails to Gravesend on the smack with Brown (II, 289 n.)
	10	"La Belle Dame" published in Hunt's *Indicator*
June	*c.* 11	Reads and corrects proofs of *Lamia* after visiting Taylor (No. 263)
	c. 18	Haydon calls (No. 265). Visits the British Institution exhibition; meets Monkhouse but declines his invitation to dinner (II, 299)
	22	Has an attack of blood spitting; sees the Gisbornes at Leigh Hunt's (II, 300 n.)
	23	Moves into Hunt's house in Mortimer Terrace (II, 300 n.)
	24	The Gisbornes call and find both him and Hunt very ill (II, 300 n.)
	27	"Has been spitting blood for several days" (Blunden, *London Mercury*, IV [1921], 143)
	28	"As Hermes once" printed in the *Indicator*
	29	Barry Cornwall sends him *Marcian Colonna* (G. H. Ford, *MLN*, LXVI [1951], 532–536)
	30	Advance copies of *Lamia* are delivered (*KC*, I, 116), one of them presented by him to Barry Cornwall, who calls (Ford, *MLN*, LXVI [1951], 534)
July	1	His Nightingale ode and other verses are printed in the

Literary Gazette. *Lamia* published July 1 or 3 (preface dated June 26)

5 Has been ordered to Italy (II, 305)

12 The Gisbornes see him ("under sentence of death") at tea at the Hunts' (II, 305 n.). Severn has "seen him many times" and will visit him "perhaps twice a week" (II, 306 f.)

14 Haydon's "bearer" calls at 2 Wesleyan Place to request the return of Chapman's Homer (II, 308)

19 *Lamia* praised by Lamb in the *New Times* (review reprinted in the *Examiner*, July 30)

20, 21 "To Autumn" printed in the London *Chronicle* from the *Literary Gazette*, July 1

22 or 23 One of the Wylie brothers calls (II, 309)

August Jeffrey's review of *Endymion* and *Lamia* appears in the *Edinburgh*

2, 9 *Lamia* praised in Hunt's *Indicator*

12 Receives an invitation to visit Shelley in Italy. Leaves Hunt's house at night and goes to the Brawnes' (II, 313 f.)

13 Writes "many Letters" (II, 314). Hunt calls (II, 317)

14 Haydon sends a messenger for Chapman's Homer. Sends his informal will to Taylor (II, 318 f.)

16 Declines Shelley's invitation (II, 322 f.). About this time, Haydon noted in 1824 (Duncan Gray and Violet Walker, *K–SMB*, No. 7 [1956], 22), he called on Haydon and told him of Shelley's letter

17 Is invited by John Aitken to visit Dunbar (II, 324 ff.)

c. 18 Is waiting to hear that Brown will accompany him (II, 327, 329)

20 Asks Abbey for money (II, 331)

1820

August	23	Abbey refuses to give him money (II, 331). Hunt's *Indicator* prints lines from "The Cap and Bells"
	30	Taylor hears that, after another hemorrhage, he now "lies in a very dangerous state" (Olive Taylor, *London Mercury*, XII [1925], 259)
September		The *New Monthly Magazine*, the *British Critic*, and others praise *Lamia*
	11	Dictates to Fanny Brawne his last letter to his sister (II, 332)
	12	Haslam spends the night with him at Hampstead (II, 333)
	13	Goes to Taylor's. Severn decides to accompany him to Italy (II, 333)
	16	Assigns the copyrights of *Endymion* (Harvard) and *Poems* with *Lamia* (Morgan Library) to Taylor and Hessey for £100 each. His passport arrives (Lowell, II, 462)
	17	Boards the *Maria Crowther* in London Docks (II, 337 f.)
	18	Sails from Gravesend at night (II, 338)
	19	Off Dover Castle (II, 342)
	20	Off Brighton; severe storms (II, 342 f.). Hunt's farewell to him printed in the *Indicator*
	21	Driven back to Dungeness and New Romney (?) (II, 340)
	22, 23	Still becalmed off Dungeness (Severn's Journal, Sharp, facing p. 55)
	28	Lands with Severn at Portsmouth; passes the day and night at Bedhampton with the Snooks (II, 346 f.)
	29	Sails from Portsmouth; contrary winds (II, 347)
	30	Off Yarmouth, Isle of Wight (II, 344). ?Lands at Studland Bay (Sharp, p. 54)

October	*c.* 1	Lands at Lulworth Cove (or perhaps Holworth Bay); writes the "Bright Star" sonnet in his copy of Shakespeare's *Poems* (Sharp, pp. 54–56)
	c. 2	Sails out of the Channel past Land's End
	21	Reaches Naples and held in quarantine (II, 348 f.)
	31	Released from quarantine and lands (II, 351); his passport registered with the Council of Public Security (Lowell, II, 486)
November	6	His passport viséed at the British Legation, Naples (Lowell, II, 496)
	7	His passport viséed by the Papal Consulate General (Lowell, II, 496)
	7 or 8	Starts for Rome in a hired carriage (Lowell, II, 496)
	12	Reaches Terracina, where his passport is finally viséed by the police (Lowell, II, 497 f.)
	15	Reaches Rome, goes into lodgings on the Piazza di Spagna, and cashes part of his draft on Taylor and Hessey. Other drafts cashed on November 23 and December 26 (*K–SMB*, No. 2 [1913], 94 f.)
	30	Writes his last known letter (No. 310)
December	10	Has a relapse (II, 361 f.)

1821

February	*c.* 20	According to Gerald Griffin (Blunden, p. 486), is visited by Valentin Llanos
	23	Dies at 11 P.M. (II, 378; *KC*, II, 94)
	24	Casts taken of his face, foot, and hand (II, 378)
	25	Autopsy performed by Drs. Clark and Luby (II, 379)
	26	Buried in the Protestant Cemetery (II, 379)
March	17	The news of his death reaches London (II, 380 f.)

Biographical Sketches of Keats's Correspondents

RICHARD ABBEY

After the death of Keats's mother in 1810, his grandmother, Mrs. John Jennings, aged seventy-four, found herself responsible for four children, aged about seven to fifteen. In July "she executed a deed by which the four children and the greater part of the money left to her by her husband were placed in the charge of two trustees,"[1] John Rowland Sandell, merchant, Broad Street Buildings, and Richard Abbey, an old friend whom she had known in her native village Colne, Lancashire, at the foot of Pendle Hill.[2] Sandell apparently took almost no part in the trusteeship, and, so Dilke writes, "was obliged to fly to Holland & there died."[3]

Abbey was living in the London parish of St. Benet, Sherehog, in the 1780's, and on February 5, 1786, he married an illiterate girl, Eleanor Jones, of St. Stephen's, Walbrook. He then became a tea broker, Size Lane, in 1789, and by 1808 the senior member of Abbey, Cocks, and Gullet, wholesale tea dealers,[4] Pancras Lane. The name of the firm was changed to Abbey and Cocks in 1811 and in 1819 to Abbey, Cocks, and Company.[5] With his wife and adopted daughter Abbey lived at 4 Pancras Lane or in a large house called Pindars on Marsh Street, Walthamstow. He removed John Keats from the Enfield school and apprenticed him to a surgeon. He gave the other brothers lodgings and work in his City countinghouse, but Tom quit because of illness, George because of a quarrel with Abbey's junior partner, one Hodgkinson, whom John detested.

When the Keats brothers went into lodgings of their own, Fanny necessarily remained with her guardian. Except for four years in the Misses Tuckey's Walthamstow school, she lived with the Abbeys until she was twenty-one. Probably they were not

[1] Adami, p. 30.

[2] *KC*, I, 306, though Abbey called her "a Native of Yorkshire."

[3] *KC*, II, 175.

[4] See Joanna Richardson, "New Light on Mr. Abbey," *K–SMB*, No. 5 (1953), 26–31, the best account yet written.

[5] *The Post Office London Directory*, 1819 and 1820, lists "Abbey, Cock, and Company," but the issue for 1814 has "Abbey and Cocks" and that for 1825 "Abbey and Cock."

actually unkind to her, but they distrusted John and his friends, always spoke contemptuously of his verses, and so far as possible kept him from visiting her and her from visiting him and his brothers. George, however, liked the whole family, even Mrs. Abbey, in spite of her "unfeeling and ignorant gabble." To Fanny, Abbey gave no liberty and little pocket money. To Keats for months at a time he gave nothing. In August, 1820, he refused to advance funds for the Italian trip, and in April, 1821, he disclaimed any responsibility for repaying the gifts of money Taylor had collected to finance it.[6]

Though John and Fanny looked upon Abbey as a tyrant, he was, as Richardson has shown, a man of prominence and public spirit in Walthamstow and London affairs. Among other activities, he was an important member of the Pattenmakers' Company, of which for two terms he was master; a representative after 1802 on the Court of Common Council; a member of the Port of London Committee in 1811; and a Commissioner of Sewers, Lamps, and Pavements in 1829. He had, however, suffered business reverses before June 3, 1824, when Fanny came of age. Much alarmed, she found him unwilling (or unable) to settle and turn over her estate. What happened next is obscure.[7] Adami asserts that Dilke "came to her help and dealt with Abbey firmly enough to obtain all that belonged to her."[8] At any rate, by January, 1827, Abbey was heavily in debt to Fanny's lawyer, James Rice, and her trustee, Dilke, and the bills were not paid until 1833. Meanwhile he had mortgaged all his business and suburban property, and by May, 1831, had left Walthamstow for London. In 1834 he appears to have been a coffee dealer at his old shop in Size Lane; in 1836 he is described as a wholesale tea dealer at 5 Barge Yard and in 1837 at 22 Budge Row. He died shortly before March 18, 1837.

BENJAMIN BAILEY[1]

"One of the noblest men alive at the present day" was Keats's description of Bailey in January, 1818, but to students today "stuffy"

[6] *KC*, I, 235.

[7] Some details are given by Fanny in *More Letters*, pp. 3–5.

[8] Page 117.

[1] The best account yet written of Bailey, as of Haydon, Reynolds, and Rice, is that in Willard B. Pope's admirable, but unfortunately unpublished, Harvard dissertation

and "pompous" seem a more fitting description. Bailey was born in Cambridgeshire, June 5, 1791. A friend of Rice and Reynolds as early as 1814, with them he came to be closely associated with the daughters, Mary, Sarah, and Thomasine, of William Leigh, who lived at Salcombe Regis near Sidmouth. During March, 1815, in the commonplace books of the Leighs they wrote numerous poems—nine by Rice and "a hundred-odd by both Bailey and Reynolds." In another manuscript, "Poems by Two Friends," given to Thomasine on December 25, 1816, there are thirty-two poems by Bailey, twenty-five by Reynolds.[2]

On October 19, 1816, Bailey matriculated at Oxford and began reading for holy orders. In the following spring he met Keats at the Reynoldses' in London, and then in the late summer saw much of him and invited him to Oxford. Throughout September Keats stayed in Bailey's Magdalen Hall quarters, where he composed *Endymion*, Book III. He left Oxford about October 5 and thereafter saw Bailey infrequently. But Bailey—he had resigned from the university on April 22, 1818—defended him in an Oxford newspaper (May, June, 1818), attempted vainly to publish in an Edinburgh magazine a reply to his assailants, and had a memorable talk with J. G. Lockhart, whom he tried to influence in favor of the poet. Before August 29, 1818, he was ordained and given a curacy near Carlisle.

Keats's friendship cooled when Bailey, after having ardently courted Mariane Reynolds, early in 1819 became engaged to Hamilton Gleig (born April 19, 1793), daughter of George Gleig, bishop of Brechin and primus of the Scots Episcopal Church. Their correspondence ended on August 14, 1819, the day on which Keats sent very stiff congratulations on the marriage, which had taken place at Stirling on April 20.[3] Thereafter Bailey was a country parson at Dallington, Northamptonshire, from December 21, 1819, till near the end of 1822, at Gayhurst and Stoke Goldington, near Olney, and Burton-on-Trent at unspecified dates, and he was living at Townfield, Durham, in 1827. At some time or other he is said to have been private chaplain to Lord Hawke of Towton

(1932). Other details have been published by me in *HLB*, IV (1950), 375–378, and *K-SJ*, VI (1957), 15–30.

[2] Pope, pp. 39 f., 42 f., 629–638.

[3] *Examiner*, May 2, 1819, p. 288.

(1774–1824). In the summer of 1827 Mrs. Bailey's bad health led him to think of going to France. With the help of Bishops Gleig and Luscombe he got a small English church (the communicants "seldom exceeded 12") at Marseilles, which he reached before July 2, 1828. His wife's ill health continued, and so they returned to England at the end of 1829.

Whether he at once became vicar at Minster, in the Isle of Thanet near Margate, Kent, is not known, but he was there in April, 1831, at which time he was planning to migrate to Ceylon as senior colonial chaplain. Almost immediately after they landed at Colombo, Mrs. Bailey died (March 31, 1832), and was buried in the Galle Face Cemetery. In spite of occasional brushes with his archdeacon and bishop, Bailey himself became archdeacon on February 27, 1846, and a tablet in St. Peter's Church, Fort, Colombo, commemorates his services and virtues.

Without any poetic inspiration at all, he wrote and published a good deal of verse, an early instance being a sonnet "To Milton" in the *Champion*, June 30, 1816, and he willed "my volumes of manuscript poems" to his daughter Janet (Mrs. Edward Ledwick Mitford). His publications, indeed, were fairly extensive, including translations from Malayan and a dictionary of that language. In a haphazard scrapbook, now at Harvard, he pasted various interesting notes, poems, letters; and among his more or less celebrated correspondents, in addition to Keats, were Sir William Rough (died 1838), chief justice of Ceylon, John Cook (1771–1824), professor of Hebrew at St. Andrews, Michael Russell (1781–1848), bishop of Glasgow and Galloway, Herbert Marsh (1757–1839), bishop of Peterborough, Michael H. T. Luscombe (1776–1846), continental bishop of the Scots Episcopal Church, Joanna Baillie (1762–1851), and Maria Jane Jewsbury (1800–1833) and her husband William K. Fletcher, who visited him in January–February, 1833.

In 1848 Milnes wrote, "Mr. Bailey died soon after Keats," a misstatement that the archdeacon hastened to point out. The long biographical letters he sent to Milnes have proved useful to all writers on Keats's life. He returned to London in October, 1852, where he died in Nottingham Place, Marylebone, on June 25, 1853.[4]

[4] See *The Times*, June 28, 1853.

FANNY BRAWNE [1]

Frances Ricketts (Mrs. Samuel) Brawne, since 1810 a widow with three children—Fanny (Frances), Samuel, Margaret—rented Brown's half of Wentworth Place in the summer of 1818 and Dilke's half from about April, 1819, to the end of 1829. In between times she lived at Elm Cottage on the corner of Red Lion Hill and Downshire Hill. Samuel and Margaret have little importance in Keats's biography, though references in his letters show that he was fond of them and their mother. Samuel was born on July 26, 1804, and died of consumption on March 28, 1828. Mrs. Brawne was severely burned at the door of her home, and died on November 23, 1829. Margaret, born April 19, 1809, married Chevalier João Antonio Pereira da Cunha, son of the Marquis de Inhambupé of Brazil, at Dieppe on November 30, 1833, and died at Lausanne on June 14, 1887.

Fanny was born in the hamlet of West End, near Hampstead, on August 9, 1800. In his copy of Milnes, Dilke notes that Keats met her "for the first time at my house." "No doubt Keats, who was daily with me," he added, "met her soon after his return" from Scotland on August 18, 1818. The date of their meeting is, however, disputed. She herself (though she was not on oath) told Fanny Keats, on September 18, 1820, "I have known your brother for two years," and hence Edgcumbe [2] thought that during his call at Wentworth Place on August 18 Keats "was probably at once introduced to the Brawnes." Lowell [3] dated the introduction "not later than some time early in September," Richardson [4] and Gittings [5] in November, a reviewer in *TLS* [6] after December 1. When-

[1] The only detailed account of the Brawnes is in Richardson.

[2] Page xxi. Fanny Brawne, writing to Thomas Medwin (*The Life of Percy Bysshe Shelley*, 1847 [ed. HBF, 1913], pp. 294, 296) around 1846, seems to say that she met Keats shortly after he returned from Scotland on August 18: "It was about this time . . . that I became acquainted with Keats. We met frequently at the house of a mutual friend, (not Leigh Hunt's,)" but evidently Dilke's. At any rate, she definitely asserts that she knew him before Tom's death on December 1: "His spirits [were] good, excepting at moments when anxiety regarding his brother's health dejected them." To be sure, she was not strictly accurate when she told Medwin (the same, p. 297), "For more than a twelvemonth before quitting England, I saw him [Keats] every day."

[3] II, 126. [4] Page 23.

[5] Pages 40 f. On September 22, 1818 (I, 370), Keats said, "I never was in love," though "the shape" of Jane Cox "has haunted me these two days." He was still fascinated by Jane as late as October 14 (I, 395).

[6] March 19, 1925, pp. 177 f.

ever the meeting occurred, Fanny was thereafter always in Keats's thoughts, though to the George Keatses he first mentioned her, in offhand manner, on December 16. Later Fanny referred to December 25, 1818, as the happiest day of her life,[7] but her exact meaning has caused further dispute. Murry[8] thinks she meant that on Christmas Day, 1818, "Keats declared his love for her and learned it was reciprocated," but that there was no formal engagement till October, 1819. Whether he is right or wrong is not very important since Keats said that "the very first week I knew you I wrote myself your vassal." But he was sick, jealous, demanding, suspicious; she was young, gay, fond of society. The two lovers were star-crossed.

Keats lived next door to the Brawnes from about the middle of October, 1819, till May, 1820, and then, desperately ill, he stayed in their home for a month in August–September. He saw Fanny for the last time on September 13. Henceforth he never wrote to her nor read her letters. More than twelve years after his death, on June 15, 1833, she married Louis Lindo, who was twelve years her junior. Lindo, born May 12, 1812, into a highly respected Sephardic Jewish family, later changed his name to Lindon. The Lindons' first child Edmund was born on July 26, 1834, Herbert Valentine on May 22, 1838, and Margaret on August 10, 1844. The family lived most of the time on the Continent—near Düsseldorf, in Bayonne, in Heidelberg, and elsewhere—till 1859, when they returned to London. There Fanny died on December 4, 1865. Her husband died on October 21, 1872, and was buried in the same grave with her in Brompton Cemetery, Kensington.

Fanny Brawne was unknown to the public until 1878. To be sure, Sir Charles W. Dilke in 1875 had referred to her as "Miss B.," Lord Houghton in 1876 as "Miss Brawn." The former, quoting out of their context phrases from a letter she had written to Brown on December 29, 1829, gave her reputation a sad blow: "When the first memoir was proposed, the woman he [Keats] had loved had so little belief in his poetic reputation, that she wrote to Mr. Dilke, 'The kindest act would be to let him rest for ever in the obscurity to which circumstances have condemned him'."[9] More

[7] Edgcumbe, pp. 55 f. [8] *Keats* (1955), p. 36.

[9] *Papers*, I, 11. Again in the *Athenaeum*, February 16, 1878, p. 218, he quoted the letter, which Brown had evidently shown to his grandfather. For the letter itself—or rather a

damaging was the publication of the now famous love letters. Harry Buxton Forman edited thirty-seven of the letters in 1878, in spite of the vigorous objections of Sir Charles Dilke, who owned them and others which he did not release.[1] The publication created a sensation, most of it equally unfavorable to the principals and to Forman, and practically all the biographers and critics long agreed that Miss Brawne cared little for Keats and was unworthy of his love.

Fortunately for her reputation today, in 1820–1824 she wrote to Fanny Keats a series of letters which much later came into the possession of Fred Holland Day (1864–1933), of Norwood, Massachusetts, and which Lowell was the first biographer to use and quote.[2] After the thirty-one letters were published under the date 1936 a new and truer picture of Miss Brawne appeared. An occasional writer like S. B. Ward[3] insists that Keats's "love affair was a bad business which brought him neither happiness nor inspiration. It was impossible that he should have been happy" with Fanny Brawne; "it was perhaps a pity they ever met." Another in a recent *TLS*[4] speaks of "those who have always refused to be coaxed by her admirers into a warm appreciation of Miss Fanny Brawne, and who continue to regard her as a conventional little Hampstead miss accidentally caught up into an emotional maelstrom which she could neither cope with nor understand." But the number of "those" is small, and few informed persons now will agree that, as R. H. Stoddard once phrased it, she was a "cold, hard, haughty young woman," who made her lover ridiculous in life and after death.[5] Instead they are likely to agree with Edgcumbe[6] that she was "a young woman of remarkable perception and imagination, keen in the observance of character and events, possessing an unusual critical faculty, and intellectually fitted to become the wife of Keats." The poet harps upon his "swooning

draft of it, now in the Keats Museum—see MBF, pp. lxii f. It has often been printed, as by S. B. Ward, *Revue anglo-américaine*, X (1932), 139–143.

[1] See I, 4; *KC*, I, xlix f.; *More Letters*, pp. 101 f.

[2] For the history of these letters see Rollins and Parrish, *Keats and the Bostonians* (Harvard University Press, 1951).

[3] *Revue anglo-américaine*, X (1932), 142 f. In the same vein Lady Gerald Wellesley, *The John Keats Memorial Volume* (1921), p. 198, speaks of Fanny's "silly slender hands that murdered" Keats.

[4] April 9, 1954, p. 232.

[5] *Appleton's Journal*, IV (1878), 382.

[6] Pages xviii f.

admiration" for her beauty. That beauty is hard to see in the familiar miniature and silhouette. But Keats saw it, and his love and admiration have made her immortal.

CHARLES BROWN [1]

Brown, who now has a sort of immortality of his own, was born, as Miss Richardson has discovered, in Lambeth, April 14, 1787, the sixth of seven sons. At fourteen he worked in a London merchant's office, and at eighteen, in partnership with his brother John, he became a merchant in St. Petersburg, while John ran the London branch of the business. After five years of prosperity, the firm went bankrupt in 1810, and Brown returned to London, suffering great privations until he became the London agent of his brother James, of the East India Company. At James's death, October, 1815, he came into enough money—over £10,000—to make possible what he called a life of literary pursuits. Already his comic opera, *Narensky; or, The Road to Yaroslaf*, produced at Drury Lane in January, 1814, had brought him £300 and lifetime free admission to that theater.

In the late summer of 1817 he was introduced to Keats, in whose letters his name then begins often to appear. The two made their famous walking tour of northern England and Scotland in June–August, 1818, and, after the death of Tom Keats on December 1, John began to "domesticate" with Brown in Wentworth Place. They were together for a short time during the summer of 1819 in the Isle of Wight, whence on August 12 they moved to Winchester. Then while Keats stayed alone, for three weeks Brown went "a-visiting" in Chichester and Bedhampton, and at some time and place during this interval he was illegally married by a priest to Abigail O'Donaghue (or Donohoo or Donaghue), his housekeeper ("our irish Servant," Keats calls her). Early in October, back in London, Keats tried to break away from Brown, only after a few days to return to his old quarters. During Keats's illness that began on February 3, 1820, Brown's kindness and

[1] For a memoir written by his son see *KC*, I, liv–lxii. Other details of his life (long after Keats's death he changed his name to Charles Armitage Brown) are summarized by me in *HLB*, IV (1950), 378 f. A good deal of information about Charles Brown, Jr., is given in *A Dictionary of New Zealand Biography* (Wellington, 1940) and Alfred Domett's *Diary*, ed. E. A. Horsman (1953), pp. 195–198.

attention were unremitting. But in May he rented his house, as usual, left Keats in Kentish Town lodgings, packed Abby off somewhere to bear her child (Charles or "Carlino"), and set out alone for Scotland. Various letters herein printed give details about why he never saw Keats again, though the unhappy poet hoped in vain that Brown would accompany him to Italy.

Sometime before November 15, 1821, Brown's ménage had been broken up, and he lamented that "my poor boy is kept aloof from me by his obstinate Mother." [2] By the following March, however, he was planning to leave Carlino with the Thomas Richardses [3] and to go alone to Italy, all this with Abby's consent. So Brown said. In 1913 Carlino's daughter Jessie (Mrs. John Brown) told a different story: "When C. A. B. discovered that she [Abby] had (unknown to him) had my Father christened a Roman Catholic, he took my Father & his nurse (travelling three days & nights) to Italy." Carlino, she added, never "saw his Mother again altho he supported her until she died many years after her husband." In Italy Brown became acquainted with Byron, Trelawny, Landor, and other celebrated persons.

In 1833 he returned briefly to England alone, and in April, 1835,[4] with his son he left Italy for good. Living at Laira Green, near Plymouth, he published a strange, but very influential, book, *Shakespeare's Autobiographical Poems* (1838), as well as a newspaper account (printed here at the end of the first volume) of part of the Scotch tour with Keats. He fully intended to publish a biography and some poems of Keats, but quarrels with Taylor, Reynolds, Dilke, and George Keats prevented. The last, indeed, empowered Dilke to invoke the copyright laws against Brown's using the poems, yet Brown did print a few in the *New Monthly Magazine* and many others in the *Plymouth and Devonport Weekly Journal*. In 1829 he composed a brief biography, which he revised to be delivered orally at Plymouth on December 29, 1836, and in 1841 he turned it and all his invaluable Keats manuscripts over to Milnes. He then migrated to New Zealand, where he died June 5, 1842. His grave on Marsland Hill, New Plymouth, disappeared when the

[2] MBF, *Some Letters . . . of Charles Brown* (1937), p. 7.

[3] See I, 121 n.

[4] Carlino (*KC*, I, lix f.) gives the date as 1834, *DNB* and Mrs. Jessie Brown (*HLB*, IV [1950], 379) as 1837. But see Sharp, pp. 165 n., 174, and John Forster, *Walter Savage Landor* (Boston, 1869), p. 499.

hill was leveled for military barracks, but was discovered in March, 1921. Shortly thereafter his grandchildren erected a tombstone on which, as on that of Reynolds, are his name and the proud description, "The Friend of Keats."

Brown wrote to Carlino, March 15, 1839, of Dilke's "infamous treachery towards me," urging, "If he should accidentally meet with you, and civilly accost you—spit in his face." [5] Dilke could never have been infamous or treacherous. Enemy to Brown though he then was, in his annotations to Milnes's biography [6] he said: "[Brown] was the most scrupulously honest man I ever knew—but wanted nobleness to lift this honesty out of the commercial kennel—He would have forgiven John what he owed him with all his heart—but had John been able & offered to pay, he would have charged interest, as he did George. He could do generous things too—but not after the fashion of the world & therefore they were not appreciated by the world. His sense of justice led him at times to do acts of generosity—at others of meanness—the latter was always noticed the former overlooked—therefore amongst his early companions he had a character for any thing rather than liberality—but he was liberal."

CHARLES COWDEN CLARKE [1]

Clarke, born on December 15, 1787, son of the master of the Enfield school which the three Keats brothers attended, greatly influenced the literary tastes and achievements of John, eight years his junior, inspired him to write verses, and introduced him to his first patron, Leigh Hunt. In a verse letter "To Charles Cowden Clarke" (No. 6), Keats rhetorically inquired, "And can I e'er these benefits forget?/ And can I e'er repay the friendly debt?" Keats's earliest non-verse letter yet found was written to Clarke on October 9, 1816, but the correspondence ended on March 25, 1817. It is worth remarking that Keats addressed him as "My daintie Davie," "C.C.C." and (twice) "My dear Charles," while he

[5] The letter is in the Keats Museum.

[6] The book is in the Pierpont Morgan Library.

[1] There is a charming sketch of Clarke and his wife by Annie (Mrs. James T.) Fields, "Two Lovers of Literature and Art," *Century Magazine*, May, 1899 (LVIII, 122–131), and a full-length biography by Richard D. Altick, *The Cowden Clarkes* (1948).

addressed all his other male friends by their surnames.[2] Clarke left Keats's circle fairly early, moving in 1817 to Ramsgate with his parents, who had given up the school. He helped with the proof-sheets of *Endymion* in the spring of 1818, but Keats's final reference to him was made in February, 1819, "I have not seen . . . C C. C. for God knows when." He thereupon ceased to have any real interest for Keats's biography until 1846. According to his own statement, he saw Keats for the last time in 1819, apparently in February.[3] How little he knew of the poet and his friends after 1817 is shown by the fact that he met Woodhouse only in August, 1823, and then first heard details of Keats's departure from London.

Clarke's father died on December 19, 1820,[4] and about a year later he himself returned to London. There in 1825 he and Henry Leigh Hunt began their publishing and bookselling business at 38 Tavistock Street, Covent Garden. When they failed in April, 1829, Clarke turned to publishing music with Joseph Alfred Novello, son of Vincent Novello, the celebrated organist and music composer, at whose house Keats had become "completely tired" of puns. In July, 1828, Clarke had married Vincent's daughter, Mary Victoria (born June 22, 1809), and had moved into the Novello home. Henceforth he and his wife knew nearly everybody worth knowing in literary and musical circles. From 1834 to 1856 he was a popular lecturer on literary subjects. With Mrs. Clarke, who in 1844–1845 published her once valuable concordance to Shakespeare's plays, he collaborated in the so-called *Shakespeare-Key* (1879) as well as in an edition of Shakespeare's works. Both husband and wife issued many other volumes before and after they moved to Nice (1856) and then to Genoa (1861). In the Villa Novello at Genoa Clarke spent the remaining years of his life, dying in his ninetieth year on March 13, 1877. Mrs. Clarke, after further publications, which included *My Long Life* (1896), died there at the age of eighty-eight on January 12, 1898.[5]

Clarke, who late in 1821 had been "thinking of writing a memoir" of Keats,[6] was of great assistance to Milnes. His love and

[2] Including Reynolds, whom in a few passages he calls "John" or "Jack."

[3] *KC*, II, 151.

[4] *Examiner*, December 24, p. 831.

[5] Nerina Medici di Marignano Gigliucci, *K-SMB*, No. 6 (1955), 18–23, gives details about the Clarkes and the Novello family in Genoa. She says that the Clarkes' graves have "disappeared."

[6] Sharp, p. 110, quoting Brown.

admiration for Keats were lifelong. When in 1853 a passage about Keats's drunkenness was published in Haydon's Journal, he sent a vigorous refutation of it to the *Examiner* (July 9). Then in January, 1861, his own "Recollections" of Keats appeared in the *Atlantic Monthly*. Soon he was urging Severn to write a life to supersede Milnes's. As Severn wisely hesitated, Clarke in 1875, a year after he had reprinted his "Recollections" in the *Gentleman's Magazine*, decided to issue it with "some additions" and illustrations in book-form. He died before the book could be prepared. Late in 1877 Mrs. Clarke told Severn of her hope to see the book published,[7] but she likewise failed, in 1878 issuing the "Recollections" of Keats, not greatly changed since 1861, in the *Recollections of Writers* by herself and her husband.

THE DILKES

At an early age Charles Wentworth Dilke—born December 8, 1789—entered the Navy Pay Office, Somerset House, and worked there till it was abolished in 1836 and he was retired on a pension. Meanwhile, about 1808, he had married Maria Dover Walker, by whom he had one son, Charles, or "Charley," or "Wentworth" (1810–1869), afterwards Sir Charles, first baronet. In 1814–1816 he published his useful six-volume edition of *Old English Plays*. With Brown, a former schoolfellow, he built in John Street, Hampstead, a double house, then called Wentworth Place, later Lawn Bank, and now the Keats House. The date at which he met Keats is uncertain, though they were friends before September, 1817. Largely because of Mrs. Dilke's kindness and charm, Wentworth Place became a home for the Keats boys and, to a much less extent, for their sister. In April, 1819, the Dilkes moved to Great Smith Street, Westminster, since Charles was entering (June 14) Westminster School. Their open disapproval of his engagement to Fanny Brawne caused Keats to see little of them during his final months in England.

Earlier Keats had been on friendly terms with other members of Dilke's family: with his parents, Mr. and Mrs. Charles Wentworth Dilke, Sr., of Chichester; with his brother William (1796–1885), who lived for a time in Wentworth House adjoining Went-

[7] Sharp, pp. 258, 260.

worth Place; and with his sister Letitia and her husband, John Snook, of Bedhampton, in whose house he and Severn spent their last night together in England.

After 1821 Dilke held together part of the old Keats circle. He supervised the financial affairs of Fanny Keats and Fanny Brawne. He likewise kept in touch with George Keats, in whose honesty and fair-dealing he firmly believed—so firmly that, after quarreling on the subject, he and Brown broke off all relations, notwithstanding their thirty years' friendship. He bought partial control of the *Athenaeum* in 1828, full control in 1830, and made that literary weekly successful, respected, and a medium for notes about Keats. He gave up the editorship, though not the ownership, in 1846, and for a time managed the *Daily News*. Maria Dilke died in 1850, his daughter-in-law Mrs. Charles Dilke in 1853. In this latter year he moved into his son's home at 76 Sloane Street. Then he wrote a number of important literary studies, particularly on the Junius letters and Pope. Retiring to a Hampshire village in 1862, he died on August 10, 1864, highly esteemed by all who knew him.

Dilke was determined to vindicate George Keats from Brown's and Haslam's slanders. His letters and papers passed to his grandson, Charles (1843–1911), the second baronet, who kept up the fight. Sir Charles not only defended George but kept in touch with the surviving members of Keats's circle. He tried to prevent publication of the love letters to Fanny Brawne, destroying some of them; welcomed contributions about Keats to the columns of the *Athenaeum*; edited a number of his grandfather's works with a memoir (1875); and willed his invaluable collection of Keats books, letters, and other relics to the Hampstead Public Library. Dilke the grandfather and Dilke the grandson were benefactors to students of the poet.

WILLIAM HASLAM

Haslam, one of the most engaging and devoted of Keats's friends, was born in 1795 or 1798, and was, according to Brown, a schoolfellow "whom Keats held dearly."[1] He was, Severn declared, "very intimate with Keats" while the latter studied at St.

[1] *KC*, II, 52. Keats, however (I, 392), says that George Keats introduced him to Haslam. Sharp, p. 12 n., dates the latter's birth 1795.

Thomas's Hospital.[2] When the elder Haslam died in March, 1819, the younger, a solicitor then living at Bethnal Green, succeeded to his position with Frampton and Sons, wholesale grocers, 34 Leadenhall Street, a fact that gave Keats great satisfaction. But with his usual dissatisfaction where the fiancées of his friends were concerned, Keats noted in September, 1819, that Haslam "is very much occupied with love and business. . . . His love is very amusing." Severn and Brown thought the lady in question "lovely" or "fair," [3] but when Keats saw the portrait Severn had painted, to him, characteristically, it represented a woman "too cunning" for her lover.

Haslam, a man of sterling character, loved Keats as a boy and as a man, and considered him a worthy rival of Shakespeare. He was an always obliging friend to whom Keats and others continually turned for help. "Our oak friend" Severn once called him.[4] His kindness to Tom Keats "during my absence and since my return," the poet wrote, "has endeared him to me for ever." He loaned money to Keats, forwarded letters for him, and in many other ways was "excessively kind." Almost at the eleventh hour he arranged for Severn to accompany Keats to Italy, having been prevented from going himself because his wife (he had married on October 16, 1819) had had, or was about to have, a child, and because he was "miserably oppressed" by business.[5] He had a large share in making the financial arrangements for the trip, act ing with Woodhouse as a witness to the copyright assignments of *Poems*, *Endymion*, and *Lamia* that provided £200, and he was almost certainly one of the two unnamed friends who gave Taylor £50 for the poet's use. Haslam was also one of the five men (one of the three personal friends) who sailed to Gravesend with Keats and Severn, and he then rushed back to London for the passport the latter had forgotten. Fanny Brawne wrote to Fanny Keats on September 18, 1820, that "his kindness [to John] cannot be described." [6]

Haslam had long been a warm friend of George Keats, but by 1820 he had adopted Brown's views. To Severn he wrote: "Avoid speaking of George to him [John]. George is a scoundrel! but talk of his friends in England, of their love, their hopes of him. Keats

[2] *KC*, II, 160. [3] *KC*, I, 241, 159. [4] II, 341.
[5] Sharp, p. 73. [6] Edgcumbe, p. 4.

must get himself well again, Severn, if but for us. I, for one, cannot afford to lose him. If I know what it is to love, I truly love John Keats." [7] When Brown learned of Keats's death, he urged Haslam to rush that news to Fanny Keats and Abbey, since he himself knew neither.

Mary Haslam died on October 6, 1822, aged 27, at Alton, Hampshire, and was buried in the parish church.[8] Much later, in May or June, 1838, Brown dined with Haslam, and found him living prosperously with another wife and a daughter Annette Augusta (who is said to have been known in London as late as 1883).[9] Haslam was of considerable assistance to Milnes in the writing of Keats's biography. He confessed, however, that Keats's letters to him "were so well, or intended to be so well taken care of" that he could find none at all,[1] and only three are known today. Fortunately he did find a number that were written to him by Severn, and they are an invaluable record of the poet's last days.

Haslam died on March 28, 1851, broken by business pressure and financial straits, but "his end was peace." [2]

BENJAMIN ROBERT HAYDON

Haydon (1786–1846) is too well known to need much comment. Keats met him at Leigh Hunt's Hampstead cottage during October, 1816, but first visited his studio at breakfast on Sunday, November 3. Haydon was then, at the age of thirty, apparently a first-class artist, a friend of the great, the triumphant defender of the Elgin Marbles. For a time Keats practically worshiped him. He was also greatly impressed by the huge painting, "Christ's Triumphant Entry into Jerusalem" (for years in the Cincinnati Art Museum, now at Mount Saint Mary's Seminary, Norwood, Ohio), wherein his face appears along with Wordsworth's, Lamb's, and Hazlitt's.[1] But he was disturbed by Haydon's quarrels with Hunt and Reynolds, and even more disturbed when in June, 1819, Haydon refused to pay a loan (not due) of £30. "I shall

[7] Sharp, pp. 72 f.

[8] The tablet over her grave calls Haslam "of Greenwich in Kent."

[9] Sharp, p. 186.

[1] *KC*, II, 189.

[2] Sharp, p. 205, quoting Mrs. Haslam. *GM*, n.s., XXXV (1851), 566, gives his age as fifty-three, his residence as Roupel-road, Upper Tulse-hill.

[1] But not, as has been said, John Howard Payne's.

perhaps still be acquainted with him," he said angrily, "but for friendship that is at an end." Soon he was writing, "I never see him." Another cause of irritation was a copy of Chapman's Homer which Keats (who thought nothing of keeping books for a year) had borrowed and lost, and for which Haydon twice sent a special messenger. Keats did attend the private exhibition of "Christ's Entry" on March 25, 1820, and during his increasing illness Haydon made several calls, only to confess that the poet "grew irritated because I would shake my head at his irregularities, and tell him that he would destroy himself." [2] Haydon took pains to retrieve his own letters after Keats's death, just how can only be guessed, and greater pains to get proper recognition in Milnes's biography of 1848, which he did not live to read. After making a pitiful entry in his enormous diary, June 22, 1846, he committed suicide. In spite of his vanity and selfishness, his is still a big name to students of Hunt, Keats, Wordsworth, Miss Mitford, and other literary personages.

LEIGH HUNT

The life of Hunt (1784–1859) is too familiar to be retold. He had grave personal faults and characteristic literary vulgarisms, but he admired and loved Keats next to Shelley, and to the end of his days lost no opportunity of praising the work of his young friend. There is little doubt that Keats met Hunt "not much after October 9, and certainly before the end of October," 1816.[1] Hunt loaned books to Keats; praised and printed his verse in the *Examiner* and the *Indicator;* introduced him to Haydon, Shelley, and other celebrities; suggested subjects for treatment; and, in fact, in every way encouraged and fostered his protégé's talents. For a time Keats venerated him as a master. Then he perceived some of Hunt's limitations, and realized how disastrous to his own reputation and style their friendship had been—how it had fastened on his name the damning label of "Cockney." Largely because of Haydon's influence, he began to criticize Hunt's ideas and behavior

[2] Penrose, p. 260.

[1] Garrod, p. lxxv. See also *KC,* I, 4 f. In his *Autobiography* (1850), II, 230, Hunt says the first meeting was at his publishing office, 8 New Road, York Buildings, but Colvin (*Keats* [New York, 1887], p. 220), called this statement "evidently only due to a slip of memory."

and even said in December, 1818, that Hunt was "vain, egotistical and disgusting in matters of taste and in morals." It is a pity that only two letters that Keats wrote to him are preserved. Though Hunt told Milnes in 1846,[2] "I hardly received above three or four letters from him in all," there must have been more. Indeed, a writer in 1892 remarked, "Of Keats's letters to Hunt I have several." [3] If these "several" were known today, they would probably give a truer idea of what Keats really thought.

At any rate it is pleasant to know that in 1820 Keats considered publishing "Hyperion" jointly with a poem or poems by Hunt; [4] and that after he had left Hunt's house in a rage on August 12, 1820, he wrote, "I feel really attach'd to you for your many sympathies with me, and patience at my lunes," signing himself "Your affectionate friend." And it is pleasanter still to read the kindly, if somewhat flamboyant, farewell to Keats, then generally thought of as a ridiculous Cockney versifier, that Hunt published in the *Indicator*, September 20, 1820, and the beautiful and generous letter he sent on March 8, 1821, to Severn, unaware of the poet's death:

> Tell him—tell that great poet and noble-hearted man—that we shall all bear his memory in the most precious part of our hearts, and that the world shall bow their heads to it, as our loves do. . . . Tell him we shall never cease to remember and love him. . . . Tell him he is only before us on the road [to immortality], as he was in everything else. . . .[5]

In 1828 Hunt published the first biographies of Keats in *Lord Byron and Some of His Contemporaries* and in John Gorton's *General Biographical Dictionary*, and still later he wrote very fine criticism of his verse, as in *Leigh Hunt's London Journal* (1835) and *Imagination and Fancy* (1844). "By his interest and sympathy" he encouraged Milnes to write a new biography, for which he supplied the texts of several poems. On its appearance in 1848 he read "with extreme pain" various slurs in Keats's letters. Hence he objected so strongly to a second edition that none appeared until eight years after his death.

THE JEFFREYS OF TEIGNMOUTH

Dr. W. C. Lake,[1] of Teignmouth, wrote to Holman on August 4, 1913, that "Margaret Jeffrey" was listed among the 146 Teign-

[2] *KC*, II, 170. [3] *Cornhill Magazine*, LXV, 501. [4] *KC*, II, 234.
[5] HBF, 1883, IV, 220–222. [1] See *HLB*, IV (1950), 390 f.

mouth taxpayers, all without addresses, in 1800, and it is generally assumed that she was the Mrs. Jeffrey to whom No. 81 was written. Earlier, on April 4, 1913, Lake had identified the Teignmouth house in which John, George, and Tom Keats lived as 20, The Strand, now Northumberland Place (today marked with a tablet), and the shop of "the Girls over at the Bonnet shop" as 35, The Strand. Whether the former was the house of Mrs. Jeffrey cannot be proved, though I think it likely that the Keats brothers lodged with, or visited, her there. Twenty, The Strand, as Hale-White[2] says, is on "a narrow street into which the sun can rarely shine.... The sitting-room occupied by the brothers is quite small and gets little light.... A more unsuitable lodging for a consumptive cannot be imagined."

Mrs. Jeffrey and her daughters Marian (or Marianne), Sarah, and Fanny were unknown to writers on Keats until in December, 1893, A. Forbes Sieveking[3] printed Nos. 81, 84, 164, 166. These four letters, three others by Tom Keats, and a manuscript of the sonnet "Blue! 'tis the life of heaven" had been put at his disposal by Launcelot Archer, of Lenham, Maidstone, Kent, who in a letter of September 20, 1893,[4] explained to him: "Miss [Marian] Jeffries was a friend of Thos Keats and I believe either nursed him or was much with him during his last illness in Devonshire. She afterwards married a Mr Prowse [of Torquay] and was mother of W. Jeffrey Prowse [born May 6, 1836] ... who wrote various poems." W. J. Prowse, he added, died "about twenty years ago" (in 1870) and from him "my father," Thomas Archer, got the eight documents. Sieveking asserted that Keats was "at one time on terms of great intimacy" with the Jeffreys. H. B. Forman wisely rejected the idea that "Mrs. Jeffrey and her daughters were family friends of the Keatses," and concluded that they met the brothers at Teignmouth, and "let their warm Devonshire hearts go out" to them. He also records a local tradition that Marian was in love with Keats.

Certainly the brothers were fond of the Jeffrey women and grateful to them, but Lowell[5] is right in saying that "anything less like love-letters than ... [Keats's Nos. 84, 164, 166] cannot well be imagined." Keats signs his letter to Mrs. Jeffrey "Yours very

[2] Page 93 n. [3] *Fortnightly Review*, LX, 728–740.
[4] Now at Harvard. [5] I, 599.

truly" in marked contrast to the "affectionate(ly)" he uses for Mrs. Wylie. Writing jointly to Marian and Sarah, he calls them "My dear Girls," sends "all our Loves to you," but ends "Yours very sincerely." In one letter to Sarah he begins "My Dear young Lady," asks her to "Give my love to your Mother," but signs himself "Ever sincerely yours"; the other salutes her as "My dear Lady" and concludes "Your sincere friend." As for Marian, when he heard of her marriage before May 31, 1819, he merely forwarded his "Comp^{ts}" (II, 113). The more ebullient George in March, 1818, wrote in a familiar, light-hearted way to "My dear Girls," "steady, quiet Marianne, and laughing thoughtless Sarah," speaks of sending them kisses, but ends "My dear Girls and Friends, Your's sincerely and truly." [6] Tom, evidently the pet of the family, writing to Marian on May 17, 18, 1818, sends "my Love to your mother and Sister" (Sarah), and concludes "Your Sincere Friend." [7]

Sarah apparently accompanied John and Tom about May 5, 1818, in the chaise to Honiton, on the first stage of their return journey to London. John wrote to her and Marian in June, then received several letters from her, but did not acknowledge them until May 31, 1819, when he had a favor to ask: "Enquire in the Villages round Teignmouth if there is any Lodging commodious for its cheapness; and let me know where it is and what price," or "give my love to your Mother and ask her to do it." It is significant that in telling Fanny Keats about his plans, he referred to the Jeffreys not as friends but as "some Acquaintances in Devonshire." The Formans assume that "your long-haired sister" of No. 166 was a fourth Jeffrey girl, an unlikely assumption since she is not mentioned in Nos. 81, 84, or 164. But whether three or four, almost nothing is known about the lives of the sisters, except that Marian wrote a book called "*Poems by Mrs. I. S. Prowse*. London: Published by Smith, Elder, and Co. Cornhill;—Baldwin and Cradock, Paternoster Row; and Sold by All Other Booksellers. MDCCCXXX." At its end there is a lengthy list of subscribers, among them Lady Noel Byron (4 copies), Sir Egerton Brydges, and Keats's Teignmouth acquaintances Captain Tonkin (2 copies), Mrs. Tonkin (4 copies), (Jacob) Bickford Bartlett, and Miss Periman. Some of Mrs. Prowse's effusions, which are up to the low standard of the 1830's, have been thought to refer to Keats or to borrow from him.

[6] *KC*, I, 13–16. [7] I, 286.

FANNY KEATS [1]

Fanny (or Frances Mary) Keats was born on June 3, 1803. After the death of her grandmother, Mrs. Jennings, in 1814, she lived with her guardian, Richard Abbey, in one or the other of his houses in Walthamstow or London except for four years (January, 1815–December, 1818) when she attended the Walthamstow school of the Misses Tuckey. Abbey made it as difficult as possible for her to see her brothers, and even offered objections to John's writing. Though John did write fairly often and visited her when he could, during his final year in Hampstead he saw little of her, and was forced to leave for Italy without telling her goodby. In almost the last sentence he penned he referred sadly to "my sister—who walks about my imagination like a ghost—she is so like Tom."

When Fanny came of age in 1824, she called upon Dilke to compel Abbey to turn over her share of her grandmother's and her dead brothers' money. After the Chancery proceedings ended in 1825, she had, according to her biographer, some £4,500, but financial troubles with Abbey and the lawyers, Rice and Reynolds, disturbed her during the next six or seven years. On March 30, 1826, she married Valentin Maria Llanos y Gutierrez (born at Valladolid, December 16, 1795).

Llanos, who is said to have known and to have spoken to Keats only three days before the latter's death, left Spain in 1814 to wander over the Continent till 1821. He apparently met Fanny Brawne and Fanny Keats in the summer of 1821—certainly before October 8. Most of his English acquaintances describe him pleasantly, though Dilke and George Keats had no respect for his business ventures. But George was flattered to have as a "friend and brother" a man of letters, and he read with enjoyment Llanos' dull novels, *Don Esteban; Or, Memoirs of a Spaniard* (1825) and *Sandoval; Or, The Freemason* (1826), as well as his *Narrative of Don Juan Van Halen's Imprisonment in the Dungeons of the Inquisition at Madrid* (1827). Presumably he knew nothing about Llanos' *Representacion al soberano pueblo Español* (1822) or his unpublished novel, "The Spanish Exile" (1828).[2]

[1] The only full account of Fanny and her family is that given by Adami. Other details, particularly about her strained relations with George Keats and Reynolds, will be found in *More Letters*.

[2] A picturesque story of a so-called breakfast given him by George Dyer, the friend of Lamb, will be found in Coventry Patmore's *Bryan Waller Procter* (Boston, 1877), pp. 77–79.

The later years of the Llanos family hardly concern readers of Keats's letters. After a visit to the Continent in 1826–1828 Fanny and Valentin moved into the half of Wentworth Place which had been the home of Keats and Brown, and for a time Fanny Brawne lived with them. They went to France in the early summer of 1833, then in October to Spain, and never saw England again. The Llanoses had three sons and three daughters, but their first daughter and first son died in infancy. During 1861–1864 they were in Italy, where they saw much of Severn. In 1879, having suffered financial reverses, Fanny received £150 from the Queen's Bounty Fund. During the next year a public subscription brought her some £300, and the government granted her a pension on the Civil List. Valentin Llanos died on August 14, 1885, Fanny on December 16, 1889, and they were buried in the same grave in the cemetery of San Isidoro, Madrid. Numerous descendants of theirs, particularly Dr. Ernesto Paradinas y Brockmann, of Avila, and his eight children, still live in Spain.[3]

GEORGE KEATS [1]

George Keats was born on February 28, 1797. Little is known of his early life except that in 1803 he was sent with John to Clarke's Enfield school, where he remained till 1811. He was then lodged and set to work in Abbey's business house, and sometime later Tom joined him. In 1816 after a quarrel with Abbey's junior partner Hodgkinson, George left Abbey's employment, and in late September the three brothers moved to 8 Dean Street, Borough, then before November 18 to 76 Cheapside, and finally before March 25, 1817, to 1 Well Walk, Hampstead. It was George who introduced John (I, 392) to some of the men now thought of as the Keats circle. "George has ever been more than a brother to me," Keats said in 1818, "he has been my greatest friend."

George escorted Tom to Teignmouth in the winter of 1817. By January, 1818, he had decided to migrate to America. He married Georgiana Wylie late in May, and on June 22 they set out for Liverpool, whence they sailed for Philadelphia. Eventually

[3] See Pope, *K–SJ*, II (1953), 117 f.

[1] For full biographical details see Kirk, Hampstead Keats, I, lxxiii–xcviii; *KC*, I, civ–cviii; *More Letters*, pp. 1–6.

they reached Hendersonville, Kentucky, where George was swindled (or so he believed) by the famous naturalist John James Audubon, and then Louisville, where his first child was born in February, 1819. His financial affairs went from bad to worse, and so, on borrowed funds, he visited England in January, 1820, managing to take back to America his own share of Tom's estate plus, his enemies said, the larger part of John's. This trip and his subsequent failure to send money to John caused Brown, Taylor, Haslam, Severn, and for a time Fanny Keats to accuse him of dishonesty and callousness.

In a few years George became a wealthy and influential citizen of Louisville, and he then paid all of John's debts. Dilke, Abbey, Fanny Brawne, and eventually Fanny Keats exonerated him of all wrong-doing. There seems no doubt that he was an honest, intelligent, high-minded man. He died suddenly on December 24, 1841, just as his wealth was melting away. The Louisville *Daily Journal* on Christmas Day called him "an inestimable member of society. There is not a man in our community whose death would be more deeply and universally mourned." Years later Lucien V. Rule declared that he "will always rank among the noblest citizens Louisville has ever had." [2]

TOM KEATS [1]

Tom, the third child of Thomas and Frances Keats, was born on November 18, 1799. No information has yet turned up about how long he attended Clarke's Enfield school, where he met Richard Hengist Horne and Charles Jeremiah Wells, or exactly when he and George lived and worked in Abbey's Pancras Lane business house. He was a tall, narrow-chested, delicate boy, "with an exquisite love of Life" (I, 293), and the letters of his brothers tell much about his tuberculous symptoms. In their solicitude for him one or the other several times took him out of London—to Lyons at a date not now known, to Margate in August, 1816, to Margate and Canterbury in April–May, 1817, to Paris in September, 1817, to Teignmouth in December, 1817–May, 1818. In Paris Tom met

[2] In L. P. Powell's *Historic Towns of the Southern States* (New York, 1904), p. 524.

[1] Since Thomas Keats, Jr., was (and is) always called Tom, he needs no more formality than Fanny Keats and Fanny Brawne.

John Scott, who got possession of his copy-book of John's verse (now at Harvard).

The three brothers lived together from late September, 1816, first at 8 Dean Street, Southwark, then at 76 Cheapside and 1 Well Walk, Hampstead. It seems odd that on June 22, 1818, John and George left Tom alone, seriously ill though he was, with the landlord-postman Bentley, though, to be sure, the Dilkes, Haslam, and other friends kept attentive eyes on him. As Tom's illness increased, Dilke sent an urgent message to Scotland. But John, himself very unwell, was already on the way home. Henceforth he devoted practically every minute to looking after Tom, thereby injuring his own health beyond repair. Before this time Wells had sent Tom, perhaps as a mere joke, a number of letters purportedly written by a girl named Amena who was in love with him. When the trick was discovered Tom's already desperate condition was made more desperate still, or at least Keats thought so, and his language about Wells and Amena was intemperate to a degree.

Tom died on December 1, 1818. His letters show him to have been, as Milnes phrases it, "of a most gentle and witty nature," and all of Keats's friends spoke of him with interest or affection. All, that is, except Bailey, who told Taylor, "From his [Tom's] character he must have lived a life of discomfort to himself & those with whom he was connected, if the character I have heard of him be just." [2] Whatever Bailey had heard or imagined was wrong. John was devoted to his brother, and George said in 1825, "No one in England understood his [John's] character perfectly but poor Tom." [3]

JOHN HAMILTON REYNOLDS [1]

One of Keats's dearest friends, Reynolds was born at Shrewsbury on September 9, 1794. Educated at Shrewsbury School and St. Paul's, London, at sixteen he became a junior clerk in the Amicable Insurance Office. Through Rice he had come to be an intimate friend of Bailey and of the three Leigh sisters before the end of 1815. The sisters introduced him to Eliza

[2] *KC*, I, 33. [3] *KC*, I, 285.

[1] The chief printed authority is G. L. Marsh, *John Hamilton Reynolds* (1928), supplemented by his articles in *Studies in Philology*, XXV (1928), 491–510, and *K–SJ*, I (1952), 47–55. By far the best biography is Pope's (see I, 63 n.).

Powell Drewe, of Exeter, whom he eventually married on August 31, 1822. Meanwhile, he had published *Safie, An Eastern Tale* (1814), *The Eden of Imagination* (1814), *An Ode* (1815), and on December 25, 1816, he and Bailey had given Thomasine Leigh their manuscript "Poems by Two Friends"—twenty-five poems by Reynolds, thirty-two by Bailey.

Reynolds met Keats at Leigh Hunt's no later than October, 1816, and in turn introduced him to Brown, Rice, Bailey, Taylor, Hessey, Dilke, and others. He favorably reviewed the *Poems* of 1817 in the *Champion;* talked about poetry with him; inspired him to write poems like "Robin Hood" and "Isabella"; prevented him from publishing the first reckless preface to *Endymion;* and in various ways exerted a good influence that partly counteracted the bad influence of Hunt. His other early publications were *The Naiad: A Tale* (1816), a farce called *One, Two, Three, Four, Five: By Advertisement* (1819), a parody of Wordsworth, *Peter Bell, A Lyrical Ballad* (1819), and a miscellany dealing with prize fighting, *The Fancy* (1820). But in November, 1817, at the urgency and with the monetary aid of Rice he took up the study of law.

After Keats's death Reynolds published *The Garden of Florence* (1821) and contributed to the *London Magazine* and other periodicals. With his brother-in-law Thomas Hood he wrote the anonymous *Odes and Addresses to Great People* (1825) and with some help from George Dance a farce called *Confounded Foreigners* (1838). In the meantime, as a member of the firm Rice and Reynolds and its successor Reynolds and Simmons, he had done much legal business, badly they thought, for the Llanoses and George Keats. Valentin Llanos, in fact, flatly accused him of dishonesty, while Dilke said in February, 1833, that his affairs had "been long desperate." [2] Taylor reported on January 9, 1835, that his only child had died, and that he "grieves much for her Loss." [3]

Reynolds' end was a bad anticlimax. R. E. Prothero (Lord Ernle) [4] asserted that from 1847 till his death on November 15, 1852, he was an assistant clerk of the County Court at Newport,

[2] *KC,* II, 9.

[3] Blunden, *Keats's Publisher* (1936), pp. 199 f. J. W. and Anne Tibble, *John Clare* (1932), p. 289, quote a letter of March 30, 1827, in which Taylor says that Reynolds "has lately lost an Infant Child." Charles Green wrote to Day (*HLB,* IV [1950], 244) on January 19, 1891, that his uncle Reynolds' one child was named Lucy.

[4] Editing Byron's *Letters and Journals,* III (1922), 46 n.

Isle of Wight—"a broken-down, discontented man . . . whose drunken habits placed him beyond the pale of society." Pope, however, shows that in its obituary the *Hampshire Independent* called him "highly respected." His tombstone in the cemetery on Church Litten proclaims him "The friend of Keats."

JOHN HAMILTON REYNOLDS' FAMILY

George Reynolds, the son of a barber named Noble Reynolds and his wife Susanna, of St. Olave, Hart Street, London, was born in December, 1764, or January, 1765. For some six years (1774–1779) he was a pupil at Christ's Hospital. On January 7, 1790, he married Charlotte Cox (born November 5,[1] 1761, died May 13, 1848), the witnesses being John Hamilton and Jane Cox.[2] From about 1794 to 1806 he served as a writing master or schoolmaster at Shrewsbury School. Returning to London in 1806, he held various positions, as master of the Lambeth Boys' Parochial School, writing master to the Female Asylum, Lambeth, usher 1810–1817 and then writing master in Christ's Hospital from May, 1817, till his retirement in March, 1835. He died on July 29, 1853. He might well have told biographers many anecdotes of Keats, who never mentions him. Many other stories ought to have been told by Mrs. Reynolds, who in 1827 published under the pseudonym of Mrs. Hamerton an edifying novel called *Mrs. Leslie and Her Grandchildren.*

George and Charlotte Reynolds had five children. Jane[3] (1791–1846) became the wife of the poet Thomas Hood (1799–1845) in 1825. Mariane[4] (1797–1874), a favorite of George Keats, after being proposed to and then jilted by Benjamin Bailey, married H. G. Green before 1833, and was the mother of the artists Charles and Townley Green. Eliza Beckford (born 1799) married Dr. George Longmore, of Upwell, Norfolk, in February, 1822,[5] and died some-

[1] So says Thomas Hood (see Walter Jerrold, *Thomas Hood* [1907], p. 204), though HBF gives the date as November 15.

[2] W. B. and R. R. B. Bannerman, *The Registers of Marriages of St. Mary le Bone, Middlesex, 1783–1792*, II (1922), 119. See also Phyllis G. Mann, *K–SJ*, V (1956), 5–7.

[3] She was born in St. Marylebone, Middlesex, on November 6, 1791—not 1792, as her tombstone has it.

[4] Her son Charles thus spells her name, though John and George Keats and the rest nearly always have "Marianne."

[5] *Ladies Monthly Museum*, XV (1822), 120.

time before December, 1870. Charlotte, born in 1802, lived until 1884.[6]

For a short while Keats was on friendly terms with all the Reynolds family, as also were Bailey, Rice, and the Dilkes. Mrs. Reynolds, Jane, and Mariane were among his correspondents. At their home on February 5, 1818, he wrote the sonnet, "Spenser! a jealous honourer of thine," which he gave to Eliza. Charlotte's piano playing is often said to have suggested "I had a dove" and "Hush! hush! tread softly." For Jane he wrote "O Sorrow!" and "On a Leander Gem Which Miss Reynolds, My Kind Friend, Gave Me." Jane, Mariane, and Charlotte are thought[7] to be addressed in "To the Ladies Who Saw Me Crown'd."

Keats's early liking for the Reynolds girls quickly changed to active dislike. The "Miss Reynoldses are very kind to me—" he said in October, 1818 (I, 394), "but they have lately displeased me much," particularly by derogatory comments on their cousin Jane Cox, or "Charmian," whom he admired. In September, 1819 (II, 187), he confessed that except for John Reynolds he is prejudiced against "all that family." He saw the "Miss Reynolds" at Mrs. Dilke's hop on January 11, 1820 (II, 241, 244), but was afraid to speak to them "for fear of some sickly reiteration of Phrase or Sentiment." The Reynolds women thoroughly disapproved of Keats's engagement to Fanny Brawne, and evidently showed their disapproval frankly. Miss Brawne had no illusions about them. Writing to Fanny Keats in November, 1821, she said: "If you live [to] the age of the Methuselem and I die tomorrow never be intimate with the Reynolds. . . . Every day I live I find out more of their malice against me."[8] The Reynolds girls quickly moved into other circles. But Rice and Dilke remained on friendly terms with them; apparently even Mrs. Dilke, after a brief quarrel, became friendly again;[9] and Hessey as late as 1860 spoke (in the past tense) kindly of them, wondering "whether any of them are still alive."[1]

JAMES RICE, JR.

Nobody can read Keats's letters without admiring James Rice, though little is known about his life. He met the three Leigh sisters,

[6] See the *Athenaeum*, December 13, 1884, p. 770.
[7] Finney, I, 180.
[8] Edgcumbe, p. 49.
[9] The same, p. 82.
[1] *KC*, II, 475.

June 26, 1814, at Sidmouth, which he was visiting for his health, and to them he introduced Bailey and later Reynolds. The three young men became intimate friends of the three girls, to whom they wrote various poems, nine by Rice having been preserved.[1] Thomasine Leigh's silhouette and miniature of Rice are in the Keats Museum.

Through Reynolds, Keats met Rice before April 17, 1817, and a lasting friendship resulted. They spent a month together in the Isle of Wight during the summer of 1819, and, being both in poor health, got on each other's nerves. But their affection and admiration were unaffected, and soon Keats was referring to Rice as "the most sensible, and even wise Man I know," and as "the wisest" of "three witty people" in his set: he "makes you laugh and think." Rice was one of the five friends who subscribed £10 to Taylor's fund for Keats, and one of the eighteen among whom Brown distributed Keats's books.

James Rice and Son, attorneys, had an office at 62 Great Marlborough Street, with James Rice, Sr., living in the parochial offices in Poland Street, Oxford Street, and his son at 50 Poland Street. In 1825 "James Rice, Junr." was one of the witnesses at the wedding of Thomas Hood and Jane Reynolds. Earlier he had persuaded Reynolds to enter the law, and ultimately took him into partnership. Rice and Reynolds were the legal advisers of P. G. Patmore, the second of John Scott, who was fatally wounded in a duel with J. H. Christie (1821). They and their successors, Reynolds and Simmons, were also Fanny Keats de Llanos' solicitors, and handled business for her, Llanos, and George Keats in a fashion that displeased, indeed alarmed, all three. The elder Rice held the position of clerk to the Magistrates and Governors of the Poor, parish of St. James, Westminster, from 1812 to 1830. He was discharged as from September 29, 1830, for "gross misconduct." The younger Rice protested to the Board on October 7 against their apparent reflections on his father's character, with the result that they sent a formal reply stating "explicitly that Whatever other offence may

[1] Pope (see I, 63 n.) reproduces them on pp. 42–47. One poem of Rice's, "Mary! I almost deemed I loved," was copied by W. P. Woodhouse into a commonplace book, now at Harvard, dated August, 1827. Two poems addressed by him to Jane Reynolds are preserved in J. H. Reynolds' commonplace book in the Bristol Public Library. Many new facts about Rice are given by Joanna Richardson, *TLS*, May 2, 1952, p. 297.

have been imputed to your Father as their Clerk, the Honor and Intigrity of his Character has been unsulled and unimpeachable."

Despite his wit, his gaiety, his work as lawyer and as clerk to the Commissioners of Land Tax for St. James's parish, Rice had for many years suffered from an incurable disease. His life, indeed, had been a long lingering ever since Keats met him. He probably retired before May, 1832, when the Llanoses and George Keats mention Reynolds' but not Rice's mismanagement of their affairs. By that time he and his father had moved to Putney, where he died early in December, 1832, aged forty, and was buried on December 9 at St. Mary's parish church. Dilke called him "the best of all who formed the associates of my early life—the best man indeed I ever knew," and George Keats agreed, "he was indeed a noble fellow." [2] Late in 1846 Reynolds echoed, "For every quality that marks the sensible Companion—the valuable Friend—the Gentleman and the Man—I have known no one to surpass him." [3] James Rice, Sr., died at Putney, January 28, 1839, aged about seventy-one.

JOSEPH SEVERN [1]

Today the most famous of Keats's friends, Severn was born at Hoxton on December 7, 1793. He was early apprenticed to William Bond, an engraver, in whose service he spent seven or eight unhappy years. He managed, however, to attend classes in painting at the Royal Academy. When or where he first met Keats has not yet been definitely ascertained, but it is not unlikely that Haslam, his lifelong friend, introduced him to Keats, then a student at Guy's Hospital, in October or November, 1815. If so, Keats's first letter to Severn is formal enough to prove that theirs was a mere casual acquaintance as late as November 1, 1816. Yet it developed soon into friendship, and Keats gave him a copy of the 1817 *Poems* "consigned" "to the Severn with all his Heart."

On occasion Severn conducted Keats around the British Museum or the art galleries, pointing out the beauties of the Elgin Marbles or the paintings of Titian. In April, 1819, his painting "Hermia and Helena," along with his beautiful miniature of Keats,

[2] *KC*, II, 10, 16. [3] *KC*, II, 178.

[1] There are unsatisfactory lives of Severn by Sharp (1892) and the Countess of Birkenhead (*Against Oblivion*, 1943), and a fictionized biography, Cecil Roberts' *The Remarkable Young Man* (New York, 1954).

was exhibited at the Royal Academy. On December 10 the Academy awarded him a gold medal, in a students' competition, for "The Cave of Despair." Severn claims that he saw Keats "many times" in the first half of 1820 and thereafter visited him "twice a week."

Ordered by the physicians to Italy, Keats at once asked Brown to accompany him but got no reply. The *Maria Crowther* was to sail on September 17, 1820, and on the thirteenth Keats went to Taylor's house for final preparations. That very day Haslam informed the delighted Taylor that Severn had decided to go with Keats, a decision which immortalized him.

From September 17, when the boat sailed to Gravesend, till February 23, 1821, when Keats died, Severn was a model cook, cleaner, entertainer, nurse, companion. His subsequent life, too, was first a crusade for Keats's reputation, and then after 1848 a sort of reminiscence of his association with the poet. As the fame of Keats grew steadily, Severn's own fame increased. He was a good man, and it is only poetic justice that Shelley's prayer in *Adonais*, "May the unextinguished Spirit of his illustrious friend... plead against Oblivion for his name," was long ago answered.

Severn married in 1828, and three of his seven children, Walter, Arthur, and Ann Mary (Mrs. Charles Thomas Newton), became artists of distinction. Twenty years after Keats's death he returned to England, where he led a financially precarious existence until 1860, on one occasion in the summer of 1853 fleeing to Jersey to escape his creditors. In January, 1861, he was appointed consul to Rome. Mrs. Severn, too ill to accompany him to Italy, died at Marseilles in April, 1862.

The remainder of his life was placid and useful. He met the Llanoses in Rome on April 6, 1861, saw much of them until their return to Spain in 1864, and then kept up a correspondence with Mme. Llanos until shortly before his death. As consul he won the respect and liking of practically everyone. All the while he continued to paint, his last works being "Isabella and the Pot of Basil" and a portrait of Keats. He died in his eighty-sixth year, some fifty-nine years after he had escorted Keats to Rome, and in 1881 his body was reinterred beside that of the poet. His tombstone, as is not always true of such objects, tells the truth: "*To the Memory of/* JOSEPH SEVERN/ *Devoted friend and death-bed companion/ of/* JOHN KEATS/ *whom he lived to see numbered among/ The Immortal*

JOHN TAYLOR AND JAMES AUGUSTUS HESSEY

Poets of England/ An Artist eminent for his representations/ of Italian Life and Nature/ British Consul at Rome from 1861 to 1872/ and Officer of the Crown of Italy/ in recognition of his services to/ Freedom and Humanity/ ——/ Died 3. Aug. 1879. aged 85./✠"

JOHN TAYLOR AND JAMES AUGUSTUS HESSEY [1]

Taylor and Hessey, whose authors included Coleridge, Carlyle, De Quincey, and Hazlitt, took over Keats's 1817 *Poems* from Charles and James Ollier soon after its appearance, and published his next two volumes. Taylor, the son of an East Retford, Nottinghamshire, bookseller, was born on July 31, 1781. Going to London in 1803, he worked for the publishers Lackington and Company, in whose establishment he met Hessey, a lad four years his junior (he was born on August 28, 1785), and the two became lifelong friends. In 1806 they established their own firm at 93 Fleet Street. Keats respected and liked Taylor and Hessey, and they in turn were thoroughly convinced of his greatness. They made him welcome in their homes, introduced him to many interesting men, defended him against the hostile reviewers, loaned him books and money, and, indeed, helped him in every possible way. They also raised the funds that made the Italian trip possible, though the sales of his books before (and after) 1820 were small.

In April, 1821, Taylor, who presently set up a new publishing office at 13 Waterloo Place, and Hessey, who continued to preside at the Fleet Street shop, bought the *London Magazine*, for a time the most brilliant of English periodicals. Later issues deteriorated, the firm lost money, and so Taylor and Hessey dissolved their partnership on June 30, 1825, arranging to sell the magazine to Henry Southern. Hessey remained as a bookseller in Fleet Street until he became bankrupt on May 19, 1829, and then started over again at 279 Regent Street as a bookseller and auctioneer. By July, 1834, he was in charge of a school at Hampstead.

Taylor was a scholarly man who wrote books on Junius, currency, banking, and Scriptural subjects, as well as antiquarian articles. Naturally he planned to write, and indeed advertised early in 1821, "Memoirs and Remains of John Keats." He dallied,

[1] The chief biographical sources are Olive M. Taylor, *London Mercury*, June, July, 1925 (XII, 158–166, 258–267), and Blunden, *Keats's Publisher* (1936).

perhaps largely because of the opposition of Severn and Brown, but in 1845 he was helpful to the biographer Milnes, to whose publisher Edward Moxon on September 30 he sold rights equal to his own in Keats's poems and letters. Taylor retired from publishing in March, 1853, and died on July 5, 1864. Hessey had moved in 1861 to Wiltshire, where he died on April 7, 1870.

RICHARD WOODHOUSE, JR.

Woodhouse, one of the most interesting and scholarly and certainly the most foresighted of Keats's friends, was born in Bath, December 11, 1788, the oldest in a family of fifteen children. After being educated at Eton, he lived in Spain and Portugal for some two years, an experience that helped him to write *A Grammar of the Spanish, Portuguese, and Italian Languages* (1815). Back in England, he studied law, and when he met Taylor and Hessey in March, 1811, he was a conveyancer, living at 2 Hare Court, Inner Temple Lane.[2] Soon he became a legal and literary adviser to the publishers.

When and how he met Keats is uncertain. At any rate, he was greatly impressed with the 1817 *Poems*, and in *Endymion* he found a genius even superior to that of the young Shakespeare. He devoted much time to his Keatsiana, collecting and copying every poem, letter, anecdote, proof-sheet he could lay his hands on. In the present edition of the letters twenty (see I, 18) otherwise unknown are printed from his transcripts. The kindness of the lawyer, who loaned Keats books and magazines, made suggestions (occasionally bad) about proofs, verses, prefaces, offered to introduce him to celebrities like the Porter sisters, and listened respectfully—with tongue in cheek—to his "rhodomontade," soon won his respect and gratitude. It was Woodhouse who arranged the copyright transfers of the *Poems*, *Endymion*, and *Lamia* that provided £200 for the Italian journey, and he was one of the small party who went to Gravesend to see Keats and Severn begin their voyage. In a letter he had authorized Keats to draw on him in Rome for money, expressing "more than a brotherly Interest in your welfare."

[1] For an account of the Woodhouse family see Joanna Richardson, *K–SMB*, No. 5 (1953), 39–44. Other details are given by Lowell and by Blunden, *Keats's Publisher* (1936).

[2] A notebook of his at Harvard has the address "2 Hare Court Temple/1st Jany 1812."

After February, 1821, Woodhouse's efforts to advance the dead poet's fame redoubled. He kept adding items to his Keatsiana, sometimes looking up Keats's friends and acquaintances himself, at others encouraging Taylor to make the visits, since he expected first Taylor and then Brown to write a biography. In an unpublished part of his notes (1873) on *Adonais* Severn described Woodhouse as "the active and discriminating friend of Keats, who had collected every written record of the Poet and to whom we owe the preservation of his finest productions." Woodhouse commissioned Hilton to paint the portrait now in the National Gallery and Giuseppe Girometti to make the beautiful medallion now in the Keats House. All the contributors to the *London Magazine* were friends or acquaintances of his, and his notes on the conversation of De Quincey, now at Harvard, are well known.

By 1829 he had developed tuberculosis, and he sought health in vain on the Continent, spending seven weeks during 1832 with Brown at Florence. Again in London, his condition steadily grew worse. He died at Bayswater on September 3, 1834, and was buried in the Temple churchyard.[3] Students of Keats today owe a heavy debt to Woodhouse.

GEORGIANA AUGUSTA WYLIE [1]

Georgiana Augusta Wylie, the daughter of James Wylie, adjutant of the Fifeshire Regiment of Fencible Infantry, was born in 1801 or 1802. Nothing has yet been discovered about her or her family before she is mentioned in a letter of Keats's on February 21, 1818. Her brothers Henry and Charles, whom Keats, oddly for him, always called by their Christian names, first appear in his letters of June 28 and October 14, 1818, and the earliest of his three known letters to her mother, for whom he had great affection, was written on August 6, 1818. Thereafter Mrs. Wylie and her sons are frequently referred to. Henry lived with his aunt and cousin, Mrs. Millar and her daughter Mary, on Henrietta Street (Mrs. Millar appears to have kept "paying guests"), Charles and Mrs. Wylie on Romney Street. Henry at least dabbled in

[3] See H. G. Woods, *Register of Burials at the Temple Church 1628–1853* (1905), p. 83, where his age is given as forty-five, the date of his burial as September 9.

[1] For fuller details see *KC*, I, xcvi–civ.

engraving, and in Louisville George Keats proudly displayed a "mezzotinto" made by him.[2] He married a Miss H——, whose physical unattractiveness Keats describes twice with more gusto than politeness, and was "wife-bound in Cambden Town" by January, 1820 (II, 68 f., 247). In August, 1828, Charles was living at 14 Godliman Street, Doctors' Commons,[3] presumably married, for before November, 1829, he had a son who was christened George Keats.[4]

Georgiana Wylie married George Keats on or about May 28, 1818. The poet had then known her "some time" and "was very fond of her." He found her "the most disinterrested woman I ever knew," whereas Dilke much later described her as "a pretty, lively ignorant girl, unaccustomed to society." To George and Georgiana, Keats's longest and brightest letters were addressed. They had eight children: Georgiana Emily (1819–1855), who married Alfred Gwathmey; Rosalind (1820–1826); Emma Frances (1823–1883), who married Philip Speed; Isabel (1825–1843); John Henry (1827–1917); Clarence George (1830–1861); Ella (1833–1888), who married George Nicholas Peay; Alice Ann (1836–1891), who married Edward M. Drane.[5] Mrs. Keats visited England once after her marriage, sailing from New York in May, 1828, and, after tending to business for her husband, returning there about February, 1829.

Her second marriage, January 5, 1843, to John Jeffrey began unhappily, and writing to her brother-in-law Alexander in 1850 she graphically described her new husband's supposed unfaithfulness and her subsequent miscarriage. Jeffrey, born in June, 1817, a Scotsman living in Lexington, Kentucky, was some sixteen years her junior. In Great Britain he had worked as a civil engineer, under David Napier, Sir John Rennie, and Isambard Kingdom Brunel. In the United States he was said to have constructed over thirty gas works, the first being in Louisville. Jeffrey, of course, took possession of what little property his wife had, including Keats's letters and autograph poems, and in 1845 he copied—or miscopied—some of these manuscripts for the use of Milnes.

[2] *More Letters*, p. 24. [3] *KC*, I, 317.

[4] *More Letters*, p. 53.

[5] A list of "living descendants of George Keats in America" is given in the *Southern Literary Messenger*, August, 1942 (IV, 356). On Clarence Keats and his family see Ophia D. Smith, *Bulletin of the Historical and Philosophical Society of Ohio*, VIII (1950), 191–194.

Jeffrey was kind to his stepchildren,[6] and Mrs. Jeffrey herself had a happy and serene old age. She died at Lexington on April 3, 1879, and was buried in the Speed lot in Cave Hill Cemetery, Louisville, on April 7. An unidentified newspaper obituary in the Harvard Keats Collection says, "She was a woman of the most sprightly, and, in her later years, the most caustic wit, and retained the unusual qualities of mind that made her famous among Kentucky women to the very last, and she was nearly 80 at her death. . . ."

Jeffrey died at Lexington on February 18, 1881. He, too, was buried in the Speed lot, where he had erected a monument "To the Memory of the Keats Family in America." He had made no will, but the Fayette County Court appointed two administrators, one being his brother Alexander, and three appraisers to dispose of his property. According to the appraisers' return, March 9, 1881, his estate amounted to $41,292, of which $3,217 was in cash, the remainder in gas and bank stocks.

[6] Miss Mabel C. Weaks, of Louisville, tells me that on May 20, 1852, Ella Keats wrote to Jeffrey: "All of your stepchildren love you as a father."

LETTERS AND PAPERS

1814–1818

NUMBERS

1–134

· I ·

GEORGE KEATS TO FANNY KEATS [1]

December (?) 1814

Address: To/ Miss. F. M. Keats

Pancras Lane

My dearest Fanny

I herewith send you a peice of silk and pastboard to make ⟨me⟩ a shade for my Eyes, which you will have the goodness when finished to return to Mr [2] Abbey's who I have no doubt will be so good as to forward it to Pancras Lane. With this you will receive a skipping-rope which I purchased in order to encourage you to jump and skipp about, to avoid those nasty Chilblanes that so troubled you last Winter, perhaps Mr Bourke will teach you the skipping-rope hornpipe, you can as well practice it in play hours by way of Amusement, and at the same time improvement. Your poor Grandmother has been very ill indeed, but she is now recovering fast, she desires her love to you. Your brothers join in their love to you, and hope you use all your endeavours to improve, particularly in music; I can assure you they love you most affectionately, and will do any thing in their power to make you happy which I have no doubt will succeed provided you will at the same time make yourself *good.*

I am now happy in subscribing myself the first Time

Dearest Sister

Your most affectionate Brother

George Keats

[1] *ALS:* Harvard. First published in *More Letters*, pp. 11 f. Fanny was evidently visiting someone, perhaps her guardian Richard Abbey at Walthamstow, during the illness of her grandmother, Alice (Mrs. John) Jennings, who died shortly before December 19, 1814. George wrote, on paper watermarked with the date 1814, from his quarters above Abbey's counting-room at 4 Pancras Lane, Cheapside. He calls the letter the first he has ever written to his sister, and it is the earliest by any member of the Keats family yet found.

[2] *Originally* Mrs.

Let me have the shade as soon as possible—in the note I say that your Brothers love you—mind—I mean to include myself—

Friday morning—

· 2 ·

TO G. F. MATHEW [1]

November 1815 [2]

Sweet are the pleasures that to verse belong,
And doubly sweet a brotherhood in song;
Nor can remembrance, Mathew! bring to view
A fate more pleasing, a delight more true
Than that in which the brother Poets [3] joy'd,
Who with combined powers, their wit employ'd
To raise a trophy to the drama's muses.
The thought of this great partnership diffuses
Over the genius loving heart, a feeling
Of all that's high, and great, and good, and healing.

[1] This epistle, taken from Keats's *Poems* (1817), pp. 53–58, was, like Nos. 5, 6, 74, sent as a letter. Woodhouse, in his Pierpont Morgan Library book of Keatsiana (compare W. W. Beyer, *Keats and the Daemon King* [New York, 1947], pp. 317–320), remarks, "The verses . . . I am informed were sent to the Misses Mathew, Cousins of the above Gentleman, then at Hastings; & that Mr M. was then with them." George Felton Mathew, born March 22, 1795, was the son of Richard Mathew, mercer and collector of the King's Taxes in the parish of St. Marylebone. For a short time Keats was on intimate terms with him and his cousins, Caroline (II, 27) and Ann Mathew. Murry, *Studies in Keats* (1930), pp. 1–6, argued that Mathew published his own verses on Keats ("To a Poetical Friend") in the *European Magazine*, October, 1816 (LXX, 365), after Keats had written his sonnet on "Solitude" and his two poems to the Mathew girls, and that the present epistle is a reply to Mathew. Murry, pp. 6–11, and for a time Blunden, *Votive Tablets* (1931), p. 253, considered Mathew's review of Keats's *Poems* (*European Magazine*, May, 1817 [LXXI, 434–437]) an "insufferable" or "embittered" expression of resentment because Keats had deserted him for Leigh Hunt, though later Blunden, *English*, I (1936), 46–55, changed his opinion, and called the review (p. 53) "greatly to Mathew's credit." Mathew wrote various other poor poems (see *KC*, II, 193–200), some of which were published by his son H. R. Mathew in 1908 and 1909. He also gave valuable aid when Milnes was writing Keats's biography. By that time he was an embittered man, barely keeping alive his wife and twelve children as a "supernumerary" at "less than £150" a year in the Poor Law administration (*KC*, II, 241). Keats's epistle, as De Selincourt, p. 395, remarks, "is interesting as suggesting the poets read by the two friends." Interesting, also, are the comments on it which Mathew sent to Milnes in 1847 (*KC*, II, 181, 186–188).

[2] Dated by Keats.

[3] Beaumont and Fletcher.

Too partial friend! fain would I follow thee
Past each horizon of fine poesy;
Fain would I echo back each pleasant note
As o'er Sicilian seas, clear anthems float
'Mong the light skimming gondolas far parted,
Just when the sun his farewell beam has darted:
But 'tis impossible; far different cares
Beckon me sternly from soft "Lydian airs," [4]
And hold my faculties so long in thrall,
That I am oft in doubt whether at all
I shall again see Phœbus in the morning:
Or flush'd Aurora in the roseate dawning!
Or a white Naiad in a rippling stream;
Or a rapt seraph [5] in a moonlight beam;
Or again witness what with thee I've seen,
The dew by fairy feet swept from the green,
After a night of some quaint jubilee
Which every elf and fay had come to see:
When bright processions took their airy march
Beneath the curved moon's triumphal arch.

But might I now each passing moment give
To the coy muse, with me she would not live
In this dark city, nor would condescend
'Mid contradictions her delights to lend.
Should e'er the fine-eyed maid to me be kind,
Ah! surely it must be whene'er I find
Some flowery spot, sequester'd, wild, romantic,
That often must have seen a poet frantic;
Where oaks, that erst the Druid knew, are growing,
And flowers, the glory of one day, are blowing;
Where the dark-leav'd laburnum's drooping clusters
Reflect athwart the stream their yellow lustres,
And intertwined the cassia's arms unite,
With its own drooping buds, but very white.
Where on one side are covert branches hung,
'Mong which the nightingales have always sung

[4] Milton, "L'Allegro," line 136. [5] Pope, *Essay on Man*, I.278.

In leafy quiet: where to pry, aloof,
Atween the pillars of the sylvan roof,
Would be to find where violet beds were nestling,
And where the bee with cowslip bells was wrestling.
There must be too a ruin dark, and gloomy,
To say "joy not too much in all that's bloomy."

Yet this is vain—O Mathew lend thy aid
To find a place where I may greet the maid—
Where we may soft humanity put on,
And sit, and rhyme and think on Chatterton;
And that warm-hearted Shakspeare sent to meet him
Four laurell'd spirits, heaven-ward to intreat him.
With reverence would we speak of all the sages
Who have left streaks of light athwart their ages:
And thou shouldst moralize on Milton's blindness,
And mourn the fearful dearth of human kindness
To those who strove with the bright golden wing
Of genius, to flap away each sting
Thrown by the pitiless world. We next could tell
Of those who in the cause of freedom fell; [6]
Of our own Alfred, of Helvetian Tell;
Of him whose name to ev'ry heart's a solace,
High-minded and unbending William Wallace.
While to the rugged north our musing turns
We well might drop a tear for him, and Burns.

Felton! without incitements such as these,
How vain for me the niggard Muse to tease:
For thee, she will thy every dwelling grace,
And make "a sun-shine in a shady place:" [7]
For thou wast once a flowret blooming wild,
Close to the source, bright, pure, and undefil'd,
Whence gush the streams of song: in happy hour
Came chaste Diana from her shady bower,

[6] These lines on freedom, says De Selincourt, p. 395, "shew Keats to be already the pupil of the *Examiner*."

[7] *The Faerie Queene*, I.iii.4.

Just as the sun was from the east uprising;
And, as for him some gift she was devising,
Beheld thee, pluck'd thee, cast thee in the stream
To meet her glorious brother's greeting beam.
I marvel much that thou hast never told
How, from a flower, into a fish of gold
Apollo chang'd thee; how thou next didst seem
A black-eyed swan upon the widening stream;
And when thou first didst in that mirror trace
The placid features of a human face:
That thou hast never told thy travels strange,
And all the wonders of the mazy range
O'er pebbly crystal, and o'er golden sands;
Kissing thy daily food from Naiad's pearly hands.

· 3 ·

THE KEATS BROTHERS TO RICHARD ABBEY [1]

13 June 1816

London June 13th 1816

We the undersigned Grand children of the late Alice Jennings, do hereby authorize Mr Richard Abbey, her executor to pay Josh Burch the sum of three Pounds, fifteen Shillings, due to him from the estate of the said Alice Jennings.

John Keats
George Keats.
Thos Keats

[1] This document, written by George Keats, is in the University of Texas Library. Perhaps Joseph Burch was the husband of "Ann Burch, of Upper Clapton, widow," who on June 29, 1825, testified in the Chancery proceedings of Rawlings *versus* Jennings that she was an intimate friend of Thomas and Frances Keats, and "that sd J. K. was born in the year 1795, vizt, on or about the 29th Oct." See Willard B. Pope, *TLS*, December 22, 1932, p. 977.

· 4 ·

GEORGE KEATS TO JOHN AND TOM KEATS [1]

August 1816

My Dear Brothers

I take the advantage of enclosing my thanks for two letters, one from each of you received this Morning in a Frank of Our Friend Wells [2]—To your's My Dear Tom I will answer on Monday or Tuesday{.} John's shall be attended to at the beginning of next Week. I most fortunately met Briggs [3] this Morning, who informed [me] C. C. C was living with Mr Towers.[4] I shall endeavour to see him—. What may occur at our meeting shall be communicat'd in my next. Wagtail is waiting & I am not over-quick or you should have more from

Your Affectionate
{George}

[1] *AL:* Harvard. Colvin, 1920, p. 37, and Lowell, I, 155, agree that after passing his examinations at Apothecaries' Hall on July 25, 1816, Keats went alone to Margate for part of August and September. The present letter (first printed in *KC*, I, 3) shows that at least for a time Tom Keats was with his brother. On its back is Keats's first draft of the sonnet, "Written in Disgust of Vulgar Superstition," at the end of which Tom added, "J Keats/ Written in 15 Minutes." G. A. R. Winston, *Guy's Hospital Reports*, XCII (1943), 102–104, suggests that Keats chose Margate because his fellow-student at Guy's, Joshua Waddington, lived there.

[2] See I, 19[illegible]

[3] A school-fellow (II, 110).

[4] John Towers, a chemist, Clarke's brother-in-law, lived at 6 Little Warner Street, Clerkenwell (see the address of No. 8). According to Blunden, *K–SJ*, III (1954), 40, he moved from London to the Isle of Thanet, Kent, in 1819.

· 5 ·

TO GEORGE KEATS

August 1816

Margate Aug[t] {1816}

My dear George,

If there be any room in this Sheet after I shall have written the prosing {verse} [1] I will say a few things to you in downright Prose—

Full many a dreary hour have I past,
My Brain bewildered, and my Mind o'er cast
With Heaviness; in seasons, when I've thought
No '⟨sperey⟩ spherey strains,[2] by me, could e'er be caught
From the blue Dome, though I to dimness Gaze
On the far depth, where sheeted Lightning plays;
Or, on the wavy Grass, out stretch'd supinely,
Pry 'mong the Stars, to strive to think divinely:
That I should never hear Apollo's song,
Though feathery clouds were floating all along
The purple West, and two bright Streaks between,
The golden Lyre itself ⟨,⟩ were faintly seen:
That the still Murmur of the honey Bee,
Would never teach a rural song to me:
That the bright glance, from Beauty's Eyelids slanting,
Would never make a lay of mine enchanting,
Or warm my Breast with ardor, to unfold
Some Tale of Love, and Arms, in time of old.
But, there are times, when those who love the Bay,
Glide from all sorrowing, far, far away:
A sudden glow comes on them; nought they see
In Water, Earth, or Air, but Poesy.
It has been said, dear George, and true I hold it,
(For Knightly Spenser to Libertas [3] told it,)

[1] This "prosing verse" was, like Nos. 2 and 6, printed in Keats's *Poems* (1817), pp. 59–67, with slight variations (see Garrod, pp. 31–34, for details). It is there dated by Keats. Copying the letter for Milnes in 1845, Jeffrey put at its head "(published)." *AL:* Harvard.

[2] Milton's *Comus*, line 1020, has "Spheary chime."

[3] Leigh Hunt is so called in Keats's "Specimen of an Induction to a Poem," line 61, and "To Charles Cowden Clarke" (see I, 110).

That, when a Poet is in ⟨shch⟩ such a trance,
In Air, he sees white Coursers, paw, and prance;
Bestridden of gay Knights, in gay Appa⟨r⟩rel,
Who, at each other tilt, in playful Quarrel;
And, what we, ignorantly, sheet lightning, call,
Is the swift opening of their wide Portal;
When the bright Warder blows his Trumpet clear,
Whose Tones reach nought on earth, but Poet's Ear.
When these enchanted Portals open wide,
And through the light, the horsemen swiftly glide;
The Poet's eye can reach those golden Halls,
And view the glory of their festivals:
Their Ladies bright, that in the distance seem
Fit for the silv'ring of a Seraphs dream:
Their rich brimed Goblets, that incessant run
Like the bright spots that move about the Sun:
{And, w}hen upheld, the Wine, from each bright Jar
{Po}urs with the lustre of a falling star.
Yet further off, are dimly seen, their bowers,
Of which, no mortal Eye can reach the Flowers;
And 't is right just—for well Apollo knows
'T would make the Poet quarrel with the Rose.
All that's reveal'd from that far seat of Blisses,
Is, the clear fountains, interchanging kisses
As gracefully descending, light, and thin,
Like silver streaks across a Dolphin's fin,
When he upspringeth from the coral Caves,
And sports, with half his Tail above the Waves.
These Wonders strange, he sees, and many more,
Whose head is pregnant with poetic lore.
Should he upon an Evening ramble fare,
With Forehead, to the soothing breezes, bare;
Would he nought see, but the dark silent blue,
With all its Diamonds trembling through, and through?
Or the coy Moon, when in the waviness
Of whitest Clouds, she doth her beauty dress,
And staidly paces, higher up, and higher,
Like a sweet Nun in Holyday Attire?
Ah yes! much more would start into his sight;

The Revelries, and Mysteries of Night:
And should I ever view them, I will tell ye
Such Tales, as needs must with Amazement spell ye.
    These are the living pleasures of the Bard;
But richer, far, Posterity's award.
What does he murmer with his latest breath,
While his proud Eye looks through the film of death?
"What, though I leave this dull, and earthly mould,
"Yet, shall my spirit, lofty converse hold
"With after times—the Patriot shall feel
"My stern alarum, and unsheath his steel:
"Or in the senate, thunder out my Numbers,
"To startle Princes from their easy slumbers.
"The Sage will mingle with each moral Theme
"My happy thoughts, sententious: he will teem
"With lofty Periods, when my Verses fire him,
"And then I'll stoop from Heaven, to inspire him.
"Lays have I left, of such a dear delight,
"That Maids will sing them on their bridal Night.
"Gay Villagers, upon a Morn of May,
"When they have tired their gentle Limbs with play,
"And formed a snowy circle on the Grass;
"Placing in midst thereof, that happy Lass
"Who chosen is their Queen; with her fine head
"Crowned with flowers, purple, white, and red:
"For there the lily, and the Musk rose, sighing,
"Are emblems true of hapless Lovers dying.
"Between her Breasts, that never yet felt trouble,
"A bunch of Violets, full blown, and double,
"Serenely sleep—She from a Casket takes
"A Little Book, and then a Joy awakes
"About each youthful heart; with stifled Cries,
"And rubbing of white hands, and sparkling Eyes.
"For she's to read a Tale of Hopes, and fears;
"One that I fostered in my youthful Years.
"The Pearls, that on each glist'ning circlet sleep,
"Gush ever and anon with silent creep,
"Lured by the innocent Dimples. To sweet rest,
"Shall the dear Babe, upon its Mother's breast

"Be lull'd with songs of Mine. Fair world Adieu!
"Thy Dales, and Hills are fading from my view:
"Swiftly, I mount, upon ⟨whi⟩ widespreading Pinions,
"Far from the narrow bounds of thy Dominions.
"Full joy I feel, while thus I cleave the Air,
"That my soft Verse will charm thy Daughters fair,
"And warm thy Sons." Ah, my dear friend, and Brother!
Could I, at once, my mad Ambition smother
For tasting Joys like these; sure I should be
Happier, and dearer to Society.
At times 't is true I've felt relief from pain,
When some bright thought has darted through my brain:
Through all that Day I've felt a greater Pleasure,
Than ⟨th⟩ if I'd brought to light a hidden Treasure.
As to my Sonnets; though none else should heed them,
I feel delighted, still, that you will read them.
Of late, too, I have had much calm enjoyment;
Stretched on the Grass, at my best lov'd employment
Of scribbling Lines for you. These things I thought,
While, in my face, the freshest Breeze I caught.
E'en now, I'm pillow'd on a bed of Flowers,
That crown a lofty Cliff, which proudly towers
Above the Ocean Waves—The Stalks, and Blades
Checquer my Tablet with their quivering shades.[4]
On one side, is a field of drooping Oats;
Through which the Poppies show their scarlet Coats;
So pert, and useless, that they bring to Mind
The scarlet Coats, that pester human kind.
And on the other side, outspread, is seen
Ocean's blue mantle, streak'd with purple & green.
Now 't is I see a Canvassed ship, and now
Mark the bright silver curling round her prow.
I see the ⟨Latk⟩ Lark, down dropping to her Nest,
And the broad winged Sea Gull, never at rest;
For when no more he spreads his feathers free,
His breast is dancing on the reastless Sea.
Now I direct my Eyes towards the west,

[4] Compare Pope, *Pastorals* ("Summer," line 4), "a quiv'ring shade," and *Windsor Forest,* line 135, "the quivering shade."

Which at this Moment, is in Sunbeams drest;
Why westward turn? 'T was but to say adieu!
'T was but to kiss my hand dear George to you!

As this may be kept for a fair Coppy I will write the three words I have time to do on the sheet [5] which will inclose this—

* * *

· 6 ·

TO C. C. CLARKE [1]

September 1816

Oft have you seen a swan superbly frowning,
And with proud breast his own white shadow crowning;
He slants his neck beneath the waters bright
So silently, it seems a beam of light
Come from the galaxy: anon he sports,—
With outspread wings the Naiad Zephyr courts,
Or ruffles all the surface of the lake
In striving from its crystal face to take
Some diamond water drops, and them to treasure
In milky nest, and sip them off at leisure.
But not a moment can he there insure them,
Nor to such downy rest can he allure them;
For down they rush as though they would be free,
And drop like hours into eternity.
Just like that bird am I in loss of time,
Whene'er I venture on the stream of rhyme;
With shatter'd boat, oar snapt, and canvass rent,
I slowly sail, scarce knowing my intent;
Still scooping up the water with my fingers,
In which a trembling diamond never lingers.

[5] Which has disappeared.

[1] From Keats's *Poems* (1817), pp. 68–75, where the date is given. For a facsimile of the original manuscript see W. H. Arnold's *Books and Letters* (New York, 1901), pp. 105–108. De Selincourt, pp. 395 f., has sufficiently annotated the borrowings from or references to Cowper, Spenser, Milton, and Shakespeare.

By this, friend Charles,[2] you may full plainly see
Why I have never penn'd a line to thee:
Because my thoughts were never free, and clear,
And little fit to please a classic ear;
Because my wine was of too poor a savour
For one whose palate gladdens in the flavour
Of sparkling Helicon:—small good it were
To take him to a desert rude, and bare,
Who had on Baiæ's shore reclin'd at ease,
While Tasso's page was floating in a breeze
That gave soft music from Armida's [3] bowers,
Mingled with fragrance from her rarest flowers:
Small good to one who had by Mulla's stream [4]
Fondled the maidens with the breasts of cream;
Who had beheld Belphœbe in a brook,
And lovely Una in a leafy nook,
And Archimago [5] leaning o'er his book:
Who had of all that's sweet tasted, and seen,
From silv'ry ripple, up to beauty's queen;
From the sequester'd haunts of gay Titania,
To the blue dwelling of divine Urania:
One, who, of late, had ta'en sweet forest walks
With him who elegantly chats, and talks—
The wrong'd Libertas, [6]—who has told you stories
Of laurel chaplets, and Apollo's glories;
Of troops chivalrous prancing through a city,
And tearful ladies made for love, and pity:
With many else which I have never known.
Thus have I thought; and days on days have flown
Slowly, or rapidly—unwilling still
For you to try my dull, unlearned quill.
Nor should I now, but that I've known you long;
That you first taught me all the sweets of song:

[2] Clarke is the only male friend whom Keats addresses by his given name in non-verse letters. See I, 14.

[3] In Tasso's *Jerusalem Delivered* an enchantress who made captives of Rinaldo and Tancred.

[4] A stream near Spenser's home at Kilcolman. See *The Faerie Queene*, IV.xi.41, VII.vi.40.

[5] For these characters see *The Faerie Queene*, Books I and II.

[6] See I, 105.

The grand, the sweet, the terse, the free, the fine;
What swell'd with pathos, and what right divine:
Spenserian vowels that elope with ease,
And float along like birds o'er summer seas;
Miltonian storms, and more, Miltonian tenderness;
Michael in arms, and more, meek Eve's fair slenderness.
Who read for me the sonnet swelling loudly
Up to its climax and then dying proudly?
Who found for me the grandeur of the ode,
Growing, like Atlas, stronger from its load?
Who let me taste that more than cordial dram,
The sharp, the rapier-pointed epigram?
Shew'd me that epic was of all the king,
Round, vast, and spanning all like Saturn's ring?
You too upheld the veil from Clio's beauty,
And pointed out the patriot's stern duty;
The might of Alfred, and the shaft of Tell;
The hand of Brutus, that so grandly fell
Upon a tyrant's head. Ah! had I never seen,
Or known your kindness, what might I have been?
What my enjoyments in my youthful years,
Bereft of all that now my life endears?
And can I e'er these benefits forget?
And can I e'er repay the friendly debt?
No, doubly no;—yet should these rhymings please,
I shall roll on the grass with two-fold ease:
For I have long time been my fancy feeding
With hopes that you would one day think the reading
Of my rough verses not an hour misspent; [7]
Should it e'er be so, what a rich content!
Some weeks have pass'd since last I saw the spires
In lucent Thames reflected: [8]—warm desires
To see the sun o'er peep the eastern dimness,
And morning shadows streaking into slimness
Across the lawny fields, and pebbly water;
To mark the time as they grow broad, and shorter;
To feel the air that plays about the hills,
And sips its freshness from the little rills;

[7] mispent *1817*. [8] Keats was writing in Margate.

To see high, golden corn wave in the light
When Cynthia smiles upon a summer's night,
And peers among the cloudlet's jet and white,
As though she were reclining in a bed
Of bean blossoms, in heaven freshly shed.
No sooner had I stepp'd into these pleasures
Than I began to think of rhymes and measures:
The air that floated by me seem'd to say
"Write! thou wilt never have a better day."
And so I did. When many lines I'd written,
Though with their grace I was not oversmitten,
Yet, as my hand was warm, I thought I'd better
Trust to my feelings, and write you a letter.
Such an attempt required an inspiration
Of a peculiar sort,—a consummation;—
Which, had I felt, these scribblings might have been
Verses from which the soul would never wean:
But many days have past since last my heart
Was warm'd luxuriously by divine Mozart;
By Arne delighted, or by Handel madden'd;
Or by the song of Erin pierc'd and sadden'd:
What time you were before the music [9] sitting,
And the rich notes to each sensation fitting.
Since I have walk'd with you through shady lanes
That freshly terminate in open plains,
And revel'd in a chat that ceased not
When at night-fall among your books we got:
No, nor when supper came, nor after that,—
Nor when reluctantly I took my hat;
No, nor till cordially you shook my hand
Mid-way between our homes:—your accents bland
Still sounded in my ears, when I no more
Could hear your footsteps touch the grav'ly floor.
Sometimes I lost them, and then found again;
You chang'd the footpath for the grassy plain.
In those still moments I have wish'd you joys
That well you know to honour:—"Life's very toys

[9] Musical instrument, piano (see II, 13). This is the last example in *NED*, the first dating from 1644.

"With him," said I, "will take a pleasant charm;
"It cannot be that ought will work him harm."
These thoughts now come o'er me with all their might:—
Again I shake your hand,—friend Charles, good night.

· 7 ·

TO C. C. CLARKE [1]

9 October 1816

Wednesday Octr 9th—

My dear Sir,

The busy time has just gone by, and I can now devote any time you may mention to the pleasure of seeing Mr Hunt—'t will be an Era in my existence—I am anxious too to see the Author of the Sonnet to the Sun,[2] for it is no mean gratification to become acquainted with Men who in their admiration of Poetry do not jumble together Shakspeare and Darwin [3]—I have coppied out a sheet or two of Verses which I composed some time ago, and find so much to blame in them that the ~~best~~ worst part will go into the fire—those to G. Mathew [4] I will suffer to meet the eye of Mr H. notwithstanding that the Muse is so frequently mentioned. I here sinned in the face of Heaven even while remembring what, I think, Horace says, "never presume to make a God appear but for an Action worthy of a God.[5] From a few Words of yours when last I saw you,

[1] *ALS:* Historical Society of Pennsylvania. Found by J. H. Birss, first printed in Holman's trade periodical, *Within the Compass of a Print Shop*, II (1932), 189 f., and reprinted by Birss in *NQ*, November 5, 1932, p. 326. For the date at which Keats met Leigh Hunt see I, 77.

[2] Holman notes: "Undoubtedly written by C.C.C." He adds that Clarke (see his *Recollections of Writers* [1878], pp. 199 f.) sent some verses, probably this sonnet, in December, 1818, to Hunt, who planned to, but did not, publish them in the *Examiner*. Keith Glenn, however (*TLS*, October 17, 1936, p. 839), believes that Keats was referring to Horace Smith's sonnet, "To the Setting Sun," afterwards published in his *Amarynthus* (1821), p. 209. Both suggestions are interesting: they would explain why "One of the earliest things JK wrote," as Clarke told Woodhouse in August, 1823 (*KC*, I, 274), "was a *Sonnet to the Moon* wh: he gave to C.C.C."

[3] Erasmus Darwin (1731–1802), physician, author of *The Botanic Garden*.

[4] See No. 2.

[5] *Ars Poetica*, line 191. MBF cites the Earl of Roscommon's translation, *Horace: Of the Art of Poetry* (1709), sig. A5, "Never presume to make a God appear,/ But for a Business worthy of a God."

I have no doubt but that you have something in your Portfolio which I should by rights see—I will put you in Mind of it—Although the Borough is a beastly place in dirt, turnings and windings; yet No 8 Dean Street [6] is not difficult to find; and if you would run the Gauntlet over London Bridge, take the first turning to the left and then the first to the right and moreover knock at my door which is nearly opposite a Meeting,[7] you would do one a Charity which as St Paul [8] saith is the father of all the Virtues—At all events let me hear from you soon—I say at all events not excepting the Gout in your fingers [9]—

Your's Sincerely
John Keats—

· 8 ·

TO C. C. CLARKE [1]

31 October 1816

Address: Mr C. C. Clarke./ Mr Towers [2]/ Warner Street/ Clerkenwell—
Postmarks: TwoPyPost Unpaid Tooley St; 12 o'Clock OC 31 1816 Nn

My dainty Davie,[3]

I will be as punctual as the Bee to the Clover—Very glad am I at the thoughts of seeing so soon this glorious Haydon [4] and all his

[6] Dean Street, Tooley Street, Borough, is identified (with a sketch-map) by Hale-White, pp. 10–12, who says that the part not now arched over by the Southern Railway in order to reach its London Bridge terminus is called Stainer Street. See I, 117 n.

[7] A Baptist chapel between Nos. 28 and 29 on the west side of Dean Street.

[8] 1 Corinthians xiii.13.

[9] Compare "my pen . . . too goutty" (II, 5).

[1] *ALS:* Berg Collection, New York Public Library. At the head of the letter (formerly owned by Owen D. Young) there is an unimportant note by James Couper, 1871.

[2] See I, 104 n.

[3] Holman observed that "My dainty Davie" appears in Burns's "To Davie Second Epistle," line 44, and "Dainty Davie" in the chorus to his "Now Rosy May." Keats owned a copy of Burns's *Poems* (*KC*, I, 258).

[4] Keats had met Haydon before this date (see *KC*, I, 4 n., and M. C. Bates, *K–SJ*, III [1954], 81 f.). Here, as Garrod, p. lxxv, makes clear, he refers to a first visit planned

ST. THOMAS'S HOSPITAL, SOUTHWARK, LONDON

From an eighteenth-century print in the Louis A. Holman Collection, Keats Room, Houghton Library

My dear Sir

I am really sorry that I have an engagement on Saturday to which I have looked forward all the Week more especially because I particularly want to look into some beautiful Scenery — for poetical purposes. I am very sensible of your kindness and hope for the pleasure of seeing you ere long at No 8 Dean Street. I know you will congratulate me when I tell you that I shall breakfast with Haydon on Sunday —

Yours sincerely

John Keats

Mr Severn

This is an autograph of John Keats

Joseph Severn

Signed by Mr Joseph Severn at Rome the 27th day of May 1877 before me

[illegible]

British Vice Consul

Rome

KEATS TO SEVERN, I NOVEMBER 1816 (*No. 9*)

Harvard Keats Collection

Novr 20th

My dear Sir—

Last Evening wrought me up, and I cannot forbear sending you the following— Yours unfeignedly John Keats—

Great Spirits now on Earth are sojourning
He of the Cloud the Cataract the Lake
Who on Helvellyn's summit wide awake
Catches his freshness from Archangel's wing
He of the Rose, the Violet the Spring
The social Smile, the Chain for freedom's sake:
And lo!—whose stedfastness would never take
A Meaner sound than Raphael's Whispering
And other Spirits are there standing apart
Upon the Forehead of the Age to come;
These, These will give the World another heart
And other pulses—hear ye not the hum
Of mighty Workings in a distant Mart?
Listen awhile ye Nations and be dumb!

Novr 20—

Removed to 76. Cheapside

KEATS TO HAYDON, 20 NOVEMBER 1816 (*No. 11*)

Harvard Keats Collection

Tuesday—

My dear Charles,

You may now look at Minerva's Ægis with impunity, seeing that my awful Visage did not turn you into a John Doe you have accordingly a legitimate title to a Copy—I will use my interest to procure it for you. I'll tell you what—I met Reynolds at Haydon's a few mornings since—he promised to be with me this Evening and Yesterday I had the same promise from Severn and I must put you in Mind that on last All hallowmas' day you gave your word that you would spend this Evening with me—so no putting off—I have done little to Endymion lately—I hope to finish it in one more attack—I believe you I went to Richards's—it was so whoreson a Night that I stopped there all the next day—His Remembrances to you. (Ext from the common place Book of my Mind—Mem—Wednesday—Hampstead—call in Warner Street—a Sketch of Mr Hunt—) I will ever consider you my sincere and affectionate friend—you will not doubt that I am yours.—

God bless you——

John Keats.

KEATS TO CLARKE, 17 DECEMBER 1816 (*No. 14*)
Harvard Keats Collection

Creation. I pray thee let me know when you go to Ollier's [5] and where he resides—this I forgot to ask you—and tell me also when you will help me waste a sullen day [6]—God 'ield you [7]—

J—K—

· 9 ·

TO JOSEPH SEVERN [1]

1 November 1816

Address: Joseph Severn Esqre/ 128 Goswell Street/ Friday Aft^{r}noon—
Postmarks: 7 o'Clock NO 1 18[16] N^{T}; TwoPyPost Unpaid Lombard St

My dear Sir,

I am nearly [2] sorry that I have an engagement on Saturday; [3] to which I have looked forward all the Week more especially because I particularly want to look into some beautiful Scenery—for poetical purposes. I am very sensible of your kindness and hope for the pleasure of seeing you ere long at No 8 Dean Street [4] I know

---

for Sunday, November 3, to Haydon's studio, a breakfast visit mentioned in the next letter.

[5] For Charles Ollier (1788–1859), the publisher, see I, 227. His shop was at 3 Welbeck Street in 1816, later at 14 Vere Street, Oxford Street.

[6] J. C. Maxwell, *NQ*, May 17, 1947, p. 215, cites Milton's sonnet "To Mr. Lawrence," line 4, "Help wast a sullen day."

[7] *Hamlet*, IV.v.41, "God 'ild you!"

[1] *ALS:* In the Frederick Locker-Lampson "Great Album," formerly owned by the late Paul M. Warburg, of New York, now deposited in the Houghton Library by its present owners, Mr. and Mrs. S. B. Grimson, of New York. The letter was first printed, with a very full discussion, by M. C. Bates, *K–SJ*, III (1954), 75–83. The last two digits of "1816" are blurred in the postmark, but Friday, November 1 (see the address and the postmark), came in 1816.

[2] It is possible (as Bates thinks) that "nearly" means "particularly," though the six examples given by *NED* seem rather to mean "closely," "personally." I suspect that Keats intended to write "very" or "really."

[3] November 2.

[4] Garrod, p. lxxv, remarks that "Keats was not long in Dean Street—he may very well have been there for no more than a week." But Keats wrote No. 7 from that address on October 9, and he added a postscript to No. 11 of November 20, "Removed to 76. Cheapside." As Bates points out, he was certainly in Dean Street for more than three weeks and probably "from late September till about the middle of November." That he had moved before November 18 is (see Lowell, I, 204 f.) proved by details in his sonnet "To My Brothers" of that date.

you will congratulate me when I tell you that I shall Breakfast with Haydon on Sunday [5]—

Your's sincerely
John Keats [6]

Mr Seve[r]n

· 10 ·

TO C. C. CLARKE [1]

8 or 11 November 1816

To C— C— C— greeting,

Whereas I have received a Note from that worthy Gentleman Mr Haydon, to the purport of his not being able to see us on this days Evening, for that he hath an order for the Orchestra to see Timon $\frac{e}{y}$ Misantrophos, and begging us to excuse the same—it behoveth me to make this thing known to you for a manifest Reason—So I rest your Hermit [2]—John Keats—

[5] November 3, the morning engagement mentioned in No. 8.

[6] After the signature is written: "This is an autograph of John Keats/ Joseph Severn/ Signed by Mr Joseph Severn at Rome/ the 27th day of May 1879 before me/ Alex. Roesler Franz/ British ViceConsul/ *Roma*"/. Severn wrote only his name, and Franz stamped the attestation with his own seal.

[1] *ALS:* Dedham (Massachusetts) Historical Society. The letter, then owned by F. Holland Day, was first printed in the Boston *Herald*, November 3, 1895, and next by Lowell, I, 202. Keats refers to an evening engagement which Haydon had canceled in order to see *Timon of Athens*. That play was presented at Drury Lane on October 28, 30, November 1, 4, 8, 11, 18. No. 9 shows that Keats breakfasted with Haydon for the first time on Sunday, November 3. Probably at that breakfast Haydon made the engagement here broken, which cannot have been for the 1st and was probably not for the 4th. As Keats visited Haydon again on November 19 (No. 11), it seems likely that the present letter was written, not on November 18, but on either November 8 or 11.

[2] *Macbeth*, I.vi.20, "We rest your hermits."

· 11 ·

TO B. R. HAYDON [1]

20 November 1816

Novr 20th

My dear Sir—

Last Evening [2] wrought me up, and I cannot forbear sending you the following—Your's unfeignedly [3] John Keats—

Great Spirits now on Earth are sojourning
He of the Cloud, the Cataract the Lake
Who on Helvellyn's summit wide awake
Catches his freshness from Archangel's wing
He of the Rose, the Violet, the Spring
The social Smile, the Chain for freedom's sake:
And lo!—whose stedfastness would never take
A Meaner Sound than Raphael's Whispering.
And other Spirits are there standing apart
Upon the Forehead of the Age to come;
These, These will give the World another heart
And other pulses—hear ye not the hum
Of mighty Workings in a distant Mart?
Listen awhile ye Nations, and be dumb.!

Novr 20—

Removed to 76. Cheapside [4]

[1] *ALS:* Formerly in Haydon's Journal, now at Harvard.

[2] Haydon refers to this evening, November 19, in his Journal (Penrose, p. 218). It was then that he made the profile sketch of Keats, dated "Nov 1816—BRH," which is reproduced by Olney, p. 294, and others.

[3] The same word is used at I, 226. For the ellipsis Haydon suggested in line 13 see the next letter. It is no doubt superfluous to say that the "Great Spirits" are Wordsworth, Hunt, and Haydon. See Garrod, p. 48, for the slight changes made in the text in the 1817 *Poems*.

[4] Evidently Keats had recently moved from 8 Dean Street (see I, 114).

· 12 ·

TO B. R. HAYDON [1]

21 November 1816

Address: Benjamin Robert Haydon/ 41 Great Marlborough Street—
Postmarks (imperfect): TwoPyPost Unpaid {Lo}mbar{d St}; 7 o'Clock
NO 21 1816 NT

Thursday Aftrn

My dear Sir,

Your Letter has filld me with a proud pleasure and shall be kept by me as a stimulus to exertion—I begin to fix my eye upon one horizon—. My feelings entirely fall in with yours' in regard to the Elipsis and I glory in it [2]—The Idea of your sending it to Wordsworth put me out of breath—you know with what Reverence—I would send my Wellwishes to him—[3]

Your's sincerely
John Keats

Great Spirits now on earth are sojourning [4]
He of the Cloud, the Cataract, the Lake

[1] *ALS:* Formerly in Haydon's Journal, now at Harvard. Keats sent No. 11 on November 20 by messenger to Haydon, who forwarded an immediate reply, probably by the same hand. [2] See line 13 and I, 117 n.

[3] Keats's signature is cut off and the following endorsement supplied: "Yours Sincerely/ John Keats/——/ The original autograph presented to/ Fras Bennock Esqr 78 Wood St/ for——Longfellow Esq. the/ American Poet—Nov. 21st 1848./ Fred W Haydon/." The signature itself, now in the Harvard Keats Collection, is endorsed: "Cut by Mrs Haydon from a letter to her husband—& handed to me by her Son Fred—November 23rd 1848 F Bennoch". Mrs. Nathaniel Hawthorne dedicated her husband's *Passages from the English Note-Books* (1870) to Bennoch, not Bennock (1812–1890), head of the wholesale trading house of Bennoch, Twentyman, and Rigg, 1848–1874, and author of *Poems, Lyrics, Songs, and Sonnets* (1877). For abundant information about him see Randall Stewart's edition, *The English Notebooks* (New York, 1941). MBF notes that Longfellow sent Bennoch an inscribed copy of his *Kavanagh* (Boston, 1849) in May, 1849.

[4] The sonnet is on a separate sheet which Keats evidently intended to be sent to Wordsworth. Instead, Haydon retained it, and waited for over a month before in a letter of December 31 (F. W. Haydon, II, 30) he forwarded Wordsworth a copy made by himself, slightly misquoting the last sentence of Keats's letter. In his reply, January 20, 1817, Wordsworth (*The Letters of William and Dorothy Wordsworth: The Later Years*, ed. De Selincourt [Oxford, 1939], III, 1367 f.) said: "The sonnet appears to be of good promise, of course neither you nor I being so highly complimented in the composition can be deemed judges altogether impartial—but it is assuredly vigorously conceived

Who on Helvellyn's summit wide awake
Catches his freshness from Archangel's wing
He of the Rose, the Violet, the Spring
The social smile, the Chain for Freedom's sake;
And lo!—whose stedfastness would never take
A meaner sound than Raphael's Whispering.
And other Spirits are there standing apart
Upon the Forehead of the age to come;
These, these will give the World another Heart
And other Pulses—hear ye not the hum
Of mighty workings?— — — — — — — — — —
Listen awhile ye Nations and be dumb!

· 13 ·

J. H. REYNOLDS TO B. R. HAYDON [1]

22 November 1816

Lambs Cond^t Street

My Dear Haydon/

Friday morng 10 oClock

As you are now getting "golden opinions from all sorts of men",[2] —it is not fitting that One who is sincerely your Friend should be found wanting. Last night when you left me—I went to my bed—And the sonnet on the other side absolutely started into my mind. I send it you, because I really *feel* your Genius, & because I know that things of this kind are the dearest rewards of Genius. It is not equal to anything you have yet had, in power, I know;—but it is sincere, & that is ⟨son⟩ a recommendation. Will you, at my desire, send a Copy to Mr Keats, & say to him, how much I was pleased with his.

Yrs Affectionately
J H Reynolds

---

and well expressed; Leigh Hunt's compliment is well deserved, and the sonnet is very agreeably concluded."

[1] *ALS:* Attached to Haydon's Journal (now owned by Willard B. Pope). Haydon visited Reynolds on the night of Thursday, November 21, and showed him the sonnet Keats had the day before sent him (No. 11). After Haydon left, Reynolds found a sonnet of his own on Haydon starting into his mind. The next morning he forwarded it in this letter, and Haydon promptly arranged for it to be printed in the *Champion*, November 24, 1816.

[2] *Macbeth,* I.vii.33.

Sonnet to Haydon

Haydon!—Thou'rt born to Immortality!—
 I look full on;—And Fame's eternal star
 Shines out o'er Ages which are yet afar;—
It hangs in all its radiance over thee!
I watch whole Nations o'er thy works sublime
Bending;—And breathing,—while their spirits glow,—
 Thy name with that of the stern Angelo
Whose Giant Genius braves the hate of Time!
But not alone in agony and strife
 Art thou majestical;—Thy fancies bring
Sweets from the sweet: [3]—The loveliness of life
 Melts from thy pencil like the breath of Spring.
Soul is with in thee:—Honours wait without thee:—
The wings of Raphael's spirit play about thee!

Novr 1816. J. H. Reynolds

[In Haydon's hand:]
Wild enthusiasm
 B R Hayd[o]n 1842

[3] Compare *Hamlet,* V.i.266. (It is impossible to tell whether a number of Reynolds' *s*'s are capital or small letters.)

· 14 ·

TO C. C. CLARKE [1]

17 December 1816

Address: Mr C. C. Clarke/ Mr Towers's/ Warner Street—/ Clerkenwell—
Postmarks: TwoPyPost Unpaid Lombard St; 2 o'Clock DE 17 1816 ANn

Tuesday—

My dear Charles,

You may now look at Minerva's Ægis with impunity, seeing that my awful Visage [2] did not turn you into a John Doree [3] you have accordingly a legetimate title to a Copy—I will use my interest to procure it for you. I'll tell you what—I met Reynolds at Haydon's a few mornings since—he promised to be with me this evening and Yesterday I had the same promise from Severn and I must put you in Mind that on last All hallowmas' day you gave you [4] word that you would spend this Evening with me [5]—so no putting off. I have done little to Endymion [6] lately—I hope to finish it in one more attack—I believe you [know] I went to Richards's [7]—it was so whoreson a Night that I stopped there all the next day—His Remembrances to you—(Ext from the common place Book of my Mind—Mem—Wednesday—Hampstead—call in Warner Street—a Sketch of Mr Hunt—I will ever consider you my sincere and affectionate friend—you will not doubt that I am your's.—

God bless you—

John Keats—

[1] *ALS:* Harvard (with the autograph "Frederick Locker 1881"). "Tuesday" was December 17.

[2] Presumably a reference to a cast of Haydon's life mask of Keats, who later (I, 174) speaks of "expurgatorizing" such masks for Bailey. [3] A fish.

[4] *NED* gives "you" as a possessive for "your," though "obs. or dial. rare." F. T. Elworthy, *The West Somerset Word-Book* (1886), p. 848, calls it very common "in speaking to children." Keats uses this possessive more than thirty times in his letters.

[5] Evidently Clarke made the promise on November 1 in replying to No. 8.

[6] That is, to "I Stood Tiptoe upon a Little Hill," which without a title begins the *Poems* of 1817. The autograph copy has at its end the date "Dec. eve 16."

[7] Thomas Richards—son of John, a livery-stable keeper—lived at 9 Providence Place near Vauxhall Gardens, and worked in the Ordnance Department in the Tower from 1804 to 1831. His brother Charles printed Keats's 1817 *Poems.* See *The Royal Kalendar* (1817), p. 235; Grant Richards, *Author Hunting* (1934), pp. 22–26; MBF, *Some Letters . . . of Charles Brown* (1937), pp. xi f.

· 15 ·

FROM B. R. HAYDON [1]

3 March 1817

My dear Keats/

Many thanks My dear fellow for your two noble sonnets [2]—*I* know not a finer image than the comparison of a Poet unable to express his high feelings to a sick eagle looking at the Sky!—when he must have remembered his former towerings amid the blaze of dazzling Sun beams, in the pure expanse of glittering clouds!—now & then passing Angels on heavenly ⟨messages⟩ errands, lying at the will of the wind, with moveless wings; or pitching downward with a fiery rush, eager & intent on the⟨ir⟩ objects of their seeking ———You filled me with fury for an hour, and with admiration for ever

B R Haydon

3 March 1817—
I shall expect you & Clarke & Reynolds to night

My dear Keats/

I have really opened My letter to tell you how deeply I feel the high enthusiastic praise with which you have ⟨sung⟩ spoken of me in the first Sonnet [3]—be assured you shall never *repent it*—the time shall

[1] *ALS:* Formerly attached to Haydon's Journal, now at Harvard.

[2] "On Seeing the Elgin Marbles" and "To Haydon." Keats, Haydon, and perhaps Reynolds saw the Elgin Marbles at the British Museum on March 1 or 2. Keats wrote the sonnets immediately thereafter, and sent copies to Haydon. Keats's 1817 *Poems* was published on March 3. He had sent Reynolds a copy a day or two in advance (see below), whereas he probably took a copy to Haydon when he and Reynolds and Clarke visited the painter on the night of March 3. An unpublished passage from Haydon's Journal, so Willard B. Pope tells me, runs: "Alluding to Keats two Sonnetts Upon my Soul I think the four first lines of the Second contain as fine an image of a Poets yearning after high feelings, as fine a Picture of restless, sweeping, searching enthusiastic [*sic*] as any in Poetry. B. R. Haydon 1817 March 3 1817."

[3] Lowell, I, 276, 279, remarks that the sonnet on the Marbles "was probably written first, although Haydon puts them the other way about in his journal," and that "in whatever order the sonnets were written, Keats was canny enough to send them to Haydon with the one written to him as the first." Garrod, pp. 477 f., agrees, for he prints the Haydon sonnet second, and calls it, following a Woodhouse transcript, "To B. R. Haydon, with the Foregoing Sonnet on the Elgin Marbles." Actually in the advance copy of the *Poems* that Keats presented to Reynolds (it was discussed in *The Times*,

come if God spare my life—when you will remember it with delight—

Once more God bless you
B R Haydon

· 16 ·

TO J. H. REYNOLDS [1]

9 March 1817

Sunday Evening [2]

My Dear Reynolds

Your kindness affects me so sensibly that I can merely put down a few mono-sentences—Your Criticism only makes me extremely anxious that I sho^d not deceive you.

It's the finest thing by God—as Hazlitt wo^d say [3] However I hope I may not deceive you—There are some acquaintances of mine [4] who will scratch their Beards and although I have, I hope, some Charity, I wish their Nails may be long—I will be ready at the time you mention in all Happiness—

There is a report that a young lady of 16 has written the new Tragedy [5] God bless her—I will know her by Hook or by Crook

May 18, 1914, and is now at Harvard) the two sonnets are written on the verso of p. 121 with "To Haydon" first. Furthermore, it had that position when it was printed in the *Examiner* and the *Champion* on March 9, 1817, and in James Elmes's *Annals of the Fine Arts*, in April, 1818 (III, 171 f.). It begins in Keats's and the *Champion* texts, "Forgive me, Haydon," but in the other two texts (supplied by Haydon) and in all modern editions it begins "Haydon! forgive me." See my notes in the *University of Missouri Studies*, XXI (1946), 163–166.

[1] A transcript in Woodhouse's letter-book, pp. 49 f., in a clerk's hand, with corrections by Woodhouse. Keats is thanking Reynolds for his unsigned review of the 1817 *Poems* in the *Champion*, Sunday, March 9, 1817. On Reynolds' authorship of the review (formerly attributed to Haydon) see J. M. Turnbull, *London Mercury*, XIX (1929), 384–394, and Rollins, *University of Missouri Studies*, XXI (1946), 163–166.

[2] Woodhouse notes, "(No date) sent by hand." But Sunday was March 9.

[3] P. G. Patmore, *My Friends and Acquaintance* (1854), III, 83–85, tells how Hazlitt, who was forbidden to drink alcohol, would smell a glass of liquor at a dinner party and put it aside untasted, with the words, "That's fine, by G—d!"

[4] Among them, no doubt, the Abbeys and their friends.

[5] Actually the new tragedy at Drury Lane, Saturday, March 8, was *Manuel* "from the pen of the Rev. Mr. [C. R.] Maturin. . . . [It] was received and announced for repetition with great applause" (*New Monthly Magazine*, VII [1817], 256 f.). Edmund Kean, however, disliked and quickly killed it.

in less than a Week—My Brother's & my Remembrances to your kind Sisters Your's most sincerely

John Keats

H
Mr J. ⟨R⟩.—Reynolds.—

· 17 ·

FROM B. R. HAYDON [1]

March 1817

Address: John Keats/ Cheapside/ 76

My dear Keats/

Consider this letter a sacred secret—Often have I sat by my fire after a day's effort, as the dusk approached, and a gauzey veil seemed dimming all things—and mused on what I had done and with a burning glow on what I would do till filled with fury I have seen the faces of the mighty dead [2] crowd into my room, and I have sunk down & prayed the great Spirit that I might be worthy to accompany these immortal beings in their immortal glories, and then I have seen each smile as it passed over me, and each shake ⟨their⟩ his hand⟨s⟩ in awful encouragement [3]—My dear Keats, the Friends who surrounded me, were sensible to what talent I had,—but no one reflected my enthusiasm with that burning ripeness of soul, my heart yearned for sympathy,—believe me from my Soul in you I have one [4] found one,—you add fire, when I am exhausted, & excite fury afresh [5]—I offer my heart & intellect & experience—at first I feared your ardor might lead you to disregard the accumulated

[1] *ALS:* Formerly attached to Haydon's Journal, now at Harvard. Haydon had been reading Keats's *Poems,* and his letter was written sometime after he got his copy on March 3.

[2] Woodruff, pp. 282 f., compares "the mighty dead" in *Endymion,* I.21, and Hazlitt's "By conversing with the *mighty dead*" (*Works,* IV [1930], 5). Compare Haydon's "filled me with fury" at I, 122.

[3] Compare his "good Genius" at I, 142.

[4] This "one" should be omitted.

[5] Compare Haydon's "a refreshed fury" at I, 135.

wisdom of ages in moral points—but the feelings put forth lately—have delighted my soul—always consider principle of more value than genius—and you are safe—⟨but⟩ because on the score of genius, you can never be vehement enough—I have read your Sleep & Poetry—it is a flash of lightening that will sound [6] men from their occupations, and keep them trembling for the crash of thunder that *will* follow—

God bless you let our hearts be buried in each other

B R Haydon

Ill be at Reynolds to night but latish

March 1817—

I confide these feelings to your honor—

· 18 ·

TO J. H. REYNOLDS [1]

17 March 1817

My dear Reynolds,

My Brothers are anxious that I sho[d] go by myself into the country—they have always been extremely fond of me; and now that Haydon has pointed out how necessary it is that I sho[d] be alone to improve myself, they give up the temporary pleasure of⟨t⟩ living with me continually for a great good which I hope will follow—So I shall soon be out of Town [2]—You must soon bring all your present troubles to a close, and so must I; but we must, like the Fox, prepare for a fresh swarm of flies.[3] Banish money—Banish sofas—Banish Wine—Banish Music—But right Jack Health—honest Jack Health, true Jack Health—banish health and banish all the world.[4] I must ⟨then⟩ myself ⟨if⟩ [5] I come this Evening I shall

[6] Hitherto printed "round," the word is exactly the same as Haydon's "made it sound" at I, 136. Evidently it means "give a call or summons to." F. W. Haydon, II, 6, printing part of the letter, reads "rouse."

[1] A transcript by Woodhouse in his letter-book, p. 42. He notes: "(Post Mark. Lombard S[t] 17 March 1817)." The letter may have been written a day earlier.

[2] He left for Southampton on April 14 (No. 21).

[3] See "The Fox and the Hedgehog," in *The Fables of Aesop* with designs by Thomas Bewick (Newcastle, 1818), p. 227.

[4] The passage is adapted from *1 Henry IV*, II.iv.520–527 (HBF, 1901).

[5] The spaces here indicate tears. Woodhouse notes, "a part of the letter torn." Perhaps Keats wrote: "I must [take care of] myself [, and it follows that] if I come this

horribly commit myself elsewhere. So I will send my excuses to them & Mrs Dilk by my Brothers

Y^r^ sincere friend John Keats

J H Reynolds
19 Lambs Conduit S^t^

· 19 ·

TO C. C. CLARKE[1]

25 March 1817

Address: M^r^/ C. C. Clarke/ Mr Towers/ Warner Street/ Clerkenwell
Postmarks: TwoPyPost Unpaid HampsteadNO (*blurred*); 7 o'Clock MR 26 1817 N^T^

Hampstead Tuesday Af^t^

My dear Charles,

When shall we see each other again? In Heaven or in Hell, or in deep Places?[2] In crooked Lane are we to meet or on Salisbury Plain? Or jumbled together at Drury Lane Door? For my part I know not where it is to be except that it may be possible to take place at Mr Novello's[3] tomorrow evening whither Mr Hunt and myself are going and wher Mr Novello requested Mr Hunt to invite you per Letter the which I offered to do. So we shall meet you there tomorrow evening—Mr H. has got a great way into a Poem on the

---

evening, I shall horribly commit myself elsewhere"—and thus endanger the "Health" of which he has been speaking.

[1] *ALS*: Found by Holman (1929) in the National Portrait Gallery of Scotland and printed in his trade journal, *Within the Compass of a Print Shop*, II (1932), 186. The letter is endorsed: "To W. F. Watson Esqre (Edinburgh—) with C Cowden Clarke's Regard, and best Wishes for Success in his interesting enterprise." William Finley Watson, bookseller (died 1881), bequeathed his collection of autographs, some 3000 items, to the National Gallery, whence in 1930 it was transferred to the National Library. Tuesday was March 25.

[2] Compare *Macbeth*, I.i.1 ff.

[3] Vincent Novello (1781–1861), organist and musical composer, became later (1828) Clarke's father-in-law. In "A Chapter on Ears," *London Magazine*, March, 1821 (E. V. Lucas, *The Works of Charles and Mary Lamb*, II [1903], 41) Lamb mentions "the evening parties, at the house of my good Catholic friend *Nov*——; who, by the aid of a capital organ, himself the most finished of players, converts his drawing-room into a chapel, his week days into Sundays, and these latter into minor heavens."

Nymphs [4] and has said a number of beautiful things I have also written a few Lines and a Sonnet on Rimini [5] which I will copy for you against tomorrow—Mr H. desires to be remembered to you—

Your's sincerely

John Keats—

N.B. we shall have a Hymn of Mr H.'s composing 4 Voices [6]—go it!

· 20 ·

TO TAYLOR AND HESSEY [1]

12 or 13 April 1817

Address: Messrs Taylor & Hessey

L.C.S. [2]

My dear Sirs

I am very unfortunate for I am just going out and have not a sheet of paper handy—so I can only beg pardon for this scrap—and thank you for your kindness which will be of little use for I will steal out of town in a day or two—excuse this shabby affair

Your's John Keats

[4] Included in his *Foliage* (1818), pp. iii–xxxvii. See I, 138 n.

[5] "On 'The Story of Rimini' " was first published by Milnes, II, 292.

[6] On this letter Clarke wrote: "This evidently should be 'N' (Novello) charles Cowden Clarke." MBF, however, refers to H. S. Milford, *The Poetical Works of Leigh Hunt* (1923), p. 728, who quotes from a letter Novello sent Hunt on June 15, 1848, concerning "the little hymn-tune which you composed in 1817." Milford notes that Novello ascribes to Hunt both the words ("To the Spirit Great and Good") and the music.

[1] *ALS:* Harvard (first printed by Lowell, I, 295). The letter, sent by messenger, was evidently written after Taylor and Hessey's decision to publish Keats's future work, a decision about which Taylor wrote to his father on April 15 (see Olive Taylor, *London Mercury*, XII [1925], 258). Keats left London on April 14 and arrived at Southampton the next morning (No. 21). "In a day or two" points to April 12 or 13.

[2] Lamb's Conduit Street, where the Reynoldses lived.

· 21 ·

TO GEORGE AND TOM KEATS [1]

15 April 1817

Tuesday Morn—

My dear Brothers,

I am safe at Southampton—after having ridden three stages outside and the rest in for it began to be very cold. I did not know the Names of any of the Towns I passed through—all I can tell you is that sometimes I saw dusty Hedges—sometimes Ponds—then nothing—then a little Wood with trees look you like Launce's Sister "as white as a Lilly and as small as a Wand" [2]—then came houses which died away into a few straggling Barns—then came hedge trees aforesaid again. As the Lamplight crept along the following things were discovered—"long heath broom furze" [3]—Hurdles here and there half a Mile—Park palings when the Windows of a House were always discovered by reflection—One Nymph of Fountain—*N.B. Stone*—lopped Trees—Cow ruminating—ditto Donkey—Man and Woman going gingerly along—William seeing his Sisters over the Heath—John waiting with a Lanthen [4] for his Mistress—Barber's Pole—Docter's Shop—However after having had my fill of these I popped my Head out just as it began to Dawn—*N.B. this tuesday Morn saw the Sun rise*—of which I shall say nothing at present. I felt rather lonely this Morning at breakfast so I went and unbox'd a Shakspeare—"There's my Comfort" [5]—I went immediately after Breakfast to Southampton Water where I enquired for the Boat to

[1] Reprinted from HBF, 1883, III, 50–52, who says that it was addressed to "Mr G. Keats, No. 1 Well Walk, Hampstead, Middx." and postmarked "16 April 1817." The original letter, formerly attached to Haydon's Journal, was owned by MBF, who adds the postmark "SOUTHAMPTON." Lowell, I, 298, remarks: "The Keats brothers must have moved there [to Hampstead] before John started on his trip, or George and Tom may have moved out on the very day that John set off for Southampton." No. 19, however, shows that they had moved before March 25. Benjamin Bentley's cottage, in which they lodged, was, says Hale-White, p. 36, "next to where The Wells Tavern now stands; the cottage was pulled down in 1849."

[2] See *The Two Gentlemen of Verona*, II.iii.22 f.

[3] See *The Tempest*, I.i.70 f.

[4] He intended to spell it "lanthern."

[5] Colvin, p. 5 n., refers to *The Tempest*, II.ii.47, 57.

the Isle of Wight as I intend seeing that place before I settle—it will go at 3, so shall I after having taken a Chop—I know nothing of this place but that it is long—tolerably broad—has bye streets—two or three Churches—a very respectable old Gate with two Lions to guard it—the Men and Women do not materially differ from those I have been in the Habit of seeing—I forgot to say that from dawn till half past six I went through a most delightful Country—some open Down but for the most part thickly wooded. What surprised me most was an immense quantity of blooming Furze on each side the road cutting a most rural dash. The Southampton water when I saw it just now was no better than a low Water Water [6] which did no more than answer my expectations—it will have mended its Manners by 3. From the Warf are seen the shores on each side stretching to the isle of Wight. You, Haydon, Reynolds &c. have been pushing each other out of my Brain by turns—I have conned over every Head [7] in Haydon's Picture—you must warn them not to be afraid should my Ghost visit them on Wednesday—tell Haydon to Kiss his Hand at Betty over the Way for me yea and to spy at her for me. I hope one of you will be competent to take part in a Trio while I am away—you need only agravate your voices [8] a little and mind not to speak Cues and all [9]—when you have said Rum-ti-ti—you must not rum any more or else another will take up the ti-ti alone and then he might be taken God shield us [1] for little better than a Titmouse. By the by talking of Titmouse Remember me particularly to all my Friends—give my Love to the Miss Reynoldses and to Fanny who I hope you will soon see. Write to me soon about them all—and you George particularly how you get on with Wilkinson's plan.[2] What could I have done without my

[6] T. C. C., *NQ*, May 8, 1943, p. 288, punctuates "Water, Water." W. W. G., the same, June 19, p. 383, thinks that Keats repeated the word "for amusement."

[7] The heads included those of Keats, Wordsworth, Hazlitt, perhaps Bewick (but *not*, as is often said, John Howard Payne), while the hands of Christ, Haydon said, were modeled from those of David Wilkie (Duncan Gray and Violet Walker, *K–SMB*, No. 7 [1956], 23).

[8] *A Midsummer Night's Dream*, I.ii.83 f., "I will aggravate my voice."

[9] The same, III.i.102 f., "You speak all your part at once, cues and all."

[1] The same, III.i.31.

[2] Kirk, Hampstead Keats, I, lxxxi, thinks that Keats means that George had "possibly a temporary position in the law office of one Wilkinson." If so, the latter was probably Charles Wilkinson, 13 New North Street, Red Lion Square. Keats inscribed a copy of his 1817 *Poems*, now in the New York Public Library, "to C. Wilkinson from the Author." He also loaned a Wilkinson £40 or £50, which George in 1825 thought had not been repaid (*More Letters*, p. 28).

Plaid? I don't feel inclined to write any more at present for I feel rather muzzy—you must be content with this fac simile of the rough plan of Aunt Dinah's Counterpane.

Your most affectionate Brother

John Keats

Reynolds shall hear from me soon.

· 22 ·

TO J. H. REYNOLDS [1]

17, 18 April 1817

Carisbrooke April 17th [2]

My dear Reynolds,

Ever since I wrote to my Brothers from Southampton [3] I have been in a taking, and at this moment I am about to become settled. for I have unpacked my books, put them into a snug corner—pinned up Haydon—Mary Queen [of] [4] Scotts, and Milton with his daughters in a row. In the passage I found a head of Shakspeare [5] which I had not before seen—It is most likely the same that George spoke so well of; for I like it extremely—Well—this head I have hung over my Books, just above the three in a row, having first discarded a french Ambassador—Now this alone is a good morning's work Yesterday I went to Shanklin, which occasioned a great debate in my mind whether I should live there or at Carisbrooke. Shanklin is a most beautiful place—sloping wood and meadow ground reaches round the Chine, which is a cleft between the Cliffs of the depth of nearly 300 feet at least.[6] This cleft is filled with trees & bushes in the narrow part; and as it widens becomes bare, if it were not for primroses on one side, which spread to the very verge of the Sea, and some fishermen's huts on the other, ⟨which⟩ perched midway in the Ballustrades of beautiful green Hedges along their

1 A transcript in Woodhouse's letter-book, pp. 43–45, made partly by Woodhouse, partly by a clerk whose copying he corrected. The clerk, for example, read "ivy" as "Joy" (twice), "ink" as "Full," and "Prunus" eluded him, but Woodhouse inserted the proper readings.

2 Woodhouse adds "(1817)."

3 See the preceding letter.

4 Woodhouse supplies "(of)."

5 See I, 142, II, 62.

6 See II, 130.

steps down to the sands.—But the sea, Jack,[7] the sea—the little waterfall—then the white cliff—then St Catherine's Hill[8]—"the sheep in the meadows, the cows in the corn." [9]—Then, why are you at Carisbrooke? say you—Because, in the first place, I sho^{d} be a^{t} twice the Expense, and three times the inconvenience—next that from here I can see your continent—from a little hill close by, the whole north Angle of the Isle of Wight, with the water between us. In the 3^{d} place, I see Carisbrooke Castle from my window,[1] and have found several delightful wood-alleys, and copses, and quick freshes [2]—As for Primroses—the Island ought to be called Primrose Island: that is, if the nation of Cowslips agree thereto, of which there are diverse Clans just beginning to lift up their heads and if an how the Rain holds whereby that is Birds eyes abate [3]—another reason [4] of my fixing is that I am more in reach of the places around me—I intend to walk over the island east—West—North South—I have not seen many specimens of Ruins—I dont think however I shall ever see one to surpass Carisbrooke Castle. The trench is o'ergrown with the smoothest turf, and the walls with ⟨Joy⟩ ivy—The Keep within side is one Bower of ⟨Joy⟩ ivy—a Co⟨l⟩lony of Jackdaws have been there many years [5]—I dare say I have seen many a descendant of some old cawer who peeped through the Bars at Charles the first, when he was there in Confinement.[6] On the road from Cowes to Newport I saw some extensive Barracks [7] which dis-

[7] Keats always addresses Reynolds by his surname, though he calls him John at I, 160 (twice), 168 f. (twice), 181.

[8] Four and a half miles west of Ventnor, and 781 feet high.

[9] See Iona and Peter Opie, *The Oxford Dictionary of Nursery Rhymes* (1951), pp. 98 f.

[1] W. H. Wadham, of Carisbrooke, decided that Keats lodged in Canterbury House, Castle Road, known in 1817 as New Village (see the postscript). Holman thought that Keats lived in the smaller house on Castle Road nearer the castle, since that castle could not be seen from Canterbury House "except from a *modern* bay window." In 1929 the houses were owned by brothers, and Holman thought that both might have been owned or at least operated by Mrs. Cook in 1817. MBF evidently disagreed with him, and I have not tried to settle the question.

[2] "Where the quick freshes are," *The Tempest*, III.ii.75 (Colvin, p. 7 n.).

[3] "If an . . . abate" has not been satisfactorily explained. Ignoto, *NQ*, June 18, 1938, p. 439, thinks that "birds' eyes" are cowslips. In his dictionary Nathaniel Bailey defined them as binding herbs.

[4] Woodhouse stops copying here and the clerk begins.

[5] They are still there.

[6] In 1647–1648.

[7] "Built there during the [Napoleonic] wars as a depot for recruits" (Hewlett, p. 103). *Leigh's New Picture of England and Wales* (1820), p. 220, mentions "the Albany Barracks, and Military Hospital" at Newport for "upwards of 3,000 soldiers."

gusted me extremely with Government for placing such a Nest of Debauchery in so beautiful a place—I asked a man on the Coach about this—and he said that the people had been spoiled—In the room where I slept at Newport I found this on the Window "O Isle spoilt by the Mil*a*tary"—I must in honesty however confess that I did not feel very sorry at the idea of the Women being a little profligate—The Wind is in a sulky fit, and I feel that it would be no bad thing to be the favorite of some Fairy, who would give one the power of seeing how our Friends got on, at a Distance [8]—I should
ink
like, of all Loves,[9] a sketch of you and Tom and George in ⟨Full⟩ which Haydon will do if you tell him how I want them—From want of regular rest, I have been rather *narvus*—and the passage in Lear [1]—"Do you not hear the Sea?"—has haunted me intensely.

On the Sea.[2]

⟨O Sea⟩[3] It keeps eternal Whisperings around
Desolate shores, and with its mighty swell
Gluts twice ten thousand Caverns; till the spell
Of Hecate leaves them their old shadowy sound.
often 'tis in such gentle temper found
That scarcely will the very smallest shell
Be moved for days from whence it sometime fell
When last the winds of Heaven were unbound.
O ye who have your eyeballs vext and tir'd
Feast them upon the wideness of the Sea
O ye whose Ears are dinned with uproar rude
Or fed too much with cloying melody—
Sit ye near some old Cavern's Mouth and brood
Until ye start as if the Sea Nymphs quired—

[8] W. W. Beyer, *Journal of English and Germanic Philology*, LI (1952), 336 f., detects a borrowing here from the translation by William Sotheby (1757–1833) of *Oberon*, X.11 f., by Christoph Martin Wieland (1733–1813). The clerk wrote "Friends got one."

[9] *A Midsummer Night's Dream*, II.ii.154, and *The Merry Wives of Windsor*, II.ii.119.

[1] IV.vi.4, "Hark, do you hear the sea?"

[2] Printed in the *Champion*, August 17, 1817, and in Milnes, II, 291. This beautiful sonnet has been sufficiently annotated by De Selincourt and Garrod.

[3] Woodhouse notes that "O Sea" is "obliterated" here.

April 18th

Will you have the goodness to do this? Borrow a Botanical Dictionary—turn to the words Laurel and Prunus [4] show the explanations to your sisters and Mrs Dilk and without more ado let them send me the Cups Basket and Books they trifled and put off and off while I was in Town—ask them what they can say for themselves—ask Mrs Dilk wherefore she does so distress me—Let me know how Jane has her health—the Weather is unfavorable for her—Tell George and Tom to write.—I'll tell you what—On the 23rd was Shakespeare born—now If I should receive a Letter from you and another from my Brothers on that day 'twould be a parlous good thing—Whenever you write say a Word or two on some Passage in Shakespeare that may have come rather new to you; which must be continually happening, notwithstandg that we read the same Play forty times—for instance, the following, from the Tempest,[5] never struck me so forcibly as at present,

"Urchins
Shall, for that vast of Night that they may work,
All exercise on thee—"

How can I help bringing to your mind the Line—

In the dark backward and abysm of time—

I find that I cannot exist without poetry—without eternal poetry—half the day will not do—the whole of it—I began with a little, but habit has made me a Leviathan—I had become all in a Tremble from not having written any thing of late—the Sonnet over leaf[6] did me some good. I slept the better last night for it—this Morning, however, I am nearly as bad again—Just now I opened Spencer, and the first Lines I saw were these.—

[4] The clerk left gaps, and Woodhouse inserted "Laurel" in ink and "Prunes" (?) and "Prunus" in pencil. If the women did look at Philip Miller and Thomas Martyn's *The Gardener's and Botanist's Dictionary*, II (1807), Part I, where nine folio pages are given to "laurel" and seventeen to "prunus" they must have been considerably confused! Jack Stillinger suggests that Keats had in mind a dictionary following William Withering's *A Systematic Arrangement of British Plants*, 4th ed. (1801), I, 231, 253, in which the laurel ("Daphne") is described as having no cup and the prunus as having petals "fixed to the cup by claws."

[5] I.ii.326–328; I.ii.50. There is a heavy second line under "vast" and a lighter line under "of Night."

[6] Woodhouse notes, "i.e. on the preceding page."

"The noble Heart that harbors vertuous thought,
And is with Child of glorious great intent,
Can never rest, until it forth have brought
Th' eternal Brood of Glory excellent—" [7]

Let me know particularly about Haydon; ask him to write to me about Hunt, if it be only ten lines—I hope all is well—I shall forthwith begin my Endymion,[8] which I hope I shall have got some way into by the time you come, when we will read our verses in a delightful place I have set my heart upon near the Castle [9]—Give my Love to your Sisters severally—To George and Tom—Remember me to Rice Mr & Mrs Dilk and all we know.——

Your sincere Friend
John Keats.

Direct J. Keats Mrs Cook's new Village
Carisbrooke

To Mr J H Reynolds 19 Lambs Conduit St.[10] London

· 23 ·

FROM B. R. HAYDON [1]

8 (?) May 1817

Address: {Jo}hn Keats/ Post. office—/ Margate.

My dear Keats/

I have been swearing to write you every hour this week—but have been so interrupted that the Post Man has rang his bell every night in vain, with a sound that made my heart quake——I think you did quite right to leave the Isle of white if you felt no relief in

[7] *The Faerie Queene*, I.v.1.

[8] For full details see "Note on the Composition of *Endymion*" in Garrod, pp. lxxxiv–lxxxix.

[9] Reynolds did not make the visit.

[10] *Apparently* "Stt."

[1] *AL:* Formerly attached to Haydon's Journal, now at Harvard. This letter was printed by F. W. Haydon, II, 2 f., with the date of May 11, 1817, at its head, and that date is also so printed by HBF and MBF, though the latter calls it a mistake for May 10. Actually, the date comes at the end: it is "May" followed by what looks like an inverted capital "U" and by some word that may begin with "T," the remainder being torn off. (It can hardly be Tuesday, May 6.) Haydon often makes an "8" that resembles an inverted "U," and Thursday, May 8, is a reasonable guess for Haydon's letter, which Keats, seventy-one miles from London, answered (No. 26) on May 10 and 11. Since Haydon says, "I have been swearing to write you every hour this week," No. 23 cannot be later than May 8 (see the next letter).

⟨having⟩ being quite alone after study—you may now devote your eight hours a day with just as much seclusion as ever——Do not give way to any forebodings they are nothing more than the over eager anxieties of a great Spirit stretched beyond its strength, and then relapsing for a time to languid inefficiency——Every man of great views, is at times thus tormented—but begin again where you left off—without hesitation or fear—*Trust in God* with all your might My dear Keats this dependance with your own energy will give you strength, & hope & comfort——In all my troubles, & wants, & distresses, here I found a refuge—from my Soul I declare to you, I never applied for help or [2] consolation, or strength—but I found it I always arose, with a refreshed fury—an iron clenched firmness, and ⟨chy⟩ chrystal piety of feeling, that sent me streaming on with a repulsive power against the troubles of life that attempted to stop me, as if I was a cannon shot, darting through feathers——never despair while there is this path open to you—by habitual exercise, you will have habitual intercourse, and constant companionship, and in every want, turn to the great Star of your hopes with a delightful confidance which will never be disappointed———I love you like my own Brother, beware for God's sake of the delusions & sophistications that is ripping up the talent & respectability of our Friend [3]—he will go out of the World the victim of his own weakness & the dupe of his own self delusions—with the contempt of his enemies ⟨of⟩ and sorrow of his Friends—the cause he undertook to support, injured by his own neglect of character his family disordered, his children neglected{,} himself, petted & his prospects ruined!—of this I am sure and keep this letter and you will find this is [4] so————I speak this in confidence & pain——I write this at breakfast—for I am able & work like a hero—and wish to God you would come up to Town for a day or two when you are inclined —that I may put your head in with glory & honor—I have rubbed in Wordsworth's & advanced the whole [5]—God bless you My dear Keats go on, dont despair, collect in{cidents,} study characters, read Shakespeare and trust in Providence—and you ⟨. . . do⟩ will do—you must, you shall—[6]

May 8 T{hursday?}

[2] *Written* or or. [3] Leigh Hunt. [4] *Written* it. [5] "Christ's Entry," of course.

[6] The signature is torn away, though F. W. Haydon, II, 3, prints it as "Ever affectionately yours,/ B. R. Haydon." His text differs very widely from that here printed.

· 24 ·

FROM B. R. HAYDON [1]

8 May 1817

My dear Keats/

I have read your delicious Poem, with exquisite enjoyment, it is the most delightful thing of the time—You have taken up the great trumpet of nature and made it sound [2] with a voice of your own—I write in a great hurry—You will realize all I wish ⟨of⟩ or expect—Success attend you my glorious fellow—& Believe me

ever & ever yours
B R Haydon

May 8, 1817

· 25 ·

TO LEIGH HUNT [1]

10 May 1817

Address: Leigh Hunt Esqre/ P— B— Shelley's Esqre/ G^{t} Marlow/ Bucks—
Postmarks (imperfect): {MARGATE} 11 MY 11 1817; E 12 MY 12 1817

Margate May 10th

My dear Hunt,

The little Gentleman that sometimes lurks in a gossips bowl ought to have come in very likeness of a *coasted* crab [2] and choaked me out-

[1] *ALS:* Formerly attached to Haydon's Journal, now at Harvard. Apparently this note (heretofore dated May 8, 1818) was dashed off after Haydon had received a letter from Keats containing the sonnet "On the Sea," and after he had written No. 23 (the first sentence of which makes a date earlier than May 8 impossible). It was not sent through the post.

[2] Exactly the same word as in "sound men from their occupations" at I, 125. Haydon's phrases could hardly apply to *Endymion,* which Keats had begun "about a Fortnight" before May 10 (see I, 139), but which in Letter 26 he "can say nothing about."

[1] *ALS:* British Museum. A facsimile of the letter is in T. J. Wise's *Ashley Library,* III (1923), between pp. 12, 13.

[2] MBF remarks that "Keats wrote 'coasted' because he was living at Margate," and cites *A Midsummer Night's Dream,* II.i.47 f., "sometime lurk I in a gossip's bowl,/ In very likeness of a roasted crab."

right for not having answered your Letter ere this—however you must not suppose that I was in Town to receive ⟨your⟩ it; no, it followed me to the isle of Wight and I got it just as I was going to pack up for Margate,[3] for reasons which you anon shall hear. On arriving at this treeless affair I wrote to my Brother George to request C. C. C. to do the thing you wot of respecting Rimini; [4] and George tells me he has undertaken it with great Pleasure; so I hope there has been an understanding between you for many Proofs——C. C C. is well acquainted with Bensley.[5] Now why did you not send the key of your Cupboard which I know was full of Papers? We would have lock'd them all in a trunk together with those you told me to destroy; which indeed I did not do for fear of demolishing Receipts. There not b[e]ing a more unpleasant thing in the world (saving a thousand and one others) [6] than to pay a Bill twice. Mind you—Old Wood's a very Varmant—sharded in Covetousness [7]—And now I am upon a horrid subject—what a horrid one you were upon last Sunday and well you handled it. The last Examiner was Battering Ram against Christianity—Blasphemy—Tertullian—Erasmus—Sr Philip Sidney.[8] And then the dreadful Petzelians and their expiation by Blood [9]—and do Christians shudder at the same thing in a Newspaper which the [1] attribute to their God in its most aggravated form? What is to be the end of this?—I must mention Hazlitt's Southey—O that he had left out the grey hairs! [2]—Or that

[3] At I, 142, Keats says, "I was but there a Week": he must have left around April 23 or 24.

[4] Clarke evidently read the proofs of *The Story of Rimini*.

[5] The second edition (1817) of the *Rimini* was "Printed by [Thomas] Bensley and Son" for Taylor and Hessey and others.

[6] See I, 139.

[7] Possibly a reference to Sir George Wood (1743–1824), the judge who presided, April, 1817, at the trial of R. G. Butt for libel (*Examiner*, April 27, p. 272). Gaynor Bradish suggests that Keats had in mind Swift's poem "Wood an Insect," which pictures William Wood (1671–1730), patentee for making all the copper halfpence and farthings in Ireland during 1722–1725, as an insect with a "coat of mail." Johnson's *Dictionary* defines "sharded" as "sheath-winged."

[8] Hunt's article "To the English People. Letter VII," in the issue of May 4, dealt with religious intolerance and ridiculed, with references to Tertullian, Erasmus, Sidney, and others, the charges of sedition and blasphemy made against the reformers.

[9] With a date line "Vienna, April 16," it tells how "Petzel, a Priest of Branau," and his disciples practise community of property and human sacrifice, and how Petzel and eighty-six "Petzelians" have been arrested and will soon be tried. See also *GM*, May, 1817 (LXXXVII, i, 459).

[1] *For* they.

[2] Reviewing Southey's *Letter to William Smith, Esq. M. P.* (1817), Hazlitt, in a characteristic tirade, said that in this publication Southey "lays open his character to the

they had been in any other Paper not concluding with such a Thunderclap—that sentence about making a Page of the feelings of a whole life appears to me like a Whale's back in the Sea of Prose.[3] I ought to have said a word on Shakspeare's Christianity—there are two, which I have not looked over with you, touching the thing: the one for, the other against: That in favor is in Measure for Measure Act. 2. S. 2 Isab. Alas! Alas!

> Why all the Souls that were; were forfeit once
> And he that might the vantage best have took,
> Found out the Remedy— [4]

That against is in Twel⟨ve⟩fth Night. Act. 3. S 2. Maria—for there is no Christian, that means to be saved by believing rightly, can ever believe such impossible Passages of grossness!' Before I come to the Nymphs [5] I must get through all disagreeables—I went to the Isle of Wight—thought so much about Poetry so long together that I could not get to sleep at night [6]—and moreover, I know not how it was, I could not get wholesome food—By this means in a Week or so [7] I became not over capable in my upper Stories, and set off pell mell for Margate, at least 150 Miles [8]—because forsooth I fancied that I should like my old Lodging here, and could contrive to do without Trees. Another thing I was too much in Solitude, and

---

scalping knife, guides the philosophic hand in its painful researches, and on the bald crown of our *petit tondu*, in vain concealed under withered bay-leaves and a few contemptible grey hairs, you see the organ of vanity triumphant—sleek, smooth, round, perfect, polished, burnished and shining, as it were in a transparency!"

[3] Hazlitt's passage is too long to quote. After demolishing Southey's change-coat opinions and actions he says: "The above passage is, we fear, written in the style of Aretin, which Mr. Southey condemns in the *Quarterly*. It is at least a very sincere style: Mr. Southey will never write so, till he can keep in the same mind for three and twenty years together. Why should not one make a sentence of a page long, out of the feelings of one's whole life?" Hazlitt meant a foolscap page, like that on which he was writing. His review of the *Letter* extended through the issues of May 11 and 18.

[4] During the arguments for and against Christianity when Haydon, Hunt, Shelley, and Keats dined with Horace Smith on January 20, 1817, Haydon, as his unpublished Journal shows (so Willard B. Pope tells me), quoted these lines plus the four that follow them in Shakespeare.

[5] "The Nymphs" is a long poem (which Shelley, writing to Hunt in March, 1818, called "delightful" and "truly *poetical*") in Hunt's *Foliage* (1818), pp. iii–xxxvii. Harvard has a copy of the book inscribed "John Keats from his affectionate friend the Author."

[6] He had been "narvus" (see I, 132).

[7] Keats went to the Isle of Wight on the afternoon of April 15 (I, 129), slept that night at Newport (I, 132), visited Shanklin on April 16 but moved to Carisbrooke, where he remained "a Week or so." He left for Margate around April 23 or 24.

[8] The distance is about 120 miles, unless he went via London.

consequently was obliged to be in continual burning of thought as an only resource. However Tom is with me at present and we are very comfortable. We intend though to get among some Trees. How have you got on among them? How are the Nymphs? [9] I suppose they have led you a fine dance—Where are you now—In Judea, Cappadocia, or the Parts of Lybia about Cyrene, Strangers from "Heaven, Hues and Prototypes [1]—I wager you have given given several new turns to the ⟨whole⟩ old saying "Now the Maid was fair and pleasant to look on" [2] as well as mad[e] a little variation in "once upon a time" perhaps too you have rather varied "thus endeth the first Lesson" [3] I hope you have made a Horse shoe business of—"unsuperfluous lift" [4] "faint Bowers" [5] and fibrous roots.[6] I vow that I have been down in the Mouth lately at this Work. These last two day however I have felt more confident—I have asked myself so often why I should be a Poet more than other Men,—seeing how great a thing it is,—how great things are to be gained by it—What a thing to be in the Mouth of Fame—that at last the Idea has grown so monstrously beyond my seeming Power of attainment that the other day I nearly consented with myself to drop into a Phæton—yet 't is a disgrace to fail even in a huge attempt, and at this moment I drive the thought from me. I began my Poem [7] about a Fortnight since and have done some every day except travelling ones—Perhaps I may have done a good deal for the time but it appears such a Pin's Point to me that I will not coppy any out—When I consider that so many of these Pin points go to form a Bodkin point (God send I end not my Life with a bare Bodkin,[8] in its modern sense) and that it requ[i]res a thousand bodkins to make a Spear bright enough to throw any light to posterity—I see that nothing but continual uphill Journeying? Now is there any thing more unpleasant (it may come among the thousand and one) [9] than to be so journeying and miss the Goal at last—But I intend to whistle all these cogitations into the Sea where I hope they will breed Storms violent enough to block up all exit from ⟨Rutla⟩ Russia. Does Shelley go on telling strange Stories of the Death of

[9] See I, 127.
[1] Compare Acts ii.10 f., "strangers of Rome, Jews and proselytes."
[2] Compare Genesis xxiv.16, Esther i.11, ii.7.
[3] The rubric in the Prayer Book.
[4] "The Nymphs," *Foliage* (1818), p. xix.
[5] The same, p. xx.
[6] The same ("fibrous mould"), p. xvii.
[7] *Endymion* (see I, 136 n.).
[8] Compare *Hamlet*, III.i.76.
[9] See I, 137.

kings? [1] Tell him there are stran{ge} Stories of the death of Poets—some have died before they were conceived "how do you make that out Master Vellum"[2] Does Mrs S—[3] cut Bread and Butter as neatly as ever? Tell her to procure some fatal Scissars and cut the th[r]ead of Life of all to be disappointed Poets. Does Mrs Hunt tear linen in half as straight as ever? Tell her to tear from the book of Life all blank Leaves.[4] Remember me to them all—to Miss Kent [5] and the little ones all— [6]

Your sincere friend
John Keats alias Junkets [7]—

You shall know where we move—

· 26 ·

TO B. R. HAYDON [1]

10, 11 May 1817

Address: Benjamin Robert Haydon/ 41 Great Marlborough Street/ London—
Postmarks: MARGATE 12 MY 12 1817; F 13 MY 13 1817

Margate Saturday Eve

My dear Haydon,

Let Fame, which all hunt after in their Lives,
Live register'd upon our brazen tombs,

[1] Colvin, p. 12 n.: "Alluding to the well-known story of Shelley dismaying an old lady in a stage-coach by suddenly, *à propos* of nothing, crying out to Leigh Hunt in the words of Richard II. [III.ii.155 f.], 'For God's sake, let us sit upon the ground,' etc."

[2] Addison, *The Drummer, Or The Haunted House*, IV.i (MBF).

[3] Mrs. Shelley, of course.

[4] So Longfellow, *Hyperion* (New York, 1839), book IV, chapter 8, writes, "It is not till Time, with reckless hand, has torn out half the leaves from the Book of Human Life. . . ."

[5] Elizabeth Kent, sister of Mrs. Leigh Hunt (see Haydon's comment at I, 259), author of *Flora Domestica* (1823) and *Sylvan Sketches* (1825), each of which refers to and quotes from Keats.

[6] According to Blunden's *Leigh Hunt* (1930) they were Thornton (1810), John (1812), Mary Florimel Leigh (1814). Children born later on (see Louis Landré, *Leigh Hunt* [Paris, 1935, 1936]) were Swinburne, Percy, Sylvan, Vincent, Julia, and Jacintha.

[7] On July 1, 1817, Hunt wrote to Clarke (*Recollections of Writers* [1878], p. 194), "What has become of Junkets I know not. I suppose Queen Mab has eaten him." Milnes, I, 44, calls "Junkets" "an appellation given him in play upon his name, and in allusion to his friends of Fairy-land." Compare "L'Allegro," line 102.

[1] *ALS:* Formerly attached to Haydon's Journal, now at Harvard.

And so grace us in the disgrace of death:
When spite of cormorant devouring time
The endeavour of this pre⟨a⟩sent breath may buy
That Honor which shall bate his Scythe's keen edge
And make us heirs of all eternity.[2]

To think that I have no right to couple myself with you in this speech would be death to me [3] so I have e'en written it—and I pray God that our brazen Tombs be nigh neighbors. It cannot be long first the endeavor of this present breath will soon be over—and yet it is as well to breathe freely during our sojourn—it is as well if you have not been teased with that Money affair—that bill-pestilence. However I must think that difficulties nerve the Spirit of a Man—they make our Prime Objects a Refuge as well as a Passion. The Trumpet of Fame is as a tower of Strength the ambitious bloweth it and is safe—I suppose by your telling me not to give way to forebodings George has mentioned to you what I have lately said in my Letters to him—truth is I have been in such a state of Mind as to read over my Lines and hate them. I am "one that gathers Samphire dreadful trade" [4] the Cliff of Poesy Towers above me—yet when, Tom who meets with some of Pope's Homer in Plutarch's Lives reads some of those to me they seem like Mice to mine.[5] I read and write about eight hours a day. There is an old saying well begun is half done" [6]—'t is a bad one. I would use instead—Not begun at all 'till half done" so according to that I have not begun my Poem and consequently (a priori) can say nothing about it.[7] Thank God! I do begin arduously where I leave off, notwithstanding occasional depressions: and I hope for the support of a High Power while I clime this little eminence and especially in my Years of more momentous Labor. I remember your saying that you had

[2] *Love's Labor's Lost*, I.i.1–7 (in line 1 "that" is changed to "which," in line 3 "then" to "so").

[3] *Written* me me. Haydon underlined "I pray . . . neighbors" and wrote opposite the verses above "I wonder if they will be. B R Haydon." Copying the letter in 1846, Haydon substituted "Perhaps they may be," after which Milnes, I, 36 n., added, "Alas! no."

[4] *King Lear*, IV.vi.15.

[5] Perhaps Keats had in mind the same, IV.vi.17 f., "The fishermen . . . Appear like mice." For his reading in Plutarch (he used one of John and William Langhorne's translations) see J. L. Lowes, *PMLA*, LI (1936), 1098–1103.

[6] See Sir Paul Harvey, *The Oxford Dictionary of English Proverbs* (1948), p. 700, and Horace, *Epistles*, I.ii.40.

[7] This sentence shows that he had *not* (see No. 24) sent Haydon extracts from *Endymion.*

notions of a good Genius presiding over you [8]—I have of late had the same thought. for things which [I] do half at Random are afterwards confirmed by my judgment in a dozen features of Propriety—Is it too daring to Fancy Shakspeare this Presider? When in the Isle of W⟨h⟩ight I met with a Shakspeare in the Passage of the House at which I lodged—it comes nearer to my idea of him than any I have seen [9]—I was but there a Week yet the old Woman made me take it with me though I went off in a hurry—Do you not think this is ominous of good? I am glad you say every Man of great Views is at times tormented as I am—

Sunday Aft. This Morning I received a letter from George by which it appears that Money Troubles are to follow us up for some time to come perhaps for always—these vexations are a great hindrance to one—they are not like Envy and detraction stimulants to further exertion as being immediately relative and reflected on at the same time with the prime object—but rather like a nettle leaf or two in your bed. So now I revoke my Promise of finishing my Poem by the Autumn which I should have done had I gone on as I have done—but I cannot write while my spirit is fe⟨a⟩vered in a contrary direction and I am now sure of having plenty of it this Summer—At this moment I am in no enviable Situation—I feel that I am not in a Mood to write any to day; and it appears that the lo⟨o⟩ss of it is the beginning of all sorts of irregularities. I am extremely glad that a time must come when every thing will leave not a wrack behind. [1] You tell me never to despair—I wish it was as easy for me to observe the saying truth is I have a horrid Morbidity of Temperament which has shown itself at intervals—it is I have no doubt the greatest Enemy and stumbling block I have to fear—I may even say that it is likely to be the cause of my disappointment. How ever every ill has its share of good—this very bane would at any time enable me to look with an obstinate eye on the Devil Himself—ay to be as proud of being the lowest of the human race as Alfred could be in being of the highest. I feel confident I should have been a rebel Angel had the opportunity been mine. I am very sure that

[8] Something on this order is said in No. 17.

[9] See I, 130 n. Bailey wrote to Milnes, May 7, 1849 (*KC*, II, 280): "A year or two after his [Keats's] death I received a book, & a fine old engraving of Shakspeare, from Mr Brown."

[1] See *The Tempest*, IV.i.156, and Caroline F. E. Spurgeon, *Keats's Shakespeare* (1928), p. 81.

you do love me as your own Brother—I have seen it in your continual anxiety for me—and I assure you that your wellfare and fame is and will be a chief pleasure to me all my Life. I know no one but you who can be fully sensible of the turmoil and anxiety, the sacrifice of all what is called comfort the readiness to Measure time by what is done and to die in 6 hours could plans be brought to conclusions.—the looking upon the Sun the Moon the Stars, the Earth and its contents as materials to form greater things—that is to say ethereal things——but here I am talking like a Madman greater things that our Creator himself made!! I wrote to Hunt yesterday [2]—scar[c]ely know what I said in it—I could not talk about Poetry in the way I should have liked for I was not in humor with either his or mine. His self delusions are very lamentable they have inticed him into a Situation which I should be less eager after than that of a galley Slave—what you observe thereon is very true must be in time. Perhaps it is a self delusion to say so—but I think I could not be deceived [3] in the Manner that Hunt is—may I die tomorrow if I am to be. There is no greater Sin after the 7 deadly than to flatter oneself into an idea of being a great Poet—or one of those beings who are privileged to wear out their Lives in the pursuit of Honor—how comfortable a feel [4] it is that such a Crime must bring its heavy Penalty? That if one be a Selfdeluder accounts will be balanced? I am glad you are hard at Work—'t will now soon be done—I long to see Wordsworth's as well as to have mine in: [5] but I would rather not show my face in Town till the end of the Year—if that will be time enough—if not I shall be disappointed if you do not write for me even when you think best—I never quite despair and I read Shakspeare—indeed I shall I think never read any other Book much—Now this might lead me into a long Confab but I desist. I am very near Agreeing with Hazlit [6] that Shakspeare is enough for us—

[2] See No. 25. [3] *Written* be be deceved.

[4] Keats no doubt took the noun "feel" from Hunt. Compare "the blind feel of *false* Philosophy," "at the feel of June," "the feel of sleep," *Foliage* (1818), pp. v, cxix, 55. Woodhouse wrote in November, 1818 (*KC*, I, 64), "I plead guilty . . . of an utter abhorrance of the word 'feel' for feeling (substantively)—But Keats seems fond of it. and will ingraft it 'in aeternum' on our language."

[5] Of course, in "Christ's Entry."

[6] Perhaps Hazlitt said so; I cannot find these exact words in his published works. Woodruff, p. 21, suggests a reference to Hazlitt's assertion (*Works*, XVI [1933], 91) that Shakespeare shows "as much knowledge of human nature, in all possible shapes, as is to be found in all other poets put together; and that, we conceive, is quite enough for one writer."

By the by what a tremendous Southean Article his last was—I wish he had left out "grey hairs" [7] It was very gratifying to meet your remarks of the Manuscript [8]—I was reading Anthony and Cleopat[ra] when I got the Paper and there are several Passages applicable to the events you commentate. You say that he arrived by degrees, and not by any single Struggle to the height of his ambition—and that his Life had been as common in particulars as other Mens—Shakspeare makes Enobarb say—Where's Antony Eros—He's walking in the garden—thus: *and spurns the rush that lies* before him, cries fool, Lepidus! In the same scene we find: "let determined things to destiny hold unbewailed their way". Dolabella says of Ant⟨h⟩ony's Messenger

"An argument that he is pluck'd when hither
He sends so poor a pinion of his wing"—Then again,
Eno—"I see Men's Judgments are
A parcel of their fortunes; and things outward
Do draw the inward quality after them,
To suffer all alike"—The following applies well to Bertram [9]
"Yet he that can endure
To follow with allegience a fallen Lord,
Does conquer him that did his Master conquer,
And earns a place i' the story" [1]

But how differently does Buonap bear his fate from Antony!
'T is good too that the Duke of Wellington has a good Word or so in the Examiner [2] A Man ought to have the Fame he deserves—and I begin to think that detracting from him as well as from Wordsworth is the same thing. I wish he had a little more taste—and did not in that respect "deal in Lieutenantry" [3] You should have heard from me before this—but in the first place I did not

[7] See I, 137 n.

[8] Discussing "Bonaparte. 'Manuscrit venu de St. Helene'" in the *Examiner*, May 4, 1817, pp. 275 f., Haydon concluded, "Never was a little book so interesting! . . . And if it be not by Napoleon, it is from an intellect of similar construction."

[9] General Count Henri Gratien Bertrand (1773–1844), Napoleon's friend and confidant (Colvin, p. 17 n.).

[1] The quotations are from *Antony and Cleopatra*, III.v.16–18, III.vi.84 f., III.xii.3 f., III.xiii.31–34, 43–46.

[2] In his review (p. 276) Haydon notes that Wellington is not mentioned in the *Manuscrit*

[3] *Antony and Cleopatra*, III.xi.38 f., "He alone/ Dealt on lieutenantry."

like to do so before I had got a little way in the 1st Book and in the next as G. told me you were going to write I delayed till I had hea[r]d from you—Give my Respects the next time you write to the North [4] and also to John Hunt [5]—Remember me to Reynolds and tell him to write, Ay, and when you sent Westward tell your Sister [6] that I mentioned her in this—So now in the Name of Shakespeare Raphael and all our Saints I commend you to the care of heaven!

Your everlasting friend
John Keats—

· 27 ·

TO TAYLOR AND HESSEY [1]

16 May 1817

Address: Messrs Taylor & Hessey/ Publishers/ Fleet Street—
Postmarks (*blurred*): MARGATE 16 MY 16 1817; F17 MY 17 1817

Margate May 16—

My dear Sirs,

I am extremely indebted to you for your liberality in the Shape of manufactu[r]ed rag value £20 and shall immediately proceed to destroy some of the Minor Heads of that spr[i]ng-headed Hydra [2] the Dun—To conquer which the knight need have no Sword. Shield Cuirass Cuisses Herbadgeon spear Casque, Greves, Pauldrons Spurs Chevron or any other scaly commodity: but he need only take the Bank Note of Faith and Cash of Salvation,[3] and set out against the

[4] To Wordsworth.

[5] Leigh Hunt's brother (1775–1848), who called himself publisher and printer of the *Examiner*.

[6] Harriett Cobley Haydon, born February 8, 1789, died December 2, 1869. She married James Haviland, M.R.C.S., of Bridgwater on August 2, 1815 (see the *Examiner*, August 20, p. 544), and had five children.

[1] *ALS:* Harvard. Woodhouse made a transcript of this letter in his letter-book, pp. 100 f.

[2] *The Faerie Queene*, II.xii.23, "Spring-headed hydres." Woodhouse first copied "that -headed" and later inserted in pencil "Sping" (*sic*).

[3] Here and in the final sentence of No. 33 Keats is paraphrasing Ephesians vi.16 f., "Taking the shield of faith . . . . And take the helmet of salvation, and the sword of the Spirit, which is the word of God."

Monster invoking the aid of no Archimago [4] or Urganda [5]—and finger me the Paper light as the Sybils Leaves in Virgil [6] whereat the Fiend skulks off with his tail between his Legs. Touch him with this enchanted Paper and he whips you his head away as fast as a Snail's Horn [7]—but then the horrid Propensity he has to put it up again has discouraged many very valliant Knights—He is such a never ending still beginning [8] sort of a Body—like my Landlady of the Bell [9]—I should conjecture that the very Spright that the "g[r]een sour ringlets makes ⟨w⟩hereof the Ewe not bites" [1] had manufactured it of the dew fallen on said sour ringlets—I think I could make a nice little Alegorical Poem called "the Dun" Where we wold have the Castle of Carelessness—the Draw Bridge of Credit—Sir Novelty Fashion'{s} [2] expedition against the City of Taylors—&c &c————I went day by day at my Poem for a Month at the end of which time the other day I found my Brain so overwrought that I had neither Rhyme nor reason [3] in it—so was obliged to give up for a few days [4]—I hope soon to be able to resume my Work—I have endeavoured to do so once or twice but to no Purpose—instead of Poetry I have a swimming in my head—And feel all the effects of a Mental Debauch—lowness of Spirits—anxiety to go on without the Power to do so which does not at all tend to my ultimate Progression—However tomorrow I will begin my next Month—This Evening I go to Cantrerbury [5]—having got tired of Margate—I was not right in my head when I came—At Cant^y I

[4] See *The Faerie Queene*, I, II, and I, 110.

[5] Urganda the Unknown, a leading character in the fifteenth-century romance, *Amadis of Gaul*.

[6] *Aeneid*, III.445–452.

[7] Compare the passage in *Venus and Adonis* quoted at I, 189.

[8] See Dryden, "Alexander's Feast," line 101.

[9] An 1823–24 directory lists among taverns and public houses in Margate the Bell, Thomas Foster, High Street.

[1] *The Tempest*, V.i.37 f. For "Ewe" Keats first wrote "yowe."

[2] Keats had in mind the Castle Joyeous and Pollente's toll bridge in *The Faerie Queene*, III.i, V.ii. Sir Novelty Fashion is a character in Colley Cibber's *Love's Last Shift*.

[3] Since Keats was buried in Shakespeare, he may have thought of this commonplace from *As You Like It*, III.ii.419.

[4] He "gave up" *Endymion* on May 11 (I, 142).

[5] Writing to Severn on May 22 (*K–SMB*, No. 1 [1910], 47; Sharp, p. 19), George Keats says, "John and Tom are at Canterbury." Again in a letter, about the same time, though undated by Sharp, p. 30, he tells Severn, "John will be in town again soon. . . . He sojourns at present at Bo Peep, near Hastings." Keats himself does not mention his stay at "Cantrerbury," but later (see I, 402, II, 65) he tells how at Hastings, where he went without Tom, he met the "lady" who has recently been identified as a Mrs. Isabella Jones. Bo-Peep is now called St. Leonards.

hope the Remembrance of Chaucer will set me forward like a Billiard-Ball [6]—I am gald [7] to hear of Mr T's health and of the Wellfare of the In-town-stayers" and think Reynolds will like his trip—I have some idea of seeing the Continent some time in the summer—

In repeating how sensible I am of your kindness I remain

Your Obedient Servt and Friend

John Keats—

I shall be very happy to hear any little intelligence in the literary or friendly way when you have time to scribble—

Messrs Taylor and Hessey.—

· 28 ·

TO TAYLOR AND HESSEY [1]

10 June 1817

Address: Messrs Taylor and Hessey/ Publishers/ Fleet Street— *Postmarks:* {TwoPyPost} Unpaid LambsConduit St; 2 o'Clock 10 JU 1817 ANn

Tuesday Morn—

My dear Sirs,

I must endeavor to lose my Maidenhead with respect to money Matters as soon as possible—and I will to—so here goes—A Couple of Duns that I thought would be silent till the beginning, at least, of next Month (when I am certain to be on my legs for certain sure) have opened upon me with a cry most "untunable" [2] never did you hear such un "gallant chiding" [3]

Now you must know I am not desolate but have thank God 25 good Notes in my fob—but then you know I laid them by to write with and would stand at Bay a fortnight ere they should grab me—In

[6] Keats once told Woodhouse (*KC*, I, 59), "he can conceive of a billiard Ball that it may have a sense of delight from its own roundness, smoothness volubility. & the rapidity of its motion," an idea, says Woodruff, pp. 179–183, that he derived from reading the manuscript of Hazlitt's old lecture "On Liberty and Necessity."

[7] *For* glad.

[1] *ALS:* Harvard. A short-hand transcript made by Woodhouse is in his Pierpont Morgan Library book of Keatsiana.

[2] *A Midsummer Night's Dream,* IV.i.128, "A cry more tuneable."

[3] The same, IV.i.118 f., "Never did I hear/ Such gallant chiding."

a Month's time I must pay—but it would relieve my Mind if I owed you instead of these Pelican duns.[4]

I am affraid you will say I have "wound about with circumstance" [5] when I should have asked plainly—However as I said I am a little maidenish or so—and I feel my virginity come strong upon me—the while I request the loan of a £20 and a £10—which if you would enclose to me I would acknowlege and save myself a hot forehead—I am sure you are confident in my responsibility—and in the sense [of] squareness that is always in me—

Your obliged friend
John Keats—

· 29 ·

TO B. R. HAYDON [1]

August 1817

Thursday Morning

My dear Haydon,

I was at Reynolds's when he received your Letter and am therefore up to Probabilities—The fact is Reynolds is very unwell—he has all kinds of distressing Symptoms, and I am on this accou[n]t rather glad that he has not spare time for one of our right Sort meetings—he would go to far for his health.

I was right glad of your Letter from Devonshire—whereby that is I hope one day to see it—right sorry that you are going back to

[4] Compare *King Lear*, III.iv.77, "Those pelican daughters." Leonidas M. Jones tells me that Reynolds used the phrases "pelican children," "a pelican thing," "Pelican daughters."

[5] *The Merchant of Venice*, I.i.154, "To wind about my love with circumstance."

[1] *ALS:* Pierpont Morgan Library (first printed by Lowell, I, 565). At its top someone has written "To B. R. Haydon." and added "1816" after "Morning." This letter, which was sent by messenger, has heretofore been assigned to February 5, 1818, a day on which Haydon, as his Journal shows, was busily working in his London studio on "Christ's Entry into Jerusalem." But when Keats wrote, Haydon had been visiting in Devonshire and was returning there "to day." Keats's reference to finishing the second book of *Endymion*, then, concerns the actual composition, not the making of a fair copy for Taylor and Hessey, and his letter belongs to the end of August before he went to visit Bailey at Oxford. Thursday was probably August 21 or 28. See my discussion in *HLB*, VII (1953), 176, and Haydon's reply of September 17 (No. 35).

day—I hope 't is not for long—I met a friend [2] the other day who had seen Wordsworth's House the other Week—You will be glad to hear that I have finished my second Book that is if this catches you at your Street-door—I have been gadding and did not see your Note [3] time to answer it sooner—Let me hear from Devon again—

Your's like a Pyramid [4]
John Keats—

My Brother George desires to be remembe[r]ed to you—

· 30 ·

TO JANE AND MARIANE REYNOLDS [1]

4 September 1817

Address: Miss Reyno{l}ds/ Mrs Earle's/ Little Hampton/ Sussex.
Postmarks: OXFORD 5 SE 5 1817; B 6 SE 6 1817

Oxf—

My dear friends,

You are I am glad to hear comfortable at Hampton where I hope you will receive the Biscuts we ate the other night at Little Brittain.[2] I hope you found them good. There you are among Sands Stocks Stones Pebbles Beaches Cliffs Rocks Deeps Shallows Weeds ships Boats (at a distance) Carrots—turnips Sun Moon and Stars and all those sort of things—here am I among Colleges, Halls Stalls plenty of Trees thank God [3]—plenty of Water thank heaven—plenty of Books thank the Muses—plenty of Snuff—thank Sir Walter Ra-

[2] Probably John Martin (see I, 166).

[3] As MBF observes, Keats first wrote "Notn" and then changed the "n" to "e" and forgot to put "in" after it.

[4] "The signature . . . reflects not Keats's mind alone; . . . there was even a scheme to erect a pyramid in what is now Trafalgar-square" (Blunden, p. 496).

[1] *ALS:* Harvard, formerly owned by John Harvey Vincent Arnold (see his sale catalog, New York, 1904). Keats was visiting Bailey, who wrote the address. Seven lines by Bailey at the top of the sheet are heavily scratched out and, unhappily, fail to reveal their secret to ultra-violet photography. The deletion must have been made before Woodhouse copied the letter in his letter-book, pp. 74–76, but he indicates no tears, and the words and letters below in curly braces are taken from his text.

[2] In which was the Reynoldses' home.

[3] Compare his comments on Margate and trees at I, 137 f.

leigh—plenty of Sagars,[4] ditto—plenty of flat Country—thank Tellus's roling pin. I'm on the Sofa—Buonapa[r]te is on the Snuff Box—but you are by the {sea} side—argal [5] you bathe—you walk—you say how beautiful—find out resemb{lan}ces between waves and Camels—rocks and dancing Masters—fireshovels and telescopes—Dolphins and Madonas—which word by the way I must acquaint you was derived from the Syriac⟨e⟩ and came down in a way which neither of you I am sorry to say are at all capaple of comprehending: but as a time may come when by your occasional converse with me you may arive at "something like prophetic strain" [6] I will unbar the Gates of my Pride and let my Condecension stalk forth like a Ghost at the Circus [7]—The Word Madon a my dear Ladies or—the Word—Mad-o-na—So I say! I am not mad—Howsumever When that aged Tamer Kewthon sold a Certain Camel Called Peter to the Overseer of the Babel Skyworks, he thus spake, adjusting his Cravat round the tip of his Chin—My dear Ten Storyupinair [8]—this here Beast though I say it as shouldn't say't [9] ⟨"⟩ not only has the Power of subsisting 40 day and 40 Nights without fire and Candle but he can sing—here I have in my Pocket a Certificate from Signor Nicolini of the King's Theatre [1] a Certificate to this effect xxxxxxxx I have had dinner since I left that effect upon you and feel to heavy in mentibus to display all the Profundity of the Polyglon [2]—so you had better each of you take a glass of cherry branday and drink to the health of Archimedes who was of so benign a disposition that he [3] never would [leave] Syracuse

[4] He mentions smoking a "Segar" at II, 98.

[5] Keats got this word, which was not in the dictionaries, from *Hamlet*, V.i.13, 21, 55.

[6] Milton, "Il Penseroso," line 174.

[7] MBF quotes M. W. Disher, *Greatest Show on Earth* (1937), p. 77: "Ghosts were rare in circuses, but one to fit this reference walked at the Royal Circus in *Halloween; or, The Castles Of Athlin And Dunbayne*, a New Grand Scotch Spectacle by J. C. Cross, the description of which is in *Circusiana*, published 1809."

[8] J. L. Lowes, *PMLA*, LI (1936), 1109 f., shows that this jocose passage on the camel and the Ten Storyupinair is based on an engraving, "The Building of Babel," in Henry Southwell's (or rather Robert Sanders') *Universal Family Bible* (1773), a copy of which Keats owned.

[9] Possibly Keats noticed this commonplace in Beaumont and Fletcher's *Wit at Several Weapons*, II.i.

[1] D. B. Green, *NQ*, March, 1955, p. 124, suggests that Keats took from the *Spectator* (an edition of which he owned), No. 405, June 14, 1712, this reference to Nicolino (or Nicolini) Grimaldi (1673–1726), who sang at the King's, later the Haymarket, Theatre.

[2] Keats, then, probably wrote No. 30 before and after dinner on September 4, and it was postmarked the next day. Gaynor Bradish suggests that, since a polygon has many sides, Keats speaks of a profound man as a "many-sided person."

[3] *Written* the.

in his Life so kept himself out of all knight errant[r]y—this I know to be a fact for it is written in the 45 Book of Winkine's treatise on Garden rollers that he trod on a fishwoman's toe in Liverpool and never begged her pardon—Now the long and the short is this—that is by comparison. for a long day may be a short year [4]—a long Pole may {be a very stupid fel}low as a Man [5]—But let us refresh ourself from this dept[h] of thinking and turn to some innocent Jocularity—the Bow cannot always be bent nor the gun always loaded if you ever let it off and the Life of Man is like a great Mountain—his breath is like a Shrewsbury Cake—he comes into the world like a Shoeblack and goes out of it like a Cobler—he eats like a Chimneysweeper, drinks like a Gingerbread Baker and breaths like Achilles—So it being that we are such sublunary creatures let us endeavour to correct all our bad Spelling all our most delightful Abominations and let us wish health to Marian and Jane whoever they be and wherever—Your's truly

John Keats—

· 31 ·

TO J. H. REYNOLDS [1]

September 1817 [2]

"Wordsworth sometimes, though in a fine way, gives us sentences in the Style of School exercises—for Instance

The lake doth glitter
Small birds twitter &c.[3]

[4] Apperson, p. 136, has a somewhat similar proverb, "A day to come shows longer than a year that's gone."

[5] MBF suggests a reference to William Pole-Tylney-Long-Wellesley, fourth Earl of Mornington (1788–1857), who is mentioned in the first poem, "Loyal Effusion," in James and Horace Smith's *Rejected Addresses*—"Long may Long Tilney Wellesley Long Pole live." After his death the *Morning Chronicle* candidly remarked that Mornington's life was "redeemed by no single virtue, adorned by no single grace."

[1] Text from Woodhouse, who copied this fragment into his book of Keats's poems (not letters), fol. 29, heading it "Lines—Rhymed in a letter to J. H. R. from Oxford."

[2] Obviously written during the first days of Keats's stay with Bailey at Oxford. Woodhouse notes "Mids^r^ 1818."

[3] Wordsworth's "Written in March, While Resting on the Bridge at the Foot of Brother's Water" begins, "The Cock is crowing,/ The stream is flowing,/ The small birds twitter,/ The lake doth glitter."

Now I think this is an excellent method of giving a very clear description of an interesting place such as Oxford is [4]—

// The Gothic looks solemn,—
The plain Doric column
Supports an old Bishop & crosier;
The mouldering arch,
Shaded o'er by a larch,
Lives next door to Wilson the hosier

———

Vicè—that is, by turns—
O'er pale visages mourns
The black-tassel trencher, or common-hat:
The Chauntry boy sings,
The steeple bell rings,
And as for the Chancellor—dominat.

———

There are plenty of trees,
And plenty of ease,
And plenty of fat deer for parsons;
And when it is venison,
Short is the benison,—
or
Then each on a leg (&) thigh fastens.

// J.K.

[4] Brown wrote to young Henry Snook on March 24, 1820 (HBF, 1883, IV, 73 f.), "I met with them [these verses of Keats] only yesterday, but they have been written long ago."

· 32 ·

TO FANNY KEATS [1]

10 September 1817

Address: Miss Keats/ Miss Kaley's School/ Walthamstow/ Essex—
Postmarks: OXFORD 12 SE 12 O 1817 O; B 13 SE 13 1817; 10 o'Clock SP 13 1817 FN[n]

Oxford Sept[r] 10th—

My dear Fanny,

Let us now begin a regular question and answer—a little pro and con; letting it interfere as a pleasant method of my coming at your favorite little wants and enjoyments, that I may meet them in a way befitting a brother.

We have been so little together since you have been able to reflect on things that I know not whether you prefer the History of King Pepin [2] to Bunyan's Pilgrims Progress—or Cinderella and her glass slipper to Moor's Almanack.[3] However in a few Letters I hope I shall be able to come at that and adapt my Scribblings to your Pleasure—You must tell me about all you read if it be only six Pages in a Week—and this transmitted to me every now and then will procue [4] you full sheets of Writing from me pretty frequently—This this I feel as a necessity: for we ought to become intimately acquainted, in order that I may not only, as you grow up love your [5] as my only Sister, but confide in you as my dearest friend. When I saw you last I told you of my intention of going to Oxford and 't is now a Week since I disembark'd from his Whipship's Coach

[1] *ALS:* British Museum. Fanny Keats attended the Ladies Boarding Academy, 12 Marsh Street, run by Mary Ann and Susanna Tuckey. Margaret Caley, 21 Marsh Street, apparently an assistant mistress who kept some of the students in her own house, took over the school after the Misses Tuckey died, and in 1852 (MBF, p. xxxv) was buried in the Tuckey vault in Walthamstow churchyard. See Adami, pp. 46 f. Keats's date may be a day or two early.

[2] Perhaps he had in mind some edition of Elizabeth Newbery's *The History of Little King Pippin* (1786). But Pepin (Pippen, Pippin) was familiar from nursery rhymes.

[3] Francis Moore (1657–1715?) issued his first almanac in 1699. Several continuations of the almanac are still published.

[4] *For* procure. [5] *For* you.

the Defiance [6] in this place. I am living in Magdalen Hall on a visit to a young Man [7] with whom I have not been long acquainted, but whom I like very much—we lead very industrious lives he in general⟨s⟩ Studies and I in proceeding at a pretty good rate with a Poem which I hope you will see early in the next year—Perhaps you might like to know what I am writing about—I will tell you—

Many Years ago there was a young handsome Shepherd who fed his flocks on a Mountain's Side called Latmus—he was a very contemplative sort of a Person and lived solitry among the trees and Plains little thinking—that such a beautiful Creature as the Moon was growing mad in Love with him—However so it was; and when he was asleep on the Grass, she used to come down from heaven and admire him excessively from [8] a long time; and at last could not refrain from carying him away in her arms to the top of that high Mountain Latmus while he was a dreaming—but I dare ⟨yo⟩ say have [9] read this and all the other beautiful Tales which have come down from the ancient times of that beautiful Greece. If you have not let me know and I will tell you more at large of others quite as delightful—

This Oxford I have no doubt is the finest City in the world [1]—it is full of old Gothic buildings—Spires—towers—Quadrangles—Cloisters Groves & [2] and is surrounded with more Clear streams than ever I saw together—I take a Walk by the Side of one of them every Evening and thank God, we have not had a drop of rain these many days—I had a long and interesting Letter from George, cross lines by a short one from Tom [3] yesterday dated Paris. They both send their loves to you—Like most Englishmen they feel a mighty preference for every thing English—the french Meadows the trees the People the Towns the Churches, the Books the every thing—although they may be in themselves good; yet when put in comparison with our green Island they all vanish like Swallows in October. They have seen Cathedrals Manuscripts. Fountains, Pictures,

[6] According to *Cary's New Itinerary* (1819), the Defiance left the Belle Sauvage, Ludgate Hill, at 7:45 A.M. and reached the Mitre Inn, Oxford, about 3 P.M.

[7] For Bailey's account (1849) of Keats's visit see *KC*, II, 269–272. Magdalen Hall was destroyed by fire on January 3, 1820.

[8] *For* for. [9] *For* you have.

[1] *Leigh's New Picture of England and Wales* (1820), p. 390, agrees: "The beauty of this city in magnificent buildings, is unequalled in the world." [2] *For* &c.

[3] At some time or other, George wrote in 1826 (*KC*, I, 301; Lowell, I, 172), Tom also "went to Lyons."

Tragedy Comedy,—with other things you may by chance meet with in this Country such a [4] Washerwomen, Lamplighters, Turnpikemen Fish kettles, Dancing Masters, kettle drums, Sentry Boxes, Rocking Horses &c and, now they have taken them over a set ⟨of⟩ of boxing gloves—I have written to George and requested him, as you wish I shou{ld,} to write to you. I have been writing very hard lately even till an utter incapacity came on, and I feel it now about my head: so you must not mind a little out of the way sayings—though bye the bye where [5] my brain as clear as a bell I think I should have a little propensity thereto. I shall stop here till I have finished the 3rd Book of my Story; which I hope will be accomplish'd in at most three Weeks from to day—about which time you shall see me. How do you like Miss Taylor's essays in Rhyme—I just look'd into the Book and it appeared to me suitable to you—especially since I remember your liking for those pleasant little things the Original Poems [6]—the essays are the more mature production of the same hand. While I was speaking about france it occured to me to speak a few Words on their Language—it is perhaps the poorest one ever spoken since the jabbering in the Tower of Ba{bel} and when you come to know that the real use and greatness of a Tongue is to be referred to its Literature—you will be astonished to find how very inferior it is to our native Speech—I wish the Italian would supersede french in every School throughout the Country for that is full of real Poetry and Romance of a kind more fitted for the Pleasure of Ladies than perhaps our own—It seems that the only end to be gained in acquiring french—is the immense accomplishment of speaking it—it is none at all—a most lamentable mistake indeed [7]—Italian indeed would sound most musically from Lips which had b[e]gan to pronounce it as early as french is cramme'd down our Mouths, as if we were young Jack daws at the mercy of an overfeeding Schoolboy.

Now Fanny you must write soon—and write all you think about, never mind what—only let me have a good deal of your writing—

[4] *For* as. [5] *For* were.

[6] Jane Taylor's *Essays in Rhyme, or Morals and Manners* (1816) and Jane and Ann Taylor's *Original Poems for Infant Minds* (1804), the first and in later editions the second published by Taylor and Hessey. Willard B. Pope, *TLS*, October 6, 1932, p. 711, notes that Mrs. Franklin P. Adams, of New York, bought at a Madrid bookstall in May, 1924, a copy of the *Essays* inscribed "John Keats to His Dear Sister."

[7] Keats rescinded this harsh judgment of French at II, 172.

You need not do it all at once—be two or three or four day about it, and let it be a diary of your little life. You will preserve all my Letters [8] and I will secure yours—and thus in the course of time we shall each of us have a good Bundle—which, hereafter, when things may have strangely altered and god knows what happened, we may read over together and look with pleasure on times past—that now are to come—Give my Respects to the Ladies [9]—and so my dear Fanny I am ever

Your most affectionate Brother
John.

If you direct—Post Office Oxford—your Letter
will be brought to me—

· 33 ·

TO JANE REYNOLDS [1]

September 1817

My dear Jane,

You must not expect that your Porcupine quill is to be shot at me with impunity—without you mean to question the existance of the Pyramids or rout Sir Isac Newton out of his Coffin. If I did not think you had a kind of preference youself [2] for Juliet I would not say a word more about it—but as I know people love to be reminded of those they most love—'t is with me a certain thing that you are merely fishing for a little proing and conning thereon—As for you [2] accusations I perhaps may answer them like Haydon in a Postscript—If you go on at this rate I shall always have you in my imagination side by side with Bayley's [3] Picture of Jeremy Taylor who always looks as if he were going to hit me a rap with a Book he hold [4] in a

[8] Adami, pp. 139 f., notes how as an old woman Fanny said that her letters from Keats had only once, and then but for a few days, been out of her possession.

[9] Her schoolmistresses.

[1] *ALS:* Berg Collection, New York Public Library, formerly owned by W. T. H. Howe (died 1939). First printed by Lowell, I, 493 f. Written at Oxford on part of an undated letter from Bailey to Jane.

[2] See I, 121 n.

[3] Perhaps the first *y* was later changed to *i*. Holman noted that the "Picture" was an engraving by Pierre Lombart (1613–1682).

[4] *For* holds.

very threatning position My head is always in imminent [5] danger—However with the armour of words and the Sword of Syllables [6] I hope to attack you in a very short time—more at length—

My love to Marianne
Your's sincerely
John Keats.

·34·

TO JANE AND MARIANE REYNOLDS [1]

14 September 1817

Address: Miss Reynolds/ Mrs Earle/ Little Hampton.
Postmarks: OXFORD 15 SE 15 1817 5{...}7; SE C 2{...} 817 [2]

Oxford Sunday Evening

My dear Jane,

You are such a literal translator that I shall some day amuse myself with looking over some foreign sentences and imagining how you would render them into english. This is an age for typical curiosities and I would advise you, as a good speculation, to study Hebrew and astonish the world with a figurative version in our native tongue. 'The Mountains skipping like Rams and the little Hills like Lambs' [3] you will leave as far behind as the Hare did the Tortoise. It must be so or you would never have thought that I really meant you would like to pro and con about those Honeycombs—no, I had no such idea, or if I had 't woud be only to tease you a little for Love. So now let me put down in black and white briefly my sentiments thereon. Imprimis—I sincerely believe that Imogen is the finest Creature; and that I should have been disappointed at hearing you prefer Juliet. Item Yet I feel such a yearning [4] towards Juliet and that I would rather follow her into Pandemonium than Imogen into Paradize—heartily wishing myself a Romeo to be

[5] *Written* immineht. [6] See I, 145 n.

[1] *ALS:* Harvard. Woodhouse made a transcript of this letter in his letter-book, pp. 19–23.

[2] There is also a blurred postmark, MINCHINHAMPTON 10, preceded by the words, written in ink, "Missent to."

[3] Psalm cxiv.4.

[4] He intended to write "yearning," but omitted at least one letter. On Juliet see also I, 156.

worthy of her and to he[a]r the Devils quote the old Proverb—'Birds of a feather flock together"—Amen. Now let us turn to the sea shore. Believe me, my dear Jane it is a great Happiness to me that you are in this finest part of the year, winning a little enjoyment from the hard World—in truth the great Elements we know of are no mean Comforters—the open Sky sits upon our senses like a sapphire Crown [5]—the Air is our Robe of State—the Earth is our throne and the sea a mighty Minstrell playing before it—able like David's Harp to charm the evil spirit from such Creatures as I am [6]—able like Ariel's to make such a one as you forget almost the tempest-cares of Life.[7] I have found in the Ocean's Musick—varying (though selfsame) more than the passion of Timotheus,[8] an enjoyment not to be put into words and "though inland far I be" [9] I now hear the voice most audibly while pleasing myself in the Idea of your Sensations. Marianne is getting well apace and if you have a few trees [1] and a little Harvesting about you I'll snap my fingers in Lucifer's eye. I hope you bathe too—if you do not I earnestly recommend it—bathe thrice a Week and let us have no more sitting up next Winter. Which is the best of Shakspeare's Plays?—I mean in what mood and with what accompenament do you like the Sea best? It is very fine in the morning when the Sun

> "opening on Neptune with fair blessed beams
> Turns into yellow gold his salt sea streams" [2]

and superb when

> "The sun from meridian height
> Illumines the depth of the sea—
> and the fishes beginning to sweat
> Cry damn it how hot we shall be" [3]

and gorgeous when the fair planet hastens—"to his home within the western foam" [4] but dont you think there is something

[5] *Comus*, line 26, has "wear their Saphire crowns."

[6] See 1 Samuel xvi.14–23. [7] See *The Tempest.*

[8] See Dryden, "Alexander's Feast."

[9] Wordsworth, "Ode: Intimations of Immortality," line 166, "Though inland far we be." [1] See I, 137 f., 149. [2] *A Midsummer Night's Dream*, III.ii.392 f.

[3] Henry Tyler, *TLS*, August 17, 1951, p. 517, called these lines "a piece of nonsense then current." Garrod, the same, August 24, p. 533, agreed, and referred to *NQ*, June 7, 1856, p. 447, where the lines are also attributed to the Swedish writers, Per Daniel Amadeus Atterbom (1790–1855) and Christian Alfred Fahlcrantz (1835–1911).

[4] Spenser, *Epithalamion*, lines 282 f.

extremely fine after sunset when there are a few white Clouds about and a few stars blinking—when the the [5] waters are ebbing and the Horison [6] a Mystery? This state of things has been so fulfilling to me that I am anxious to hear whether it is a favorite with you—so when you and Marrianne club your Letter to me put in a word or to about it—I am glad that you will spend a little time with the Dilks—tell Dilk that it would be perhaps as well if he left a Pheasant or Partrige alive here and there to keep up a supply of Game for

n

next season—tell him to rei⟨gn⟩ in if possible all the Nimrod of his disposition, he being a mighty hunter befor the Lord [7]—of the Manor. Tell him to shoot far [8] and not have at the poor devils in a furrow—when they are flying he may fire and nobody will be the wiser. Give my sincerest Respects to Mrs Dilk saying that I have not forgiven myself for not having got her the little Box of Medicine I promised for her after dinner flushings. and that had I remained at Hampstead I would have made precious havoc with her house and furniture—drawn a great harrow over her garden—poisoned Boxer [9]—eaten her Cloathes pegs,—fried her Cabbages fricaceed (how is it spelt?) her radishes—ragouted her Onions—⟨bl⟩ belaboured her beat root—outstripped her scarlet Runners—parlez vou'd with her french Beans—devoured her Mignon or Mig[n]onette —metamorphosed her Bell handles—splinterd her looking glasses—bullock'd at her cups and saucers—agonized her decanters—put old Philips [1] to pickle in the Brine tub—disorganized her Piano—dislocated her Candlesticks—emptied her wine bins in a fit of despair—turned out her Maid to Grass and Astonished Brown—whose Letter to her on these events I would rather see than the original copy of the Book of Genesis. Should you see Mr W. D.[2] remember {me} to him—and to little Robinson Crusoe [3]—and to Mr Snook [4]—Poor Bailey scar[c]ely ever well has gone to bed very so so,[5] and

[5] *Sic.*

[6] Garrod, p. xviii, believes that Keats pronounced this word to rime with *Morrison*, a pronunciation "hateful to think" about.

[7] See Genesis x.9.

[8] J. C. Maxwell, *NQ*, May 17, 1947, p. 215, reads "fa[i]r."

[9] Her dog (MBF).

[1] "The gardener," Dilke noted in his copy of Milnes.

[2] William Dilke, brother of Keats's friend.

[3] Probably Dilke's nephew, Henry or John Snook.

[4] John Snook (1780–1863), of the Old Mill House, Bedhampton, married Letitia Dilke (1784–1865), sister of Keats's friend, on November 26, 1804. They had two sons, Henry (1805–1879) and "the boy" John (1807–1887). See Guy Murchie, *K-SJ*, III (1954), 1–6.

[5] In William Barnes Rhodes's *Bombastes Furioso*, which Keats knew, the king sings

p{leased} that I am writing to you. To your Brother John (whom henceforth I shall consider as mine) and to you my dear friends [6] Marrianne and Jane I shall ever feel grateful for having made known to me so real [7] a fellow as Bailey. He delights me in the Selfish and (please god) the disenterrested part of my disposition. If the old Poets have any pleasure in looking down at the Enjoyers of their Works, their eyes must bend with double satisfaction upon him—I sit as at a feast when he is over them and pray that if after my death any of my Labours should be worth saving, they may have as "honest a Chronicler [8] as Bailey. Out of this his Enthusiasm in his own pursuit and for all good things is of an exalted kind—worthy a more healthful frame and an untorn Spirit. He must have happy years to come—he shall not die by God [9]—A Letter from John the other day was a chief Happiness to me. I made a little mistake when just now I talked of being far inland: how can that be when Endymion and I are at the bottom of the Sea? [1] Whence I hope to bring him in safety before you leave the Sea Side and if I can so contrive it you shall be greeted by him on the Sands and he shall tell you all his adventures: which at having finished he shall thus proceed. "My dear Ladies, favorites of my gentle Mistress, how ever my friend Keats may have teazed and vexed you believe me he loves you not the less—for instance I am deep in his favor and yet he has been hawling me through the Earth and Sea with unrelenting Perseverence—I know for all this that he is mightily fond of me, by his contriving me all sorts of pleasures—nor is this the least fair Ladies—this one of meeting you on desart shore and greeting you in his Name—He sends you moreover this little scroll"—

"My dear Girls,

I send you per favor of Endymion the assurance of my esteem of you and my utmost wishes for you Health and Pleasure—being ever—Your affectionate Brother. John Keats—

George and Tom are well— [2]

(Remberences to little Britain)

---

in the opening scene, "We are but middling;—that is, but so, so," and Fusbos replies, "Only so so? O monstrous, doleful thing."

[6] *Written* firends.

[7] A word denoting the highest praise: see I, 282 n.

[8] *Henry VIII*, IV.ii.72, "such an honest chronicler as Griffith."

[9] Holman noted the borrowing from *Tristram Shandy*, vol. VI, chapter 8.

[1] See *Endymion*, book III, of which by September 21 (I, 166) Keats had written 800 lines.

[2] At the end of the transcript Woodhouse wrote in shorthand "Miss Reynolds/ Mrs. Earle."

· 35 ·

FROM B. R. HAYDON [1]

17 September 1817

My dear Keats/

I am delighted to hear you getting on with your Poem, success to it and to you with all my heart & soul and liver—will you oblige ⟨oblige⟩ me by going to Magdalen College, and ask for the Porter—and will you enquire of him about a Young Man [2] who was copying when I was at Oxford the Altar piece there by Moralez.[3]—I am anxious to know about that Young Man, the copy promised something—will you if you can see the Young Man, and ascertain what his wishes in Art *are*—if he has *ambition*, if he seems to possess *power*—if he wishes to *be great*——all of which you can soon see——In these cases should any friend be disposed to assist him up to London & to support him for a Year I'll train him in the Art, with no o{ther} remuneration [4] but the pleasure of seeing him advance—I'll put him in the right way, and do every thing to advance him—read this part of the *letter to the Porter*—and do oblige me by exerting your Yourself perhaps Mr Bailey will also feel an interest—give my kind remembrance to him—

Yours ever Dear
Keats—B. R. Haydon

Sp. 17. 1817—

41 as usual— [5]

[1] *ALS:* Formerly attached to Haydon's Journal, now at Harvard. A reply to No. 29. Like various other letters of Haydon's it was not sent by the post. Keats received it on September 20 (I, 166).

[2] MBF notes that the young man was Charles Cripps, who was baptized in Iffley Church on November 27, 1796, and whose third child was born at Iffley in 1831. He is not mentioned in Haydon's published Journal.

[3] The altar-piece was not by Luis de Morales (*c.* 1509–1586), "El Divino," Spanish painter, but, according to MBF, by Francisco Ribalta (1555–1628), and Cripps's copy of it now hangs in St. Denys' Church, Northmoor.

[4] Haydon usually charged pupils 200 guineas for three years' instruction.

[5] See the address of No. 37.

· 36 ·

TO J. H. REYNOLDS [1]

21 September 1817

My dear Reynolds./ Oxford Sunday Morn

So you are determined to be my mortal foe—draw a Sword at me, and I will forgive—Put a Bullet in my Brain, and I will shake it out as a dewdrop from the Lion's Mane; [2]—put me on a Gridiron, and I will fry with great complancency—but, oh horror! to come upon me in the shape of a Dun! Send me Bills! as I say to my Taylor send me Bills and I'll never employ you more [3]—However,
drives:
needs must when the devil ⟨deuces⟩ and for fear of "before and behind Mr Honeycomb" [4] I'll proceed—I have not time to elucidate the forms and shapes of the grass and trees; for, rot it! I forgot to bring my mathematical case with me; which unfortunately contained my triangular Prism so that the hues of the grass cannot be dissected for you— [5]

For these last five or six days, we have had regularly a Boat on the Isis, and explored all the streams about, which are more in number than your eye lashes. We sometimes skim into a Bed of rushes, and there become naturalized riverfolks,—there is one particularly nice nest which we have christened "Reynolds's Cove"—in which we have read Wordsworth and talked as may be. I think I see you and Hunt meeting in the Pit.—What a very pleasant fellow he is, if he would give up the sovereignty of a Room pro bono—What Evenings we might pass with him, could we have him from Mrs H—Failings I am always rather rejoiced to find in a Man than sorry

[1] A transcript in Woodhouse's letter-book, pp. 46–48, by a clerk with corrections by Woodhouse, who adds the date "(21 Septr 1817)."

[2] *Troilus and Cressida,* III.iii.224 f., "like a dew-drop from the lion's mane,/Be shook to air."

[3] At his death Keats owed his tailor £30 or £40: see II, 319 n.

[4] See Goldsmith, *The Good Natur'd Man,* III.i.252–254. The hero's name is Honeywood, which Keats perhaps confused with the Will Honeycomb of the *Spectator.*

[5] Jack Stillinger thinks that in his letter Reynolds had quoted the famous passage in *Rasselas,* chapter 10: "The business of a poet . . . is to examine, not the individual, but the species; . . . he does not number the streaks of the tulip, or describe the different shades in the verdure of the forest."

for; for they bring us to a Level—He has them,—but then his makes-up are very good. He agrees with the Northe[r]n Poet in this, "He is not one of those who much delight to season their fireside with personal talk" [6]—I must confess however having a little itch that way. and at this present I have a few neighbourly remarks to make—The world, and especially our England, has within the last thirty year's been vexed and teased by a set of Devils, whom I detest so
-most
much that I al⟨ways⟩ hunger after an acherontic promotion to a Torturer, purposely for their accomodation; These Devils are a set of Women, who having taken a snack or Luncheon of Literary scraps, set themselves up for towers of Babel in Languages Sapphos in Poetry—Euclids in Geometry—and everything in nothing. Among such the Name of Montague [7] has been preeminent. The thing has made a very uncomfortable impression on me.—I had longed for some real feminine Modesty in these things, and was therefore gladdened in the extreme on opening the other day one of Bayley's Books—a Book of Poetry written by one beautiful Mrs Philips, a friend of Jeremy Taylor's, and called "the matchless Orinda" [8]—You must have heard of her, and most likely read her Poetry—I wish you have not, that I may have the pleasure of treating you with a few stanzas—I do it at a venture:—You will not regret reading them once more. The following to her friend Mrs M. A. at parting you will Judge of.

═══

–1–

I have examined and do find
  of all that favour me
There's none I grieve to leave behind
  But only, only thee
To part with thee I needs must die
Could parting sep'rate thee and I.

[6] Wordsworth's "Personal Talk" begins, "I am not One who much or oft delight/ To season my," etc.

[7] Keats is here taking a farewell of an earlier favorite like Mrs. Tighe (see II, 18), though he names only Elizabeth (Robinson) Montagu (1720–1800), a famous bluestocking.

[8] Katherine Fowler (Mrs. James) Philips (1631–1664). "To Mrs. M. A. at Parting" is in her *Poems* (1710), pp. 94–96. M. A. was Mary Aubrey (Mrs. William Montagu).

–2–

But neither chance nor Compliment
  Did *element* our Love;
'Twas sacred sympathy was lent
  Us from the Quire above.
That friendship fortune did create,
Still fears a wound from time or fate.

3

Our chang'd and mingled souls are grown
  To such acquaintance now,
That if each would resume her own
  Alas! we know not how.
We have each other so engrost
That each is in the union lost

–4–

And thus we can no absence know
  Nor shall we be confin'd;
Our active souls will daily go
  To learn each others mind.
Nay should we never meet to sense
Our souls would hold intelligence.

5

Inspired with a flame divine
  I scorn to court a stay;
For from that noble soul of thine
  I ne'er can be away.
But I shall weep when thou dost grieve
Nor can I die whilst thou dost live

6

By my own temper I shall guess
  At thy felicity,
And only like my happiness
  Because it pleaseth thee.
Our hearts at any time will tell
If thou, or I be sick or well.

–7–

All honour sure I must pretend,
All that is good or great;
She that would be Rosania's friend,
Must be at least compleat,†
If I have any Bravery,
'Tis cause I have so much of thee.

† A compleat friend—this Line sounded very oddly to me at first.

8

Thy Leiger Soul in me shall lie,
And all thy thoughts reveal;
Then back again with mine shall flie
And thence to me shall steal.
Thus still to one another tend;
Such is the sacred name of friend.

9–

Thus our twin souls in one shall grow,
And teach the world new Love,
Redeem the age and sex, and show
A Flame Fate dares not move:
And courting death to be our friend,
too
Our Lives together ⟨We⟩ shall end

10

A Dew shall dwell upon our Tomb
of such a Quality
That fighting Armies thither come
Shall reconciled be
We'll ask no ⟨etip⟩ epitaph but say
Orinda and Rosannia.

In other of her Poems there is a most delicate fancy of the Fletcher Kind—which we will con over together: So Haydon is in Town—I had a letter [9] from him yesterday—We will contrive as the Winter comes on—but that [is] neither here nor there. Have you heard from Rice? Has Martin met with the Cumberland Beggar or been wondering at the old Leech gatherer? [1] Has he a turn for fossils? that is, is he capable of sinking up to his Middle in a Morass?—I have longed to peep in and see him at supper after some tolerable fatigue. How is Hazlitt? We were reading his Table [2] last night—I know he thinks himself not estimated by ten People in the world—I wishe he knew he is—I am getting on famous with my third Book —have written 800 lines thereof, and hope to finish it next week—Bailey likes what I have done very much—Believe me, my Dear Reynolds, one of my chief layings-up is the pleasure I shall have in showing it to you; I may now say, in a few days—I have heard twice from my Brothers, they are going on very well, and send their Remembrances to you. We expected to have had notices from little Hampton this Morning—we must wait till Tuesday.[3] I am glad of their Days with the Dilks.[4] You are I know very much teased in that precious London, and want all the rest possible; so [5] shall be content with as brief a scrall—a word or two—till there comes a pat hour.—

Send us a few of your Stanzas to read in "Reynolds's cove" Give my Love and respects to your Mother and remember me kindly to all at home. Yours faithfully

John Keats

I have left the doublings for Bailey who is going to say that he will write to you to Morrow [6]

[9] No. 35.

[1] Wordsworth's "Old Cumberland Beggar" and "Resolution and Independence." Martin was a partner in the publishing and bookselling firm, Rodwell and Martin, 46 New Bond Street (see Blunden, p. 490). Born in 1791, he retired from business in 1826, became librarian at Woburn Abbey in 1836, and died in 1855.

[2] Woodhouse notes "(round Table)." Hazlitt and Hunt collaborated in *The Round Table* (1817), a two-volume collection of essays.

[3] September 23.

[4] Dilke records that Jane and Mariane Reynolds came from Littlehampton "and stayed a few days with us at my sister's [see I, 159] at Bedhampton" (HBF).

[5] Woodhouse emends to "so I."

[6] For the letter Bailey wrote on the "doublings" see *KC*, I, 6 f. Among other things he says, "I have not heard from Little Hampton since their [the two Reynolds girls'] return from Mrs Snookes. . . . There is one passage of Keats's 3^d^ Book [*Endymion*, III. 766–806] which beats all he has written. It is on *death*. He wrote it last night—Tell me if you agree with me when you hear it."

· 37 ·

TO B. R. HAYDON [1]

28 September 1817

Address: B. R. Haydon/ 41 Great Marlborough Street/ London
Postmarks: OXFORD 28 SE 28 1817; B 29 SE 29 1817

Oxford Septr 28th—

My dear Haydon,

I read your last to the young Man whose Name is Crips.[2] He seemed more than ever anxious to avail himself of your offer. I think I told you we asked him to ascertain his Means. He does not possess the Philosophers stone—nor Fortunatus' purse, nor Gyges' ring [3]—but at Bailey's suggestion, whom I assure you is a very capital fellow, we have stummed [4] up a kind of contrivance whereby he will be enabled to do himself the benifits you will lay in his Path —I have a great Idea that he will be a tolerable neat brush. 'T is perhaps the finest thing that will befal him this many a year: for he is just of an age to get grounded in bad habits from which you will pluck him. He brought a Copy of Mary Queen of Scotts. it appears to me that he has coppied the bad style of the painting as well as couloured the eyebals yellow like the original. He has also the fault that you pointed out to me in Hazlitt [5]—on the constringing and diffusing of substance. However I really believe that he will take fire at the sight of your Picture—and s⟨t⟩et about things. If he can get ready in time to return to Town with me which will be in a few days—I will bring [him] to you. You will be glad to hear that

[1] *ALS:* Formerly attached to Haydon's Journal, now at Harvard. Sealed with a Tassie's head of Shakespeare.

[2] See No. 35.

[3] Keats probably learned about Gyges, the Lydian monarch, and his ring of invisibility from Lempriere's *Classical Dictionary* rather than from Plato. Probably, too, he had read Thomas Dekker's *Old Fortunatus* or seen a stage-adaptation of it.

[4] *NED* defines as "?set going, worked up."

[5] Hazlitt's portrait of Lamb is in the National Portrait Gallery. To readers he is best known as a painter from Southey's words, December 14, 1803 (Howe, pp. 71 f.): "Hazlitt, whom you saw at Paris, has been here. . . . He has made a very fine picture of Coleridge for Sir George Beaumont, which is said to be in Titian's manner: he has also painted Wordsworth, but so dismally, though Wordsworth's face is his idea of physiognomical perfection, that one of his friends, on seeing it exclaimed, 'At the gallows—deeply affected by his deserved fate—yet determined to die like a man.' "

within these last three weeks I have written 1000 lines—which are the third Book of my Poem.[6] My Ideas with respect to it I assure you are very low—and I would write the subject thoroughly again. but I am tired of it and think the time would be better spent in writing a new Romance which I have in my eye for next summer—Rome was not built in a Day.[7] and all the good I expect from my employment this summer is the fruit of Experience which I hope to gather in my next Poem. Bailey's kindest wishes and my vow of being

Yours eternally.
John Keats—

· 38 ·

TO BENJAMIN BAILEY [1]

8 October 1817

Address: Mr B— Bailey/ Magdalen Hall./ Oxford—
Postmarks: C OC 8 1817; 7 o'Clock OC 8 1817 NT

Hamps[t]ead Octr Wednesday

My dear Bailey,

After a tolerable journey I went from Coach to Coach to as far as Hampstead where I found my Brothers—the next Morning [2] finding myself tolerably well I went to Lambs Conduit Street and delivered your Parcel—Jane and Marianne were greatly improved Marianne especially she has no unhealthy plumpness in the face—but she comes me healthy and angular to the Chin—I did not see John I was extrem{e}ly sorry to hear that poor Rice after having had capital Health During his tour, was very ill. I dare say you have heard from him. From No 19 [3] I went to Hunt's and Haydon's who live now neighbours.[4] Shelley was there—I know nothing about

[6] Actually 1033 lines. [7] See I, 174.

[1] *ALS:* Harvard. Bailey endorsed it, "I think this letter will be a groundwork for a defence of poor Keats's having had *Hunt for a Patron.*—which is so shamelessly insisted on by the writers of Blackwds. B B—" John Taylor, to whom he sent this letter and others on May 8, 1821 (*KC*, I, 243), added from *Hamlet*, I.iii.5 f., 9, "As for Hamlet & the trifling of his favour Hold it a Fashion & a toy in blood The perfume &c." There is also a transcript of this letter in Woodhouse's letter-book, pp. 76–79.

[2] Apparently October 6. [3] See the address of No. 22.

[4] Haydon had moved (see the seventh sentence below) to 22 Lisson Grove North, now said to be 1 Rossmore Road. On September 27, 1817, he wrote in his unpublished

any thing in this part of the world—every Body seems at Logger-heads. There's Hunt infatuated—theres Haydon's Picture in statu quo. There's Hunt walks up and down his painting room criticising every head most unmercifully—There's Horace Smith [5] tired of Hunt. The web of our Life is of mingled Yarn" [6] Haydon having removed entirely from Marlborough street Crips must direct his Letter to Lisson Grove North Paddington. Yesterday Morning while I was at Brown's in came Reynolds—he was pretty bobbish we had a pleasant day—but he would walk home at night that cursed cold distance. Mrs Bentley's children [7] are making a horrid row—whereby I regret I cannot be transported to your Room to write to you. I am quite disgusted with literary Men and will never know another except Wordsworth—no not even Byron—Here is an instance of the friendships of such—Haydon and Hunt have known each other many years—now they live pour ainsi dire jealous Neigh-bours. Haydon says to me Keats dont show your Lines to Hunt on any account or he will have done half for you—so it appears Hunt wishes it to be thought. When he met Reynolds in the Theatre John told him that I was getting on to the completion of 4000 Lines. Ah! says Hunt, had it not been for me they would have been 7000! If he will say this to Reynolds what would he to other People? Haydon received a Letter a little while back on this subject from some Lady—which contains a caution to me through him on this subject—Now is not all this a most paultry thing to think about? You may see the whole of the case by the following extract from a Letter I wrote to George in the spring [8] "As to what you say about my being a Poet, "I can retu[r]n no answer but by saying that the high Idea I have "of poetical fame makes me think I see it towering to high above "me. At any rate I have no ⟨wi⟩ right to talk until Endymion is "finished—it will be a test, a trial of my Powers of Imagination and "chiefly of my invention which is a rare thing indeed—by which I

Journal (so Willard B. Pope tells me), "I left my old Lodgings this day. . . . After a short time I came into my new habitation."

[5] See I, 192 f.

[6] Colvin, p. 33 n., compares *All's Well That Ends Well*, IV.iii.83 f. (with "of a mingled").

[7] The Keats brothers were now lodging in the house of Benjamin Bentley, a postman, in Well Walk. See the Index for further references to him and his family.

[8] This letter, which George and Tom had preserved, is now unknown. Perhaps it contained the statement, "I have forgotten all surgery," quoted in Brown's *Life of John Keats* (*KC*, II, 56).

"must make 4000 Lines of one bare circumstance and fill them with "Poetry; and when I consider that this is a great task, and that "when done it will take me but a dozen paces towards the Temple "of Fame—it makes me say—God forbid that I should be without "such a task! I have heard Hunt say and may[9] be asked—why "endeavour after a long Poem? To which I should answer—Do not "the Lovers of Poetry like to have a little Region to wander in where "they may pick and choose, and in which the images are so numer-"ous that many are forgotten and found new in a second Reading: "which may be food for a Week's stroll in the Summer? Do not they "like this better than what they can read through before Mrs Wil-"liams comes down stairs? a Morning work at most. Besides a long "Poem is a test of Invention which I take to be the Polar Star of "Poetry, as Fancy is the Sails, and Imagination the Rudder.[1] Did "our great Poets ever write short Pieces? I mean in the shape of "Tales—This same invention seems i{n}deed of late Years to have "been forgotten as a Poetical excellence{.} But enough [2] of this, I "put on no Laurels till I shall have finished Endymion, and I hope "Apollo is {not} angered at my having made a Mockery at him at "Hunt's" [3] You see Bailey how independant my writing has been—Hunts dissuasion was of no avail—I refused to visit Shelley, that I might have my own unfetterd scope—and after all I shall have the Reputation of Hunt's elevé—His corrections and amputations will by the knowing ones be trased in the Poem—This is to be sure the vexation of a day—nor would I say so many Words about it to any but those whom I know to have my wellfare and Reputation at Heart—Haydon promised to give directions for those Casts [4] and you may expect to see them soon—with as many Letters You will soon hear the dinning of Bells—never mind you and Gleg [5] will defy the foul fiend [6]—But do not sacrifice your heal[t]h to Books do take it kindly and not so voraciously. I am certain if you are your own Physician your stomach will resume its proper strength and then

[9] Woodhouse has "(I) may."

[1] But at II, 154, he is steering "by the rudder of information."

[2] *Written* enought.

[3] See the "Ode to Apollo" ("God of the golden bow") and the two "Laurel Crown" sonnets (Garrod, pp. 430–432, 527 f.). [4] See I, 121.

[5] George Robert Gleig (1796–1888), later Bailey's brother-in-law, student at Magdalen Hall, Oxford, novelist, historian, inspector-general of military schools (1846–1857), and chaplain-general of the forces (1844–1875).

[6] Compare *King Lear*, III.iv.101.

what great Benefits will follow. My Sister wrote a Letter to me which I think must be at $\frac{e}{y}$ post office Ax Will [7] to see. My Brothers kindest remembrances to you [8]—we are going to dine at Brown's where I have some hopes of meeting Reynolds. The little Mercury I have taken has corrected the Poison and improved my Health [9]—though I feel from my employment that I shall never be again secure in Robustness—would that you were as well as

your sincere friend & brother

John Keats

The Dilks are expected to day—

· 39 ·

TO BENJAMIN BAILEY [1]

28–30 October 1817

Address: Mr B. Bailey/ Magdal{e}n Hall/ O{xfor}d.
Postmark: C NO 1 817

My dear Bailey,

So you have got a Curacy! good—but I suppose you will be obliged to stop among your Oxford favorites during term-time—never mind. When do you p[r]each your first sermon tell me—for I shall propose to the two R s [2] to hear it so dont look into any of the old corner oaken pews for fear of being put out by us—Poor

[7] Presumably the college porter.

[8] Bailey did not know Tom, of whose character he professed to have heard only bad things. See *KC*, I, 33, II, 279.

[9] See I, 369.

[1] *ALS:* Harvard. The first two paragraphs, with the lines from *Endymion*, were written on October 28. In them Keats says that he has been confined at Hampstead for a fortnight, or from about October 10 to October 24, and that Saturday, October 25, "was my first day in town." He entertained Rice on October 27, and thought of seeing the Reynoldses "tomorrow," October 29, as he did (No. 40). Returning that night, he found a second letter from Bailey, and (I, 176) "finished my Letter [No. 39] to him immediately." The long postscript, however, was added on October 30 ("yesterday I called at Lambs —St"), and the letter was not postmarked until November 1. (Colvin, p. 36, guessed the date to be "about November 1," MBF as "October.") Bailey enclosed No. 39 in his letter of October 15, 16, 1848, to Milnes (*KC*, II, 262).

[2] Presumably Rice and Reynolds. Bailey's first curacy was at Carlisle (II, 66).

Johnny Martin [3] cant be there He is ill—I suspect—but that's neither here nor there—all I can say I wish him as well through it as I am like to be. For this fortnight I have been confined at Hampstead—Saturday evening was my first day in town—when I went to Rices as we intend to do every Saturday till we know not when—Rice had some business at Highgate yesterday—so he came over to me and I detained him for the first time of I hope 24860 times. We hit upon an old Gent.[4] we had known some few years ago and had a veray pleausante daye, In this World there is no quiet nothing but teasing and snubbing and vexation—my Brother Tom look'd very unwell yesterday and I am for shipping him off to Lisbon. perpaps I ship there with him. I have not seen Mrs Reynolds since I left you—wherefore my conscience smites me—I think of seeing her tomorrow have you any Message? I hope Gleg [5] came soon after I left. I dont suppose I've w[r]itten as many Lines [6] as you have read Volumes or at least Chapters since I saw you. However, I am in a fair way now to come to a conclusion in at least three Weeks when I assure you I shall be glad to dismount for a Month or two—although I'll keep as tight a reign as possible till then nor suffer myself to sleep. I will copy for you the opening of the 4 Book [7] —in which you will see from the Manner I had not an opportunity of mentioning any Poets, for fear of spoiling the effect of the passage by particularising them!

Muse of my Native Land. Loftiest Muse!
O First born of the Mountains, by the hues
Of Heaven on the spiritual air begot—
Long didst thou sit alone in northern grot
While yet our England was a wolfish den;
Before our forests heard the talk of Men;
Before the first of Druid⟨'⟩s was a child.—
Long didst thou sit amid our regions wild
Wrapt in a deep, prophetic Solitude.
There came a hebrew voice of solemn Mood
Yet wast thou patient: then sang forth the Nine
Apollo's Garland; yet didst thou divine

[3] See I, 166. [4] That is, an old poet.
[5] For Gleig see I, 170 n. [6] Of *Endymion.*
[7] The printed poem (1818) has several variants of diction and punctuation. See Garrod, p. 158, for details.

Such homebred Glory, that they cry'd in vain
"Come hither Sister of the Island." Plain
Spake fair Ausonia, and once more she spake
A higher Summons—still didst thou betake
darling
Thee to thy⟨self and to thy⟩ hopes. O thou has won
A full accomplishment—the thing is done
Which undone these our latter days had risen
On barren Souls. O Muse thou knowst what prison
Of flesh and bone curbs and confines and frets
Our Spirits Wings: despondency besets
Our Pillows and the fresh tomorrow morn
Seems to give {forth} its light in very scorn
Of our dull uni{nspired} snail paced lives.
Long have I said "how happy he who shrive{s}
To thee"—but then I thought on Poets gone
And could not pray—nor can I now—so on
I move to the end in Humbleness of Heart..—

Thus far had I written when I received your last which made me at the sight of the direction caper for despair—but for one thing I am glad that I have been neglectful—and that is, therefrom I have received a proof of your utmost kindness which at this present I feel very much—and I wish I had a heart always open to such sensations—but there is no altering a Man's nature and mine must be radically wrong for it will lie dormant a whole Month—This leads me to suppose that there are no Men thouroughly wicked—so as never to be self spiritualized into a kind of sublime Misery—but alas! 't is but for an Hour—he is the only Man "who has kept watch on Man's Mortality" [8] who has philantrophy enough to overcome the disposition [to] an indolent enjoyment of intellect—who is brave enough to volunteer for uncomfortable hours.x [9] You remember in Hazlit's essay on commonplace people—He says they read the Edinburgh and Quarterly and think as they do" [1] Now with respect to Wordsworth's Gipseys I think he is right and yet I think Hazlitt is right [2]

[8] Wordsworth, "Ode: Intimations of Immortality," line 202 (with "That hath kept watch o'er," etc.).

[9] The *x* calls attention to the second postscript.

[1] "On Common-place Critics," *The Round Table* (1817), II, 204 ("He reads the *Edinburgh* and *Quarterly Reviews*, and thinks as they do").

[2] He probably intended *righter:* see the phraseology at I, 319, 324, II, 69.

and yet I think Wordsworth is rightest. Wordsworth had not been idle he had not been without his task—nor had they Gipseys—they in the visible world had been as picturesque an object as he in the invisible. The Smoke of their fire—their attidudes—their Voices were all in harmony with the Evenings—It is a bold thing to say and I would not say it in print—but it seems to me that if Wordsworth had though[t] a little deeper at that Moment he would not have written the Poem at all—I should judge it to ⟨has⟩ have been written in one of the most comfortable Moods of his Life—it is a kind of sketchy intellectual Landscape—not a search after Truth—nor is it fair to attack him on such a subject—for it is with the Critic as with the poet had Hazlitt thought a little deeper and been in a good temper he would never have spied an imaginary fault there.[3] The Sunday before last [4] I asked Haydon to dine with me. when I thought of settling all Matters with him in regard to Crips and let you know about it—now although I engaged him a Fortnight before—he sent illness as an excuse—he never will come—I have not been well enough to stand the chance of a Wet night, and so have not seen him nor been able to expurgatorize those Masks [5] for you—but I will not spaek: your speakers are never dooers—then Reynolds—every time I see him and mention you he puts his hand to his head and looks like a son of Niobe's—but he'll write soon. Rome you know was not built in a day [6]—I shall be able, by a little perseverence to read your Letters off hand. [7] I am affraid your health will suffer from over study before your examination—I think you might regulate the thing according to your own Pleasure—and I would too They [8] were talking of your being up at Christmas—will it be before you have passed? There is nothing my dear Bailey I should rejoice at more that [9] to

[3] Keats is discussing Hazlitt's note to "On Manner," *The Round Table*, I, 120–122, which runs in part: "Mr Wordsworth, who has written a sonnet to the King ["November 1813"] on the good that he has done in the last fifty years, has made an attack [in "Gipsies," 1807] on a set of gipsies for having done nothing in four and twenty hours. . . . And why should they, if they were comfortable where they were? . . . What had he himself been doing in these four and twenty hours? Had he been admiring a flower, or writing a sonnet? . . . [The gipsies are] a better answer to the cotton manufactories than Mr W. has given in the '*Excursion*'. . . . We should be sorry to part with Mr Wordsworth's poetry, because it amuses and interests us: we should be still sorrier to part with the tents of our old friends, the Bohemian philosophers, because they amuse and interest us more."

[4] Presumably on October 12 for October 26.

[5] That is, to get copies of Keats's life mask (I, 121, 170) from Haydon.

[6] See I, 168.

[7] On Bailey's villainous handwriting see I, 188, II, 272.

[8] The Reynoldses (on October 29).

[9] *For* than.

see you comfortable with a little Pæòna [1] Wife—an affectionate Wife I have a sort of confidence would do you a great happiness May that be one of the many blessings I wish you—Let me be but [t]he 1/10 of one to you and I shall think it great—My Brother Georges kindest wishes to you. My dear Bailey I am

your affectionate friend.
John Keats

I should not like to be Pages in your way when in a tolerable hungry mood—you have no Mercy—your teeth are the Rock tarpeian [2] down which you capsise Epic Poems like Mad—I would not for 40 shillings [3] be Coleridge's Lays [4] in your way. I hope you will soon get through this abominable writing in in the schools—and be able to keep the terms with more comfort in the hope of retu[r]ning to a comfortable and quiet home out of the way of all Hopkinses and black beetles [5]—When you are settled I will come and take a peep at your Church—your house—try whether I shall have grow[n] two lusty for my chair—by the fire side—and take a peep at my cardials Bower —A Question is the best beacon towards a little Speculation. You ask me after my health and spirits—This Question ratifies in my Mind what I have said above—Health and Spirits can only belong unalloyed to the selfish Man—the Man who thinks much of his fellows can never be in Spirits—when I am not suffering for vicious beastliness I am the greater part of the [6] week in spirits.

xYou must forgive although I have only written 300 Lines—they would have been five but I have been obliged to go to town. yesterday I called at Lambs—St [7] Jane look'd very flush when I first went in but was much better before I left.

[1] "Peona, his sweet sister," *Endymion*, I.408 ff.

[2] *Coriolanus*, III.i.213, "Bear him to the Rock Tarpeian." Bailey's chief enthusiasms were Milton and Wordsworth.

[3] Compare *Twelfth Night*, II.iii.19, and *The Merry Wives of Windsor*, I.i.205.

[4] Presumably his *Lay Sermons*.

[5] Richard Van Fossen notes that Henry John Hopkins matriculated at Magdalen Hall on March 17, 1815, proceeded A.B. in 1819, and died in 1854 (Joseph Foster, *Alumni Oxonienses* [1888], II, 688). He suggests that "black beetles" may have been a slang phrase for the Oxford beadles. Partridge defines "black beetles" as "the lower classes."

[6] *Written* he.

[7] That is, 19 Lamb's Conduit Street (see the addresses of Nos. 18 and 40).

· 40 ·

TO JANE REYNOLDS [1]

31 October 1817

Address: Miss Jane Reynolds/ 19 Lamb's Conduit Street
Postmark: 7 o'Clock OC 31 1817 N^T

My dear Jane,

When I got home the other night there was a letter from Bailey —and so very kind a one after all my indolence that I felt a very repentance—and finished my Letter [2] to him immediately. I hope you are getting well quite fast I send you a few lines from my fourth Book [3] with the desire of helping away for you five Minutes of the day—

O Sorrow
Why dost borrow
The natural hue of health from vermil Lips?
To give maiden blushes
To the white rose bushes?
Or ist thy dewy hand the daisy tips?

—

O Sorrow
Why dost borrow
The lutrous [4] passion from a Lover's eye?
To give the glow worm light?
Or on a moonless night
To tinge ⟨the⟩ on syren shores the salt sea Spry?

O Sorrow
Why dost borr{ow}
The mellow ditties from a mourning tongue?
To give 't at Evening pale
Unto the Nightingale
That thou may'st listen the cold dews *among?*

[1] *ALS:* Yale (formerly owned by F. H. Day and then by Mitchell Kennerley, New York, and first printed by Lowell, I, 421–423).

[2] That preceding.

[3] *Endymion,* IV.146–181, which varies somewhat from the text in No. 41 and from the printed text of 1818 (see Garrod, pp. 163 f.).

[4] lustrous *1818* (see I, 181).

—

O Sorrow
Why dost borrow
Hearts lightness from the Merriment of May?
A Lover would not tread
A Cowslip on the head
Though he should dance from eve till *peep of day.*
Nor any drooping flower
Held sacred for thy bower
Wherever he may sport himself and play.

—

To Sorrow
I bad good morrow
And thought to leave her far away behind
But cheerly cheerly
She loves me dearly—
so
She is to me ⟨too⟩ constant and so kind
I would deceive her
And so leave her
But Ah! she is to constant and too kind!

Give our [5] Love to Marianne—

Your's sincerely.
John Keats

[5] The three Keats brothers'.

· 41 ·

TO BENJAMIN BAILEY [1]

3 November 1817 [2]

Address: Mr B. Bailey/ Magdalen Hall/ Oxford
Postmarks: TwoPyPost Unpaid LOMBARD St; C NO 5 817; 8 o'Clock NO 5 1817 M^n^

Monday—Hampstead

My dear Bailey,

Before I received your Letter I had heard of your disappointment—an unlook'd for piece of villainy.[3] I am glad to hear there was an hindrance to your speaking your Mind to the Bishop: for all may go straight yet—as to being ordained—but the disgust consequent cannot pass away in a hurry—it must be shocking to find in a sacred Profession such barefaced oppression and impertinence —The Stations and Grandeurs of the World have taken it into their heads that they cannot commit themselves towards and inferior in rank—but is not the impertinence from one above to one below more wretchedly mean than from the low to the high? There is something so nauseous in self-willed yawning impudence in the shape of conscience—it sinks the Bishop of Lincoln [4] into a smashed frog putrifying: that a rebel against common decency should escape the Pillory! That a mitre should cover a Man guilty of the most coxcombical, tyranical and indolent impertinence! I repeat this word

[1] *ALS:* Harvard. Sending part of the letters he had received from Keats to Taylor on May 8, 1821 (*KC*, I, 243 f.), Bailey observed, "I have made occasional observations on the outsides which may serve as memoranda." No. 41, which he retained and later inserted in his Ceylon scrapbook (see Rollins, *K–SJ*, VI [1957], 18), he endorsed "Respecting Hunt's Conduct to Keats—" The letter from "I will speak of something else" through "I dont relish his abuse" is in Woodhouse's letter-book, pp. 79 f., copied by his clerk, corrected by himself, and headed, "Outside sheet of a letter to B.B. . . . " The original has a Tassie's Shakespeare-head seal.

[2] If Keats actually wrote the letter on Monday, November 3, he posted it two days later. The section beginning "Yesterday Rice" may well have been a November 4 continuation of the letter.

[3] Bailey's curacy is mentioned at II, 66. Hewlett, p. 115, explains: "There was some difficulty about his ordination in time to take up the curacy. The blame for the delay was apparently put upon the Bishop of Lincoln." Nos. 43, 55, 67, 83, 86 indicate that Bailey remained at Oxford till the middle of June, 1818. See the changed addresses of Nos. 99 and 181. He was not ordained until early in August, 1818 (*KC*, I, 28, 32).

[4] (Sir) George Pretyman Tomline (1750–1827).

for the offence appears to me most especially *impertinent*—and a very serious return would be the Rod—Yet doth he sit in his Palace. Such is this World—and we live—you have surely in [5] a continual struggle against the suffocation of accidents—we must bear (and my Spleen is mad at the thought thereof) the Proud Mans Contumely [6]—O for a recourse somewhat human independant of the great Consolations of Religion and undepraved Sensations. of the Beautiful. the poetical in all things—O for a Remedy against such wrongs within the pale of the World! Should not those things be pure enjoymen{t} should they stand the chance of being contaminated by being called in as antagonists to Bishops? Would not earthly thing do? By Heavens my dear Bailey, I know you have a spice of what I mean—you can set me and have set it in all the rubs [7] that may befal me you have I know a sort of Pride which would kick the Devil on the Jaw Bone and make him drunk with the kick—There is nothing so balmy to a soul imbittered as yours must be, as Pride—When we look at the Heavens we cannot be proud—but shall stocks and stones [8] be impertinent and say it does not become us to kick them? At this Moment I take your hand let us walk up ⟨your⟩ yon Mountain of common sense now if our Pride be vainglorious such a support woud fail—yet you feel firm footing —now look beneath at that parcel of knaves and fools. Many a Mitre is moving among them. I cannot express how I despise the Man who would wrong or be impertinent to you—The thought that we are mortal makes us groan I will speak of something else or my Spleen will get higher and higher—and I am not a bearer of the two egded Sword.[9] I hope you will recieve an answer from Haydon soon—if not Pride! Pride! Pride! I have received no more subscription [1]—but shall soon have a full health Liberty and leisure to give a good part of my time to him—I will certainly be in time for him—We have promised him one year let that have elapsed and then do as we think proper. If I did not know how impossible it is, I should say 'do not at this time of disappointments disturb yourself about others'—There has been a flaming attack upon Hunt in the Endin-

[5] *For* surely been in. [6] *Hamlet*, III.i.71.

[7] Compare the same, III.i.65.

[8] Compare Milton's sonnet on the Piedmont Massacre, line 4, "worship't Stocks and Stones."

[9] R. H. Knox cites Psalm cxlix.6.

[1] To pay for Cripps's studying under Haydon (I, 161).

burgh Magazine [2]—I never read any thing so virulent—accusing him of the greatest Crimes—dep[r]eciating his Wife his Poetry—his Habits—his company, his Conversation—These Philipics are to come out in Numbers—calld 'the Cockney School of Poetry' There has been but one Number published—that on Hunt to which they have prefixed a Motto from one Cornelius Webb Poetaster—who unfortunately was of our Party occasionally at Hampstead and took it into his head to write the following—something about—"we'll talk on Wordsworth Byron—a theme we never tire on and so forth till he comes to Hunt and Keats. In the Motto they have put Hunt and Keats in large Letters [3]—I have no doubt that the second Number was intended for me: but have hopes of its non appearance from the following advertisement in last Sunday's Examiner.[4] "To Z. The writer of the Article signed Z in Blackwood's Ed[i]nburgh magazine for October 1817 is invited to send his address to the printer of the Examiner, in order that Justice may be executed of the proper person" I dont mind the thing much—but if he should go to such lenghts with me as he has done with Hunt I mu[s]t infalibly call him to an account—if he be a human being and appears in Squares and Theatres where we might possibly meet—I dont relish his abuse

[2] "On the Cockney School of Poetry. No I," *Blackwood's Edinburgh Magazine*, October, 1817 (II, 38–41). Between this sentence and that preceding there is a line across the whole page.

[3] Cornelius Francis Webb, or Webbe (*c.* 1790–*c.* 1848), published many verses in the *New Monthly Magazine* (1814–1817) and the *London Magazine* (1820), as well as several volumes of poems, tales, and essays. His books were praised by many critical journals (among them the *Theatrical Inquisitor*, XVI [1820], 207–209, to which he contributed); C. C. Clarke opens various chapters of *Adam, The Gardener* (1834), pp. 85, 100, 122, 145, 160, 228, by quoting from his *Lyric Leaves* (1832); and he himself often quotes and praises Keats. The fullest account of his work is that by G. L. Marsh, *Philological Quarterly*, XXI (1942), 323–333. *Blackwood's* headed the first (October, 1817 [II, 38–41]) and the second (November, 1817 [II, 194–201]), but not the third (July, 1818 [III, 453–456]), article on the Cockney School with a quotation from a lost poem of Webb's: "Our talk shall be (a theme we never tire on)/ Of Chaucer, Spenser, Shakespeare, Milton, Byron,/ (Our England's Dante)—Wordsworth—Hunt, and Keats,/ The Muses' son of promise; and of what feats/ He yet may do." The phrase, "The Muses' son of promise," was applied to Keats in ridicule by very many later writers. As one illustration Charles H. Terrot, in *Common Sense: A Poem* (Edinburgh, 1819), remarks in a note: "Mr. John Keates, the muse's child of promise, is a rising poet of the Cockney School; who, if he had but an ear for rhyme, a little knowledge of grammar, and sufficient intellect to distinguish sense from nonsense, might perhaps do very well." *Blackwood's* continued to insult his memory long after his death.

[4] November 2, p. 693. Two longer "advertisements" to "Z." appeared in the *Examiner*, November 16, p. 729, and December 14, p. 788. They had no effect. Z. replied to Hunt in *Blackwood's*, January, 1818 (II, 414–417), refusing to give his name and indulging in further abuse.

Yesterday Rice and I were at Reynolds—John was to be articled tom[or]row I suppose by this time it is done.[5] Jane was much better—At one time or other I will do you a Pleasure and the Poets a little Justice—but it ought to be in a Poem of greater moment than Endymion—I will do it some day—I have seen two Letters of a little Story [6] Reynolds is writing— I wish he would keep at it—Here is the song [7] I enclosed to Jane if you can make it out in this cross wise writing.

O Sorrow
Why dost borrow
The natural hue of health from vermil Lips?
To give maiden blushes
To the white Rose bushes
Or ist thy dewy hand the daisy tips?

O Sorrow
Why dost borrow
The Lustrous Passion from an orbed eye?
To give the glow worm Light?
Or on a moonless night
To tinge on syren shores the salt sea spry?

O Sorrow
Why dost borrow
The ⟨mo⟩ tender ditties from a mourning tongue?
To give at Evening pale
Unto the Nightingal
That thou mayest listen the cold dews among?

[5] HBF quotes Dilke's note in his personal copy of Milnes's biography: "Rice suggested that he [Reynolds] should become a lawyer, and his relation, Mr. Fladgate,—himself a literary man in early life and editor of the 'Sun' newspaper consented to receive him as an Articled Pupil, and dear generous noble James Rice—the best, and in his quaint way one of the wittiest and wisest men I ever knew—paid the fee or stamp or whatever it is called—about £110 I believe—and promised if he ever succeeded to his father's business to take him as partner. He not only kept his word, but in a few years gave up the business to him. Reynolds unhappily threw away this certain fortune. The Frank Fladgate here mentioned was Mr. Fladgate's eldest son, then Articled to his father." Francis Fladgate, Sr., died on November 5, 1821, aged 48 (*Examiner*, November 11, p. 720).

[6] *The Fancy.*

[7] It has several variants from the text in No. 40, as well as from *Endymion.*

O Sorrow
Why dost borrow
Heart's lightness from the Merriment of May?
A Lover would not tread
A Cowslip on the head
Though he should dance from eve till peep of day;
Nor any drooping flower
Held sacred to thy bower
Wherever he may sport himself and play.

To Sorrow
I bade {good morrow,}
And thought to leave her far away behind
But cheerly, cheerly,
She loves me dearly—
She is to me so constant, and so kind—
I would deceive her
And so leave her
But ah! she is too constant and too kind.

O that I had Orpheus lute—and was able to cha[r]m away all your Griefs and Cares—but all my power is a Mite—amid all you troubles I shall ever be—

your sincere and affectionate friend
John Keats

My brothers remembrances to you
Give my respects to Gleig and Whitehead [8]

[8] For Gleig see I, 170 n. Whitehead (see also I, 212, 244) was the Reverend Joseph Charles Frederick Whitehead, of Eccleston, Lancashire. He entered Magdalen Hall, Oxford, December 14, 1812, aged 28, and died (*GM*, XCV, i [1825], 649) on May 21, 1825, at Newton Heath, near Manchester.

· 42 ·

TO THE DILKES [1]

5 or 12 (?) November 1817

My dear Dilke

Mrs Dilke or Mr Wm Dilke whoever of you shall receive this present have the kindness to send pr Bearer—"*Sybilline Leaves*" [2] and you petitioner shall ever pray as in duty bound.
Given under my hand this Wendnesday Morning of Novr 1817.[3]

John Keats

Vivant Rex et Regina—amen—

· 43 ·

TO BENJAMIN BAILEY [1]

22 November 1817

Address: Mr B. Bailey/ Magdalen Hall/ Oxford—
Postmarks: LEATHERHEAD; O 22 NO 22 1817

My dear Bailey,

I will get over the first part of this (*un*said) [2] Letter as soon as possible for it relates to the affair of poor Crips—To a Man of your nature, such a Letter as Haydon's must have been extremely cutting

[1] *ALS:* Keats Museum (first printed in *Papers,* I, 2). There is a facsimile in Williamson, plate XII. This informal note was addressed to C. W. Dilke, his wife, and his brother William. The last, says Colvin, p. 26 n., "served in the Commissariat department in the Peninsula, America, and Paris," and "died in 1885 at the age of 90."

[2] Coleridge's book was published in August, 1817.

[3] Wednesdays in November came on November 5, 12, 19, 26. On the 25th Keats was at Burford Bridge, and probably the 5th or the 12th was the day on which he wrote.

[1] *ALS:* Harvard. Nos. 43 and 44 have hitherto been printed in reverse order, but Lowell, I, 446 f., is correct in calling No. 43 earlier. No. 43 was written in the late morning or early afternoon of November 22 ("I am just arrived at Dorking. . . . Direct Burford Bridge near dorking"), and was postmarked at Leatherhead, the post town some three miles distant. Keats stayed in the Fox and Hounds (today the Burford Bridge Hotel) at the foot of Box Hill. No. 44 was written there late at night on the 22nd after he "went up Box Hill this Evening . . . came down—and wrote some lines" of *Endymion.* The letter is endorsed by Bailey: "Extracts from this letter might be made with great credit to the ⟨poor⟩ unfortunate writer's memory. BB." There is also a transcript by a clerk in Woodhouse's letter-book, pp. 80–83, with corrections by Woodhouse.

[2] Colvin, p. 40 n., suggested the reading "unpaid," which HBF, 1895, adopted. HBF, 1901, rightly explained the word as a pun on the legal use of "said": " 'This said letter' . . . would be Haydon's to Bailey: 'this *un*said letter' " the present one.

—What occasions the greater part of the World's Quarrels? simply this, two Minds meet and do not understand each other time enough to p[r]aevent any shock or surprise at the conduct of either party—As soon as I had known Haydon three days I had got enough of his character not to have been surp[r]ised at such a Letter as he has hurt you with. Nor when I knew it was it a principle with me to drop his acquaintance although with you it would have been an imperious feeling. I wish you knew all that I think about Genius and the Heart—and yet I think you are thoroughly acquainted with my innermost breast in that respect or you could not have known me even thus long and still hold me worthy to be your dear friend. In passing however I must say of one thing that has pressed upon me lately and encreased my Humility and capability of submission and that is this truth—Men of Genius are great as certain ethereal Chemicals operating on the Mass of neutral intellect—by [3] they have not any individuality, any determined Character. I would call the top and head of those who have a proper self Men of Power—

But I am running my head into a Subject [4] which I am certain I could not do justice to under five years s[t]udy and 3 vols octavo—and moreover long to be talking about the Imagination—so my dear Bailey do not think of this unpleasant affair if possible—do not—I defy any ha[r]m to come of it—I defy—I'll shall write to Crips this Week and reque[s]t him to tell me all his goings on from time to time by Letter whererever I may be—it will all go on well—so dont because you have suddenly discover'd a Coldness in Haydon suffer yourself to be teased. Do not my dear fellow. O I wish I was as certain of the end of all your troubles as that of your momentary start about the authenticity of the Imagination. I am certain of nothing but of the holiness of the Heart's affections and the truth of Imagination—What the imagination seizes as Beauty must be truth [5] —whether it existed before or not—for I have the same Idea of all our Passions as of Love they are all in their sublime, creative of essential Beauty—In a Word, you may know my favorite Speculation

[3] *For* but. [4] The subject is discussed again in No. 118 to Woodhouse.

[5] All readers will be reminded of the ending of the "Ode on a Grecian Urn." According to W. J. Bate, *The Stylistic Development of Keats* (New York, 1945), p. 45 n., Truth usually means to Keats "the joint 'identity,' character, reality, and beauty of a phenomenon," and because of "its identity with beauty . . . the Imagination alone can conceive it."

by my first Book and the little song I sent in my last—which is a representation from the fancy of the probable mode of operating in these Matters [6]—The Imagination may be compared to Adam's dream [7]—he awoke and found it truth. I am the more zealous in this affair, because I have never yet been able to perceive how any thing can be known for truth by consequitive [8] reasoning—and yet it must be—Can it be that even the greatest Philosopher ever ⟨when⟩ arrived at his goal without putting aside numerous objections—However it may be, O for a Life of Sensations rather than of Thoughts! [9] It is 'a Vision in the form of Youth' a Shadow of reality to come—and this consideration has further conv[i]nced me for it has come as auxiliary to another favorite Speculation of mine, that we shall enjoy ourselves here after by having what we called happiness on Earth repeated in a finer tone and so repeated—And yet such a fate can only befall those who delight in sensation rather than hunger as you do after Truth—Adam's dream will do here and seems to be a conviction that Imagination and its empyreal reflection is the same as human Life and its spiritual repetition. But as I was saying—the simple [1] imaginative Mind may have its rewards in the repeti[ti]on of its own silent Working coming continually on the spirit with a fine suddenness—to compare great things with small [2]—have you never by being surprised with an old Melody—in a delicious place—by a delicious voice, fe[l]t over again your very speculations and surmises at the time it first operated on your soul—do you not remember forming to youself the singer's face more beautiful that [3] it was possible and yet with the elevation of the Moment you did not think so—even then you were mounted on the Wings of Imagination so high—that the Prototype must be here after—that delicious face you will see—What a time! I am continually

[6] "O Sorrow" (I, 181). [7] In *Paradise Lost*, VIII.452–490 (Colvin, p. 42 n.).

[8] Woodhouse has "*so*."

[9] Garrod, *Keats* (Oxford, 1926), pp. 32 f., explains that Keats was thinking of Wordsworth and Coleridge: "O for the pure gospel of the *Lyrical Ballads!*" W. W. Beyer, *Journal of English and Germanic Philology*, LI (1952), 337 n., says, "Here Keats uses 'Sensations' in the sense of 'intuitive perceptions through the senses'," and in his *Keats and the Daemon King* (New York, 1947), pp. 124 f., 306–308, he elaborately discusses the letter. Equally elaborate is the analysis in N. F. Ford's *The Prefigurative Imagination of John Keats* (Stanford University Press, 1951), pp. 20–38.

[1] The word looks like "semple."

[2] *Paradise Lost*, II.921 f., "to compare/ Great things with small." See also the same, X.306, and *Paradise Regained*, IV.563 f.

[3] *For* than.

running away from the subject—sure this cannot be exactly the case with a complex Mind—one that is imaginative and at the same time careful of its fruits—who would exist partly on sensation partly on thought—to whom it is necessary that years should bring the philosophic Mind [4]—such an one I consider your's and therefore it is
drink
necessary to your eternal Happiness that you not only ⟨have⟩ this old Wine of Heaven which I shall call the redigestion of our most ethereal Musings on Earth; but also increase in knowledge and know all things. I am glad to hear you are in a fair Way for Easter —you will soon get through your unpleasant reading and then!— but the world is full of troubles and I have not much reason to think myself pesterd with many—I think Jane or Marianne has a better opinion of me than I deserve—for really and truly I do not think my Brothers illness connected with mine—you know more of the real Cause than they do—nor have I any chance of being rack'd as you have been [5]—you perhaps at one time thought there was such a thing as Worldly Happiness to be arrived at, at certain periods of time marked out—you have of necessity from your disposition been thus led away—I scarcely remember counting upon any Happiness —I look not for it if it be not in the present hour—nothing startles me beyond the Moment. The setting sun will always set me to rights —or if a Sparrow come before my Window I take part in its existince and pick about the Gravel. The first thing that strikes me on hea[r]ing a Misfortune having befalled another is this. 'Well it cannot be helped. he will have the pleasure of trying the resources of his spirit, and I beg now my dear Bailey that hereafter should you observe any thing cold in me not to but [6] it to the account of heartlessness but abstraction—for I assure you I sometimes feel not the influence of a Passion or Affection during a whole week—and so long this sometimes continues I begin to suspect myself and the genuineness of my feelings at other times—thinking them a few barren Tragedy-tears—My Brother Tom is much improved—he is

[4] Compare Wordsworth, "Ode: Intimations of Immortality," line 190.

[5] Lowell, I, 513, explains that the Reynolds girls feared lest "Keats's recent ill-health pointed to consumption, and considered that he was taking it bravely. Bailey's being racked refers to the non-success of one of his love affairs. Keats thinks himself safe from ever being in Bailey's position, and he does not believe himself touched by tuberculosis. What it all seems to point to is that Keats feared he might have contracted syphilis"—an idea that she (with other biographers) proceeds to refute.

[6] *For* put.

going to Devonshire—whither I shall follow him—at present I am just arrived at Dorking to change the Scene—change the Air and give me a spur to wind up my Poem, of which there are wanting 500 Lines.[7] I should have been here a day sooner but the Reynoldses persuaded me to spop [8] in Town to meet your friend Christie [9]—There were Rice and Martin—we talked about Ghosts—I will have some talk with Taylor and let you know—when please God I come down a[t] Christmas—I will find that Examiner if possible. My best regards to Gleig—My Brothers to you and M[rs] Bentley [10]

Your affectionate friend
John Keats—

I want to say much more to you—a few hints will set me going
Direct Burford Bridge near dorking

· 44 ·

TO J. H. REYNOLDS [1]

22 November 1817

Saturday

My Dear Reynolds,

There are two things which tease me here—one of them Crips—and the other that I cannot go with Tom into Devonshire—however I hope to do my duty to myself in a week or so;· and then Ill try

[7] At the end of the first draft of *Endymion* is written "Burford Bridge, Nov. 28, 1817."

[8] *For* stop.

[9] Jonathan Henry Christie, who on February 16, 1821, mortally wounded John Scott, editor of the *London Magazine*, in a duel that resulted directly from J. G. Lockhart's *Blackwood's* reviews. Scott died on February 27. Christie was tried for wilful murder on April 13, and found not guilty. On April 28 Bailey wrote (*KC*, I, 237): "He is as fine & honorable a man as I ever was acquainted with." Christie lived until April 15, 1876. According to Andrew Lang, *The Life and Letters of John Gibson Lockhart* (1897), I, 199, Christie liked Keats so much that on January 27, 1818, he was asked by Lockhart "to write a little review of him."

[10] *For* Bentley's.

[1] Heretofore this letter has been printed before No. 43, although Lowell, I, 446 f., long ago proved that order incorrect. Keats wrote No. 43, on November 22, after he had "just arrived at Dorking" and before he had written another line of *Endymion*. When he began to write No. 44, however, he had had time to see and "like this place," Burford Bridge, "very much," he had walked up Box Hill in the evening, and had come down to compose "some lines" (he quotes ten) of *Endymion*. Lowell was naturally puzzled when she saw No. 44 printed with the postmarks "LEATHERHEAD and 22 NO 1817." She had no way of knowing that it is a transcript in Woodhouse's letter-book, pp. 50–52, by a clerk with corrections by Woodhouse, who noted the date of writing as "(Leatherhead 22[d] Nov[r] 1817)." Keats was at Burford Bridge, and his letter in all probability was mailed on November 23 at Leatherhead, some three miles away.

what I can do for my neighbour—now is not this virtuous? on returning to Town—Ill damn all Idleness—indeed, in superabundance of employment, I must not be content to run here and there on
two penny
little ⟨too many⟩ errands—but turn Rakehell i e go a *making* [2] or Bailey will think me just as great a Promise keeper as *he* thinks you—for my self I do not,—and do not remember above one Complaint against you for matter o' that—Bailey writes so abominable a hand, to give his Letter a fair reading requires a little time; so I had not seen when I saw you⟨,⟩ last, his invitation to Oxford at Christmas—I'll go with you [3]—You know how poorly Rice was—I do not think it was all corporeal—bodily pain was not used to keep him silent. Ill tell you what; he was hurt at what your Sisters said about his joking with your Mother he was, soothly to sain [4]—It will all blow over. God knows, my Dear Reynolds, I should not talk any sorrow to you—you must have enough vexations—so I won't any more. If I ever start a rueful subject in a Letter to you—blow me! Why dont you—Now I was a going to ask a very silly Question neither you nor any body else could answer, under a folio, or at least a Pamphlet—you shall judge—Why dont you, as I do, look unconcerned at what may be called more particularly Heart-vexations? They never surprize me—lord! a man should have the fine point of his soul taken off to become fit for this world—I like this place very much—There is Hill & Dale and a little River—I went up Box hill this Evening after the Moon—you a' seen the Moon—came down—and wrote some lines.[5] Whenever I am separated from you, and not engaged in a continued Poem—every Letter shall bring you a lyric—but I am too anxious for you to enjoy the whole, to send you a particle. One of the three Books I have with me is Shakespear's Poems: I neer found so many beauties in the sonnets—they seem to be full of fine things said unintentionally—in the intensity of working out conceits—Is this to be borne? Hark ye!

When lofty trees I see barren of leaves
erst
Which ⟨not⟩ from heat did canopy the he⟨a⟩rd,

[2] Woodhouse suggests "masking." [3] See I, 187. They did not go.

[4] Compare "sooth to seyne," *Troilus and Criseyde*, III.430, and *The Shepherd's Calendar*, "May," line 158.

[5] Lowell, I, 445 f., thinks that they included the moon passage in *Endymion*, IV.496–502. The "little River" is the Mole.

And Summer's green all girded up in sheaves,
Borne on the bier with white and bristly beard.[6]

He has left nothing to say about nothing or any thing: for look at Snails, you know what he says about Snails, you know where he talks about "cockled snails" [7]—well, in one of these sonnets, he says —the chap slips into—no! I lie! this is in the Venus and Adonis: [8] the Simile brought it to my Mind.

Audi—As the snail, whose tender horns being hit,
Shrinks back⟨s⟩ into his shelly cave with pain,
And there all smothered up in shade doth sit,
Long after fearing to put forth again:
So at his bloody view her eyes are fled,
Into the deep dark Cabins of her head.

He overwhelms a genuine Lover of Poesy with all manner of abuse, talking about—

"a poets rage
And stretched metre of an antique song" [9]—

Which by the by will be a capital Motto for my Poem [1]—wont it?— He speaks too of "Time's antique pen"—and "aprils first born flowers"—and "deaths eternal cold" [2]—By the Whim King! I'll give you a Stanza,[3] because it is not material in connection and when I wrote it I wanted you to——give your vote, pro or con.—

Christalline Brother of the Belt of Heaven,
Aquarius! to whom King Jove ha'th [4] given
Two liquid pulse streams! s'tead of feather'd wings—
fan
Two ⟨fair⟩ like fountains—thine illuminings
For Dian play:
Dissolve the frozen purity of air;

[6] Sonnet 12, lines 5–8. (The 1806 edition of Shakespeare's *Poetical Works* now in the Keats Museum was given to Keats by Reynolds in 1819.)

[7] *Love's Labor's Lost*, IV.iii.338, "the tender horns of cockled snails."

[8] Lines 1033–1038 (slightly misquoted).

[9] Sonnet 17, lines 11 f.

[1] It appears on the title-page of *Endymion.*

[2] Sonnets 19, line 10 ("thine antique pen"), 21, line 7, 13, line 12.

[3] The so-called stanza forms lines 581–590 of *Endymion*, book IV. Of it Colvin, 1920, p. 153, remarks: "Certainly one of the weakest things in the poem: pity Reynolds had not been there indeed, to give his vote *contra.*"

[4] has *Endymion.*

Let thy white shoulders silvery and bare
Show cold through wa⟨r⟩tery pinions: make more bright
The Star-Queen's Crescent on her marriage night:
Haste Haste away!—

Now I hope I shall not fall off in the winding up,[5]—as the Woman said to the—   [6]—I mean up and down. I see there is an advertizement in the chronicle to Poets—he is so overloaded with poems on the late Princess.[7]—I suppose you do not lack [8]—send me a few —lend me thy hand to laugh a little [9]—send me a little pullet sperm,[1] a few finch eggs [2]—and remember me to each of our Card playing Club [3]—when you ⟨did⟩ die you will all be turned into Dice, and be put in pawn with the Devil—for Cards they crumple up like any King [4]—I mean John in the stage play what pertains Prince Arthur —I rest

Your affectionate friend
John Keats

Mr John Hn Reynolds
Lambs Conduit St[t] [5]

19

London.

Give my love to both houses [6]—hinc atque illinc.[7]

[5] He finished on November 28 (I, 187 n.).

[6] Woodhouse's clerk left the blank space, which someone later filled with an undecipherable penciled conjecture.

[7] Charlotte Augusta died on November 6. The advertisement appeared in the *Morning Chronicle*, November 20, p. 2: "We are so overwhelmed with *Monodies*, *Elegies* and *Epitaphs*, that we must intreat our Poetical Correspondents to grant us indulgence.—Our stock on hand would literally fill a volume. We wish to pay respect to every Correspondent, but there are some effusions that ought to have been addressed to a less fastidious Editor. —We shall select some of the Essays for insertion."

[8] That is, lack poems on the princess, for at this time Reynolds was in charge of the poetry department of the *Champion*.

[9] *1 Henry IV*, II.iv.2.

[1] *The Merry Wives of Windsor*, III.v.32 f., "I'll no pullet-sperm in my brewage."

[2] *Troilus and Cressida*, V.i.41, "Finch-egg!"

[3] Evidently the Saturday Club at Rice's (I, 202).

[4] *King John*, V.vii.31, "all my bowels crumble up to dust." The clerk wrote "King," Woodhouse changed it to "Thing" and then back to "King."

[5] Perhaps the superscript *t* is a plus sign calling attention to the postscript, which is written horizontally in the margin.

[6] *Romeo and Juliet*, III.i.94, 103 f., 111, "A plague o' both your houses!"

[7] Virgil, *Georgics*, III.257.

· 45 ·

TO GEORGE AND TOM KEATS [1]

21, 27 (?) December 1817

Hampstead Sunday
22 December 1818

My dear Brothers

I must crave your pardon for not having written ere this & & I saw Kean return to the public in Richard III, & finely he did it,[2] & at the request of Reynolds I went to criticise his Luke in Riches [3] —the critique is in todays champion,[4] which I send you with the Examiner in which you will find very proper lamentation on the obsoletion of christmas Gambols & pastimes: but it was mixed up with so much egotism of that drivelling nature that pleasure is entirely lost.[5] Hone the publisher's trial, you must find very amusing; & as Englishmen very ⟨amusing⟩ encouraging—his *Not Guilty* is a thing, which not to have been, would have dulled still more Liberty's Emblazoning—Lord Ellenborough has been paid in his own coin—Wooler & Hone have done us an essential service [6]—I have had two

[1] A very puzzling transcript, apparently of a journal letter, by Jeffrey, which I have discussed in the *HLB*, VII (1953), 175. Jeffrey dated it Sunday, December 22, 1818, but the year should be 1817, while Sunday was December 21. Keats may have begun to write earlier than December 21, for Jeffrey omitted some words (possibly even a page or two) after the first sentence, indicating that fact by "& &." (Remarkably enough, J. G. Speed, editing the letters in 1883, p. 7, made the identical omission.) At any rate, the second sentence of the transcript was written in the morning, while that beginning "I have had two" was written late at night, presumably on the 21st.

[2] Kean was absent from Drury Lane for about six weeks in November and December. The playbill for December 8 mentions his "continued and severe indisposition" (see Keats's words at I, 245, about "poor Kean"). He returned to the stage in *Richard III* on December 15, and, said the *Theatrical Inquisitor*, XI (1817), 485, "never acted better."

[3] On December 18 he played Luke (Jeffrey has "Duke") Traffic in Sir James Bland Burges' *Riches: Or, The Wife and Brother. A Comedy* (an adaptation of Massinger's *City Madam*, for which see Burges' *Dramas* [1817], II, 295–422). William Godwin (so Lewis Patton tells me) noted in his diary that at *Riches* on June 18 he saw Lamb, Talfourd, and Keats.

[4] His critique of Kean is reprinted in the Hampstead Keats, V, 227–232.

[5] Hunt's essays, "Christmas and Other Old National Merry-Makings Considered, with Reference to the Nature of the Age, and to the Desirableness of Their Revival" appeared in the issues of December 21 and 28, pp. 801–803, 817–819.

[6] William Hone (1780–1842), writer and bookseller, was tried, December 18–20, on three charges for publishing scandalous libels. Lord Ellenborough (1750–1818), lord chief justice, who in February, 1813, had sentenced John and Leigh Hunt to prison,

very pleasant evenings with Dilke yesterday & today; & am at this moment just come from him & feel in the humour to go on with this, began in the morning, & from which he came to fetch me. I spent Friday evening with Wells [7] & went the next morning to see *Death on the Pale horse*. It is a wonderful picture, when West's age is considered; But there is nothing to be intense upon; no women one feels mad to kiss; no face swelling into reality. the excellence of every Art is its intensity, capable of making all disagreeables evaporate, from their being in close relationship with Beauty & Truth [8] —Examine King Lear & you will find this examplified throughout; but in this picture we have unpleasantness without any momentous depth of speculation excited, in which to bury its repulsiveness— The picture is larger than Christ rejected [9]—I dined with Haydon the sunday after you left,[1] & had a very pleasant day, I dined too (for I have been out too much lately) with Horace Smith & met his

---

presided at the second and third trials (Keats is referring to the third as reported in the *Examiner*, December 21, pp. 806 f.), and according to Lord Campbell, *The Lives of the Chief Justices* (1857), III, 225, the final verdict of not guilty was "followed by a tremendous burst of applause, which he could not even attempt to quell," while it was popularly believed "that Lord Ellenborough was killed by Hone's trial, and he certainly never held up his head in public after." Thomas Jonathan Wooler (1786?—1853), journalist and politician, editor of the *Black Dwarf* (1817–1824), had been tried before another judge on June 5 for libeling the ministry, and was acquitted (*Examiner*, June 8, pp. 361, 366–368).

[7] Charles Jeremiah Wells (1800–1879) was a school-fellow of Tom Keats. He and the poet were for a time intimate (Keats wrote an early sonnet to him), but his cruel joke on Tom with the "Amena" letters brought their friendship to an end. Of *Joseph and His Brethren* (published in 1824) Wells said in 1845, "I wrote it in six weeks to compel Keats to esteem me and admit my *power*, for we had quarrelled, and everybody who knew him must feel I was in fault." See the sketch of him by HBF, Boston Bibliophile Society, *Twelfth Year Book* (Boston, 1913), pp. 75–116.

[8] Compare "Beauty must be truth," I, 184. Colvin, 1920, p. 253, says the present sentence is "worth whole treatises and fit, sketchy as it is, to serve as text to most of what can justly be discoursed concerning problems of art in relation to nature,—of realism, romance, and the rest." For discussions of "intense" and "intensity" see Murry, *Studies in Keats* (1930), p. 55, and Finney, I, 244 f.

[9] Benjamin West (1738–1820), an American, was president of the Royal Academy. "Mr. West's Exhibition" at 125 Pall Mall "under the immediate patronage of His Royal Highness the Prince Regent" was advertised for weeks in the papers. Closing at the old king's death, it reopened in February, 1820, under the patronage of George IV, and ran until West himself died on March 10. Though Leigh Hunt, in his libel on the Prince Regent, called West "a wretched Foreigner," R. H. in the *Examiner*, April 9, 1820, p. 237, said, "The world has seldom possessed a better man, and not very often a greater Artist." In his comments on "Death on the Pale Horse" Keats is following Hazlitt's criticism in the *Edinburgh Magazine*, December, 1817 (Hazlitt, *Works*, XVIII [1933], 135–140). Both pictures he mentions are now in the Academy of Fine Arts, Philadelphia.

[1] Haydon's Journal ignores this dinner. George and Tom Keats went to Teignmouth some time after November 22 (I, 187), probably early in December. Jack Stillinger thinks that, since in the letter up to this point no date earlier than December 14 is reerred to, George and Tom left on the morning of the 14th.

two Brothers [2] with Hill & Kingston & one Du Bois,[3] they only served to convince me, how superior [4] humour is to wit in respect to enjoyment—These men say things which make one start, without making one feel, they are all alike; their manners are alike; they all know fashionables; they have a mannerism in their very eating & drinking, in their mere handling a Decanter—They talked of Kean & his low company—Would I were with that company instead of yours said I to myself! I know such like acquaintance will never do for me & yet I am going to Reynolds, on wednesday [5]—Brown & Dilke walked with me & back from the Christmas pantomime.[6] I had not a dispute but a disquisition with Dilke, on various subjects; several things dovetailed in my mind, & at once it struck me, what quality went to form a Man of Achievement especially in Literature & which Shakespeare posessed so enormously—I mean *Negative Capability*,[7] that is when man is capable of being in uncertainties, Mysteries, doubts, without any irritable reaching after fact & reason—Coleridge, for instance, would let go by a fine iso-

[2] Horace Smith (1779–1849), poet, novelist, wit, and intimate friend of Hunt and Shelley, is now best known for the *Rejected Addresses*, which he and his brother James (1775–1839) published in 1812. He met Keats and Shelley, apparently in December, 1816, at Hunt's Hampstead cottage. Keats wrote at least one letter to him (No. 63), appreciated his witticisms, but was not on intimate terms with him. The third brother was Leonard Smith (1778–1837). Since "They talked of Kean" the dinner was probably a day or two after December 15.

[3] Thomas Hill (1760–1840), dry-salter, was a well-known book collector and *bon vivant*. In a letter of February 2, 1818, Wordsworth (De Selincourt, *The Letters of William and Dorothy Wordsworth: The Middle Years* [Oxford, 1937], II, 804 f.) refers to John Kingston as the comptroller of stamps. *The Royal Kalendar* for 1818 calls him deputy comptroller and "accomp. gen."; that for 1819, one of the commissioners. Keats heartily disliked him, as later references in the letters show. Edward Dubois (1774–1850), wit and man of letters, editor of the *Monthly Mirror* and other magazines, wrote *My Pocket Book* (1807), satirizing the travels of Sir John Carr (1772–1832), part of which, in its second edition, 1808, Keats (II, 16) found amusing.

[4] Jeffrey has "suporior."

[5] December 24. Jeffrey plainly omitted something here, for the next sentence cannot have been written before the night of December 26.

[6] The pantomimes were always first performed at Drury Lane and Covent Garden on the day after Christmas. Keats, Brown, and Dilke saw the Drury Lane pantomime (see No. 48), *Harlequin's Vision, Or, The Feast of the Statue*, which was presented twenty-nine times. Very likely they did so on December 26; or if they went on December 27, this part of the letter was written on December 28 before Keats attended Haydon's "immortal dinner" (I, 197 f.).

[7] There are many discussions of this famous phrase, as Woodhouse's in October, 1818 (No. 119), W. J. Bate's *Negative Capability: The Intuitive Approach in Keats* (Harvard University Press, 1939), C. L. Finney's in *Vanderbilt Studies in the Humanities* (Nashville, 1951), pp. 174–196, and Barbara Hardy's in *NQ*, July 5, 1952, pp. 299–301. See also Bate's comments in G. B. Harrison's *Major British Writers* (New York, 1954), II, 299 n., and George Watson's edition of Coleridge's *Biographia Literaria* (1956), p. 256.

lated verisimilitude [8] caught from the Penetralium [9] of mystery, from being incapable of remaining content with half knowledge. This pursued through Volumes would perhaps take us no further than this, that with a great poet the sense of Beauty overcomes every other consideration, or rather obliterates all consideration.
Shelley's poem is out & there are words about its being objected too, as much as Queen Mab was.[1] Poor Shelley I think he has his Quota of good qualities, in sooth la!! [2] Write soon to your most sincere friend & affectionate Brother

(Signed) John

Messrs Keats
Teignmouth Devonshire

· 46 ·

TO B. R. HAYDON [1]

31 December 1817

Address: Benjamin Robert Haydon/ Lisson Grove North/ Paddington
Postmarks: 4 o'Clock JA 1 1818 EV; TwoPyPost Unpaid SOHampstead (*blurred*)

Hampstead Decr 31st

My dear Haydon,

I forgot on Sunday [2] to ask you for Cripps's direction as you might chance to know—on monday you were out in the Sun. I shall be with you shortly to have a talk about him. I thoughtlessly gave

[8] Jeffrey has "insolated verisimilature."

[9] Colvin, p. 48 n., comments: "An admirable phrase!—if only *penetralium* were Latin." Milnes, II, 52, wrote "that inmost penetralium of Fame," a fact that should have given pause to Garrod, *Keats* (Oxford, 1926), p. 33 n., who tried "to believe that Keats knew better" and wrote "penetralia." In 1897 Andrew Lang, *The Life and Letters of John Gibson Lockhart*, I, 197 f., had cited the word as proving that Keats "had no classical education."

[1] Shelley's struggles with the Olliers (see I, 227) over *Laon and Cythna*, copies of which were "out" early in December, may be followed in N. I. White's *Shelley* (New York, 1940), I, 547–552. Frightened by its apparent approval of incest and its irreligious tone, they tried to call in the copies already issued, forced Shelley to make elaborate changes by cancel leaves, and then published the poem in January as *The Revolt of Islam*. Keats probably heard about these matters from Godwin, who (Lewis Patton tells me) noted in his diary for December 25 "Meet Keats." [2] See *Antony and Cleopatra*, IV.iv.8.

[1] *ALS:* Wisbech Museum, Cambridgeshire; first printed by MBF, 1935, from a transcript made by F. H. Day and sent by Holman.

[2] December 31 was Wednesday, Sunday was December 28 (the date of Haydon's "immortal dinner").

you a promise for Sunday [3]—now I have just received a 'yes' from a friend of mine to pass that said day here [4]—so be lenient and your petitioner shall ever pray &c I met Wordsworth [5] on Hampstead Heath this Morning.

Your⟨s⟩ affectionate friend
John Keats

· 47 ·

TO CALLERS ON JOHN TAYLOR [1]

January 1818 (?) [2]

To any friend who may call

Mr Taylor's Compt^s to any Ladies or gentlemen his friends who may call, and begs they will pardon him for being led away by an unavoidable engagement, which will detain him till eleven o'clock to night

· 48 ·

TO GEORGE AND TOM KEATS [1]

5 January 1818

Address: Messrs Keats/ Post Office/ Teignmouth/ Devonshire
Postmarks: 7 o'Clock 5 J[A] N^T; [Pe]nny Post [U]npaid [B]road St PO; C JA 5 818

Featherstone Buildgs Monday

My dear Brothers,

I ought to have written before, and you should have had a long Letter last week; [2] but I undertook the Champion for Reynolds who

[3] January 4. [4] Severn and Wells spent the day with him (I, 196).

[5] T. O. Mabbott, *NQ*, May 10, 1941, pp. 328 f., argues that Keats had met Wordsworth at Monkhouse's (see I, 198 n.) around December 15. On December 31, by the way, there was a very heavy fog in London and its vicinity (*GM*, January, 1818 [LXXXVIII, i, 78]). [1] *ALS:* Harvard.

[2] Lowell, I, 547 f., who owned and first printed the note, dated it (a mere guess) about January, 1818. In his letter-book, pp. 101 f., Woodhouse—who pays no attention to chronological arrangement—copied it after No. 28 with the following explanation: "Keats Persuaded Mr Taylor to accompany him one afternoon to Hampstead & ⟨left⟩ wrote for him the following note—"

[1] *ALS:* Carl H. Pforzheimer, Jr., New York. The text has been kindly verified by Dr. Kenneth Neill Cameron.

[2] An odd remark, since part of No. 45 was written to them not earlier than December 27. Here Keats was writing, as he says later, in Wells's quarters (see I, 197) in 17 Feather-

is at Exeter. I wrote two articles, one on the Drury Lane Pantomime, the other on the Covent Garden New Tragedy,[3] which they have not put in.[4] The one they have inserrted is so badly puncuated [5] that, you perceive, I am determined never to write more without some care in that particular. Wells tells me, that you are licking your Chops Tom, in expectation of my Book coming out; I am sorry to say I have not began my corrections yet: tomorrow I set out. I called on Sawrey [6] this morning. He did not seem to be at all out at any thing I said and the enquiries I made with regard to your spitting of Blood: and moreover desired me to ask you to send him a correct accou[n]t of all your sensations and symptoms concerning the Palpitation and the spitting and the Cough—if you have any. Your last Letter gave me at [7] great Pleasure for I think the Invalid is in a better spirit there along the Edge [8]—and as for George I must immediately, now I think of it, correct a little misconception of a part of my last Letter. The Miss Reynolds have never said one word against me about you,[9] or by any means endeavoured to lessen you in my estimation. That is not what I refered to: but the manner and thoughts which I knew they internally had towards you—time will show. Wells and Severn dined with me yesterday: we had a very pleasant day [1]—I pitched upon another bottle of claret—Port —we enjoyed ourselves very much were all very witty and full of

---

stone Buildings, a street running from High Holborn to Bedford Street. His letter is badly penned and crossed, with several pen strokes that have to be guessed at. It is endorsed "Various old letters," "Copied July 1845," presumably by Jeffrey, who in his transcript as usual misread many words and omitted words and sentences at random.

[3] *Harlequin's Vision, Or, The Feast of the Statue* was presented on December 26, 1817, and twenty-eight times thereafter. *Retribution* was first performed on January 1, 1818, and again on January 2, 5, 9, 12, 16, 21.

[4] They *were* "put in" as two articles (see the postscript) in the issue of January 4, and are reprinted in the Hampstead Keats, V, 247–256. Keats wrongly entitled the second "Don Giovanni."

[5] *Sic.* Keats is referring to his critique on Kean's acting published in the *Champion* for December 21, 1817 (see I, 191), for he had not seen the January 4 issue until he had finished this letter.

[6] Solomon Sawrey, surgeon (1765–1825), lived (according to an 1823–1824 directory) at 28 Bedford Row. He was a specialist in and the author of two books about venereal diseases. The long passage from "I called on Sawrey" to "time will show" is omitted in the transcript Jeffrey sent to Milnes. Since it deals with the Misses Reynolds, Jeffrey's omission at the beginning of No. 45 may have concerned the same subject.

[7] *For* a.

[8] Escarpment.

[9] MBF observes that what Keats meant was "to assure his brothers that the Misses Reynolds had not said anything *to* him *against* George."

[1] See Keats's apology to Haydon in No. 46.

Rhyme—we played a Concert [2] from 4 o'clock till 10—drank your Healths the Hunts and N. B Severn Peter Pindars.[3] I said on that day the only good thing I was ever guilty of—we were talking about Stephens [4] and the 1^{s} Gallery. I said I wondered that careful Folks would go there for although it was but a Shilling still you had to pay through the Nose. I saw the Peachey family [5] in a Box at Drury one Night. I have got such a curious [6]—or rather I had such, now I am in my own hand. I have had a great deal of pleasant time with Rice lately, and am getting initiated into a little Cant—they call dr[i]nking deep dying scarlet, and when you breathe in your wartering [7] they bid you cry hem and play it off—they call good Wine a pretty tipple, and call getting a Child knocking out an apple, [8] stopping at a Tave[r]n they call hanging out—Where do you sup? is where do you hang out? [9] This day I promised to dine with Wordsworth and the Weather is so bad that I am undecided for he lives at Mortimer street I had an invitation to meet him at Kingstons—but not liking that place I sent my excuse—What I think of doing to day is to dine in Mortimer Street (wordsth) [1] and sup here in Feathers^{ne} Buildg^{s} as Mr Wells has invited me—On Saturday I called on Wordsworth before he went to Kingston's and was surp[r]ised to find him with a stiff Collar. I saw his Spouse and I think his Daughter [2]—I forget whether I had written my last before my Sunday Evening [3] at Haydon's—no I did n{o}t or I should have told you Tom

[2] "Each one . . . imitated vocally some musical instrument" (HBF, 1895).

[3] Peter Pindar, or John Wolcot (1738–1819), satirist, died on January 14, 1819.

[4] Not yet identified. Jack Stillinger suggests the possibility that Keats is referring to Miss Stephens, who acted Lucy Bertram in *Guy Mannering* at Covent Garden on January 3 and earlier.

[5] *The Post Office London Directory* for 1819 and 1820 lists only Richard Peachey and Son, furnishing ironmongers, 1 Hanover Street. Pigot's *Commercial Directory* for 1823–1824 gives four others, among them James Peachey, attorney, 17 Salisbury Court. One Peachey, perhaps this James, was a schoolfellow of Keats.

[6] That is, a bad pen, which he changed at this point.

[7] He is slightly misquoting (and misspelling) *1 Henry IV*, II.iv.16–18, "They call drinking deep, dyeing scarlet; and when you breathe in your watering, they cry 'hem!' and bid you play it off." (Noted by A. D. Atkinson, *TLS*, September 28, 1933, p. 652.)

[8] Partridge gives only this example.

[9] Still used in much the same way to mean "reside, lodge." J. O. Halliwell[-Phillipps], *A Dictionary of Archaic and Provincial Words* (1847), defines it as "to give a party."

[1] He did: see I, 202. Wordsworth was staying with Thomas Monkhouse (see below).

[2] Kathleen Coburn, *The Letters of Sara Hutchinson* (1954), p. 114 n., thinks he saw Miss Hutchinson, who with Wordsworth and his wife was visiting Monkhouse. At this time Dora Wordsworth was at Rydal Mount.

[3] December 28. Since No. 45 does not mention Haydon's "immortal dinner," it was written either on December 27 or in the morning or early afternoon of the next day.

of a y{oung} Man you met at Paris at Scott's [4] of the n{ame of} Richer [5] I think—he is going to Fezan in Africa there to proceed [6] if possible like Mungo Park [7]—he was very polite to me and enquired very particularly after you—then there was Wordsworth, Lamb, Monkhouse, [8] Landseer, [9] Kingston and your humble Sarvant. Lamb got tipsey and blew up Kingston—proceeding so far as to take the Candle across the Room hold it to his face and show us wh-a-at-sor^t-fello he-waas I astonished Kingston at supper with a pertinacity in favour of drinking—keeping my two glasses at work in a knowing way—I have seen Fanny twice lately—she enquired particularly af[t]er you and wants a Co-partnership Letter from you—she has been unwell but is improving—I think she will be quick—Mrs Abbey was saying that the Keatses were ever indolent—that they would ever be so and that it was born in them—Well whispered fanny to me 'If it is born with us how can we help it—She seems very anxious for a Letter—⟨She as⟩ I asked her what I should

[4] Tom and George Keats were at Paris in September, 1817 (I, 154). It was on this visit that John Scott met them and acquired Tom's so-called "copy-book," which is now at Harvard.

[5] Joseph Ritchie (1788?–1819), surgeon, "late private secretary to Sir Charles Stuart, has undertaken to reach the Niger and Tombuctoo by a new route. . . . The present Bashaw of Tripoli has intimated his readiness to co-operate with the British government in the promotion of their plans" (*Annals of Philosophy*, July, 1818 [XII, 72 f.]). Ritchie's travels and death are described at length in Captain George Francis Lyon's *A Narrative of Travels in Northern Africa, in the Years 1818, 19, and 20* (1821). On a government exploring mission Ritchie went to Malta in September, 1818, sailed on October 10 for Tripoli, where Lyon joined him on November 25, and the two set out on their explorations on February 7, 1819. Ritchie died, November 20, at Murzuk, the capital of Fezzan, and Lyon turned over all his papers to the government after he reached London on July 29, 1820. A letter of 1818 in which Ritchie praised Keats as likely "to be the great poetical luminary of the age to come" was printed by Lowell, I, 282, and then by David Garnett in the *New Statesman*, June 10, 1933, p. 763. (On F. H. Day and the eight Ritchie letters see Rollins and Parrish, *Keats and the Bostonians* [Harvard University Press, 1951], pp. 168 f.) Ritchie's poem, "A Farewell to England," was printed in the *Monthly Magazine*, June, 1820 (XLIX, 426 f.), the *London Magazine*, April, 1821 (III, 388), in Alaric Watts's *Poetical Album*, 1828, pp. 44 f., and in *The Lyre*, 1830, pp. 121 f. (1841 ed., pp. 119 f.). See also I, 416 n.

[6] *Written* proceid.

[7] African explorer (1771–1806).

[8] Thomas Monkhouse (1783–1825), to whom Keats wrote one letter (No. 89), a merchant of Budge Row, lived for a time at 48 Mortimer Street and then at 28 Queen Anne Street, Cavendish Square. He was a cousin of Mrs. Wordsworth and her sister Sara Hutchinson. Miss Hutchinson's *Letters* (1954) abounds in information about him and about his wife, Jane Horrocks (daughter of a Preston counselor and M.P.), whom she disliked. He is mentioned often, too, in the letters of Wordsworth and Lamb and in Crabb Robinson's diary.

[9] John Landseer (1769–1852), painter and engraver, had three sons: Charles (1799–1879), painter; Sir Edwin Henry (1802–1873), animal painter; and Thomas (1795–1880), engraver. Keats perhaps refers to Thomas.

get for her, she said a Medal of the Princess.[1] I called on Haslam —we dined very snugly together—he sent me a Hare last Week which I sent to M[rs] Dilk. Brown is not come back[2]—I and Dilk are getting capital Friends—he is going to take the Champion[3]— he has sent his farce to Covent Garden[4]—I met Bob Harris in the Slips at Covent Garden[5]—we had a good deal of curious chat—he came out with his old humble Opinion—The Covent Garden Pantonine[6] is a very nice one—but they have a middling Harlequin, a bad Pantaloon, a worse Clown and a shocking Columbine who is one of the Miss Dennets.[7] I suppose you will see my Critique on the new Tragedy in the next Weeks Champion[8]—It is a shocking bad one. I have not seen Hunt, he was out when I called—M[rs] Hunt looks as well as ever I saw her after her Confinement[9]—There is an article in the sennight Examiner—on Godwin's Mandeville signed E. K. I think it Miss Kents[1]—I will send it. There are fine Subscriptions going on for Hone.[2] You ask me what degrees there are between Scotts Novels and those of Smollet—They appear to me to be quite distinct in every particular—more especially in

[1] See I, 190 n.

[2] He was with the Snooks at Bedhampton, Hampshire (I, 206 n.).

[3] He became its dramatic critic before January 23 (I, 214).

[4] *Written* Consent Garden. Nothing is known of Dilke's farce.

[5] The slips are the sidings from which scenery was pushed on the stage. Thomas Harris, manager of Covent Garden for many years, died on October 1, 1820, aged 82 (London *Courier*, October 4), and was succeeded by his son Henry. Whether Bob Harris was related to them I cannot say, but it is apparently his "old humble Opinion" about the bad actors that Keats proceeds to give.

[6] So apparently.

[7] *Harlequin Gulliver, Or, The Flying Island* was first produced (after *George Barnwell*) on December 26, 1817, and often thereafter. As Keats saw it following John Dillon's "new Tragedy," *Retribution, Or, The Chieftain's Daughter*, he must have been at Covent Garden on either January 1 or 2. Hence the "middling" harlequin was Mr. Bologna (whom the *European Magazine*, January, 1817 [LXXI, 64], calls "decidedly our best Harlequin"), the "bad" pantaloon Mr. Ryalls, the "worse" clown Mr. Norman, the "shocking" Columbine Miss Frances Dennett. If he had gone there on December 29 or earlier or on January 5 (when the present letter was written), he would have seen the famous Joseph Grimaldi (who between those dates had suffered "a severe Indisposition") as the clown, Norman as the pantaloon. The three Miss Dennetts, formerly of the Theatre Royal, Dublin, had made their début at Covent Garden on September 11, 1816. Keats saw them twice in another pantomime and liked them. They were often warmly praised by Hazlitt (*Works*, XVIII [1933], 209 f., 298 f., 324), as well as by Reynolds in the *Champion*, February 2, 1817.

[8] See the postscript and I, 196, n.4.

[9] With Percy Shelley Hunt.

[1] E. K. in the *Examiner*, December 28, 1817, pp. 826 f., was not Bessy Kent, Mrs. Leigh Hunt's sister, but (as MBF noted) Shelley ("Elfin Knight").

[2] See I, 191 n.

their Aim—Scott endeavours to th[r]ow so interesting and ramantic a colouring into common and low Characters as to give them a touch of the Sublime—Smollet on the contrary pulls down and levels what with other Men would continue Romance. The Grand parts of Scott are within [3] the reach of more Minds that [4] the finest humours in Humphrey Climker [4]—I forget whether that fine thing of the Sargeant is Fielding's or Smollets but it gives me more pleasure that [4] the whole Novel of the Antiquary—you must remember what I mean. Some one says to the [5] Sargeant "thats a non sequiter," "if you come to that" replies the Sargeant "you're another." [6] I see by Wells Letter, Mr Abbey does not overstock you with Money—you must insist—I have not seen Loveless [7] yet—but expect it on Wednesday—I am affraid it is gone. Severn tells me he has an order for some drawings for [8] the Emperor of Russia I was at a Dance at Redhall's [9] and passed a pl[e]asant time enough—drank deep and won 10.6 at cutting for Half Guinies there was a younger Brother of the Squibs [1] made him self very conspicuous after the Ladies had retired from the supper table by giving Mater Omnium—Mr Redhall said he did not understand any thing but plain english—where at Rice egged the young fool on to ⟨sary⟩ say the World plainly out. After which there was an enquirey about the derivation of the Word C—t [2] when while two parsons and Grammarians were setting together and settling the matter Wm Squibs interrupting them said a very good thing—'Gentleman says he I have always understood it to be a Root and not a Derivitive.' On proceeding to the Pot in the Cupboard it soon became full on which the Court door was opened

[3] *Written* willing. [4] *For* than *and* Clinker.

[5] Some word that looks like "Rasher" or "Railier" is here deleted.

[6] Fielding, *Tom Jones*, IX.vi.

[7] Can this, asks W. J. Bate, be a reference to Lovelace in Richardson's *Clarissa?* Or to Lovelace, the rake-hero of Colley Cibber's *Love's Last Shift* or its sequel, Sir John Vanbrugh's *The Relapse*, which was rewritten in Sheridan's *A Trip to Scarborough* (first produced at Drury Lane, February 24, 1777)? J. G. Speed, editing the letters at New York in 1883 (p. 5 n.), says, "The word is not legible, but he evidently referred to some play of the day."

[8] *Written* fror. Alexander I (1777–1825). Sharp, p. 25 n., merely quotes this sentence without details.

[9] See II, 13.

[1] G. Squibb, auctioneer, Boyle Street, Saville Row, is the only person with that surname in *The Post Office London Directory* for 1819.

[2] Keats observed the taboo that, according to Partridge, has since about 1700 made it a legal offense to print the word in full. The whole passage from "Mater" was garbled or omitted by HBF, 1895, 1901, and J. G. Speed, editing the letters in 1883.

Frank Floodgate [3] bawls out, Hoollo! here's an opposition pot—Ay, says Rice in one you have a Yard for your pot, and in the other a pot for your Yard [4]—Bailey was there and seemed to enjoy the Evening Rice said he cared less about the hour than any one and the p[r]oof is his dancing—he cares not for time, dancing as if he was deaf. Old Redall not being used to give parties had no idea of the Quantity of wine that would be drank and he acually put in readiness on the kitchen Stairs 8 dozen—E[v]ery one enquires after you —an{d every} one desires their remembrances to you You must get well Tom and then I shall feel 'Whole and general as the casing Air.' [5] Give me as many Letters as you like and write to Sawrey soon—I received a short Letter from Bailey about Crips and one from Haydon ditto—Haydon thinks he improves very much Here a happy twelveth days [6] to you and may we pass the next together —Mrs Wells desires [7] particularly to Tom and her respects to George —and I desire no better than to be ever your most affectionate

Brother John—

I had not opened the Champion before—I find both my articles in it—

·49·

TO JOHN TAYLOR [1]

10 January 1818

Saturday Morning

My dear Taylor,

Several things have kept me from you lately:—first you had got into a little hell, which I was not anxious to reconnoitre [2]—Secondly, I have made a vow not to call again without my first book: [3] so

[3] Really Fladgate (see I, 181 n.).

[4] Partridge, *Shakespeare's Bawdy* (1947), p. 225, remarks that from 1590 to 1780 "*yard* was perhaps the most generally used literary term for 'penis'," but was obsolete by 1850.

[5] Colvin, p. 238 n., compares *Macbeth*, III.iv.23, "As broad and general as the casing air." See also I, 269.

[6] *Or perhaps* days' (January 6).

[7] Probably he meant "desires remembrances" or "desires her love." Was Mrs. Wells the mother of C. J. Wells?

[1] A transcript in Woodhouse's letter-book, p. 2, with the note: "No date. Post Brand. 10 January 1818.—"

[2] For Leigh Hunt's dispute with Taylor and Hessey over transferring to them the profits of *Rimini* see Shelley's *Complete Works*, ed. Roger Ingpen and W. E. Peck, IX (1926), 289 f.

[3] Of *Endymion*. He seems to have carried the copy of Book I to Taylor on January 20 (I, 206 f.).

you may expect to see me in four days. Thirdly, I have been racketing too much, & do not feel over well—I have seen Wordsworth frequently—Dined with him last Monday [4]—Reynolds, I suppose you have seen—Just scribble me thus many lines, to let me know you are in the land of the living,[5] & well. Remember me to the fleet Street Household [6]—And should you see any from Percy Street,[7] give my kindest regards to them.

Your sincere friend John Keats.

Mr J. Taylor
Bond Street.

· 50 ·

TO B. R. HAYDON [1]

10 January 1818

Address: Benjamin Robert Haydon/ Lisson Grove North/ Paddington
Postmarks: TwoPyPost Unpaid SOHampstead; To be Delivered by 10 o'Clock on Sund Morn; 7 o'Clock JA 10 1818 N{T}

Saturday Morn—

My dear Haydon,

I should have seen you ere this, but on account of my sister being in Town: so that when I have sometimes made ten paces towards you, Fanny has called me into the City; and the Xmas Holyday[s] are your only time to see Sisters, that is if they are so situated as mine. I will be with you early next week—to night it should be, but we have a sort of a Club every Saturday evening [2]—to morrow—but I have on that day an insuperable engagement [3]—Crips has been down to me, and appears sensible that a binding to you would be of the greatest advantage to him—if such a thing be done it cannot be before £150 or £200 are secured in subscriptions to him—I will write to Bailey about it, give a Copy of the Subscribers names to every one I know who is likely to get a £5 for

[4] January 5 (I, 197). [5] See Job xxviii.13. [6] That is, to the Hesseys.
[7] That is, to the De Wints and Hilton. See I, 296 n.
[1] *ALS:* Formerly attached to Haydon's Journal, now at Harvard.
[2] On this club see I, 172, 190.
[3] He was in town on January 11 and 12 (I, 204).

him. I will leave a Copy at Taylor and Hesseys, Rodwell [4] and Martin and will ask Kingston and C° to cash up. Your friendship fo{r} me is now getting into its teens—and I feel the past. Also evey [5] day older I get—the greater is my idea of your atchievements in Art: and I am convinced that there are three things to rejoice at in this Age—The Excursion Your Pictures, and Hazlitt's depth of Taste.[6]

Your's affectionately
John Keats

· 51 ·

FROM B. R. HAYDON [1]

11 January 1818

My dear Keats/

I feel greatly delighted by your high opinion, allow me to add sincerely a fourth to be proud of—*John Keats' genius!*—this I speak from my heart—You & Bewick [2] are the only men I ever liked with all my heart, for Wordsworth being older, there is no equality tho I reverence him & love him devotedly—and now you know my peculiar feelings in wishing to have a notice when you cannot keep an engagement with me; there can never be as long as we live any ground of dispute between us—My Friendship for you is beyond its teens, & beginning to ripen to maturity—I always saw through your motive at once & you shall always find me a devoted & affectionate Brother——with respect to Cripps, I sincerely think it would be for our mutual advantage to have him bound, I would

[4] See I, 166 n.

[5] One of the almost innumerable cases in which Keats omitted an *r*.

[6] See I, 205. In his copy of Hazlitt's *Characters of Shakespear's Plays* (1817) Keats wrote after the author's name on the title-page, " . . . he hath a kind of taste" (see the Hampstead Keats, V, 280 n.).

[1] *AL:* Formerly attached to Haydon's Journal, now at Harvard. It is a draft of a prompt reply to Keats's letter of January 10 (No. 50), which reached Haydon on the morning of January 11. As No. 52 proves, Keats was in town on January 11 and 12, and when he returned to Hampstead he found No. 51 lying "on the table."

[2] "Bewick" is heavily scratched out in different ink. In the *Examiner*, March 7, 1819, p. 157, Haydon says that Bewick (1795–1866) became his pupil in 1816. *DNB* remarks that "his artistic promise was greater than his performance."

instruct him for the first two years, and then in the last he would be a great assistance to me I will subscribe £5—it is all I can afford, and all which ought to be expected of me, as I will do all in my power to inform him—I like him much he is docile & industrious & improves rapidly—I hope we shall succeed in getting the money—do your utmost & so will I—In the mean time I will go on with his Studies—with respect to our meeting the sooner My dear Keats the better—but accept this engagement as long as we live—every Sunday at *three* I shall be happy to see you as long as I live and you live, and as long as I have a bit of beef to give you when you have other engagements more important, come the sunday following &c

* * *

· 52 ·

TO GEORGE AND TOM KEATS [1]

13, 19 January 1818

Tuesday Hampstead 1818

My dear Brothers

I am certain I think of having a letter tomorrow morning for I expected one so much this morning, having been in town two days,[2] at the end of which my expectations began to get up a little, I found two on the table, one from Bailey & one from Haydon,[3] I am quite perplexed in a world of doubts & fancies—there is nothing stable in the world—uproar's your only musick,[4] I do not mean to include Bailey in this & so I dismiss him from this, with all the oprobrium he deserves, that is in so many words, he is one of the noblest men alive at the present day.[5] In a note to Haydon about a week ago, (which I wrote with a full sense of what he had done, and how he had never manifested any little mean drawback in his value of me) I said if there were three things superior in the modern world, they

[1] A transcript by Jeffrey, who dated it "Tuesday Hampstead 1818/ April 21."

[2] If the first sentence of No. 55 is to be taken literally, Keats returned home late on the night of January 12.

[3] The preceding letter.

[4] Compare "How Many Bards," line 14, "Make pleasing music, and not wild uproar."

[5] With the characterization compare his words at II, 66 f.

were "the Excursion." "Haydon's pictures" & "Hazlitts depth of Taste" [6] So I do believe—Not thus speaking ⟨that⟩ with any poor vanity that works of genius were the first things in this world. No! for that sort of probity & disinterestedness which such men as Bailey possess, does hold & grasp the tip top of any spiritual honours, that can be paid to any thing in this world—And moreover having this feeling at this present come over me in its full force, I sat down to write to you with a grateful heart, in that I had not a Brother, who did not feel & credit me, for a deeper feeling & devotion for his uprightness, than for any marks of genius however splendid I was speaking about doubts & fancies—I Mean there has been a quarrel of a severe nature between Haydon & Reynolds & another ("the Devil rides upon a fiddle stick") [7] between Hunt & Haydon—the first grew from the sunday [8] on which Haydon invited some friends to meet Wordsworth. Reynolds never went, & never sent any Notice about it, this offended Haydon more than it ought to have done—he wrote a very sharp & high note to Reynolds & then another in palliation—but which Reynolds feels as an aggravation of the first —Considering all things—Haydons frequent neglect of his Appointments &c. his notes were bad enough to put Reynolds on the right side of the question but then Reynolds has no powers of sufferance; no idea of having the thing against him; so he answered Haydon in one of the most cutting letters I ever read; exposing to himself all his own weaknesses, & going on to an excess, which whether it is just or no, is what I would fain have unsaid, the fact is they are both in the right & both in the wrong.

The quarrel with Hunt I understand thus far. M[rs] H. was in the habit of borrowing silver of Haydon, the last time she did so, Haydon asked her to return it at a certain time—She did not—Haydon sent for it; Hunt went to expostulate on the indelicacy &c. they got to words & parted for ever—All I hope is at some time to bring them all together again—Lawk! Molly there's been such doings [9]—Yesterday evening I made an appointment with Wells,

[6] See I, 203. The note was written four, not seven, days earlier.

[7] *1 Henry IV*, II.iv.534 f.

[8] December 28, 1817, the "immortal dinner." On the quarrels between Haydon and Reynolds and Haydon and Hunt see also I, 210.

[9] D. B. Green, *NQ*, December 24, 1949, p. 558, compares *Humphry Clinker* (Smollett's *Works* [1899–1901], III, 63), "O Molly! you that live in the country have no deception of our doings at Bath."

to go to a private theatre & it being in the neighbourhood of Drury Lane, & thinking we might be fatigued with sitting the whole evening in one dirty hole; I got the Drury Lane ticket & therewith we divided the evening with a Spice of Richard III [1]—Good Lord,! [2] I began this letter nearly a week ago, what have I been doing since —I have been—I mean not been sending last sunday's paper [3] to you I believe because it was not near me—for I cannot find it, & my conscience presses heavy on me for not sending it; You would have had one last thursday but I was called away, & have been about somewhere ever since. Where. What. well I rejoice almost that I have not heard from you, because no news is good news.—I cannot for the world recollect why I was called away, all I know is, that there has been a dance at Dilke's & another at the London Coffee House; [4] to both of which I went. But I must tell you in another letter the circumstances thereof—for though a week should have passed since I wrote on the other side it quite appalls me—I can only write in scraps & patches,[5] Brown is returned from Hampstead [6] —Haydon has returned an answer [7] in the same style—they are all dreadfully irritated against each other. On sunday [8] I saw Hunt & dined with Haydon, met Hazlitt & Bewick [9] there; & took Haslam with me—forgot to speak about Crips though I broke my engagement to Haslams on purpose—Mem. Haslam came to meet me, found me at Breakfast, had the goodness to go with me my way—I have just finished the revision of my first book, & shall take it to

[1] This evening of January 12 is more fully described in No. 56 (I, 215 f.). The "ticket," as MBF observes, is probably Brown's life admission to Drury Lane Theatre.

[2] That Keats is now writing on Monday, January 19, is shown by his references to "nearly a week ago" and to dining with Haslam at Haydon's, a dinner on January 18 vouched for by statements at I, 214.

[3] The *Examiner*.

[4] Operated by Leech and Company, wine merchants, 24 Ludgate Hill. Keats went to dances three times in January, 1818, on February 19, 1819, and on January 11, 1820. Because he asked his sister on February 27, 1819 (II, 42), "to teach me a few common dancing steps," his biographers assume that at least up to that time he could not dance. A non-dancer could hardly have made the comment about Rice's "dancing as if he was deaf" (I, 201), or have expressed an intention of not leaving Scotland "without having got the Highland fling"(I, 307).

[5] Compare *Hamlet*, III.iv.102, "A king of shreds and patches."

[6] Keats meant either "to Hampstead" or "from Hampshire," for Brown had been at Bedhampton (I, 199).

[7] Presumably to Reynolds.

[8] January 18; see I, 214.

[9] Bewick wrote to his brother and sister on February 11, 1818 (Thomas Landseer, *Life and Letters of William Bewick* [1871], I, 41), that he had been "at two or three very intellectual dinners" with Horace Smith, "Keats the poet," Hazlitt, Haydon, John Hunt, and others.

Taylor's tomorrow [10]—intend to persevere—Do not let me see many days pass without hearing from you

Your most affectionate Brother

(signed) John—

Mess[rs] Keats
Teignmouth Devonshire

· 53 ·

TO B. R. HAYDON [1]

23 January 1818

Friday 23rd—

My dear Haydon,

I have a complete fellow-feeling with you in this business [2]—so much so that it would be as well to wait for a choice out of *Hyperion* —when that Poem is done there will be a wide range for you—in Endymion I think you may have many bits of the deep and sentimental cast—the nature of *Hyperion* will lead me to treat it in a more naked and grecian Manner—and the march of passion and endeavour will be undeviating—and one great contrast between them will be—that the Hero of the written tale being mortal is led on, like Buonaparte, by circumstance; whereas the Apollo in Hyperion being a fore-seeing God will shape his actions like one. But I am counting &c.

Your proposal pleases me—and, believe me, I would not have my Head in the shop windows from any hand but yours—no by Apelles!

I will write Taylor [3] and you shall hear from me

Your's ever John Keats—

[10] See the promise he made to Taylor about the *Endymion* manuscript on January 10 (I, 201 f.).

[1] *ALS:* British Museum.

[2] Keats is replying to a letter he received from Haydon on January 19 about Taylor's proposal that Haydon make a drawing to be used as the frontispiece to *Endymion* (see I, 208, 213). His letter was sent by messenger.

[3] See the next letter.

· 54 ·

TO JOHN TAYLOR [1]

23 January 1818

Friday 23rd

My dear Taylor,

I have spoken to Haydon about the Drawing [2]—he would do it with all his Art and Heart too if so I will it—however he has written thus to me—but I must tell you first, he intends painting a finished picture from the Poem—thus he writes

"When I do any thing for your poem, it must be effectual—an honor to both of us—to hurry up a sketch for the season won't do. I think an engraving from your head, from a Chalk drawing of mine—done with all my might—to which I would put my name, would answer Taylor's Idea more than the other indeed I am sure of it—this I will do & this will be effectual and as I have not done it for any other human being—it will have an effect" [3]

What think you of this? Let me hear—I shall have my second book in readiness forthwith—

Your's most sincerely
John Keats—

If Reynolds calls tell him three lines would be acceptable for I am squat [4] at Hampstead

[1] Printed from a facsimile in the Anderson Galleries catalog of the W. H. Arnold library, November, 1924, item 507. The letter was sent, like No. 53, by messenger. There is also a transcript by Woodhouse in his letter-book, pp. 102 f.

[2] See Nos. 53 and 56.

[3] Actually Haydon did nothing, and the book appeared without illustrations.

[4] See this word at I, 318, 321.

· 55 ·

TO BENJAMIN BAILEY [1]

23 January 1818

Address: Mr B. Bailey/ Magdalen Hall/ Oxford—
Postmarks: 7 o'Clock JA 23 1818 NT; A JA 23 818

My dear Bailey, Friday Jany 23rd

Twelve days have pass'd since your last reached me—what has gone through the myriads of human Minds since the 12th [2] we talk of the immense number of Books, the Volumes ranged thousands by thousands—but perhaps more goes through the human intelligence in 12 days than ever was written. How has that unfortunate Family lived through the twelve? [3] One saying of your's I shall never forget—you may not recollect it—it being perhaps said when you were looking on the surface and seeming of Humanity alone, without a thought of the past or the future—or the deeps of good and evil—you were at the moment estranged from speculation and I think you have arguments ready for the Man who would utter it to you—this is a formidable preface for a simple thing—merely you said; "*Why should Woman suffer?*" [4] Aye. Why should she? 'By heavens I'd coin my very Soul and drop my Blood for Drachmas."! [5] These things are, and he who feels how incompetent the most skyey Knight errantry [6] its [7] to heal this bruised fairness is like a sensitive leaf on the hot hand of thought. Your tearing, my dear friend, a spirit-
to
less and gloomy Letter up ⟨and⟩ rewrite to me is what I shall never forget—it was to me a real thing.[8] Things have happen'd lately

[1] *ALS:* Harvard (with a Tassie's Shakespeare-head seal). There is also a transcript of this letter by a clerk in Woodhouse's letter-book, pp. 83–85, with corrections by Woodhouse.

[2] This sentence indicates that he returned late in the night of January 12.

[3] Bailey put an X in the margin opposite this sentence, which he underlined. On the address fold he wrote: "This letter opens the excellent feelings of an excellent heart. 'The unfortunate family' mentioned was most kindly treated by poor Keats. BB."

[4] Underlined, apparently by Keats. Woodhouse's clerk underlined it and the sentence mentioned in note 3.

[5] *Julius Caesar*, IV.iii.72 f., "By heaven, I had rather coin my heart," etc.

[6] The word looks like "errartry." [7] *For* is.

[8] Compare his use of "real" at I, 160, 325.

of great Perplexity—You must have heard of them—Reynolds and Haydon retorting and recrimminating—and parting for ever—the same thing has happened between Haydon and Hunt[9]—It is unfortunate—Men should bear with each other—there lives not the Man who may not be cut up, aye hashed to pieces on his weakest side. The best of Men have but a portion of good in them—a kind of spiritual yeast in their frames which creates the ferment of existence—by which a Man is propell'd to act and strive and buffet with Circumstance. The sure way Bailey, is first to know a Man's faults, and then be passive, if after that he insensibly draws you towards him then you have no Power to break the link. Before I felt interested in either Reynolds or Haydon—I was well read in their faults yet knowing them I have been cementing gradually with both —I have an affection for them both for reasons almost opposite— and to both must I of necessity cling—supported always by the hope that when a little time—a few years shall have tried me more fully in their esteem I may be able to bring them together—the time must come because they have both hearts—and they will recollect the best parts of each other when this gust is overblown.[1] I had a Message from you through a Letter to Jane[2]⟨,⟩ I think about Cripps —there can be no idea of binding[3] till a sufficient sum is sure for him—and even then the thing should be maturely consider'd by all his helpers. I shall try my luck upon as many fat-purses as I can meet with—Cripps is improving very fast—I have the greater hopes of him because he is so slow in devellopment—a Man of great executing Powers at 20—with a look and a speech almost stupid is sure to do something. I have just look'd th[r]ough the second side of your Letter—I feel a great content at it. I was at Hunt's the other day, and he surprised me with a real authenticated Lock of *Milton's Hair.*[4] I know you would like what I wrote thereon—so here it is—*as they say of a Sheep in a Nur*sery Book

On seeing a Lock of Milton's Hair—

[9] On these quarrels see also I, 205. Haydon wrote of Hunt in 1824 (Duncan Gray and Violet Walker, *K–SMB*, No. 7 [1956], 24): "After we separated His wife wished me to return, but as I knew him to the core—I declined."

[1] Possibly a reminiscence of "Il Penseroso," line 128, "When the gust hath blown his fill."

[2] Reynolds.

[3] That is, of apprenticing him to Haydon (I, 203).

[4] On Hunt's collection of locks of hair, see T. R. Leigh-Hunt, *The John Keats Memorial Volume* (1921), pp. 107–109. The collection is now in the library of the University of Texas. Keats saw it on January 21. The underlining here and in the next sentence may be Bailey's.

Ode. [5]

Chief of organic Numbers!
Old scholar of the spheres!
Thy spirit never slumbers,
But rolls about our ears
For ever and for ever.
O, what a mad endeavour
Worketh he
Who, to thy sacred and ennobled hearse,
Would offer a burnt sacrifice of verse
And Melody!

How heavenward thou soundedst [6]
Live Temple of sweet noise;
And discord unconfoundedst: [6]
Giving delight new joys,
And Pleasure nobler pinions—
O where are thy Dominions!
Lend thine ear
To a young delian oath—aye, by thy soul,
By all that from thy mortal Lips did roll;
And by the kernel of thine earthly Love,
Beauty, in things on earth and things above,[7]
When every childish fashion
Has vanish'd from my rhyme
Will I grey-gone in passion,
Give to an after-time
Hymning and harmony
Of thee, and of⟨f⟩ thy Works and of thy Life:
But vain is now the burning and the strife—
Pangs are in vain—until I grow high-rife
With Old Philosophy
And mad with glimpses at futurity!

[5] Omitted in other texts of the poem.

[6] Other texts have "soundest" and "unconfoundest." See Garrod, pp. 478–480, for further variants.

[7] In his manuscript collection of Keats's poems (which Garrod calls "W²"), fol. 155, Woodhouse pencils in "I swear" as a new line and on the opposite page writes, "Should there not be a short line to rhyme with 'ear' at the end of this page, such as— 'I swear'? —" These words are also penciled in the original letter, and Garrod, p. 479, adopts them, beginning a new stanza with "When every childish fashion."

For many years my offerings must be hush'd:
When I do speak I'll think upon this hour,
Because I feel my forehead hot and flush'{d,}
Even at the simplest vassal of thy Po{wer—}
A Lock of thy bright hair!
Sudden it came,
And I was startled when I heard thy name
Coupled so unaware—
Yet, at the moment, temperate was my blood:
Methought I had beheld it from the flood.
Jany 21st

This I did at Hunt's at his request—perhaps I should have done something better alone and at home—I have sent my first book to the Press—and this afternoon shall begin preparing the second [8]—my visit to you will be a great spur to quicken the Proceeding—I have not had your Sermon [9] returned—I long to make it the subject of a Letter to you—What do they say at Oxford?
I trust you and Gleig pass much fine time together. Remember me to him and Whitehead. My Brother Tom is getting stronger but his Spitting of blood continues—I sat down to read King Lear yesterday, and felt the greatness of the thing up to the writing of a Sonnet [1] preparatory thereto—in my next you shall have it There were some miserable reports of Rice's health—I went and lo! Master Jemmy had been to the play the night before and was out at the time—he always comes on his Legs like a Cat—I have seen a good deal of Wordsworth. Hazlitt is lectu[r]ing on Poetry at the Surry institution—I shall be there next Tuesday.[2]

Your most affectionate Friend
John Keats—

[8] See No. 54. Bailey wrote to Taylor on February 22, 1818 (*KC*, I, 11), "Keats I expect here in his way to Devon," but the visit did not take place (see I, 240 f.).

[9] *A Discourse Inscribed to the Memory of the Princess Charlotte Augusta*, published anonymously by Taylor and Hessey (1817). It was praised by Coleridge and was reviewed by Dilke in the *Champion*, March 22, 1818 (*KC*, I, 8, 10, 20).

[1] See I, 214 f.

[2] January 27. Hazlitt's lectures at the Surrey Institution, Blackfriars Road, began on January 13 and ended on March 3.

· 56 ·

TO GEORGE AND TOM KEATS [1]

23, 24 January 1818

Friday 23[d] January 1818

My dear Brothers.

I was thinking what hindered me from writing so long,[2] for I have many things to say to you & know not where to begin. It shall be upon a thing most interesting to you my Poem. Well! I have given the 1st book to Taylor; he seemed more than satisfied with it, & to my surprise proposed publishing it in Quarto if Haydon would make a drawing of some event therein, for a Frontispeice. I called on Haydon,[3] he said he would do anything I liked, but said he would rather paint a finished picture, from it, which he seems ⟨to say⟩ eager to do; this in a year or two will be a glorious thing for us; & it will be, for Haydon is struck with the 1st Book. I left Haydon & the next day received a letter from him, proposing to make, as he says, with all his might, a finished chalk sketch of my head, to be engraved in the first style & put at the head of my Poem, saying at the same time he had never done the thing for any human being, & that it must have considerable effect as he will put the name to it—I begin to day to copy my 2nd Book "thus far into the bowels of the Land" [4]—You shall hear whether it will be Quarto or non Quarto, picture or non Picture.[5] Leigh Hunt I showed my 1st Book to, he allows it not much merit as a whole; says it is unnatural & made ten objections to it in the mere skimming over. He says the conversation is unnatural & too high-flown for the Brother & Sister. Says it should be simple forgetting do ye mind, that they are both overshadowed by a Supernatural Power, & of

[1] A transcript by Jeffrey, with the date "1818" changed to "1819."

[2] He had finished and presumably mailed a letter (No. 52) to them only four or five days before. See also the first sentence of No. 64.

[3] About January 21. For Haydon's abortive plans see I, 208.

[4] *Richard III*, V.ii.3.

[5] *Endymion* was "non Quarto, non Picture." Blunden, p. 495, cites the advice of Byron, October 30, 1815 (*Letters and Journals*, ed. R. E. Prothero [1922], III, 242), to Hunt: "Don't let your bookseller publish [*Rimini*] in *quarto;* it is the worst size possible for circulation. I say this on bibliopolical authority."

force could not speak like Franchesca in the Rimini. He must first prove that Caliban's poetry is unnatural,—This with me completely overturns his objections—the fact is he & Shelley are hurt & perhaps justly, at my not having showed them the affair officiously & from several hints I have had they appear much disposed to dissect & anatomize, any trip or slip I may have made.—But whose afraid Ay! Tom! demme if I am.[6] I went last tuesday,[7] an hour too late, to Hazlitt's Lecture on poetry, got there just as they were coming out, when all these pounced upon me. Hazlitt, John Hunt & son,[8] Wells, Bewick, all the Landseers,[9] Bob Harris, Rox of the Burrough[1] Aye & more; the Landseers enquired after you particularly—I know not whether Wordsworth has left town [2]—But sunday I dined with Hazlitt & Haydon, also that I took Haslam with me [3]—I dined with Brown lately. Dilke having taken the Champion, Theatricals [4] was obliged to be in Town. Fanny has returned to Walthamstow—Mr Abbey appeared very glum, the last time I went [to] see her, & said in an indirect way, that I had no business there—Rice has been ill, but has been mending much lately—I think a little change has taken place in my intellect lately—I cannot bear to be uninterested or unemployed, I, who for so long a time, have been addicted to passiveness—Nothing is finer for the purposes of great productions, than a very gradual ripening of the intellectual powers—As an instance of this—observe—I sat down yesterday to read King Lear once again the thing appeared to demand the prologue of a Sonnet, I wrote it [5] & began to read—(I know you would like to see it)

"On sitting down to King Lear once Again"
O golden tongued Romance with serene Lute!
Fair plumed syren! Queen! if[6] far away!
Leave melodizing on this wintry day,

[6] Keats is quoting from Horace Smith's *Nehemiah Muggs*, which he had read in manuscript (see I, 227, 234), "Pooh! Nonsense! damme! who's afraid." See also I, 246.

[7] January 20. Hazlitt's lectures were advertised as beginning precisely at 7 P.M. (*Literary Gazette*, January 10, 1818, p. 32).

[8] Henry Leigh Hunt. [9] See I, 198 n.

[1] *The Post Office London Directory* for 1819 and 1820 lists George Rokes, 247 Borough, and Richard Rokes, 7 Blackman Street, Borough, "undertakers." A slightly later directory gives the names as Richard and Henry Rokes and the addresses as 2 Blackman Street and 247 High Street, Borough.

[2] He had. [3] The dinner was on January 18 (I, 206). [4] See I, 199.

[5] See his comments to Bailey at I, 212.

[6] *Correctly* Queen of. (Garrod, p. 482, is cited. See him for details.)

Shut up thine olden volume [7] & be mute.
Adieu! for once again the fierce dispute,
Betwixt Hell torment [8] & impassioned Clay
Must I burn through; once more [9] assay
The bitter sweet of this Shakespeareian fruit
Cheif Poet! & ye clouds of Albion.
Begettors of our deep eternal theme,
When I am through the old oak forest gone [1]
Let me not wander in a barren dream
But when I am consumed with [2] the Fire
Give me new Pheonix-wings to fly at my desire

So you see I am getting at it, with a sort of determination & strength, though verily I do not feel it at this moment—this is my fourth letter [3] this morning & I feel rather tired & my head rather swimming—so I will leave it open till tomorrow's post.—— [4]

I am in the habit of taking my papers to Dilkes & copying there; so I chat & proceed at the same time. I have been there at my work this evening, & the walk over the Heath takes off all sleep, so I will even proceed with you—I left off short in my last,[5] just as I began an account of a private theatrical [6]—Well it was of the lowest order, all greasy & oily, insomuch that if they had lived in olden times, when signs were hung over the doors; the only appropriate one for that oily place would have been—a guttered Candle—they played John Bull The Review. & it was to conclude with Bombastes Furioso [7]

[7] pages *Garrod.* [8] Betwixt damnation *Garrod.* [9] more humbly *Garrod.*

[1] When through the old oak Forest I am gone *Garrod.*

[2] in *Garrod.* [3] Remarkably enough they are all (Nos. 53–56) preserved.

[4] The remainder of the letter was written late in the evening of January 24.

[5] He refers to No. 52 (see I, 206), and then tells what plays he saw with Wells on January 12.

[6] The *British Stage, and Literary Cabinet*, December, 1819 (IV, 61), says a private theater is one "where the audience are admitted gratis, and the performers pay for playing." In other issues, as January, 1817, July, 1818, July and August, 1819 (I, 23, II, 159, III, 209 f., 247), it describes private theaters, like one in Gough Street, Gray's Inn Lane, and another in Wilson Street, Gray's Inn Lane, in language that closely parallels Keats's remarks. The *Theatrical Inquisitor*, December, 1818 (XIII, 412–414), however, gives a more favorable verdict on plays "represented in private, by unprofessional persons, for their own amusement and that of their friends."

[7] Jeffrey's bad copying obscures the fact that the private theater had announced at least three plays: the younger George Colman's *John Bull, Or, The Englishman's Fire-side* (1803), a five-act comedy, and *The Review, Or, The Wags of Windsor: A Musical Farce* (1801), in two acts, and William Barnes Rhodes's *Bombastes Furioso* (1810), a burlesque tragic opera in one act. The last was "not played." Keats saw only the first act of *John Bull*, then went to Drury Lane to see *Richard III* with Kean, and returned to wait in vain

—I saw from a Box the 1st Act of John Bull, then I went to Drury & did not return till it was over; when by Wells'[8] interest we got behind the scenes. there was not a yard wide all the way round for actors, scene shifters & interlopers to move in; for 'Note Bene'[9] the Green Room was under the stage & there was I threatened over & over again to be turned out by the oily scene shifters—there did I hear a little painted Trollop own, very candidly, that she had failed in Mary, with a "damned if she'd play a serious part again, as long as she lived," & at the same time she was[1] habited as the Quaker in the Review—there was a quarrel & a fat good natured looking girl in soldiers Clothes wished she had only been a man for Tom's sake[2]—One fellow began a song but an unlucky finger-point from the Gallery sent him off like a shot, One chap was dressed to kill for the King in Bombastes. & he stood at the edge of the scene in the very sweat of anxiety to show himself, but Alas the thing was not played. the sweetest morsel of the night[3] moreover was, that the musicians began pegging & fagging away at an overture—never did you see faces more in earnest, three times did they play it over, dropping all kinds of correctness & still did not the curtain draw up —Well then they went into a country-dance then into a region they well knew, into their old boonsome[4] Pothouse. & then to see how pompous o' the sudden they turned; how they looked about, & chatted; how they did not care a Damn; was a great treat—I hope I have not tired you by this filling up of the dash in my last,[5]—Constable the Bookseller has offered Reynolds ten gineas a sheet to write for his magazine. it is an Edinburgh one which, Blackwoods

---

for *Bombastes Furioso.* Incidentally, Drury Lane and Covent Garden began performances at 6:30 till the end of the season on June 20, 1817, and at 7:00 with the new season starting September 6.

[8] Jeffrey has "Well's."

[9] *Sic.* Keats may have meant "take notice," or he may be referring to *Nota Bene*, "a rather amusing farce . . . admirably performed" (*British Stage, and Literary Cabinet*, January, 1817 [I, 7]) at Drury Lane on December 12 and 13, 1816. According to W. C. Oulton, *A History of the Theatres of London* (1818), I, 348, the work of E. T. Hookham, on its first night the audience showed "much disapprobation" and "on the second night . . . [it] was finally condemned.—*Not published.*"

[1] Jeffrey has "was she was."

[2] Mary Thornberry in *John Bull;* "the merry young Quaker," Grace Gaylove, heroine of *The Review;* and Phoebe Whitethorne, a female "dressed as a private soldier," in *The Review.* "Tom," I suppose, was the actor who played the Honourable Tom Shuffleton in *John Bull.*

[3] *2 Henry IV*, II.iv.396 f.

[4] Not in *NED*, but compare "boon companion."

[5] For the dash see I, 206.

started up in opposition to.[6] Hunt said he was nearly sure that the 'Cockney School' was written by Scott,[7] so you are right Tom!— There are no more little bits of news I can remember at present I remain

My dear Brothers Your very affectionate Brother
(signed) John

Messrs Keats
Teignmouth Devonshire.[8]

[6] Archibald Constable (1774–1827) published the *Scots Magazine* (1801–1817), to which Reynolds certainly contributed in 1818–1819 (it was then called the *Edinburgh Magazine, and Literary Miscellany*), and the *Edinburgh Review, or Critical Journal* (beginning in October, 1802). In opposition to the latter William Blackwood (1776–1834) founded in April, 1817, *Blackwood's Edinburgh Magazine*, which in its seventh number, October, 1817, contained Lockhart's first article on the Cockney School of Poetry. Reynolds "has become an edinburgh Reviewer," Keats wrote in December, 1818 (II, 7), and Leonidas M. Jones (*K–SJ*, VI [1957], 102) has identified as his contribution the elaborate review of Hazlitt in the *Scots Magazine*, December, 1818, January, February, 1819 (see II, 24 n.). Discussing the dullness of that magazine, J. G. Lockhart, *Peter's Letters to His Kinsfolk* (2nd ed., Edinburgh, 1819), II, 227 f., conceded that it had a few good articles by Hazlitt "and a few better still by a gay writer of the name of Reynolds." The latter, he said, "is certainly a very promising writer, and might surely do better things than copying the Cockneys."

[7] The reference cannot be to Sir Walter. Hunt and John Scott had waged a bitter war about Byron in the *Champion* and the *Examiner* during 1816. Naturally Hunt suspected his old enemy (whom Tom Keats had met in Paris) of having written the Cockney School attacks, a suspicion widely held. John Scott wrote to the publisher, Robert Baldwin, January 24, 1819, of having seen two issues of *Blackwood's:* "I sent to England for them because some one had said (I was told) that *I* had written the scandalous article on Mr. Hunt! Articles I read with disgust and abhorrence." Haydon at first thought that "Z." was the author and playwright Daniel Terry (1780?–1829) and next Christopher North (Penrose, pp. 228, 251). De Quincey, too (see H. A. Eaton, *Thomas De Quincey* [New York, 1936], p. 282), identified him as "North." It has long been known that J. G. Lockhart was the guilty man. His latest biographer, Marion Lochhead (1954), makes no effort to defend him, but speaks, p. 39, of his "remorse" in later life.

[8] Jeffrey added for Milnes's information: "(Note—Mr Abbey mentioned in the previous letter [No. 56] was Guardian to the Keats family)."

·57·

TO JOHN TAYLOR [1]

30 January 1818

Address: John Taylor Esqre/ 91 [2] New Bond Street
Postmarks: TwoPyPost Unpaid SOHampstead; 7 o'Clock JA 30 1818 N^{T}

My dear Taylor, Friday

These Lines, as they now stand, about Happiness have rung in my ears like a 'chime a mending'. [3] see here,

Behold
Wherein Lies happiness Pœona? fold—

This appears to me the very contrary of blessed. I hope this will appear to you more elegible.

Wherein lies Happiness? In that which becks
Our ready Minds to fellowship divine;
A fellowship with essence, till we shine
Full alchymized and free of space. Behold
The clear Religion of heaven—fold &c— [4]

You must indulge me by putting this in for setting aside the badness of the other, such a preface is necessary to the Subject. The whole thing must I think have appeared to you, who are a consequitive Man, as a thing almost of mere words—but I assure you that when I wrote it, it was a regular stepping of the Imagination towards a
Argument
Truth. My having written that ⟨Passage⟩ will perhaps be of the greatest Service to me of any thing I ever did—It set before me at once the gradations of Happiness even like a kind of Pleasure Thermometer [5]—and is my first Step towards the chief Attempt in the

[1] *ALS:* Pierpont Morgan Library. On it Woodhouse notes: "Postmark Jany 30. 1818." Woodhouse also made a transcript in his letter-book, p. 3.

[2] Followed by a slant line.

[3] He might also have quoted the "like a" (*Troilus and Cressida*, I.iii.159).

[4] So printed in *Endymion*, I.777–781. For details see Garrod, p. 88.

[5] For comments on "versions" of the pleasure thermometer see E. R. Wasserman, *The Finer Tone* (Baltimore, 1953), pp. 69, 196, 207.

Drama [6]—the playing of different Natures with Joy and Sorrow.

Do me this favor and believe Me, Your sincere friend

John Keats

I hope your next Work [7] will be of a more general Interest—I s[u]ppose you cogitate a little about it now and then.[8]

· 58 ·

TO J. H. REYNOLDS [1]

31 January 1818

My Dear Reynolds Hampstead Saturday

I have parcelld out this day for Letter Writing—more resolved thereon because your Letter will come as a refreshment and will have (sic parvis &c) [2] the same effect as a Kiss in certain situations where people become over-generous. I have read this first sentence over, and think it savours rather; however an inward innocence is like a nested dove; [3] or as the old song says.

1

O blush not so, O blush not so [4]
or I shall think ye knowing;
And if ye smile, the blushing while
Then Maidenheads are going.

2

There's a blush for want, and a blush for shan't
And a blush for having done it,

[6] On Keats's plans to write great drama see II, 139, 234.

[7] *The Identity of Junius with a Distinguished Living Character Established*, 2nd ed. (1818). See I, 237 n.

[8] At the foot of the page Woodhouse has written "To/ John Taylor, Esqre/ 91 New Bond S^{t}/."

[1] A transcript in Woodhouse's letter-book, pp. 53–55, by a clerk, with corrections by Woodhouse, who supplies the date "31 Jany 1818—"

[2] Virgil, *Eclogues*, I.24. Woodhouse corrected his clerk's bad Latin here.

[3] Compare Isaac Watts (*Poetical Works*, ed. Samuel Johnson [1807], III, 90), "But Thomas and William, and such pretty names,/ Should be cleanly, and harmless, as doves, or as lambs,/ Those lovely sweet innocent creatures."

[4] For variants in other texts see Garrod, p. 542. Oddly enough, Swinburne, writing to W. M. Rossetti on May 23, 1870 (so Cecil Y. Lang tells me), called the poem a "short bawdy song which was unfit for publication."

There's a blush for thought, and a blush for naught
And a blush for just begun it.

3

O sigh not so, O sigh [5] not so
For it sounds of Eve's sweet Pipin
By those loosen'd hips,[6] you have tasted the pips
o
And f⟨a⟩ught in an amorous nipping.

4

Will ye play once more, at nice cut core
For it only will last our youth out,
And we have the prime, of the Kissing time
We have not one sweet tooth out.

–5– [7]

There's a sigh for yes, and a sigh for no,
And a sigh for "I can't bear it"—
O what can be done, shall we stay or run
O cut the sweet apple and share it?

Now I purposed to write to you a serious poetical Letter—but I find that a maxim I met with the other day is a just one "on cause mieux [8] quand on ne dit pas *causons*" I was hindered however from my first intention by a mere muslin Handkerchief very neatly pinned—but "Hence vain deluding &c" [9] Yet I cannot write in prose, It is a sun-shiny day and I cannot so here goes,

Hence Burgundy, Claret & port [1]
Away with old Hock and Madeira
Too couthly [2] ye are for my sport
There's a Beverage brighter and clearer

[5] Woodhouse and Garrod, p. 542, interpret both "sigh's" as a Cockney pronunciation of "say," and substitute that word.

[6] Garrod miscredits this text with reading "lips."

[7] The clerk wrote "5" at the foot of page 53 and then "–5–" before the stanza at the top of page 54.

[8] His *x*'s often look like "œ."

[9] Milton, "Il Penseroso," line 1.

[1] It is hardly possible to reproduce exactly the indentions. For variant readings in other texts see Garrod, pp. 480 f.

[2] Opposite this word Woodhouse wrote "so" (that is, *sic*); perhaps Keats meant "familiar." Garrod reads "earthly."

Instead of a pitiful rummer
My Wine overbrims a whole Summer
My bowl is the sky
And I drink at my eye
Till I feel in the brain
A delphian pain—
The[n] follow my Caius [3] then follow
On the Green of the Hill
We will drink our fill
Of golden sunshine
Till our brains intertwine
With the glory and grace of Apollo!

God of the Meridian
And of the East and West
To thee my soul is flown
And my body is earthward press'd—
It is an awful mission
A terrible division
And leaves a gulph austere
To be filled with worldly fear—
Aye, when the Soul is fled
To high above our head
Affrighted do we gaze
After its airy maze—
As doth a Mother wild
When her young infant child
Is in an eagle's claws—
And is not this the cause
of Madness? God of Song
Thou bearest me along
Through sights I scarce can bear
O let me, let me share
With the hot Lyre and thee
The staid Philosophy.
Temper my lonely hours
And let me see thy bowr's
More unalarm'd!—

[3] "Caius" means Reynolds, who sometimes used that signature (see I, 228 n.).

My Dear Reynolds, you must forgive all this ranting—but the fact is I cannot write sense this Morning—however you shall have some —I will copy my last Sonnet.

When I have fears that I may cease to be [4]
  Before my pen has glean'd my teeming brain,
Before high piled Books in charactery
  Hold like full garners the full ripen'd grain—
When I behold upon the night's starr'd face
  Huge cloudy symbols of a high romance
And feel that I may never live to trace
  Their shadows with the magic hand of Chance:
And when I feel, fair creature of an hour,
  That I shall never look upon thee more
Never have relish in the fairy power
  Of unreflecting Love: then on the Shore
    Of the wide world I stand alone and think
    Till Love and Fame to Nothingness do sink.—

I must take a turn, and then write to Teignmouth—Remember me to all, not excepting yourself.

Your sincere friend,
John Keats.

Mr J. H Reynolds.
Little Britain
Christs Hospital.

[4] In the margin Woodhouse, who was verifying transcripts of letters made by his clerk, picked up the wrong letter, added the postscript "Give my love to both houses—hinc atque illinc," and then deleted it, seeing that it belongs to No. 44.

· 59 ·

TO J. H. REYNOLDS [1]

3 February 1818

Hampstead Tuesday.

My dear Reynolds,

I thank you for your dish of Filberts—Would I could get a basket of them by way of desert every day for the sum of two pence— [2] Would we were a sort of ethereal Pigs, & turn'd loose to feed upon spiritual Mast & Acorns—which would be merely being a squirrel & feed [3] upon filberts. for what is a squirrel but an airy pig, or a filbert but a sort of archangelical acorn. About the nuts being worth cracking, all I can say is that where there are a throng of delightful Images ready drawn simplicity is the only thing. the first is the best on account of the first line, and the "arrow—foil'd of its antler'd food" [4]—and moreover (and this is the only ⟨only⟩ word or two I find fault with, the more because I have had so much reason to shun it as a quicksand) the last has "tender and true" [5]—We must cut this, and not be rattlesnaked into any more of the like—It may be said that we ought to read our Contemporaries. that Wordsworth &c should have their due from us. but for the sake of a few fine imaginative or domestic passages, are we to be bullied into a certain Philosophy engendered in the whims of an Egotist [6]—Every man has his speculations, but every man does not brood and peacock over them till he makes a false coinage and deceives himself—

[1] A transcript by Woodhouse in his letter-book, pp. 28–30. His clerk also copied most of the first three sentences again on p. 55, but Woodhouse deleted them, noting "This letter is already copied—See page 28." On pp. 30 and 55 he gives the date as "Feby 3. 1818."

[2] Woodhouse here inserts "(2 Sonnets on Robin Hood sent by R. by the 2^{dy} post)." The sonnets, beginning "The trees in Sherwood forest are old and good" and "With coat of Lincoln green and mantle too," were afterwards printed in the *Yellow Dwarf*, February 21, 1818, p. 64, and in Reynolds' book, *The Garden of Florence* (1821), pp. 124–127.

[3] *For* feeding.

[4] Sonnet 1, line 5, "No arrow found,—foil'd of its antler'd food."

[5] Sonnet 2, line 8, "His green-wood beauty sits, tender and true." For the last three words Reynolds in his 1821 text substituted "young as the dew."

[6] W. J. Bate, in *Major British Writers*, ed. G. B. Harrison (New York, 1954), II, 299 n., observes: "Keats, in his contrast of Wordsworth with the Elizabethans, is following Hazlitt, for whom much of the poetry of the Romantic movement, especially that of Wordsworth, was subjective self-expression."

Many a man can travel to the very bourne of Heaven,[7] and yet want confidence to put down his halfseeing. Sancho will invent a Journey heavenward as well as any body.[8] We hate poetry that has a palpable design upon us—and if we do not agree, seems to put its hand in its breeches pocket. Poetry should be great & unobtrusive, a thing which enters into one's soul, and does not startle it or amaze it with itself but with its subject.—How beautiful are the retired flowers! how would they lose their beauty were they to throng into the highway crying out, "admire me I am a violet! dote upon me I am a primrose! Modern poets differ from the Elizabethans in this. Each of the moderns like an Elector of Hanover governs his petty state, & knows how many straws are swept daily from the Causeways in all his dominions & has a continual itching that all the Housewives

Emperors

should have their coppers well scoured: the antients were ⟨Emperors

of vast

of large⟩ Provinces, they had only heard of the remote ones and scarcely cared to visit them.—I will cut all this—I will have no more of Wordsworth or Hunt in particular—Why should we be of the tribe of Manasseh, when we can wander with Esau? [9] why should we kick against the Pricks,[1] when we can walk on Roses? Why should we be owls, when we can be Eagles? Why be teased with "nice Eyed wagtails," [2] when we have in sight "the Cherub Contemplation"? [3] —Why with Wordsworths "Matthew with a bough of wilding in his hand" [4] when we can have Jacques "under an oak &c" [5]—The secret of the Bough of Wilding will run through your head faster than I can write it—Old Matthew spoke to him some years ago on some nothing, & because he happens in an Evening Walk to imagine the figure of the old man—he must stamp it down in black & white, and it is henceforth sacred—I don't mean to deny Wordsworth's grandeur & Hunt's merit, but I mean to say we need not be teazed with grandeur & merit—when we can have them un-

[7] *Hamlet*, III.i.79 f.

[8] Jack Stillinger thinks that the reference may be, not to *Don Quixote*, but to *Le depart de Sancho Panza*, a divertisement performed after the first act of the opera *Griselda*, King's Theatre, January 10 and 13.

[9] He refers to Genesis and to Judges vi.15, vii.23, etc. (compare II, 135).

[1] Acts ix.5, xxvi.14.

[2] Hunt, *Foliage* (1818), p. xxxiii.

[3] Milton, "Il Penseroso," line 54.

[4] Wordsworth, "The Two April Mornings," lines 59 f.

[5] *As You Like It*, II.i.31.

contaminated & unobtrusive. Let us have the old Poets, & robin Hood Your letter and its sonnets gave me more pleasure than will the 4th Book of Childe Harold [6] & the whole of any body's life & opinions. In return for your dish of filberts, I have gathered a few Catkins, I hope they'll look pretty.

To J. H. R. In answer to his Robin Hood Sonnets.

"No those days are gone away &c"— See Coll: p 58 [7]

I hope you will like them they are at least written in the Spirit of Outlawry.—Here are the Mermaid lines

"Souls of Poets dead & gone, &c"— [8] ib. p 61.

I will call on you at 4 tomorrow, and we will trudge together for it is not the thing to be a stranger in the Land of Harpsicols. [9] I hope also to bring you my 2d book [1]—In the hope that these Scribblings will be some amusement for you this Evening—I remain copying ⟨still⟩ on the Hill

Yr sincere friend and Coscribbler
John Keats.

[6] Byron's fourth canto was published in April, 1818.

[7] This and the following page reference are to Woodhouse's own manuscript of Keats's poems (which Garrod calls W2). In this letter Woodhouse gives only the first line of each poem.

[8] E. F. Madden, *Harper's New Monthly Magazine*, LV (1877), 361, has the following important comments based upon a now lost letter of Keats shown him by George Keats's daughter, Mrs. Philip Speed:

"In one of the letters from Keats to his brother he alludes to an evening at the 'Mermaid' with Horace Twiss and Horace Smith, saying their being together at this place revived thoughts of Ben Jonson, Fletcher, Beaumont, and others who used to assemble there in days of yore. Upon the occasion in question Keats composed the lines commencing,

"'Souls of poets dead and gone,
What Elysium have ye known,
Happy field or mossy cavern,
Fairer than the Mermaid tavern?'

" 'Reynolds, Dilke, and others,' says Keats, 'were pleased with this beyond any thing I ever did.'

"In this letter Keats alludes to the fondness of Twiss for repeating extempore verses —written, however, at home—and incloses a very clever take-off on him and his verses by Horace Smith."

(For what may be the "take-off" on Twiss, see W. G. Lane, *MLN*, LXX [1955], 22–24.)

[9] *NED* has examples of this word (harpsicord) from 1616 to 1773. MBF suggests that Keats and Reynolds were going to another musical evening at the Novellos'.

[1] Of *Endymion*.

·60·

TO JOHN TAYLOR [1]

5 February 1818

Address: John Taylor Esqre/ 91 New Bond Street
Postmarks: TwoPyPost Unpaid Ludgate Hill; 7 o'Clock FE 5 1818 N[T]

Fleet Street Thurs—Morn

My dear Taylor,

I have finish'd coppying my Second Book [2] but I want it for one day to overlook it—and moreover this day I have very particular employ in the affair of Cripps—so I tresspass on your indulgence and take advantage of your good nature—

You shall hear from me or see me soon—I will tell Reynolds of your engagement—tomorrow.

Your's unfeignedly [3]
John Keats—

·61·

TO GEORGE AND TOM KEATS [1]

14 (?) February 1818

Hampstead Saturday Night

My dear Brothers

When once a man delays a letter beyond the proper time, he delays it longer for one or two reasons; first because he must begin in a very commonplace style, that is to say, with an excuse; & secondly things & circumstances become so jumbled in his mind, that he knows not what, or what not, he has said in his last—I shall visit you as soon as I have copied my poem [2] all out, I am now much beforehand with the printer, they have done none yet, & I am half

[1] *ALS:* Harvard. Woodhouse copied this letter in his letter-book, p. 103.

[2] Of *Endymion,* which he had begun on January 23 (I, 212).

[3] This phrase also concludes No. 11.

[1] A transcript by Jeffrey, who supplied under "Hampstead . . . Night" the incorrect date "February 16 1819" with "9" written over "8." On the date see I, 228 n.

[2] *Endymion.*

afraid they will let half the season by before the printing, I am determined they shall not trouble me when I have copied it all.—Horace Smith has lent me his manuscript called "Nehemiah Muggs, an exposure of the Methodists" perhaps I may send you a few extracts [3]—Hazlitts last Lecture was on Thompson, Cowper & Crabbe, he praised Cowper & Thompson [4] but he gave Crabbe an unmerciful licking [5]—I think Hunts article of Fazio—no it was not, but I saw Fazio the first night,[6] it hung rather heavily on me—I am in the high way of being introduced to a squad of people, Peter Pindar,[7] Mrs Opie.[8] Mrs Scott [9]—Mr Robinson a great friend of Coleridges called on me [1]—Richards tell[s] me that my Poems are known in the west country & that he saw a very clever copy of verses, headed with a Motto from my Sonnet to George [2]—Honors rush so thickly upon me that I shall not be able to bear up against them. What think you, am I to be crowned in the Capitol,[3] am I to be made a Mandarin—No! I am to be invited, Mrs Hunt tells me, to a party at Ollier's to keep Shakespeares birthday Shakespeare would stare to see me there [4]—The Wednesday before last [5] Shelley, Hunt

[3] He sent extracts (54 lines) on a separate sheet which Jeffrey copied: see below.

[4] James Thomson (1700–1748). Keats's own spelling was "Thompson" (II, 78).

[5] Hazlitt lectured on eight Tuesdays, January 13, 20 (Keats missed this lecture: see I, 214), 27, February 3, 10, 17, 24, March 3.

[6] *Fazio* by Henry Hart Milman (1791–1868) was presented at Covent Garden on February 5. The London *Courier*, February 6, says that it "experienced throughout a most favourable reception."

[7] See I, 197.

[8] Amelia Alderson (Mrs. John) Opie (1769–1853), novelist and poet.

[9] Caroline Colnaghi (Mrs. John) Scott, who admired Keats's work as early as July, 1817 (MBF, p. xv), and whom George and Tom Keats met in Paris in 1817 (I, 198). Keats disliked her husband (II, 364).

[1] Henry Crabb Robinson (1775–1867), diarist, who fails to mention the visit in his published or unpublished journals.

[2] "Many the wonders I this day have seen," published in the 1817 *Poems*. The West Country verses have not yet been found.

[3] Compare Reynolds to Haydon, August 26, 1816 (Leonidas M. Jones, *K-SJ*, VI [1957], 98 f.), "your name will be put up in the Capital. . . . Honours shall be heaped upon you."

[4] Because of the insulting letter (first printed in the *Athenaeum*, June 7, 1873, p. 725) Charles and James Ollier, Keats's original publishers, had sent to George Keats on April 29, 1817. In it (see MBF, pp. 100 f.) they expressed "regret that your brother ever requested us to publish his book," which a gentleman had told them that he considered "no better than a take in," and relief that George was about to spare them "the unpleasant necessity" of having "any further connexion with it." The letter was no doubt written by James Ollier, for Charles had expressed his admiration of the 1817 *Poems* in a sonnet (see Colvin, 1920, p. 131, and Hewlett, p. 77), while in his collection of stories, *Inesilla* (1824), he mentions Keats very eulogistically (see Rollins, *NQ*, March, 1953, p. 118). Keats must have heard of Charles Ollier's invitation when he dined with the Hunts (I, 39) on February 11.

[5] February 4.

& I wrote each a Sonnet on the River Nile, some day you shall read them all.[6] I saw a sheet of Endymion & have all reason to suppose they will soon get it done.[7] there shall be nothing wanting on my part. I have been writing at intervals many songs & Sonnets,[8] & I long to be at Teignmouth, to read them over to you: however I think I had better wait till this Book is off my mind; it will not be long first,

Reynolds has been writing two very capital articles in the Yellow Dwarf on popular Preachers [9]—All the talk here is about Dr Croft the Duke of Devon &c [1] Your most affectionate Brother

(signed) John.

Messrs Keats

Teignmouth Devon.

(The following Extracts from Horace Smith's Manuscript are on a loose sheet enclosed in the previous letter of date Hampstead. February 16th—) [2]

[6] In January, 1847 (*KC*, II, 181 f.), Leigh Hunt sent Milnes copies of his sonnet ("It flows through old hush'd Ægypt and its sands") and Keats's ("Son of the old moon-mountains African"), and misinformed him that Shelley's was "Ozymandias." Only in 1876 did Milnes learn that Shelley's Nile sonnet was "Month after month the gather'd rains descend" (the same, II, 352). Meanwhile, Milnes in 1848, had printed, I, 99 f., Hunt's and Keats's. All critics consider Keats's inferior to Hunt's.

[7] These remarks indicate that, once again, Jeffrey made large omissions from a letter written on more than one day. When Keats began the letter, the printers had done nothing on *Endymion*, and he was fearing an indefinite delay; before he finished it, he had seen one printed sheet, and he thought that the printers would soon have the entire poem set up.

[8] Among them were "To a Lady Seen for a Few Moments at Vauxhall," "To Spenser," "Blue! 'tis the life of heaven," as well as the poems at I, 225.

[9] "Pulpit Oratory" appeared in the *Yellow Dwarf*, February 7, 14, 28, April 4, pp. 46–48, 51–53, 67 f., 108 f., the first three articles being signed "Caius."

[1] Sir Richard Croft (1762–1818) was widely accused of negligence after the death of the Princess Charlotte Augusta in childbirth, November 6, 1817, though only two days later (Robert Huish, *Memoirs of . . . Charlotte Augusta* [1818], pp. 547 f.) the Prince Regent had sent him a message applauding "the zealous care and indefatigable attention" he had given the princess, and expressing "entire confidence in the medical skill and ability which he displayed." Croft was also defended by William Cooke in *An Address to British Females* (1817), but the gossip preyed on his mind, so that he shot himself on February 12, 1818. His suicide revived the old rumor that Elizabeth Hervey (1760–1824), widow of John Thomas Foster, and later the second wife of William Cavendish, fifth Duke of Devonshire (1748–1811), and Georgiana Spencer (1757–1806), the duke's first wife, had in 1790 exchanged their infant son and daughter with the connivance of Croft, a scandalous report repeated by Vicary Gibbs in *The Complete Peerage*, IV (1916), 348 n. Keats read about these things in the *Examiner*, February 15, 1818, pp. 105, 109.

[2] This caption and the lines that follow it are in Jeffrey's hand. Part of Smith's satire was later printed in the *London Magazine*, February, March, June, 1821 (III, 200–202, 280–282, 648–650), where, however, only eight of the lines ("Is it that addled . . . appear

——Poem. Nehemiah Muggs—An Exposure of the Methodists——

Muggs had long wished to be a father
And told his wish without succeeding
At length Rose brought him two together
And there I think she show'd her breeding

Behold them in the Holy place
With others all agog for Grace
Where a perspiring preacher vexes
Sundry old women of both sexes

Thumping as though his zeal were pushing
To make a convert of the cushion

But in their hurry to proceed ⟨each reached the doo⟩
Each reached the door at the same minute
Where as the[y] scuffled for the lead
Both struggling stuck together in it

Shouting rampant amorous hymns
Under pretext of singing Psalms

———

He shudder'd & withdrew his eye
Perk'd up his head some inches higher
Drew his chair nearer to the fire
And hummed as if he would have said
Pooh! Nonsense! damme! who's afraid
Or sought by bustling up his frame
To make his courage do the same
Thus would some blushing trembling Elves
Conceal their terrors from themselves
By their own cheering wax the bolder
And pat themselves upon the shoulder

A Saints' a sort of human Mill
That labours when the body's still

---

to sparkle") quoted by Keats are included. The one real variant in the printed text of these lines is "dark as charcoal" in line 7.

And gathers grist with inward groans
And creaking melancholy moans
By waving heavenward o'er his head
His arms & working them for bread

Is it that addled brains perchance
When the skull's dark with ignorance
Like rotten eggs surveyed at night
Emit a temporary light?
Or is it that a heated brain
When it is rubbed against the grain,
Like a Cats' back though black as charcoal
Will in the gloom appear to sparkle

New Missions sent
To make the Antipodes relent
Turn the Anthropophagetic race
To sucking lambs & babes of grace
Or tempt the hairy Hebrew rogues
To cut their beards & Synagogues

This grave advertisement was seen
"Wanted a serious Shopman, who
To Gospel principles is true
Whose voice for Hymns is not too gruff
Who can grind brick dust, mix up snuff
And has an undisputed Nack in
Fearing the Lord & making Blacking

(The above in all probability is published but they are copied to show John Keats Choice in the selection of Extracts)

· 62 ·

TO J. H. REYNOLDS [1]

19 February 1818

Address: Mr John Reynolds/ Little Britain/ Christ's Hospital
Postmarks: TwoPyPost Unpaid HampsteadNO; 7 o'Clock FE 19 1818 N^T; *another blurred*

My dear Reynolds,

I have an idea that a Man might pass a very pleasant life in this manner—let him on any certain day read a certain Page of full Poesy or distilled Prose and let him wander with it, and muse upon it, and reflect from it, and bring home to it, and prophesy upon it, and dream upon it—untill it becomes stale—but when will it do so? Never—When Man has arrived at a certain ripeness in intellect any one grand and spiritual passage serves him as a starting post towards all "the two-and thirty Pallaces" [2] How happy is such a "voyage of conception,' what delicious diligent Indolence! [3] A doze upon a Sofa does not hinder it, and a nap upon Clover engenders ethereal finger-pointings—the prattle of a child gives it wings, and the converse of middle age a strength to beat them—a strain of musick conducts to 'an odd angle of the Isle' [4] and when the leaves whisper it puts a 'girdle round the earth.[5] Nor will this sparing touch of noble Books be any irreverance to their Writers—for perhaps the honors paid by Man to Man are trifles in comparison to the Benefit done by great Works to the 'Spirit and pulse of good' [6] by their mere passive existence. Memory should not be called knowledge—Many have original Minds who do not think it—they are led away by Custom—Now it appears to me that almost any Man may like the Spider [7] spin from his own inwards his own airy Citadel—

[1] *ALS:* Robert H. Taylor, Yonkers, New York (formerly owned by A. S. W. Rosenbach). Woodhouse also made a transcript in his letter-book, pp. 23–25.

[2] Keats could hardly have known anything about Buddhism (as has been suggested) or about the medieval Indian story-book, *Vikrama's Adventures*, in which thirty-two stories about King Vikrama are told by the thirty-two statuettes that supported his throne.

[3] MBF compares II, 77.

[4] *The Tempest*, I.ii.223.

[5] *A Midsummer Night's Dream*, II.i.175, "I'll put a girdle round about the earth."

[6] Wordsworth, "The Old Cumberland Beggar," line 77.

[7] D. B. Green, *NQ*, November 11, 1950, pp. 499–501, shows that this long passage on the spider and the bee is borrowed from Pliny and Swift.

the points of leaves and twigs on which the Spider begins her work are few and she fills the Air with a beautiful circuiting: man should be content with as few points to tip with the fine Webb of his Soul and weave a tapestry empyrean—full of Symbols for his spiritual eye, of softness for his spiritual touch, of space for his wandering of distinctness for his Luxury—But the Minds of Mortals are so different and bent on such diverse Journeys that it may at first appear impossible for any common taste and fellowship to exist ⟨bettween⟩ between two or three under these suppositions—It is however quite the contrary—Minds would leave each other in contrary directions, traverse each other in Numberless points, and all [8] last greet each other at the Journeys end—A old Man and a child would talk together and the old Man be led on his Path, and the child left thinking—Man should not dispute or assert but whisper results to his neighbour, and thus by every germ of Spirit sucking the Sap from mould ethereal every human might become great, and Humanity instead of being a wide heath of Furse [9] and Briars with here and there a remote Oak or Pine, would become a grand democracy of Forest Trees. It has been an old Comparison for our urging on—the Bee hive—however it seems to me that we should rather be the flower than the Bee—for it is a false notion that more is gained by receiving than giving [1]—no the receiver [2] and the giver are equal in their benefits—The f[l]ower I doubt not receives a fair guerdon from the Bee—its leaves blush deeper in the next spring—and who shall say between Man and Woman which is the most delighted? Now it is more noble to sit like Jove that [3] to fly like Mercury—let us not therefore go hurrying about and collecting honey-bee like, buzzing here and there impatiently from a knowledge of what is to be arrived at: but let us open our leaves like a flower and be passive and receptive [4]—budding patiently under the eye of Apollo and taking hints from evey noble insect that favors us with a visit—sap will be given us for Meat and dew for drink—I was led into these thoughts, my dear Reynolds, by the beauty of the morning operating on a sense of Idleness—I have not read any Books—the Morning

[8] *For* at.

[9] Possibly he had in mind *The Tempest*, I.i.70 f., "long heath, brown furze."

[1] Acts xx.35.

[2] He wrote "recever" with a dot for the missing "i."

[3] *For* than.

[4] No doubt Wordsworth's "wise passiveness" (as in "Expostulation and Reply") was in his mind.

said I was right—I had no Idea but of the Morning and the Thrush said I was right—seeming to say—

> 'O thou whose face hath felt the Winter's wind;
>   Whose eye has [5] seen the Snow clouds hung in Mist
> And the black-elm tops 'mong the freezing Stars
> To thee the Spring will be a harvest-time—
> O thou whose only book has [5] been the light
> Of supreme darkness which thou feddest on
> Night after night, when Phœbus was away
> To thee the Spring shall be a tripple morn—
> O fret not after knowledge—I have none
> And yet my song comes native with the warmth
> O fret not after knowledge—I have none
> And yet the Evening listens—He who saddens
> At thought of Idleness cannot be [6] idle,
> And he's awake who thinks himself asleep.'

Now I am sensible all this is a mere sophistication, however it may neighbour to any truths, to excuse my own indolence [7]—so I will not deceive myself that Man should be equal with jove—but think himself very well off as a sort of scullion-Mercury or even a humble Bee—It is not [8] matter whether I am right or wrong either one way or another, if there is sufficient to lift a little time from your Shoulders. Your affectionate friend

John Keats—

[5] Woodhouse reads "hath."
[6] *Written* be be.
[7] Woodhouse has "indulgence."
[8] *For* no.

· 63 ·

TO HORACE SMITH [1]

19 February 1818 [2]

Address: Horace Smith Esqre/ Knightsbridge
Postmark: Hampstead . . . (*blurred*)

Hampstead—Thursd—Morn.

My dear Sir,

My Brothers are expecting me every day in devonshire,[3] and I have some days work before I can go thither: so I am hardy enough to nullify the day I had expected to pass with you, and trespassing enough to ask your indulgence therefore—

I am being greatly amused with your Poem—it has a full leven of Wit and imaginative fun [4]—I thank you for it now and will return it to Reynolds. Remember me to Shelley and Kingston. Your's very sincerely

John Keats

[1] *ALS:* Keats Museum. There is a facsimile in the guide-book, *Keats House and Museum*, 3rd ed., revised (Hampstead, n.d.), after p. 16.

[2] The comments made in the next letter indicate that Thursday was February 19.

[3] Actually Keats left London on March 4 (I, 240 n.).

[4] "Nehemiah Muggs": see I, 214 n.

·64·

TO GEORGE AND TOM KEATS [1]

21 February 1818

Address: Mess[rs] Keats/ Post office/ Teignmouth/ Devon— [2]
Postmarks: TwoPyPost Unpaid HampsteadNO; B FE 21 818; 7 o'Clock FE 21

Hampstead Saturday— [3]

My dear Brothers,

I am extremely sorry to have given you so much uneasiness by not writing: however you know good news is no news or vice versa—I do not like to write a short Letter to you—or you would have had one long before [4]—The Weather although boisterous to day has been very much milder—and I think Devonshire is no[t] the last place to receive a temperate change—The occasion of my writing to day is the enclosed Letter by the Post Mark from Miss Wylie [5]—does she expect you in town George? I have been abominably id[l]e since you left—but have just turned over a new leaf—and used as a marker a Letter of excuse to an invitation from Horace Smith.[6] I received a Letter from Haydon the other day [7] in which he says, his essays on the elgin Marbles are being translated into italian—the which he superintends. I did not mention that I had seen the British Gallery—there are some nice things by Stark and Bathsheba by Wilkie

[1] *ALS:* Harvard. Jeffrey endorsed it, "Copied July 1845," and only his transcript of the original has heretofore been printed by the editors. After his note another hand has added "John Keats—/ Poet—"

[2] Jeffrey gave the address at the close of his transcript, ending it "Teignmouth/ Dover."

[3] Jeffrey has "Saturday/ February 21st 1818—"

[4] Actually he had written No. 61 just seven days (or less) before. Compare also the odd apology with which he begins No. 56.

[5] Afterwards George's wife. Jeffrey has "W—."

[6] Jeffrey transposes this and the preceding sentence. Keats's letter to Smith (No. 63) was apparently written, but not mailed, on February 19.

[7] Jeffrey has "the other day from Haydon." Eric George, *The Life and Death of Benjamin Robert Haydon* (1948), pp. 85 f., notes that Haydon's *Examiner-Champion* letter on the Marbles was translated into both Italian and French.

which is condemned [8]—I could not bear Leslie's Uriel [9]—Reynolds has been very ill for some time—confined to the house—and had Leeches applied to the chest—When I saw him on Wednesday [1] he was much the same—and he is in the worst place in the world for amendment—among the strife of womens tongues in a hot and parch'd room—I wish he would move to Butler's [2] for a short time. The Thrushes and Blackbirds have been singing me into an idea that it was spring, and almost that Leaves were on the trees—so that black clouds and boisterous winds seem to have muster'd and collected to full Divan [3] for the purpose of convincing me to the contrary—I have not been to Edmonton all this While, and there is not a day but Le Mesurier's image reproaches me for it—and I suppose the Haughtons think us dead—I will shortly go and set matters to rights thereabouts [4] Taylor says my Poem shall be out

[8] The directors of the British Institution, Pall Mall, in the exhibition beginning on February 2, awarded James Stark (1794–1859) a prize of £50 for his "nice things" called "Penning the Flock" and "Lambeth, Looking towards Westminster Bridge." "Bathsheba" by Sir David Wilkie (1785–1841) was "condemned" in the *Champion*, February 15, 1818, p. 109, and the *Examiner*, p. 107, of the same date. The *New Monthly Magazine*, March, 1818 (IX, 155–158), however, after calling the February exhibition "the best exhibition which has ever been presented to the public by this patriotic institution," described Wilkie's picture as "calculated greatly to aggrandize his fame." Later, April (IX, 256 f.), it called Stark's "Lambeth" "a charming picture" showing Nature "in her most happy and becoming garment."

[9] The name was changed by Milnes, I, 102—or by his copyist—to "Alston's." Keats knew Charles Robert Leslie (1794–1859) and confused him with his teacher Washington Allston (1779–1843). (Holman suggested that Keats met Leslie at Dawlish.) The *New Monthly* for April (IX, 255 f.) was "astonished to hear" that Leslie's "Christ Raising the Widow's Son at Nain" had "received the first premium from the Directors" of the British Institution, as "It appears to be without almost all the requisites of a fine painting." (Leslie himself tells of winning the *second* prize.) Allston's "Uriel in the Sun" (which is praised in Elmes's *Annals of the Fine Arts*, III [1819], 109–111, 145), was awarded a prize of £150 by the directors, and was bought by the Marquis of Stafford, from whom it passed to the Duke of Sutherland, then to the Dana Collection, Cambridge, Massachusetts, and ultimately to the Fogg Art Museum of Harvard, where it now reposes ignominiously in storage. "Uriel" is impressively reproduced as Plate XLI in E. P. Richardson's *Washington Allston* (Chicago, 1948).

[1] February 18.

[2] He did so later (I, 275 n.). MBF notes that Charles Butler entered Guy's Hospital as a student a day before Keats (September 30, 1815), and passed the examination at Apothecaries' Hall along with him on July 25, 1816; Blunden, p. 496, that "Mrs. Butler was a relation, perhaps the aunt, of Eliza Drewe, who became Mrs. J. H. Reynolds," and who is mentioned by Thomas Hood.

[3] Compare Scott's *Rob Roy*, chapter 12, "To meet the family . . . in full divan."

[4] Jeffrey omits "I have not been . . . to rights thereabouts." I have not identified Le Mesurier and the Haughtons, whom Keats mentions nowhere else. Possibly the former was connected in some way with Thomas Le Mesurier, of Newton Longville, Bucks, and Haughton-le-Skerne, Durham, several of whose sons attended Oxford (Joseph Foster, *Alumni Oxonienses* [Oxford, 1888], III, 947), and the latter with Moses Haughton, Jr.

in a Month. I think he'll be out before it [5]—The Thrushes are singing now—af it [6] they would speak to the Winds because their big brother Jack, the spring was'nt far off—I am reading Voltaire [7] and Gibbon, although I wrote to Reynolds the other day to prove reading of no use [8]—I have not seen Hunt since.[9] I am a good deal with Dilke and Brown—we are very thick—they are very kind to me—they are well—I don't think I could stop in Hampstead [1] but for their neighbourhood. I hear Hazlitt's Lectures regularly—his last was on Grey Collins, Young &c and he gave a very f{ine} piece of discriminating criticism on Swift, Vo{ltaire} And Rabelais—I was very disappointed at his treatment of Chatterton [2]—I generally meet with many I know there. Lord Byron's 4th Canto [3] is expected out—and I heard somewhere that Walter Scott has a new Poem in readiness [4]—I am sorry that Wordsworth has left a bad impression whereever [5] he visited in Town—by his egotism, Vanity and bigotry—yet he is a great Poet if not a Philosopher.[6] I have not yet read Shelly's Poem [7]—I don't suppose you have it at the Teignmouth Libraries—These double Letters must come rather heavy—I hope you have a moderate portion of Cash—but dont fret at all [8] if you have not—Lord I intend to play at cut and run [9] as well as Falstaff—that is to say before he got so lusty—I have not time to chequer work this

(1772?–1848?), miniature painter and engraver. The *Examiner*, July 19, 1818, p. 464, announced the death on July 7 of one Isaac Lemesurier, aged 53, of Edmonton.

[5] The *Monthly Magazine*, April, 1818 (XLV, 256), announced that "Mr. Keats will shortly publish, Endymion, a poem," and the book appeared towards the end of April. "He'll [Jeffrey has "he will"] be out before it" perhaps means that the second edition of Taylor's book on Junius (see I, 219) was about ready for publication.

[6] Jeffrey has "as if."

[7] Keats owned copies of Voltaire's *Dictionnaire philosophique* and *Essai sur les mœurs et l'esprit des nations*.

[8] See No. 62.

[9] Perhaps he omitted a date like January 21 (I, 210).

[1] *Written* Hampsteat.

[2] "Probably Keats's disappointment at his treatment of Chatterton was conveyed to Hazlitt . . . for he prefaced his next lecture by 'I am sorry that what I said . . . should have given dissatisfaction to some persons, with whom I would willingly agree in all such matters'" (Hewlett, pp. 138 f.). See also Howe, p. 221. The lectures were given on February 17 and 24.

[3] Of *Childe Harold* (see I, 225 n.).

[4] Actually Scott published *The Heart of Midlothian* in the following June.

[5] Jeffrey has "where-ever." (The hyphen occurs only to divide the word at the end of a line.)

[6] Quoting this sentence, Howe, p. 222 n., remarks: "This, all said and done, was Hazlitt's opinion."

[7] See I, 194 n. [8] The words look like "attall."

[9] Partridge explains, "decamp hurriedly."

Letter for I should like to be sure of the 4 o Clock Post—So [10] I remain praying for your hea[l]th; my dear Brothers, your affectionate Brother—

John—

· 65 ·

TO JOHN TAYLOR [1]

27 February 1818

Address: John Faylor [2] Esqre/ New bond Street

Hampstead 27 Feby–
⟨London T⟩ [3]

My dear Taylor,

Your alteration strikes me as being a great improvement—the page looks much better. And now I will attend to the Punctuations you speak of—the comma should be at *soberly*,[4] and in the other passage the comma should follow *quiet*, .[5] I am extremely indebted to you for this attention and also for your after admonitions—It is a sorry thing for me that any one should have to overcome Prejudices in reading my Verses—that affects me more than any hypercriticism on any particular Passage. In *Endymion* I have most likely but moved into the Go-cart from the leading strings. In Poetry I have a few Axioms, and you will see how far I am from their Centre. 1st I think Poetry should surprise by a fine excess and not by Singularity—it should strike the Reader as a wording of his own highest thoughts, and appear almost a Remembrance—2nd Its touches of Beauty should never be half way therby making the reader breathless instead of content: the rise, the progress, the setting of imagery should like the Sun come natural natural too him—shine over him and set soberly although in magnificence leaving him in the Luxury of twilight—but it is easier to think what Poetry should be than to write it—and this leads me on to another axiom. That if Poetry comes not as naturally as the Leaves to a tree it had better not come

[10] Jeffrey omits "I have not. . . . So."

[1] *ALS:* Pierpont Morgan Library. On the first page some enthusiast—see the facsimile in the catalog of J. Pearson and Company, London, 1912, lot 92—penciled, "Finest letter of Keats Extant." There is a transcript of this letter in his letter-book, pp. 4 f., by Woodhouse, who gives the date "1818."

[2] *For* Taylor.

[3] He wrote either "London T" or "London L."

[4] See *Endymion*, I.149.

[5] The same, I.247.

at all.[6] However it may be with me I cannot help looking into new countries with 'O for a Muse of fire to ascend!' [7]—If Endymion serves me as a Pioneer perhaps I ought to be content. I have great reason to be content, for thank God I can read and perhaps understand Shakspeare to his depths, and I have I am sure many friends, who, if I fail, will attribute any change in my Life and Temper to Humbleness rather than to Pride—to a cowering under the Wings of great Poets rather than to a Bitterness that I am not appreciated. I am anxious to get Endymion [8] printed that I may forget it and proceed. I have coppied the 3rd Book and have begun the 4th. On running my Eye over the Proofs—I saw one Mistake I will notice it presently and also any others if there be any—There should be no comma in 'the raft branch down sweeping from a tall Ash top' [9] —I have besides made one or two alteration{s} and also altered the 13 Line Page 32 [1] to make sense of it as you will see. I will take care the Printer shall not trip up my Heels—There should be no dash after Dryope in the [2] Line 'Dryope's lone lulling of her Child.[3] Remember me to Percy Street.

Your sincere and obligd friend
John Keats—

P.S. You shall have a sho[r]t *Preface* in good time—

· 66 ·

FROM B. R. HAYDON [1]

4 March 1818

March 4. 1818

My dear Keats/ I shall certainly go mad!—In a field at Stratford upon Avon, in a field that belonged to Shakespeare; they have found a gold ring and seal [2] with the initial thus—*a true* WS *Lover's Knot*

[6] Here, as often, Keats is indebted to Hazlitt (*Works*, IV [1930], 24).
[7] *Henry V*, Prologue, line 1, "O for a Muse of fire, that would ascend."
[8] Someone has underlined this word in pencil. [9] *Endymion*, I.334 f.
[1] Garrod, p. lxxxvii: "[This change] can no longer be identified—the thirteenth line of page 32 of the edition of 1818 shows no changes from Keats' own MS."
[2] Originally "this" (Woodhouse has "the"). [3] *Endymion*, I.495.
[1] *ALS:* Formerly attached to Haydon's Journal, now at Harvard. It was sent by messenger.
[2] The *Monthly Magazine*, February, 1818 (XLV, 6), remarked: "A few years since, at no great distance from the garden of New Place, Stratford, a massy gold ring was dug

between;[3] if *this* is not Shakespeare who is it?—a true lovers Knott!!—I saw an impression to day, and am to have one as soon as possible—As sure as you breathe, & that he was the first of beings the Seal belonged to him—Oh Lord!— B R Haydon

· 67 ·

TO BENJAMIN BAILEY

13 March 1818[1]

Address: Mr B. Bailey/ Magdalen Hall/ Oxford—
Postmark (*blurred*): TEIGNMOUTH . . .

My dear Bailey, Teignmouth Friday

When a poor devil is drowning, it is said he comes thrice to the surface, ere he makes his final sink if however, even at the third rise, he can manage to catch hold of a piece of weed or rock, he stands a fair chance,—as I hope I do now, of being saved. I have sunk twice in our Correspondence, have risen twice and been too idle, or something worse, to extricate myself—I have sunk the third time and just now risen again at this two of the Clock P.M. and saved myself from utter perdition—by beginning this, all drench'd as I am and fresh from the Water—and I would rather endure the present inconvenience of a Wet Jacket, than you should keep a laced one in store for me. Why did I not stop at Oxford in my Way?—How can you ask such a Question? Why did I not promise to do so? Did I

---

up,—on one side of which was a seal, with the following characters on it:— [the seal is reproduced]. This seal is now in possession of Mr. Wheeler. . . . There seems little doubt but it must have belonged to the Bard." Halliwell-Phillipps likewise found little doubt when he reproduced the seal ring in *The Life of William Shakespeare* (1848), p. 298. MBF notes that the ring is still to be seen in the museum at Shakespeare's birthplace.

[3] Haydon drew a sketch of the seal with "W S" in a double circle.

[1] *ALS:* Harvard. There is a transcript by Woodhouse in his letter-book, pp. 95–99. Oddly enough, he misdated it and the original "Septr 1818," thereby causing Milnes, I, 215–221, to believe that, after his return from Scotland, Keats rejoined Tom at Teignmouth. Keats left London from the Swan with Two Necks, Lad Lane, at 7:30 P.M. on March 4 (*Cary's New Itinerary* for 1819; *KC*, I, 12), and, though the trip to Exeter normally took about twenty-seven hours, because of a violent storm (see the *Monthly Magazine*, April, 1818 [XLV, 275–277]) he could hardly have reached that city before the morning of Friday, March 6. He may have gone to Teignmouth on that day or the next. When he wrote No. 67 he had already had three "abominable" days of rain, and that his "Friday" is March 13 is told at I, 246, "I wrote to Bailey yesterday."

not in a Letter to you make a promise to do so? Then how can you be so unreasonable as to ask me why I did not? This is the thing—(for I have been rubbing up my invention; trying several sleights—I first polish'd a cold, felt it in my fingers tried it on the table, but could not pocket it: I tried Chilblains, Rheumatism, Gout, tight Boots, nothing of that sort would do, so this is, as I was going to say, the thing.—I had a Letter from Tom saying how much better he had got, and thinking he had better stop—I went down to prevent his coming up—Will not this do? Turn it which way you like—it is selvaged all round—I have used it these three last days to keep out the abominable Devonshire Weather—by the by you may say what you will of devonshire: the thuth [2] is, it is a splashy, rainy, misty snowy, foggy, haily floody, muddy, slipshod County—the hills are very beautiful, when you get a sight of 'em—the Primroses are out, but then you are in—the Cliffs are of a fine deep Colour, but then the Clouds are continually vieing with them—The Women like your London People in a sort of negative way—because the native men are the poorest creatures in England—because Government never have thought it worth while to send a recruiting party among them. When I think of Wordswo[r]th's Sonnet 'Vanguard of Liberty! ye Men of Kent!' [3] the degenerated race about me are Pulvis Ipecac. Simplex [4] a strong dose—Were I a Corsair I'd make a descent on the South Coast of Devon, if I did not run the chance of having Cowardice imputed to me: as for the Men they'd run away into the methodist meeting houses, and the Women would be glad of it—Had England been a large devonshire we should not have won the Battle of Waterloo—There are knotted oaks—there are lusty rivulets there are Meadows such as are not—there are vallies of femminine Climate—but there are no thews and Sinews—Moor's Almanack [5] is here a curiosity—A[r]ms Neck and shoulders may at least be⟨e⟩ seen there, and The Ladies read it as some out of the way romance—Such a quelling Power have these thoughts over me, that I fancy the very Air of a deteriorating quality—I fancy the flowers, all precocious, have an Acrasian [6] spell about them—I feel able to beat off the devonshire waves like soap froth—I think it well

[2] *For* truth. [3] "To the Men of Kent. October 1803."

[4] Hale-White, p. 88: "Nauseating, for Pulvis Ipecac. Simplex in strong doses is an emetic." [5] See I, 153 n.

[6] For Acrasia see *The Faerie Queene*, II.i.51–55, xii.69, III.i.2.

for the honor of Brittain that Julius Cæsar did not first land in this County—A Devonshirer standing on his native hills is not a distinct object—he does not show against the light—a wolf or two would dispossess him. I like, I love England, I like its strong Men—Give me a "long brown plain" for my Morning [7] so I may meet with some of Edmond Iron side's desendants—Give me a barren mould so I may meet with some shadowing of Alfred in the shape of a Gipsey, a Huntsman or as [8] Shepherd. Scenery is fine—but human nature is finer [9]—The Sward is richer for the tread of a real, nervous, english foot—the eagles nest is finer for the Mountaineer has look'd into it—Are these facts or prejudices? Whatever they are, for them I shall never be able to relish entirely any devonshire scenery—Homer is very fine, Achilles is fine, Diomed is fine, Shakspeare is fine, Hamlet is fine, Lear is fine, but dwindled englishmen are not fine—Where too the Women are so passable, and have such english names, such as Ophelia, Cordelia &—that they should have such Paramours or rather Imparamours [1]—As for them I cannot, in thought help wishing as did the cruel Emperour,[2] that they had but one head and I might cut it off to deliver them from any horrible Courtesy they may do their undeserving Countrymen—I wonder I meet with no born Monsters—O Devonshire, last night I thought the Moon had dwindled in heaven—I have never had your Sermon [3] from Wordsworth but Mrs Dilke lent it me—You know my ideas about Religion—I do not think myself more in the right than other people and that nothing in this world is proveable. I wish I could enter into all your feelings on the subject merely for one short 10 Minutes and give you a Page or two to your liking. I am sometimes so very sceptical as to think Poetry itself a mere Jack a lanthern to amuse whoever may chance to be struck with its brilliance—As Tradesmen say every thing is worth what it will fetch, so probably every mental pursuit takes its reality and worth from the ardour of the pursuer—being in itself a nothing—Ethereal thing [4] may at least be thus real, divided under three heads—Things real—

[7] Woodhouse queries "Money." [8] *For* a. [9] See I, 415.

[1] Apparently a coinage by Keats.

[2] Joan Grundy, *RES*, n.s., VI (1955), 52, thinks that Keats borrowed this comment on Caligula from William Browne's *Britannia's Pastorals*, 1613, I.v.271–274 (*Poems*, ed. Bullen [1894], I, 147). But Jack Stillinger is correct in assigning it to the *Spectator*, Nos. 16, 246, 435 (March 19, December 12, 1711, July 19, 1712).

[3] See I, 212. [4] Woodhouse reads "thing(s)."

things semireal—and no things—Things real—such as existences of Sun Moon & Stars and passages of Shakspeare—Things semireal such as Love, the Clouds &c which require a greeting of the Spirit to make them wholly exist—and Nothings which are made Great and dignified by an ardent pursuit—Which by the by stamps the burgundy mark on the bottles of our Minds, insomuch as they are able to "*consec*[*r*]*ate whate'er they look upon*" [5] I have written a Sonnet here of a somewhat collateral nature—so don't imagine it an a propos des bottes.

Four Seasons fill the Measure of the year; [6]
  Four Seasons are there in the mind of Man.
He hath his lusty spring when fancy clear
  Takes in all beauty with an easy span:
He hath his Summer, when luxuriously
  He chews the honied cud of fair spring thoughts,
Till, in his Soul dissolv'd they come to be
  Part of himself. He hath his Autumn ports
And Havens of repose, when his tired wings
  Are folded up, and he content to look
On Mists in idleness: to let fair things
  Pass by unheeded as a threshhold brook.
    He hath his Winter too of pale Misfeature,
    Or else he would forget his mortal nature.

Aye this may be carried—but what am I talking of—it is an old maxim of mine and of course must be well known that evey [7] point of thought is the centre of an intellectual world—the two uppermost thoughts in a Man's mind are the two poles of his World he revolves on them and every thing is southward or northward to him through their means—We take but three steps from feathers to iron. Now my dear fellow I must once for all tell you I have not one Idea of the truth of any of my speculations—I shall never be a Reasoner because I care not to be in the right, when retired from bickering and in a proper philosophical temper—So you must not stare if in any future letter I endeavour to prove that Appollo as he had a cat gut string⟨s⟩ to his Lyre used a cats' paw as a Pecten—and further from said

[5] Compare Shelley, "Hymn to Intellectual Beauty," lines 13 f., "Spirit of Beauty, that dost consecrate/ With thine own hues all thou dost shine upon."

[6] See Garrod, p. 534, for striking variants in other texts.

[7] Keats often spells the word thus.

Pecten's reiterated and continual teasing came the term Hen peck'd. My Brother Tom desires to be remember'd to you[8]—he has just this moment had a spitting of blood poor fellow—Remember me to Greig[9] and Whitehed—

Your affectionate friend
John Keats—

· 68 ·

TO J. H. REYNOLDS[1]

14 March 1818

Teignmouth Saturday[2]

Dear Reynolds.

I escaped being blown over and blown under & trees & house[s] being toppled on me.[3]—I have since hearing of Brown's accident had an aversion to a dose of parapet.[4] and being also a lover of antiquities I would sooner have a harmless piece of herculaneum sent me quietly as a present, than ever so modern a chimney pot tumbled onto my head—Being agog to see some Devonshire, I would have taken a walk the first day, but the rain wo^{d} not let me; and the second, but the rain wo^{d} not let me; and the third; but the rain forbade it—Ditto 4 ditto 5—ditto—So I made up my Mind to stop in doors, and catch a sight flying between the showers; and behold I saw a pretty valley—pretty cliffs, pretty Brooks, pretty Meadows, pretty trees, both standing as they were created, and blown down as they are uncreated—The green is beautiful, as they say, and pity it is that it is amphibious—mais! but alas! the flowers here wait as

[8] See I, 171 n. [9] *For* Gleig.

[1] A transcript in Woodhouse's letter-book, pp. 56–58, by a clerk, with corrections by Woodhouse.

[2] Woodhouse adds "14 March 1818."

[3] He refers to the terrific storm of March 4 and his trip to Exeter (see *KC*, I, 12). Details are given about the former in all the papers and magazines, like the *Examiner*, March 8, p. 160, and the *Champion*, March 8, p. 158.

[4] In a note in his copy of Milnes, Dilke says: "This alludes to an accident which befell Brown many years before and which must have been about that time first mentioned to Keats and Reynolds. A parapet stone fell and struck Brown on the *calf of the leg*—a narrower escape a man could not well have. Apparently no great harm done—but it got worse and worse and it was doubtful at last whether he would not have lost the limb. This was years before he knew either Keats or Reynolds" (MBF).

naturally for the rain twice a day as the Muscles do for the Tide.—so we look upon a brook in these parts as you look upon a dash in your Country—there must be something to support this, aye fog, hail, snow rain—Mist—blanketing up three parts of the year—This devonshire is like Lydia Languish,[5] very entertaining when at smiles, but cursedly subject to sympathetic moisture. You have the sensation of walking under one great Lamplighter: and you cant go on the other side of the ladder to keep your frock clean, and cosset your superstition. Buy a girdle—put a pebble in your Mouth—loosen your Braces—for I am going among Scenery whence I intend to tip you the Damosel Radcliffe [6]—I'll cavern you, and grotto you, and waterfall you, and wood you, and water you, and immense-rock you, and tremendous sound you, and solitude you. Ill make a lodgment on your glacis by a row of Pines, and storm your covered way with bramble Bushes.[7] Ill have at you with hip and haw small-shot, and cannonade you with Shingles—Ill be witty upon salt fish,[8] and impede your cavalry with clotted cream. But ah Coward! to talk at this rate to a sick man, or I hope to one that was sick—for I hope by this you stand on your right foot.—If you are not—that's all,—I intend to cut all sick people if they do not make up their minds to cut sickness—a fellow to whom I have a complete aversion, and who strange to say is harboured and countenanced in several houses where I visit—he is sitting now quite impudent between me and Tom—He insults me at poor Jem Rice's—and you have seated him before now between us at the Theatre—where I thought he look'd with a longing eye at poor Kean.[9] I shall say, once for all, to my friends generally and severally, cut that fellow, or I cut you—I went to the Theatre here [1] the other night, which I

[5] The sentimental heroine of Sheridan's *Rivals*.

[6] Of course a reference to Mrs. Ann Radcliffe (1764–1823).

[7] Norman Holland reminds me that all these military terms are a reminiscence of Uncle Toby's vocabulary in *Tristram Shandy* (ed. Douglas Grant, Harvard University Press, 1951). Compare "giving such clear ideas of the differences and distinctions between the scarp and counterscarp,—the glacis and covered way,—the half-moon and ravelin" (vol. II, chapter 1); "the talus of the glacis" (VI, 21); "When the duke of *Marlborough* made a lodgment,—my uncle *Toby* made a lodgment too" (VI, 22); "[The morning] was that of the storm of the counterscarp" (VI, 24).

[8] The *New Monthly Magazine*, May, 1817 (VII, 364), tells of a Teignmouth merchant who imported and sold "30,000 quintals of Newfoundland fish" on which he made a profit of £10,000.

[9] On Kean's illness see I, 191 n.

[1] Pigot's London and provincial commercial directory, 1823–24, says that in Teignmouth "a good theatre is open during the summer months."

forgot to tell George, and got insulted, which I ought to remember to forget to tell any Body; for I did not fight, and as yet have had no redress—"Lie thou there, sweetheart!" [2] I wrote to Bailey yesterday,[3] obliged to speak in a high way, and a damme who's affraid.[4] —for I had owed him [5] so long; however, he shall see I will be better in future. Is he in Town yet? I have directed to Oxford as the better chance. I have copied my fourth Book,[6] and shall write the preface soon. I wish it was all done; for I want to forget it and make my mind free for something new—Atkins the Coachman, Bartlet the Surgeon,[7] Simmons the Barber, and the Girls over at the Bonnet shop [8] say we shall now have a Month of seasonable Weather. warm, witty, and full of invention [9]—Write to me and tell me you are well or thereabouts, or by the holy Beaucœur,—which I suppose is the virgin Mary, or the repented Magdalen, (beautiful name, that Magdalen) Ill take to my Wings and fly away to any where but old or Nova Scotia [1]—I wish I had a little innocent bit of Metaphysic in my head, to criss-cross this letter: but you know a favorite tune is hardest to be remembered when one wants it most and you, I know, have long ere this taken it for granted that I never have any speculations without assoc[i]ating you in them, where they are of a pleasant nature and you know enough to [2] me to tell the places where I haunt most, so that if you think for five minutes after having read this you will find it a long letter and see written in the Air above you,

⟨Remember me to all⟩

Your most affectionate friend
John Keats.

Remember me to all. Tom's remembrances to you.

Mr John H Reynolds
Little Brittain
Christs Hospital
London.

[2] *2 Henry IV*, II.iv.197, "sweetheart, lie thou there."

[3] In No. 67 Keats's "long" silence dated only from January 23.

[4] See I, 214 n.

[5] Woodhouse emends to "owed him a letter."

[6] Of *Endymion*.

[7] Pigot's 1823–24 directory lists Jacob Bartlett, surgeon, Regent's Place. Dr. W. C. Lake, of Teignmouth, writing to Holman on April 4, 1913 (see Rollins, *HLB*, IV [1950], 390), called him "(Jacob) Bickford Bartlett."

[8] See I, 248 n.

[9] *Twelfth Night*, III.ii.46 f., "no matter how witty, so it be eloquent and full of invention."

[1] See I, 245 n.

[2] Woodhouse emends to "(of)."

· 69 ·

FROM GEORGE KEATS [1]

18 March 1818

Address: Jno Keats/ —Post Office—/ Teignmouth/ Devonshire
[*In the upper right corner is written*] 18 March. 1818
Postmark (*imperfect*): B MR 18 818

Pancras Lane [2]—March 18—1818.

My dear John—

Poor Tom—who could have imagined such a change? I have indeed been sanguine; whenever he has occured to my thoughts he has appeared nearly in good health, every answer I have given to enquiring Friends, has been, "much better" and "improving every day" I can hardly beleive this melancholy news, Having so long accustomed myself to think altogether otherwise—I hope and trust that your *kind* superintendance will prevent any violent bleeding in future, and consequently that this alarm may prove in the end advantageous; Tom must never again presume on his strength, at all events untill he has *completely* recover'd. John Reynolds is little better,[3] in many respects worse, he has a very bad rheumatic Fever, and suffers constant pain: it is not said that he is dangerously ill, but I cannot help thinking that so many evils acting upon his most irritable disposition; deadening his hopes of his advance in business, consequently all his hopes, must make this illness somewhat dangerous.—I called yesterday but he was not sufficiently well to be seen. His Sisters are well—Your letter was most welcome to him—Bailey's in Town for a few days, on business for Glegg [4]—I have not seen him.—Mrs Scott desires her compliments to you and Tom, I have repeatedly called on Taylor & Hessey and have never found

[1] *ALS:* Harvard. Brown had this letter when on January 20, 1830 (Keats Museum), he quoted from it to Dilke.

[2] George was writing from Abbey's place of business.

[3] He has a) instead of a comma. Reynolds seems for a time to have been almost chronically ill. MBF, p. 119 n., quotes an undated letter of his to Hessey in which he complains of "leading a life of pain, sleeplessness & bleeding," and asks for the loan of "Hazlitts first lecture" and "a proof of Keats' Poem," *Endymion*, to read.

[4] *For* Gleig (I, 170 n.).

them at home, or you should long since have known the progress of your book. Brown has I understand written to you and given you the pleasant information that the printer's are in immediate want of the Fourth book and preface—By the time you have received this I have no doubt but T & H will have received them—the inclosed 20 pounds N° 834 dated 3rd Feby—1818. will reach you before you are quite aground. I am about paying your's as well as Tom's bills, of which I shall keep regular accounts and for the sake of justice and a future proper understanding I intend calculating the probable amount Tom and I are indebted to you, something of this kind must be done, or at the end of two or three years we shall be all at sixes and sevens. let me know when you want Money. I have paid Hodgkinson [5] who desires his best rems—I'll write Tom soon give my love to him—rems to Miss M & C [6]—and love to the Miss J's [7]—Miss Wylie as usual desires her *respects* to you, and *best wishes* to Tom—R Draper [8] has been teazing throughout the writing of this to my great annoyance—

Good bye for the present

Your most affectionate Brother

—George.

· 70 ·

TO B. R. HAYDON

21 March 1818 [1]

Address: B R Haydon Esq—/ Lisson Grove North/ Paddington/ Middx

Postmarks: TEIGNMOUTH . . . ; . . . o'Clock MR 23 1818 FNn; G 23 MR 23 1818

My dear Haydon— Teignmouth Saturd—Morn

In sooth, I hope you are not too sanguine about that seal—in sooth I hope it is not Brumidgeum—in double sooth I hope it is his—and in tripple sooth I hope I shall have an impression. Such a

[5] Abbey's junior partner.

[6] Possibly "the Girls over at the Bonnet shop" (I, 246).

[7] The Misses Jeffrey (I, 78 ff.).

[8] Possibly one of Abbey's clerks.

[1] *ALS:* Harvard. This letter, dated March 23 by HBF, 1895, and March 14 by MBF, was instead written on March 21, the date given by Colvin, p. 85. Keats arrived in Teign-

piece of intelligence came doubly welcome to me while in your own County and in your own hand—not but I have blown up said County for its urinal qualifications—the 6 first days I was here it did nothing but rain and at that time having to write to a friend I gave Devonshire a good blowing up—it has been fine for about three days and I was coming round a bit; but to day it rains again—with me the County is [2] yet upon its good behaviour—I have enjoyed the most delightful Walks these three fine days beautiful enough to make me content here all the summer could I stay.

I

For their's [3] Bishop's teign
And king's teign
And Coomb at the clear teign head.
Where close by the Stream
You may have your cream
All sp[r]ead upon barley bread—

II

There's Arch Brook
And there's larch Brook
Both turning many a Mill
 And cooling the drouth
 Of the salmon's mouth
And fattening his silver gill

II

There is Wild wood
A Mild hood
To the sheep on the lea o the down
Where the golden furse
With its green than,[4] spurs
Doth Catch at the Maiden's gown

---

mouth on March 6 or 7. He says that "the 6 first days" after his arrival it rained, and that "having to write to a friend I gave Devonshire a good blowing up." That blowing up was sent to Bailey on March 13 (No. 67). The present letter speaks of these six rainy days and "about three days" of good weather, and "to day it rains again." The language clearly proves it to have been written several days after No. 68, and "Saturday" must be March 21. Actually, too, the postmark, March 23, is evidence for the date of March 21, although Haydon's letter which answers it (No. 73), dated March 25, is postmarked April 2.

[2] *For* is not?

[3] there's *Garrod* (though on pp. 553–555 he refers only to this one text).

[4] *For* thin (*Garrod*).

There is newton marsh
With its spear grass harsh—
A pleasant summer level
Where the Maidens sweet
Of the Market Street
Do meet in the dusk to revel

|||

Theres the Barton rich
With dyke and ditch
And hedge for the thrush to live in
And the hollow tree
For the buzzing bee

in.

And a bank for the Wasp to hive ⟨him⟩

||||

And O, and O
The Daisies blow
And the Primroses are waken'd
And the violet white
Sits in silver plight
And the green bud's as long as the spike end

|||

Then who would go
Into dark soho
And chatter with dack'd hair'd critics [5]
When he can stay
For the new mown hay

P

And startle the dappled ⟨Th⟩rickets

Here's some doggrel for you{—}Perhaps you would like a bit of B—hrell— [6]

[5] "Dock-haired," short-haired, perhaps an oblique reference to Hazlitt. For a different explanation see Garrod, p. 555 n.

[6] "Bitchrell," so Haydon (I, 257) interpreted it. Haydon, however (Penrose, p. 238), and F. W. Haydon, II, 8, printed it as "botheral." The poem, according to Gittings, *The Mask of Keats* (1956), pp. 90 f., is based on Chatterton's "Mynstrelles songe" ("Mie husbande, Lorde Thomas") in *Ælla.*

I

Where be ye going you devon Maid
  And what have ye there ithe Basket?
Ye tight little fairy—just fresh from the dairy
  Will ye give me some cream if I ask it—

II

I love you [7] Meads and I love your flowers
                                mainly.
  And I love your junkets ⟨huge⟩ly
But 'hind the door, I love kissing more
  O look no[t] so disdainly!

III

I love your Hills and I love your dales
  And I love your flocks a bleating—
But O on the hether to lie together
  With both our hearts a beating.

IIII

I'll put your Basket all safe in a *nook*
                    w
  And your sha⟨l⟩l I hang up *on this* [8] *willow*
And we will sigh in the daisy's eye
  And kiss on a grass green pillow.

I know not if this rhyming fit has done any thing—it will be safe with you if worthy to put among my Lyrics How does the Work go on? I should like to bring out my Dentatus [9] at the time your Epic makes its appearance. I expect to have my Mind soon clear for something new. Tom has been much worse: but is now getting better.—his remembrances to you—I think of seeing the dart and Plymouth—but I dont know. It has as yet been a Mystery to me how and when Wordsworth went—I cant help thinking he has retu{r}ned to his Shell—with his beautiful Wife and his enchanting Sister—It is a great Pity that People should by associating themselves with the

[7] your *Garrod* (p. 544).   [8] the *Garrod.*

[9] The name of a picture, with which (Penrose, pp. 92 f.) Haydon won the British Institution prize of one hundred guineas in May, 1810. Haydon's "Epic" was "Christ's Entry."

fine[st] [1] things, spoil them—Hunt has damned Hampstead [and] [1] Masks and Sonnets and italian tales—Wordsworth ha[s] [1] damned the lakes—Millman has damned the old drama [2]—West [3] has damned—wholesale—Peacock [4] has damned sattire Ollier has damn'd Music [5]—Hazlitt has damned the bigotted and the blue-stockined [6] how durst the Man?! he is your only good damner and if ever I am damn'd—⟨damn me if⟩ [7] I shoul'nt like him to damn me—It will not be long ere I see you, but I thought I would just give you a line out of Devon—

Your's affectionately
John Keats

Rember me to all we know

[1] These letters are covered by the seal. In 1828 Haydon considered publishing a thin quarto called "Leigh Hunt & some of his companions" (see A. L. Strout, *Studia Neophilologica*, XXVI [1954], 93, 95). To William Blackwood on March 1 J. G. Lockhart wrote: "What will make you laugh most in Haydon's book will be some letters of Keats in one of which he says 'Hunt has damned Hampstead, Sonnets, & Italian tales, & also poor *me*.'" W. H. Ainsworth on March 2 sent further details: "The most curious portion are certain MS letters of Johnny Keats's from which it was evident that the writer entertain'd the meanest opinion of Leigh and attributed his want of success to his precarious puffery. The first part will I suspect be out in the course of a few days. . . . I will send you an early copy if you desire it."

[2] See I, 227 n. [3] See I, 192 n.

[4] Thomas Love Peacock (1785–1866), satirical novelist and poet.

[5] Blunden, p. 496, records that "Charles Ollier was an amateur flute-player."

[6] Hazlitt said (*Works*, VIII [1931], 236), "I have an utter aversion to *blue-stockings*."

[7] These words are scratched out apparently by Keats (they were omitted by Haydon when he transcribed the letter in his Autobiography [Penrose, pp. 236–238], but both he and F. W. Haydon, II, 9, printed "I should like him to damn me"), thereby changing the meaning of a sentence that has been misquoted dozens of times. Keats, who admired the "damning" letter to William Gifford, would hardly have wished to be damned by Hazlitt.

· 71 ·

TO TAYLOR AND HESSEY [1]

21 March 1818

Address: Messrs Taylor & Hessey/ Booksellers &c—/ Fleet Street/ London—
Postmarks: TEIGNMOUTH . . . (*blurred*); G 23 MR 23 1818

My dear Sirs, Teignmouth Saturday Morn—

I had no idea of your getting on so fast—I thought of bringing my 4th Book to Town all in good-time for you, especially after the late unfortunate chance.[2]

I did not however for my own sake delay finishing the copy which was done a few days after my arrival here. I send it off to day, and will tell you in a Post script at what time to send for it from the Bull and Mouth [3] or other Inn. You will find the Preface and dedication, and the title Page as I should wish it to stand—for a ramance [4] is a fine thing notwithstanding the circulating Libraries. My respectes to Mrs Hessey and to Percy Street—

Your's very sincerely—
John Keats

P.S. I have been advised to send it to you—you may expect it on Monday for I send it by the Postman to Exeter at the same time with this Letter. Adieu

[1] *ALS:* Victoria and Albert Museum.
[2] Possibly he is referring to Tom's severe illness.
[3] R. Greenwood's coffee-house and hotel on Bull and Mouth Street, Aldersgate Street.
[4] In his transcript in his letter-book, p. 6, Woodhouse (he has "romance") notes: "It had been suggested that a romance was an improper title for the book."

· 72 ·

TO JAMES RICE [1]

24 March 1818

Address: Mr James Rice Junr/ Poland Street/ Oxford Street/ London—
Postmarks: TEIGNMOUTH . . . ; G 26 MR 26 1818

Teignmouth Tuesday,

My dear Rice,

Being in the midst of your favorite Devon, I should not by rights, pen one word but it should contain a vast portion of Wit, Wisdom, and learning—for I have heard that Milton ere he wrote his Answer to Salmasius came into these parts, and for on [2] whole Month, rolled himself, for three whole hours [3] in a certain meadow hard by us—where the mark of his nose at equidistances is still shown. The exhibitor of said Meadow further saith that after these rollings, not a nettle sprang up in all the seven acres for seven years and that from said time a new sort of plant was made from the white thorn, of a thornless nature very much used by the Bucks of the present day to rap their Boots withall—This accou[n]t [4] made me very naturally suppose that the nettles and thorns etherealized by the Scholars rotatory motion and garner'd in his head, thence flew after a {n}ew fermentation against the luckless Salmasius and accasioned his well known and unhappy end.[5] What a happy thing it would be if we could settle our thoughts, make our minds up on any matter in five Minutes and remain content—that is to build a sort of mental Cottage of feelings quiet and pleasant—to have a sort of Philosophical Back Garden, and cheerful holiday-keeping front one—but Alas! this never can be: ⟨the⟩ for as the material

[1] *ALS:* Harvard. When Woodhouse copied this letter in his letter-book, pp. 111–113, it had only two of the tears noticed below.

[2] *For* one. [3] Woodhouse queries "hours [per day?]."

[4] Keats had trouble with this word: see I, 196, II, 81.

[5] "The general success of Milton's *Defence* . . . reduced Salmasius to utter chagrin, cost him the favor of the Queen [Christina of Sweden], and so undermined his health that he shortly died" (Walter Mac Kellar, *The Latin Poems of John Milton* [New Haven, Connecticut, 1930], pp. 41 f.). For further details about Claudius Salmasius (1588–1653) see David Masson, *The Life of John Milton,* IV (1877), 537–540.

Cottager knows there are such places as france and Italy and the Andes and the Burning Mountains—so the spiritual Cottager has knowledge of the terra semi incognita of things unearthly; and cannot for his Life, keep in the check rein—Or I should stop here quiet and comfortable in my theory of Nettles. You will see however I am obliged to run wild, being attracted by the Loadstone Concatenation.[6] No sooner had I settle the notty point of Salmasius that [7] the Devil put this whim into my head in the likeness of one of Pythagora's questionings 'Did Milton do more good or ha[r]m to the world? He wrote let me info[r]m you (for I have it from a friend, who had it of [8]—) he wrote Lycidas, Comus, Paradise Lost and other Poems, with much delectable prose—he was moreover an active friend to Man all his Life and has been since his death. Very good—but my dear fellow I must let you know that as there is ever the same quantity of matter constituting this habitable globe—as the ocean notwithstanding the enormous changes and revolutions taking place in some or other of its demesnes—notwithstanding Waterspouts whirpools and mighty Rivers emptying themselves into it, it still is made ⟨of⟩ up of the same bulk—nor ever varies the number of its Atoms [9]—And as a certain bulk of Water was instituted at the Creation—so very likely a certain portion of intellect was spun forth into the thin Air for the Brains of Man to prey upon it—You will see my drift without any unnecessary parenthesis. That which is contained in the Pacific and [1] lie in the hollow of the Caspian—that which was in Miltons head could not find Room in Charles the seconds—he like a Moon attracted ⟨the⟩ Intellect to its flow—it has not ebbd yet—but has left the shore pebble all bare —I mean all Bucks [2] Authors of Hengist [3] and Castlereaghs of the present day—who without Miltons gormandizing might have been all wise Men—Now for as much as—I was very peedisposed [4] to a

[6] A. D. Atkinson, *NQ*, August 4, 1951, pp. 343–345, shows that Keats referred to the Andes, the Burning Mountains, the *Terra semi-incognita*, and magnets because he had been reading Buffon's *Natural History* and Robertson's *History of America*.

[7] *For* settled, knotty, *and* than.

[8] He intended to, but did not actually, write "from" or "of."

[9] Atkinson finds the source of these details about "habitable globe," bulk of water, the Caspian Sea, and others also in Buffon and Robertson.

[1] MBF accepts the conjecture "can't." Woodhouse has "could not."

[2] A reference to the trifling dramatist (II, 85) Charles Bucke (1781–1846).

[3] An anonymous play, *Hengist, Or The Fifth Century, An Historical Melodrama* (1816).

[4] *For* predisposed.

Country I had heard you speak [5] so highly of, I took particular notice of every thing during my journey and have bought some folio asses skin for Memorandums—I have seen evey thing but the wind—and that they say becomes visible by taking a dose of Acorns or sleeping on [6] night in a hog trough with your tail to the Sow Sow west. Some of the little Barmaids look'd at me as if I knew Jem Rice—but when I took {a glass of} [7] Brandy they were quite convinced. One asked whether {you pres}er{v}ed [8] a secret she gave you on the nail—another how my [9] buttons of your Coat were buttoned in general—I {told} her it used to be four—but since you had become acqu{ain}ted with one Martin [1] you had reduced it to three and had been turning this third one in your Mind—and would do so with finger and thumb only you had taken to snuff—I have met with a Brace or twain of little Long heads [2]—not a bit o' the german—all in the neatest little dresses, and avoiding all the pudd[l]es—but very fond of peppermint drops, laming [3] ducks, and seeing little Girls affairs. Well I cant tell! I hope you are showing poor Reynolds the way to get well—send me a good account of him and if I can I'll send you one of Tom—Oh! for a day and all well! I went yesterday to dawlish fair— [4]

Over the hill and over the dale,
And over the bourn to Dawlish—
Where Gingerbread Wives have a scanty sale
And gingerbred nuts are smallish—

Rantipole Betty she ran down a hill
And kik'ed up her pettic[o]ats fairly
Says I I'll be Jack if you will be Gill—
So she sat on the Grass debonnairly—

[5] From the fact that Keats's copy (now at Harvard) of *Guzman d'Alfarache* (1634) is inscribed "John Keats From his Friend J^s Rxxx 20th April 1818" (see *KC*, I, 256, II, 366), Holman conjectured that Rice spent the week-end of April 18–20 (Saturday–Monday) in his favorite "Country" with Keats, and, from Holman, Lowell, I, 616–618, borrowed the conjecture.

[6] *For* one.

[7] Woodhouse and Lowell, I, 610, read "(Cherry?)."

[8] Woodhouse has "(you preserv?)—ed."

[9] *For* many.

[1] See I, 166 n.

[2] Partridge defines as shrewd or cunning persons, which cannot be the meaning here, and Jack Stillinger suggests that the Jeffrey sisters are referred to. Rice and his set were much given (see I, 197) to "a little Cant." The next phrase eludes explanation.

[3] *Perhaps for* lanning (lanner) ducks.

[4] It was held only on Easter Monday, which in 1818 came on March 23.

Here's somebody coming, here's sombody coming!
Says I 't is the Wind at a parley
So without any fuss any hawing and humming
She lay on the grass debonnai[r]ly—

Here's somebody here and here's somebody *there!*
Say's I hold your tongue you young Gipsey.
So she held her tongue and lay plump and fair
And dead as a venus tipsy—

O who would'nt hie to Dawlish fair
O who would'nt stop in a Meadow
O would [5] not rumple the daisies there
And make the wild fern for a bed do—

Tom's Remembrances and mine to all—
Your sincere friend
John Keats

· 73 ·

FROM B. R. HAYDON [1]

25 March 1818

Address: John Keats Esq/ Teignmouth/ Devonshire/ ⟨Post office⟩
Postmark: C AP 2 818

March 25th 1818

My dear Keats/ Your bi——ell [2] as you call it, is beautiful & I take it as a great friendly kindness to remember me in that way—as often as you feel inclined to give vent remember I am ⟨al⟩ready [always] with pleasure to receive the result—Surely you will not leave Devonshire without going to Plymouth the country round which is most exquisite—I will give you letters and promise you a kind & a welcome

[5] *For* who would.

[1] *ALS:* Formerly attached to Haydon's Journal, now at Harvard. Unless Haydon's date is erroneous, he received No. 70 on March 23, replied to it two days later, and then forgot to mail his reply till more than a week had passed.

[2] F. W. Haydon, II, 9, prints "Your versicles are beautiful"!

reception—Do go my dear Keats, and if you consent let me know & I will write my Friends immediately, and go round by the Totness road which is very fine, & come home by Ashburton, and then by Bridgewater where I have a Sister [3] who will be most happy to see you—I am getting on well, & have got my Christ [4] better than I have ever had it yet—and in a good state to compleat it—I am most happy to hear your Poem is advancing, to publication, God grant it the most compleat success, and may its reputation equal your genius—Devon[s]hire has somehow or other the character of being rainy, but I must own to you I do Not think it is more so than any other County, and pray remember the time of year; it has rained in Town almost incessantly ever since you went away, the fact is you dog you carried the rain with you ⟨and even⟩ as Ulysses did the Winds and then opening your rain bags you look round with a knowing wink, and say 'curse this Devonshire how it rains! —Stay till the Summer, and then bask in its deep blue summer Sky, and lush grass, & tawny banks, and silver bubbling rivers—you must not leave Devonshire without seeing some of its Scenery rocky, mossy, craggy with roaring rivers & as clear as crystal—it will do your mind good———

Shakespeare in speaking of somebody who is gradually dying makes some one say—"how is he?"—still ill nature & sickness *debate it at their leisure*" [5]—is this not exquisite?—When I die I'll have [6] my Shakespeare placed on my heart, with Homer in my right hand & Ariosto in the other, Dante under my head, Tasso at my feet & Corneille under my ——I hate that Corneille, a heartless ⟨tried⟩ tirade maker—I leave my other side that is my right one, for you, if you realize all of which your Genius is capable, as I am sure you will—write me if you go to Devonshire [7]—Mrs Scott "con occhi neri" [8] is as interesting as ever & desires to be remembered—I have

[3] See I, 145 n. [4] In "Christ's Entry into Jerusalem."

[5] *All's Well That Ends Well,* I.ii.69 f., 74 f., "How long is't, . . . Since the physician at your father's died?" ". . . Nature and sickness," etc.

[6] About six lines are heavily scratched out here. All I can read is: "Lear placed on my head, Macbeth in my hand, Othello on my heart, Romeo & Juliet on my lips, and the . . . up with the other, & the Midsummer Dream on one side of my head & the Tempest on the other." The deleted words are not in F. W. Haydon, II, 9 f., whose changes in what he does print are amazing.

[7] Or rather Plymouth (see I, 257).

[8] For Keats's comment on this phrase see I, 265. He had met Mrs. John Scott after February 14 (I, 227). Both she and her husband (see W. M. Parker, *TLS,* July 8, 1939, p. 405) greatly admired Keats's verse.

heard nothing of Wordsworth ever since he went, which I take to be unkind—Haslitt is going to lecture at Crown & anchor [9] I am sorry for it, tho' he will get money, it is letting his talents down a little—What affectation in Hunts title—"*Foliage*"! [1]—I met that horrid creature Miss Kent, [2] looking like a fury & an old maid, mixed—Yours ever d^r Keats

B R Haydon

·74·

TO J. H. REYNOLDS [1]

25 March 1818

[Teignmouth, 25 March 1818.] [2]

Dear Reynolds, as last night I lay in bed,
There came before my eyes that wonted thread
Of Shapes, and Shadows and Remembrances,
That every other minute vex and please:
Things all disjointed come from North and south,
Two witch's eyes above a cherub's mouth,
Voltaire with casque and shield and Habergeon,
And Alexander with his night-cap on—
Old Socrates a tying his cravat;
And Hazlitt playing with Miss Edgworth's cat; [3]

[9] "The Lectures on Poetry, delivered by this Gentleman with such success at the Surrey Institution, he is now re-delivering at the Crown and Anchor" (*Examiner*, March 29, 1818, p. 201). See also Howe, p. 227. The Crown and Anchor was Edward Ottey's tavern in the Strand. The spelling "Haslitt" occurs also in *Annals of the Fine Arts*, IV (1820), 543–549.

[1] *Foliage; Or Poems Original and Translated* was published by the Olliers in 1818.

[2] See I, 140. According to Haydon's own boast (see Duncan Gray and Violet Walker, *K–SMB*, No. 7 [1956], 24), Miss Kent "pretended to be dying for me."

[1] A transcript in Woodhouse's letter-book, p. 74, by a clerk, with corrections by Woodhouse. It begins, "See Below*"; then the letter is given, and is followed by "*Dear Reynolds! as last night I lay in bed,/ There came before my eyes &^c See the lines pa: 65 of the/ Collection of K's Poetry." The reference is to Woodhouse's manuscript of Keats's poems which Garrod calls W^2. That manuscript, fols. 65–68, contains the entire poem and most of the letter, with one sentence in short-hand. I print the prose from the first of Woodhouse's books, listing the variants in "W^2," and the poem from the second. Milnes, I, 113, printed the letter before the verses.

[2] Supplied by Woodhouse.

[3] Woodruff, pp. 25 f., thinks it likely that Hazlitt met Miss Edgeworth, who was in Paris, while he was studying at the Louvre during the latter part of 1802. For her love of cats he cites Emily Lawless, *Maria Edgeworth* (New York, 1904), pp. 84 f.

And Junius Brutus [4] pretty well so, so,[5]
Making the best of 's way towards Soho.
Few are there who escape these visitings—
P'erhaps one or two, whose lives have patent wings;
And through whose curtains peeps no hellish nose,
No wild boar tushes, and no Mermaid's toes:
But flowers bursting out with lusty pride;
And young Æolian harps personified,
Some, Titian colours touch'd into real life.—
The sacrifice goes on; the pontif knife
Gloams [6] in the sun, the milk-white heifer lows,[7]
The pipes go shrilly, the libation flows:
A white sail shews above the green-head cliff
Moves round the point, and throws her anchor stiff.
The Mariners join hymn with those on land.—
You know the Enchanted Castle [8] it doth stand
Upon a Rock on the Border of a Lake
Nested in Trees, which all do seem to shake
Urganda's [9]
From some old Magic like ⟨the witch's⟩ sword.
O Phœbus that I had thy sacred word
To shew this Castle in fair dreaming wise
Unto my friend, while sick and ill he lies.
You know it well enough, where it doth seem
A mossy place, a Merlin's Hall, a dream.
You know the clear lake, and the little Isles,
The Mountains blue, and cold near neighbour rills—
All which elsewhere are but half animate
Here do they look alive to love and hate;
To smiles and frowns; they seem a lifted mound
Above some giant, pulsing underground.

[4] Junius Brutus Booth (1796–1852), actor. [5] Slang for "tipsy" (see I, 288).

[6] Woodhouse notes "so." The word should be "Gleams."

[7] De Selincourt, p. 538, comments: "An interesting anticipation of the *Ode on a Grecian Urn*, and in . . . [lines 76 f.] we have another anticipation of the same poem. . . . The picture in lines 23–25 suggests *Endymion*, ii.78–82."

[8] Colvin, p. 91 n., says that Keats must have seen an engraving by François Vivarès (1709–1780) and William Woollett (1735–1785). Hewlett, p. 156, adds that the picture was at William Wells's home, Redleaf, near Sevenoaks, Kent. A. D. Atkinson, *NQ*, August 4, 1951, p. 345, thinks some details are also suggested by Claude's "Sacrifice to Apollo."

[9] See I, 146 n.

Part of the building was a chosen See
Built by a banish'd santon [1] of Chaldee:
+ The other part two thousand years from him
Was built by Cuthbert de Saint Aldebrim;
Then there's a little wing, far from the sun,
Built by a Lapland Witch [2] turn'd maudlin nun—
And many other juts of aged stone
Founded with many a mason-devil's groan.
The doors all look as if they oped themselves,
The windows as if latch'd by fays & elves—
And from them comes a silver flash of light
As from the Westward of a summer's night;
Or like a beauteous woman's large blue eyes
Gone mad through olden songs and Poesies—
See what is coming from the distance dim!
A golden galley all in silken trim!
Three rows of oars are lightening moment-whiles
Into the verdurous bosoms of those Isles.
Towards the shade under the Castle Wall
It comes in silence—now tis hidden all.
The clarion sounds; and from a postern grate
An echo of sweet music doth create
A fear in the poor herdsman who doth bring
His beasts to trouble the enchanted spring:
He tells of the sweet music and the spot
To all his friends, and they believe him not.
O that our dreamings all of sleep or wake
Would all their colours from the sunset take:
From something of material sublime,
Rather than shadow our own Soul's daytime
In the dark void of Night. For in the world
We jostle—but my flag is not unfurl'd

+ Here the following line is written and erased. "Poor Man he left the Terrace Walls of Ur.

[1] "A kind of dervish or priest, regarded as a saint" (De Selincourt, p. 539). Gittings, *The Mask of Keats* (1956), p. 101, observes that Santons appear in William Beckford's *Vathek*.

[2] De Selincourt cites *Paradise Lost*, II.662–666. See also F. E. Farley, "Three 'Lapland Songs'," *PMLA*, XXI (1906), 37.

On the Admiral staff [3]—and to philosophize
I dare not yet!—Oh never will the prize,
High reason, and the lore of good and ill
Be my award. Things cannot to the will
Be settled, but they tease us out of thought.
Or is it that Imagination brought
Beyond its proper bound, yet still confined,—
Lost in a sort of Purgatory blind,
Cannot refer to any standard law
Of either earth or heaven?—It is a flaw
In happiness to see beyond our bourn—
It forces us in Summer skies to mourn:
It spoils the singing of the Nightingale.
Dear Reynolds. I have a mysterious tale
And cannot speak it. The first page I read
Upon a Lampit Rock of green sea weed
Among the breakers—'Twas a quiet Eve;
The rocks were silent—the wide sea did weave
An untumultuous fringe of silver foam
Along the flat brown sand. I was at home,
And should have been most happy—but I saw
Too far into the sea; where every maw
The greater on the less feeds evermore:—
But I saw too distinct into the core
Of an eternal fierce destruction,[4]
And so from Happiness I ⟨was⟩ far was gone.
Still am I sick of it: and though to day
I've gathered young spring-leaves, and flowers gay
Of Periwinkle and wild strawberry,
Still do I that most fierce destruction see,
The shark at savage prey—the hawk at pounce,
The gentle Robin, like a pard or ounce,
Ravening a worm [5]—Away ye horrid moods,

[3] J. L. Lowes, *PMLA*, LI (1936), 1100, shows that "flag . . . staff" comes from North's Plutarch (1676), p. 178.

[4] De Selincourt, p. 539: "Keats returns to the problem of Nature's cruelty in a letter written a year later [II, 79 f.], and shows himself far more able to grapple with it."

[5] For borrowings from Goethe's *Werther* in the passage "I was at home . . . Ravening a worm," see D. B. Green, *NQ*, September 16, 1950, p. 411.

Moods of one's mind![6] You know I hate them well,
You know I'd sooner be a clapping bell
To some Kamschatkan missionary church,[7]
Than with these horrid moods be left in lurch—
Do you get health—and Tom the same—I'll dance,
And from detested moods in new Romance
Take refuge—Of bad lines a Centaine dose
Is sure enough—and so "here follows prose."[8]—

My Dear Reynolds.

In hopes of cheering you through a Minute or two I was determined nill he will he[9] to send[1] you some lines so you will[2] excuse the unconnected⟨ness⟩ subject, and careless verse—You know, I am sure, Claude's Enchanted Castle and I wish you may be pleased with my remembrance of it—The Rain is Come on again—I think with me Devonshire stands a very poor chance, I shall damn it up hill and down dale, if it keeps up to the average of 6 fine days in three weeks.[3] Let me have better news of you.

Your affectionate friend
John Keats.

Toms Rememb[s] to you. Rem[r]
us to all—[4]

M[r] J. H Reynolds
Little Britain
Christs Hospital London

[6] De Selincourt notes the "reminiscence of the title given by Wordsworth to some poems" in *Poems in Two Volumes* (1807). See also "Moods of my own Mind" at I, 287.

[7] As Atkinson (see above), pp. 345 f., remarks, many of Keats's details "suggest that thoughts of the sea and travel were in his head." Keats, he says, had been reading Buffon's *Natural History* (1792), where Kamchatka is often mentioned, and Robertson's *History of America*, where there is a graphic description of "that most hateful land" of America on the shore of the Sea of Kamchatka.

[8] *Twelfth Night*, II.v.154.

[9] nil-he will-he *W*².

[1] scribble *W*².

[2] So you'll *W*².

[3] I shall damn . . . three weeks *in short hand W*².

[4] *W*² omits the postscript.

·75·

TO B. R. HAYDON [1]

8 April 1818

Address: B R Haydon Esqr/ Lisson Grove North/ Paddington Middx
Postmarks: TEIGNMOUTH . . . ; 10 o'Clock AP 10 1818 FN^{n}; G 10 AP 10 1818

Wednesday— [2]

My dear Haydon,

I am glad you were pleased with my nonsense [3] and if it so happen that the humour takes me when I have set down to prose to you I will not gainsay it. I should be (god forgive me) ready to swear because I cannot make use of you [4] assistance in going through Devon if I was not in my own Mind determined to visit it thoroughly at some more favorable time of the year. But now Tom (who is getting greatly better) is anxious to be in Town therefore I put off my threading the County. I purpose within a Month to put my knapsack at my back and make a pedestrian tour through the North of England, and part of Scotland—to make a sort of Prologue to the Life I intend to pursue—that is to write, to study and to see all Europe at the lowest expence.[5] I will clamber through the Clouds and exist. I will get such an accumulation of stupendous recollolections that as I walk through the suburbs of London I may not see them—I will stand upon Mount Blanc and remember this coming Summer when I intend to straddle ben Lomond—with my Soul!—galligaskins are out of the Question—I am nearer myself to hear your Christ is ⟨having⟩ being tinted into immortality—Believe me Haydon your picture is a part of myself—I have ever been too sensible of the labyrinthian path to eminence in Art (judging from Poetry) ever to think I understood the emphasis of Painting. The

[1] *ALS:* Formerly attached to Haydon's Journal, now at Harvard. Addressed by Tom Keats.

[2] Another hand wrote "1817" before "Wednesday," and still another puts under that "1817" "(Postmark 1818!)."

[3] See No. 70. [4] See I, 121 n.

[5] On his plans for travel see also I, 268, 343 n., and the Index.

innumerable compositions and decompositions which take place between the intellect and its thousand materials before it arrives at that trembling delicate and snail-horn [6] perception of Beauty—I know not you many havens of intenseness—nor ever can know them—but for this I hope not [7] you atchieve [8] is lost upon me: for when a Schoolboy the abstract Idea I had of an heroic painting—was what I cannot describe I saw it somewhat sideways large prominent round and colour'd with magnificence—somewhat like the feel [9] I have of Anthony and Cleopatra. Or of Alcibiades, leaning on his Crimson Couch in his Galley, his broad shoulders imperceptibly heaving with the Sea [1]—That [2] passage in Shakspeare is finer than this

'See how the surly Warwick mans the Wall' [3]

I like your consignment of Corneille—that's the humor of it [4]—They shall be called your Posthumous Works. I don't understand you bit of Italian.[5] I hope she will awake from her dream and flourish fair—my respects to her [6]—The Hedges by this time are beginn[in]g to leaf—Cats are becoming more vociferous—young Ladies that wear Watches are always looking at them—Women about forty five think the Season very back ward—Lady's Mares have but half an allowance of food—It rains here again, has been doing so for three days—however as I told you I'll take a trial in June July or August next year—

I am affraid Wordsworth went rather huff'd out of Town—I am sorry for it. he cannot expect his fireside Divan to be infallible he cannot expect but that every Man of worth is as proud as himself. O that he had not fit with a Warrener [7] that is din'd at King-

[6] See I, 189 n. Compare also Hazlitt (*Works*, V [1930], 51), "In Shakspeare there is a continual composition and decomposition of its elements, a fermentation of every particle in the whole mass. . . ."

[7] *For* nought. [8] The "t" is changed from "d."

[9] On this noun see I, 143 n.

[1] J. L. Lowes, *PMLA*, LI (1936), 1100, shows that the reference is to North's Plutarch (1676), p. 171.

[2] *For* What. [3] *3 Henry VI*, V.i.17. [4] *Henry V*, II.i.101.

[5] On Mrs. Scott's black eyes see I, 258.

[6] The next five sentences, as MBF points out, resemble (see Lowell, II, 428 f.) Leigh Hunt's "A Now, Descriptive of a Hot Day," *Indicator*, June 28, 1820, pp. 300–303, in writing which he had some aid from Keats.

[7] *The Merry Wives of Windsor*, I.iv.28, "He hath fought with a warrener" (Colvin, p. 95 n.). Blunden, p. 497, sees "a hit at the set of John Warren, who published some volumes of verse by Reynolds and others."

ston's. I shall be in town in about a fortnight [8] and then we will have a day or so now and then before I set out on my northern expedition—we will have no more abominable Rows [9]—for they leave one is [1] a fearful silence having settled the Methodists let us be rational—not upon compulsion [2]—no if it will out let it—but I will not play the Basoon any more delibe[r]ately—Remember me to Hazlitt, and Bewick [3]—Your affectionate friend

John Keats—

·76·

TO J. H. REYNOLDS [1]

9 April 1818

My Dear Reynolds. Th^y^ Morn^g^ [2]

Since you all agree that the thing [3] is bad, it must be so—though I am not aware there is any thing like Hunt in it, (and if there is, it is my natural way, and I have something in common with Hunt) look it over again and examine into the motives, the seeds from which any one sentence sprung—I have not the slightest feel of humility towards the Public—or to any thing in existence,—but the eternal Being, the Principle of Beauty,—and the Memory of great Men—When I am writing for myself for the mere sake of the Moment's enjoyment, perhaps nature has its course with me—but a Preface is written to the Public; a thing I cannot help looking upon as an Enemy, and which I cannot address without feelings of Hos-

[8] He and Tom actually left Teignmouth on May 4 or 5 (see No. 81).

[9] F. W. Haydon, II, 10–12, printing the letter, explains: "Keats appears to allude here to the violent political and religious discussions of the set, as much as to an absurd practice they had, when they met, of amusing themselves after dinner by a concert, each imitating a different instrument. The fun was as boisterous by all accounts as the discussions were heated."

[1] *For* in.

[2] Compare *1 Henry IV*, II.iv.261, 263 f., 266 (J. C. Maxwell, *NQ*, May 17, 1947, p. 215).

[3] The words "and Bewick" are scratched out, probably by F. W. Haydon, who does not print them.

[1] A transcript by a clerk in Woodhouse's letter-book, pp. 58–60, with corrections by Woodhouse.

[2] The clerk put above these words "Teignmouth April 9th 1818." and Woodhouse enclosed that addition in red-ink parentheses.

[3] The original preface to *Endymion*, now in the Pierpont Morgan Library, is printed by Garrod, pp. lxxxviii f.

tility—If I write a Preface in a supple or subdued style, it will not be in character with me as a public speaker—I wo[d] be subdued before my friends, and thank them for subduing me—but among Multitudes of Men—I have no feel of stooping, I hate the idea of humility to them—

I never wrote one single Line of Poetry with the least Shadow of public thought.

Trojan

Forgive me for vexing you and making a ⟨troqan⟩ Horse of such a Trifle, both with respect to the matter in Question, and myself—but it eases me to tell you—I could not live without the love of my friends—I would jump down Ætna for any great Public good [4]—but I hate a Mawkish Popularity.—I cannot be subdued before them—My glory would be to daunt and dazzle the thousand jabberers about Pictures and Books—I see swarms of Porcupines with their Quills erect "like lime-twigs set to catch my Winged Book" [5] and I would fright 'em away with a torch—You will say my preface is not much of a Torch. It would have been too insulting "to begin from Jove" [6] and I could not [set] [7] a golden head upon a thing of clay—if there is any fault in the preface it is not affectation: but an undersong of disrespect to the Public.—if I write another preface. it must be done without a thought of those people—I will think about it. If it should not reach you in four—or five days—tell Taylor to publish it without a preface, and let the dedication simply stand "inscribed to the memory of Thomas Chatterton." I had resolved last night to write to you this morning—I wish it had been about something else—something to greet you towards the close of your long illness—I have had one or two intimations of your going to Hampstead for a space; and I regret to see your confounded Rheumatism keeps you in Little Brittain where I am sure the air is too confined—Devonshire continues rainy. As the drops beat against the window, they give me the same sensation as a quart of cold water offered to revive a half drowned devil—No feel of the clouds dropping fatness; but as if the roots of the

drench'd

Earth were rotten cold and ⟨dead⟩—I have not been able to go

[4] On doing good for the world compare I, 293, 387. Keats had Empedocles in mind.

[5] *2 Henry VI*, III.iii.16, "Like lime-twigs set to catch my winged soul."

[6] Herrick's "Evensong," line 1, in *Hesperides* (*Poems* [1902], p. 124).

[7] Woodhouse emends to "(set)."

to Kents' Ca[ve][8] at Babbicun—however on one very beautiful day I had a fine Clamber over the rocks all along as far as that place: I shall be in Town in about Ten days.—We go by way of Bath on purpose to call on Bailey.[9] I hope soon to be writing to you about the things of the north, purposing to wayfare all over those parts. I have settled my accoutrements in my own mind, and will go to gorge wonders: However we'll have some days together before I set out—

I have many reasons for going wonder-ways: to make my winter chair free from spleen—to enlarge my vision—to escape disquisitions on Poetry and Kingston Criticism.—to promote digestion and economise shoe leather—I'll have leather buttons and belt; and if Brown holds his mind, over the Hills we go.—If my Books will help me to it,—thus will I take all Europe in turn,[1] and see the Kingdoms of the Earth and the glory of them [2]—Tom is getting better he hopes

nurses [3]

you may meet him at the top o' the hill—My Love to your ⟨Neases⟩. I am ever

Your affectionate Friend,
John Keats.

J H Reynolds Esq
Little Brittain
Christs Hospital
London

[8] Woodhouse has "Ca(ve?)." Kents Cavern in Babbacombe, Torquay, famous for the bones and flint implements it provided for the Torquay Museum and the British Museum, was perhaps a greater "sight" in 1818 than it is today. Keats did visit it later: see II, 167 f.

[9] Actually he left Teignmouth on May 4 or 5 (No. 81), going by Honiton and Bridport, while Bailey remained in Oxford.

[1] See I, 264 n. [2] Luke iv.5 f.; Matthew iv.8.

[3] Woodhouse notes "(his sisters)."

·77·

TO J. H. REYNOLDS [1]

10 April 1818 [2]

Friday

My dear Reynolds/.

I am anxious you sho^d find this Preface [3] tolerable. if there is an affectation in it 'tis natural to me.—Do let the Printer's Devil cook it—and 'let me be as the casing air.' [4]

You are too good in this Matter—were I in your state, I am certain I should have no thought but of discontent and illness—I might tho' be taught patience: I had an idea of giving no Preface; however, don't you think this had better go?—O, let it—one should not be too timid—of committing faults.

The Climate here weighs us [down] [5] completely—Tom is quite low spirited—It is impossible to live in a country which is continually under hatches—Who would live in the region of Mists, Game Laws indemnity Bills &^c when there is such a place as Italy? It is said this England from its Clime produces a Spleen, able to engender the finest Sentiment—and covers the whole face of the Isle with Green [6]—so it aught, I'm sure.—I should still like the Dedication simply, as I said in my last.

I wanted to send you a few songs written in your favorite Devon ——it cannot be—Rain! Rain! Rain! I am going this morning to take a fac-simile of a Letter of Nelson's, [7] very much to his honor—you will be greatly pleased when you see it—in about a Week [8]—What a spite it is, one cannot get out the little way I went yesterday

[1] A transcript in Woodhouse's letter-book, p. 61, by a clerk, with corrections by Woodhouse.

[2] The letter is dated by Woodhouse and his clerk "(Teignm^o Apl 10. 1818.)—"

[3] It was published with *Endymion*.

[4] See I, 201 n.

[5] Woodhouse supplies "(down)."

[6] A reference to *The Spleen. An Epistle Inscribed to his particular Friend Mr. C. J. . . . By the late Mr. Matthew Green, of the Custom-house* (1737). On Green (1696–1737) see H. R. Smith, *NQ*, June, July, 1954, pp. 250–253, 284–287.

[7] On Keats's interest in Nelson see Hewlett, p. 116.

[8] See I, 283 n.

I found a lane bank'd on each side with store of Primroses, while the earlier bushes are beginning to leaf.

I shall hear a good Account of you soon

Your affectionate Friend

John Keats.

My Love to all and remember me to Taylor.

John H Reynolds Esq: Little Brittain Christs Hospital London.

· 78 ·

TO JOHN TAYLOR [1]

24 April 1818

Address: John Taylor Esqre/ Taylor & Hessey's/ Booksellers &c/ Fleet Street

Postmarks: TEIGNMOUTH . . . ; G 27 AP 27 1818

Teignmouth Friday

My dear Taylor,

I think I Did very wrong to leave you to all the trouble of Endymion—but I could not help it then—another time I shall be more bent to all sort of troubles and disagreeables—Young Men for some time have an idea that such a thing as happiness is to be had [2] and therefore are extremely impatient under any unpleasant restraining —in time however, of such stuff is the world [3] about them, they know better and instead of striving from Uneasiness greet it as an habitual sensation, a pannier which is to weigh upon them through life.

And in proportion to my disgust at the task is my sense of your kindness & anxiety—the book [4] pleased me much—it is very free

[1] *ALS:* Pierpont Morgan Library. There is also a transcript in Woodhouse's letter-book, pp. 7 f., with the "Errata" omitted. On the original letter Taylor penciled the date of receipt "27 Ap."

[2] See I, 186.

[3] *Written* would. Keats first wrote "about him, he knows . . . greets . . . weigh upon him."

[4] An advance copy of *Endymion*, which Colvin, 1920, p. 163, Lowell, I, 619, Hewlett, p. 159, and MacGillivray (*Keats* [Toronto, 1949], p. 4) say was published towards the end of April. The *Champion*, April 22, p. 271, lists it as "Just published." In some copies of *Endymion* there is a list of books just published dated May 1. On April 13 Sara Hutchinson (*Letters*, ed. Kathleen Coburn [1954], p. 133) wrote: "Little Keats too I see is in the

from faults; and although there are one or two words I should wish replaced, I see in many places an improvement greatly to the purpose—

I think those speeches which are related—those parts where the speaker repeats a speech—such as Glaucus' repetition of Circe's words, should have inverted commas to every line—In this there is a little confusion. If we divide the speeches into *identical* and *related:* and to the former put merely one inverted comma at the beginning and another at the end; and to the latter inverted commas before every line, the book will be better understood at the first glance. Look at pages 126 and 127 you will find in the 3 line the beginning of a *related* speech marked thus "Ah! art awake [5]—while at the same time in the next page the continuation of the *identical speech* is mark'd in the same manner "Young Man of Latmos [6]—You will find on the other side all the parts which should have inverted commas to every line—

I was purposing to travel over the north this Summer—there is but one thing to prevent me—I know nothing I have read nothing and I mean to follow Solomon's directions of 'get Wisdom—get understanding' [7]—I find cavalier days are gone by. I find that I can have no enjoyment in the World but continual drinking of Knowledge—I find there is no worthy pursuit but the idea of doing some good for the world [8]—some do it with their society—some with their wit—some with their benevolence—some with a sort of power of conferring pleasure and good humour on all they meet and in a thousand ways all equally dutiful to the command of Great Nature—there is but one way for me—the road lies though [9] application study and thought. I will pursue it and to that end purpose retiring for some years. I have been hovering for some time between an exquisite sense of the luxurious and a love for Philosophy [1]—were I calculated for the former I should be glad—but as I am not I shall turn all my soul to the latter. My Brother Tom is getting better and I hope I shall see both him and Reynolds well before I retire from

publishing line—but the Title of his Poem has no charms for me—however beautiful it may be I am sure it cannot awaken my interest or sympathies—I wonder anybody should take such subjects now-a-days." Probably she was expressing Wordsworth's sentiments.

[5] III. 429. [6] III.449. [7] Proverbs iv.5.

[8] Compare his words to Reynolds at I, 267. [9] *For* through.

[1] "By 'philosophy' he does not mean metaphysics but knowledge and the fruits of reading generally" (Colvin, 1920, p. 266).

the World. I shall see you soon and have some talk about what Books I shall take with me—

Your very sincere friend
John Keats

Hessey
Remember me to ⟨Heffey⟩ —Woodhouse and Percy Street

Errata—

Page 4 line 4 place the comma after *old*
Page 60 line 12 for *head* read *bead* [2]
— 66 — 5 place a comma after *dim*
— 88 — 13 for 'my kindest' read 'delicious'
— 90 — 10 for 'honour' read 'horror' [2]
— 98 leave out the inverted commas in lines 12 and 14
⟨— 122 line 12 for 'utmost' read 'tiptop'⟩
Page 166 line 17 for '*is it*' read '*is 't*'
— 151 — 3 dele comma
— 177 there should be a white space after the 5th line
— 185 [3] line 13 a note of exclam. after longing instead of the full stop.
— 205 — 6 — dele inverted commas after ha!"

There is a great mistake in the 1st line page 195—it should read thus—"Favour from thee and so *I kisses gave*
To the void air &c"
Page 194 line 3 for not of interrog. put not of exclam

I cannot discover any other error—the preface is well without those thing you have left out—Adieu—

Parts that should have inverted commas to every line [4]

Page 47 from line 12 to line 7 in the next page
— 126— 3— 17
— 132— the 4 from the bottom to line 5 in page 134

[2] According to HBF, these words were followed by crosses "probably made by Taylor to indicate that those corrections at all events were to be included" on the printed errata slip. The crosses are no longer on the letter but the corrections were made.

[3] Changed from "195."

[4] Written on the bottom "doubling."

Those abreviations of *is 't* of *is it* and *done 't* for *done it* are of great
consequence
more last words [5]

Page 47 line 10 for *scene* read *screne*
— 201 — 6 from the bottom for the note of exclam
put a note of interrog—
— 90 — 3 for done it read done 't

·79·

TO J. H. REYNOLDS [1]

27 April 1818

Teignmouth Monday [2]

My dear Reynolds.

It is an awful while [3] since you have heard from me—I hope I may not be punished, when I see you well, and so anxious as you always are for me, with the remembrance of my so seldom writing when you were so horribly confined—the most unhappy hours in our lives are those in which we recollect times past to our own blushing—If we are immortal that must be the Hell—If I must be immortal, I hope it will be after having taken a little of "that watery labyrinth" in order to forget some of my schoolboy days & others since those.[4]

I Have heard from George at different times how slowly you were recovering. it is a tedious thing—but all Medical Men will tell you how far a very gradual amendment is preferable; you will be strong after this, never fear.—We are here still enveloppd in clouds—I lay awake last night—listening to the Rain with a sense of being drown'd and rotted like a grain of wheat—There is a continual courtesy between the Heavens and the Earth.—the heavens

[5] Written on the top "doubling."

[1] A transcript in Woodhouse's letter-book, pp. 62 f., by a clerk, with corrections by Woodhouse.

[2] Woodhouse adds "27 April 1818."

[3] Only seventeen days (see No. 77); but compare his remarks in Nos. 48 and 56.

[4] *Paradise Lost*, II.584 f., "Her watrie Labyrinth, whereof who drinks,/ Forthwith his former state and being forgets."

rain down their unwelcomeness, and the Earth sends it up again to be returned to morrow. Tom has taken a fancy to a Physician here, Dr Turton,[5] and I think is getting better—therefore I shall perhaps remain here some Months.[6]—I have written to George for some Books—shall learn Greek, and very likely Italian—and in other ways prepare myself to ask Hazlitt in about a years time the best
to be
metaphysical road I can take.—For although I take poetry ⟨of the⟩ Chief, there is something else wanting to one who passes his life among Books and thoughts on Books—I long to feast upon old Homer as we have upon Shakespeare. and as I have lately upon Milton.[7]—if you understood Greek, and would read me passages, now and then, explaining their meaning, 't would be, from its mistiness, perhaps a greater luxury than reading the thing one's self.—I shall be happy when I can do the same for you.—I have written for my folio Shakespeare, in which there is the first few stanzas of my "Pot of Basil": [8] I have the rest here finish'd, and will copy the whole out fair shortly—and George will bring it to you—The Compliment is paid by us to Boccace, whether we publish or no: [9] so there is content in this world—mine [1] is short—you must be deliberate about yours: you must not think of it till many months after you are quite well:—then put your passion to it,—and I shall be bound up with you in the shadows of mind, as we are in our matters of human life—Perhaps a Stanza or two will not be too foreign to your Sickness.

[5] William Turton (1762–1835), M.B., conchologist, author of various medical and scientific books, whose collection of shells is now in the Smithsonian Institute at Washington.

[6] But see I, 283 n.

[7] Among Keats's books as listed by Brown in 1821 (*KC*, I, 253–260) were Hazlitt's *Essay on the Principles of Human Action* (1805), an edition of Shakespeare, various works in Italian or translated from Italian, an Italian-French dictionary, a Greek grammar, but not Homer or Milton.

[8] His facsimile reproduction (1808) of the first folio, now in the Keats Museum, contains two autograph poems by him but not the "Isabella" lines. See also the last two sentences of No. 80.

[9] Reynolds called at Well Walk on October 13, 1818, took the manuscript of "Isabella" with him, and, after reading it, wrote the next day (*KC*, I, 43 f.), urging Keats to publish it at once, for "I can never write anything now—my mind is taken the other way." Keats and Reynolds had planned to issue jointly a volume containing poems based on Boccaccio. Keats published only "Isabella," but Reynolds in 1821 included two "stories" from Boccaccio ("The Garden of Florence" and "The Ladye of Provence") in *The Garden of Florence*, pp. 1–28, 153–175, with touching comments on his dead friend.

[1] Woodhouse explains, "(ie my Poem)."

'Were they unhappy then? It cannot be:
Too many tears &c &c ——
——
But for the general award of love &c } 2 Stanzas [2]

⟨5th line "W⟩

═══

She wept alone for Pleasures &c &c 1 Stanza—

The 5th line ran thus "What might have been too plainly did she see." [3]—

═══

I heard from Rice this morning—very witty—and have just written to Bailey [4]—Don't you think I am brushing up in the letter way? and being in for it,—you shall hear again from me very shortly:—if you will promise not to put hand to paper for me until you can do it with a tolerable ease of health—except it be a line or two—Give my Love to your Mother and Sisters Remember me to the Butlers—not forgetting Sarah

Your affectionate friend
John Keats

Mr J H Reynolds
Mr [5] Butlers
2 Spencer Place
Kennington Common.

· 80 ·

TO J. H. REYNOLDS [1]

3 May 1818

Teignmouth May 3d [2]

My dear Reynolds.

What I complain of is that I have been in so an uneasy a state of Mind as not to be fit to write to an invalid. I cannot write to any length under a dis-guised feeling. I should have loaded you with an

[2] See "Isabella," stanzas 12, 13 (which were given in full in the original letter).

[3] As printed, stanza 30 begins "She weeps," etc., and line 5 runs "His image in the dusk she seem'd to see." See Garrod, p. 225, for other readings.

[4] The letter is not known.

[5] The initial looks like "W," though Woodhouse's clerk surely intended to write "Mr." Earlier Keats had expressed the wish that the ailing Reynolds would "move to Butler's for a short time" (I, 236).

[1] A transcript in Woodhouse's letter-book, pp. 64–70, by a clerk, with corrections by Woodhouse. [2] Woodhouse adds "1818."

addition of gloom, which I am sure you do not want. I am now thank God in a humour to give you a good groats worth—for Tom, after a Night without a Wink of sleep, and overburdened with fever, has got up after a refreshing day sleep and is better than he has been for a long time; and you I trust have been again round the Common [3] without any effect but refreshment.—As to the Matter I hope I can say with Sir Andrew "I have matter enough in my head" in your favor [4] And now, in the second place, for I reckon that I have finished my Imprimis, I am glad you blow up the weather—all through your letter there is a leaning towards a climate-curse. and you know what a delicate satisfaction there is in having a vexation anathematized: one would think there has been growing up for these last four thousand years, a grandchild Scion of the old forbidden tree, and that some modern Eve had just violated it; and that there was come with double charge, "Notus and Afer black

Sierra-

with thunderous clouds from ⟨Sera⟩leona" [5]—I shall breathe worsted stockings [6] sooner than I thought for. Tom wants to be in Town—we will have some such days upon the heath like that of last summer and why not with the same book: or what say you to a black Letter Chaucer printed in 1596: aye I've got one huzza! [7] I shall have it bounden gothique a nice sombre binding—it will go a little way to unmodernize. And also I see no reason, because I have been away this last month, why I should not have a peep at your Spencerian [8]—notwithstanding you speak of your office, in my thought a little too early, for I do not see why a Mind like yours is not capable of harbouring and digesting the whole Mystery of Law as easily as Parson Hugh does Pepins [9] —which did not hinder him from his poetic Canary—Were I to study physic or rather Medicine again,—I feel it would not make the least difference in my

[3] Kennington Common, where the Butlers (I, 275) lived.

[4] *The Merry Wives of Windsor*, I.i.127 f. (Abraham Slender speaks), "I have matter in my head against you."

[5] *Paradise Lost*, X.702 f. (HBF, 1889).

[6] That is, return to the house of the postman, Benjamin Bentley, and his noisy children.

[7] MBF notes that such an edition is unknown, and that Keats probably meant 1598.

[8] "The Romance of Youth," later published in Reynolds' *Garden of Florence* (1821), pp. 29–92.

[9] Sir Hugh Evans, in *The Merry Wives of Windsor*, I.ii.11 f., says, "I will make an end of my dinner; there's pippins and cheese to come" (Colvin, p. 104 n.). The "poetic Canary" that follows probably means, as in the same play, II.ii.61, 64, "quandary."

is
Poetry; when the Mind is in its infancy a Bias ⟨in⟩ in reality a Bias, but when we have acquired more strength, a Bias becomes no Bias. Every department of knowledge we see excellent and calculated towards a great whole. I am so convinced of this, that I am glad at not having given away my medical Books, which I shall again look over to keep alive the little I know thitherwards; and moreover intend through you and Rice to become a sort of Pip-civilian.[1] An extensive knowlege is needful to thinking [2] people—it takes away the heat and fever; and helps, by widening speculation, to ease the Burden of the Mystery: [3] a thing I begin to understand a little, and which weighed upon you in the most gloomy and true sentence in your Letter. The difference of high Sensations with and without knowledge appears to me this—in the latter case we are falling continually ten thousand fathoms deep and being blown up again with-
bare
out wings and with all [the] horror of a ⟨Case⟩ shoulderd Creature —in the former case, our shoulders are fledge⟨d⟩, [4] and we go thro'
air
the same ⟨Fir⟩ and space without fear. This is running one's rigs on the score of abstracted benefit—when we come to human Life and the affections it is impossible [5] how a parallel of breast and head
treading
can be drawn—(you will forgive me for thus privately ⟨heading⟩
tread
out [6] my depth and take it for treading as schoolboys ⟨head⟩ the water⟨s⟩)—it is impossible to know how far knowlege will console

[1] According to Henry Ellershaw, *Keats* (Oxford, 1922), p. 204, "The first part of the word refers to what has been said above, pip being short for pippin, the second part means one expert in law, 'an epitome in law.' " J. M. Murry, *TLS*, July 9, 1938, p. 466, says that Keats means " 'an undistinguished sort of lawyer.' 'Pip'—the spot on a non-court card; 'civilian'—a student of civil law." Roberta D. Cornelius, the same, August 6, p. 520, replies that "pip" means a small seed, as of an apple; Keats was "carrying in his mind the image of the apple and thinking that under the tutelage of Rice and Reynolds he might become a kind of embryo civilian."

[2] Woodhouse substituted "thinking" for the clerk's "them [?] King."

[3] Wordsworth, "Lines Composed a Few Miles Above Tintern Abbey," line 38. For other borrowings here from that poem, lines 31–41, see C. L. Rivers, *NQ*, March 31, 1951, p. 142.

[4] J. C. Maxwell, *NQ*, May 17, 1947, p. 215, notes the reminiscences of *Paradise Lost*, II.933 f., III.627, and *King Lear*, III.iv.112, "a bare, forked animal as thou art."

[5] Woodhouse adds "[to know]."

[6] Woodhouse has "*sic*" (that is, Keats omitted "of").

us
⟨as⟩ for the death of a friend and the ill "that flesh is heir to⟨o⟩[7]—With respect to the affections and Poetry you must know by a sympathy my thoughts that way; and I dare say these few lines will be but a ratification: I wrote them on May-day—and intend to finish the ode all in good time.—

Mother of Hermes! and still youthful Maia!
May I sing to thee
As thou wast hymned on the shores of Baiæ?
Or may I woo thee
In earlier Sicilian? or thy smiles
Seek as they once were sought, in Grecian isles,
By Bards who died content in [8] pleasant sward,
Leaving great verse unto a little clan?
O give me their old vigour, and unheard,
Save of the quiet Primrose, and the span//
Of Heaven, and few ears// rounded by thee
My song should die away// content as ⟨this⟩ theirs//
Rich in the simple worship of a day.—// [9]

You may be anxious to know for fact to what sentence in your Letter I allude. You say "I fear there is little chance of any thing else in this life." You seem by that to have been going through with
zest
a more painful and acute ⟨test⟩ the same labyrinth that I have—I have come to the same conclusion thus far. My Branchings out therefrom have been numerous: one of them is the consideration of Wordsworth's genius and as a help, in the manner of gold being the meridian Line of worldly wealth,—how he differs from Milton.—And here I have nothing but surmises, from an uncertainty whether Miltons apparently less anxiety for Humanity proceeds from his seeing further or no than Wordsworth: And whether Wordsworth has in truth epic passion⟨s⟩, and martyrs himself to the

[7] *Hamlet*, III.i.63. [8] Garrod, p. 487, has "on."

[9] Woodhouse puts a capital "R" above "rounded" and notes: "Perhaps the lines sho^{d} be divided as shewn in red Ink. R. W." (Garrod follows the division indicated by his slant lines. In his *Keats* [Oxford, 1926], p. 76, he says that Keats's poem was suggested by Barnabe Barnes's Ode XI, *Parthenophil and Parthenope* [1593], sig. Q3^{v}, which begins, "Louely *Maya Hermes* mother.")

human heart, the main region of his song [1]—In regard to his genius alone—we find what he says true as far as we have experienced and we can judge no further but by larger experience—for axioms in philosophy are not axioms until they are proved upon our pulses: We read fine——things but never feel them to thee [2] full until we have gone the same steps as the Author.—I know this is not plain; you will know exactly my meaning when I say, that now I shall relish Hamlet more than I ever have done—Or, better—You are sensible no man can set down Venery as a bestial or joyless thing until he is sick of it and therefore all philosophizing on it would be mere wording. Until we are sick, we understand not;—in fine, as Byron says, "Knowledge is Sorrow"; [3] and I go on to say that "Sorrow is Wisdom"—and further for aught we can know for certainty! "Wisdom is folly"—So you see how I have run away from Wordsworth, and Milton; and shall still run away from what was in my head, to observe, that some kind of letters are good squares others handsome ovals, and others some orbicular, others spheroid —and why should there not be another species with two rough edges like a Rat-trap? I hope you will find all my long letters of that species, and all will be well; for by merely touching the spring delicately and etherially, the rough edged will fly immediately into a proper compactness, and thus you may make a good wholesome loaf, with your own leven in it, of my fragments—If you cannot find this said Rat-trap sufficiently tractable—alas for me, it being an impossibility in grain for my ink to stain otherwise: If I scribble long letters I must play my vagaries. I must be too heavy, or too light, for whole pages—I must be quaint and free of Tropes and figures—I must play my draughts as I please, and for my advantage and your erudition, crown a white with a black, or a black with a white, and move into black or white, far and near as I please—I must go from Hazlitt to Patmore,[4] and make Wordsworth and Coleman [5] play at leap-frog—or keep one of them down a whole half

[1] Compare Wordsworth, *The Recluse*, I.i.793 f., "the Mind of Man—/ My haunt, and the main region of my song."

[2] The clerk had "till thee full," which Woodhouse changed to "to thee full." In the next clause he queries, "we have overgone."

[3] *Manfred*, I.i.10, "Sorrow is knowledge." See "sorrow is joy," etc., at I, 358.

[4] Peter George Patmore (1786–1855), author, intimate friend of Hazlitt and Lamb, father of Coventry Patmore. On January 19, 1863, Coventry Patmore (*Memoirs and Correspondence*, ed. Basil Champneys [1900], I, 66) asked Milnes to omit this reference, which he considered disparaging. Accordingly the words "from Hazlitt . . . garter," which appeared in Milnes, I, 137, were omitted in the 1867 edition.

[5] The playwright George Colman the younger (1762–1836).

holiday at fly the garter [6]—"From Gray to Gay, from Little to Shakespeare" [7]—Also as a long cause requires two or more sittings of the Court, so a long letter will require two or more sittings of the Breech wherefore I shall resume after dinner.—

Have you not seen a Gull, an orc, a sea Mew,[8] or any thing to bring this Line to a proper length, and also fill up this clear part; that like the Gull I may *dip* [9]—I hope, not out of sight—and also, like a Gull, I hope to be lucky in a good sized fish—This crossing a letter is not without its association—for chequer work leads us naturally to a Milkmaid,[1] a Milkmaid to Hogarth Hogarth to Shakespeare Shakespear to Hazlitt—Hazlitt to Shakespeare [2] and thus by merely pulling an apron string we set a pretty peal of Chimes at work—Let them chime on while, with your patience,— I will return to Wordsworth—whether or no he has an extended vision or a circumscribed grandeur—whether he is an eagle in his nest, or on the wing—And to be more explicit and to show you how tall I stand by the giant, I will put down a simile of human life as far as I now perceive it; that is, to the point to which I say we both have arrived at—' Well—I compare human life to a large Mansion of Many Apartments,[3] two of which I can only describe, the doors of the rest being as yet shut upon me—The first we step into we call the infant or thoughtless Chamber, in which we remain as long as we do not think—We remain there a long while, and notwithstanding the doors of the second Chamber remain wide open, showing a bright appearance, we care not to hasten to it; but are at

[6] "A game in which the players leap from one side of a 'garter' or line of stones over the back of one of their number" (*NED*, citing Keats as the first of two examples).

[7] J. R. Sutherland, *TLS*, January 8, 1944, p. 19, notes the borrowing from Pope's *Essay on Man*, IV.380, "From grave to gay, from lively to severe," and suggests that Keats wrote "from Lillo to Shakespeare." But, as Mabel A. E. Steele, the same, July 15, p. 343, points out, Keats probably wrote "Little" (Thomas Little being the pseudonym of Thomas Moore), since Woodhouse painstakingly corrected the transcript made by his clerk.

[8] J. C. Maxwell, *NQ*, May 17, 1947, p. 215, compares *Paradise Lost*, XI.835, "The haunt of . . . Orcs, and Sea-mews clang."

[9] Woodhouse inserts: "(Here the first page of the letter is crossed—and the 2 first lines to this mark‡ [that is, after "Gull I may"] are written in the clear space left as a margin—& the word 'dip' is the first word that *dips* into the former writing—"

[1] Possibly he was thinking of "the Milkmaid singeth blithe" and "Dancing in the Chequer'd shade" in "L'Allegro," lines 65, 96.

[2] Woodruff, p. 43, remarks: "Reynolds could be counted on . . . to recognize that the headings referred to essays in *The Round Table*, the *Characters of Shakespear's Plays*, and 'On Shakspeare and Milton' in *The Lectures on the English Poets*."

[3] Compare John xiv.2. This "Mansion of Life letter" is elaborately discussed by C. D. Thorpe, *The Mind of John Keats* (New York, 1926), pp. 43–47.

length imperceptibly impelled by the awakening of the thinking principle—within us—we no sooner get into the second Chamber, which I shall call the Chamber of Maiden-Thought, than we become intoxicated with the light and the atmosphere, we see nothing but pleasant wonders, and think of delaying there for ever in delight: However among the effects this breathing is father of is that
heart
tremendous one of sharpening one's vision into the ⟨head⟩ and nature of Man—of convincing ones nerves that the World is full of Misery and Heartbreak, Pain, Sickness and oppression [4]—whereby This Chamber of Maiden Thought becomes gradually darken'd and at the same time on all sides of it many doors are set open—but all dark—all leading to dark passages—We see not the ballance of good and evil. We are in a Mist—*We* are now in that state—We feel the "burden of the Mystery," [5] To this point was Wordsworth come, as far as I can conceive when he wrote 'Tintern Abbey' and it seems to me that his Genius is explorative of those dark Passages. Now if we live, and go on thinking, we too shall explore them. he is a Genius and superior [to] [6] us, in so far as he can, more than we, make discoveries, and shed a light in them—Here I must think Wordsworth is deeper than Milton—though I think it has depended more upon the general and gregarious advance of intellect, than individual greatness of Mind—From the Paradise Lost and the other Works of Milton, I hope it is not too presuming, even between ourselves to say, his Philosophy, human and divine, may be tolerably understood by one not much advanced in years, In his time englishmen were just emancipated from a great superstition—and Men had got hold of certain points and resting places in reasoning
opposed
which were [7] too newly born to be doubted, and too much ⟨oppressed⟩ by the Mass of Europe not to be thought etherial and authentically divine—who could gainsay his ideas on virtue, vice, and Chastity in Comus, just at the time of the dismissal of Cod-pieces [8] and a

[4] Finney, II, 464, detects borrowings here from Wordsworth's *Excursion*, V.1207 ff. Compare also "The Fall of Hyperion," I.147–149, " 'None can usurp this height,' returned that shade,/ 'But those to whom the miseries of the world/ Are misery, and will not let them rest'."

[5] See I, 277 n.

[6] Woodhouse inserts "(to)."

[7] Woodhouse emends "we" to "were." Possibly Keats was thinking of the "Landing Places" in Coleridge's *The Friend* (1809, 1810).

[8] *NED* "dismisses" them with an example from 1761.

hundred other disgraces? who would not rest satisfied with his hintings at good and evil in the Paradise Lost, when just free from the inquisition and burrning in Smithfield? The Reformation produced such immediate and great⟨s⟩ benefits, that Protestantism was considered under the immediate eye of heaven, and its own remaining Dogmas and superstitions, then, as it were, regenerated, constituted those resting places and seeming sure points of Reasoning—from that I have mentioned, Milton, whatever he may have thought in the sequel, appears to have been content with these by his writings —He did not think into the human heart, as Wordsworth has done —Yet Milton as a Philosop⟨h⟩er, had sure as great powers as Wordsworth—What is then to be inferr'd? O many things—It proves there is really a grand march of intellect—, It proves that a mighty providence subdues the mightiest Minds to the service of the time being, whether it be in human Knowledge or Religion—I have often pitied a Tutor who has to hear "Nome: Musa"—so often dinn'd into his ears—I hope you may not have the same pain in this scribbling—I may have read these things before, but I never had even a thus dim perception of them; and moreover I like to say my lesson to one who will endure my tediousness for my own sake—After all there is certainly something real in the World—Moore's present to Hazlitt is real—I like that Moore, and am glad ⟨that⟩ I saw him at the Theatre just before I left Town.[9] Tom has spit a leetle [1] blood this afternoon, and that is rather a damper—but I know—the truth is there is something real in the World Your third Chamber of Life

[9] Howe, pp. 227 f., says: "We do not know what Moore's present to Hazlitt can have been, unless it was a copy of the 'Fudge Family in Paris,' which Moore sent at this time, and which, as a tribute of respect from a fashionable poet to the leading spirit of *The Yellow Dwarf*, was not unacceptable." Howe owned a copy of *The Fudge Family* (3rd ed., 1818) inscribed to Hazlitt by Moore on April 27, 1818, "as a small mark of respect for his literary talents & political principles." It was small indeed, not "real" in the emphatic sense in which Keats used the word: compare his "there is something real in the World" (in the next sentence), "so real a fellow" (I, 160), "it was to me a real thing" (I, 209), "Things like these . . . are real" (I, 325). When he wrote this letter Keats had not met Thomas Moore (II, 11), and, as Holman acutely noted, Keats and Reynolds could hardly have known of his gift of a book six days after it was made, particularly since Reynolds was ill in London, Keats a visitor at Teignmouth. Hazlitt disliked and disparaged Moore (see P. G. Patmore, *My Friends and Acquaintance* [1854], III, 136–138), while Moore was far too poor to make a "real" present. Holman is certainly correct in thinking the present a gift of money and the giver Peter Moore (1753–1828), M.P., one of the managers of Drury Lane Theatre, a rich man who patronized Sheridan. Keats would almost inevitably have seen Peter Moore "at the Theatre just before I left Town."

[1] Woodhouse notes "so" (that is, *sic*).

shall be a lucky and a gentle one—stored with the wine of love—and the Bread of Friendship—When you see George if he should not have recēd a letter from me tell him he will find one at home most likely—tell Bailey I hope soon to see him—Remember me to all The leaves have been out here, for MONY [2] a day—I have written to George for the first stanzas of my Isabel [3]—I shall have them soon and will copy the whole out for you.

Your affectionate friend
John Keats.

Mr John H Reynolds
Little Britain
Christs Hospital London.—

· 81 ·

TO MRS. MARGARET JEFFREY [1]

4 or 5 May 1818 [2]

Honiton.

My dear Mrs. Jeffrey,—My Brother has borne his Journey thus far remarkably well. I am too sensible of your anxiety for us not to send this by the Chaise back for you. Give our goodbyes again to Marrian and Fanny. Beleive me we shall bear you in Mind and that I shall write soon.

Yours very truly,
John Keats.

[2] Woodhouse underscores here, as at I, 323, to show that it is correct.

[3] See I, 274.

[1] A. F. Sieveking published the texts of Nos. 81, 84, 164, 166 in the *Fortnightly Review*, LX (1893), 729–735. Only the originals of Nos. 84 and 164 are now known, and a comparison of them with the 1893 printings shows that Sieveking was a pretty accurate transcriber.

[2] John and Tom Keats left Teignmouth soon after No. 80 was written, probably on May 4 or 5, and the present letter was written on the first stage of their journey and sent back by the chaise. They seem to have spent the first night or two at Bridport (see the next letter). They were back in London before May 11 when, according to Haydon's Journal (see Hewlett, p. 383), Keats brought a friend of his, "a noodle," to dine with Haydon and Bewick.

· 82 ·

TOM KEATS TO MARIAN JEFFREY [1]

17, 18 May 1818

Address: Miss Mary Ann Jeffrey/ Teignmouth/ Devonshire
Postmarks: [7] o'Clock MY 19 1818 N^T^; C MY 19 818

Hampstead Sunday [2]

May 1818

My Dear Maryann

We received your Mothers Letter by Mrs Atkins which prevented my writing so soon as I had intended that the Letter might accompany the Book John promis'd you, and be deliver'd by M^rs^ A on her return—I thank you all for your kind solicitude—the rest of the journey pass'd off pretty well after we had left Bridport in Dorsetshire—I was very ill there and lost much blood—we travell'd a hundred miles in the two last days—I found myself much better at the end of the journey than when I left *Tartarey* alias Teignmouth —the Doctor [3] was surprised to see me looking so well, as were all my Friends—they insisted that my illness was all mistaken Fancy and on this presumption excited me to laughing and merriment which has deranged me a little—however it appears that confinement and low spirits have been my chief enemeis and I promise myself a gradual recovery—this will be gratefull news to you—Our leave-taking was more formal than it might have been: and at the time I cursed the Doctor,[4] but now I think it better as it happen'd —I was at the Window to stop you as you return'd from the Cottage but you did not come our way—it did not require John's assurance to convince me that you felt our departure—Your Sister must indeed have been au desespoire that she could not eat a Bun—she lost her appetite and that was not all—the Bun lost an honor—instead of being masticated by a pair of *Ivory Teeth* it was destined perhaps to some hungry pityless voracious maw, or perhaps to

[1] *ALS:* Harvard. The letter, which has the embossed seal of "Albert Forbes Sieveking. F. S. A. 12 Seymour Street W," was first printed (in part) by Lowell, II, 4 f., and (in full) in *KC*, I, 21–24.

[2] Sunday was May 17.

[3] Sawrey (I, 196).

[4] Turton (I, 274).

⟨some⟩ a more fearful destiny—there are a thousand arguments for a sophist for and against—It may be cowardly to attack a poor unfortunate lumped Combination of Doe and flour—but as it has to do with a point in Philosophy I must put in this opinion: that, as material Bodies sometimes feed upon the things they nourish, so Miss S. J.[5] may one day find herself, by the treacherous machinations of this son of paste, prematurely possessed of an unpleasant compliment of hollow teeth; which to carry on the discussion may be argued for and against—in their * favour we might say—they
tend
⟨go⟩ to the maintenance of a very respectable class in Society the Dentists, Barber, and whatnot—the greatest objection to them is that they bring on Lisping and denote old age which as * Chaucer calls it an affectation in a coarse old monk cannot but be still more despiseable in a Young Lady—I hope Mr Stanbury vet.[6]—is elected to twenty Pounds a year and that Waltzing will be admitted to the Teignmouth and other Town and Country Ball rooms in Sarah's time.—I calculate it will be by then she has attained the age of Fifty Six and that's no age at all—Convey my Compliments to Miss Michell and thank her for the present—remember me to Captain Tonkin and Mr Bartlett[7] if he should Come in your way in the
goes
Labyrinthe of Teignmouth—tell Captain T if he ⟨puts⟩ his projected Tour to Italy we may perhaps meet—this leads me to a developement of my plan which I am fond to think about if I should alter it—in {five}[8] weeks I shall be here alone and I hope well—John {will}[8] have set out on his Northern Expedition George o{n his}[8] Western and I shall be preparing for mine to the South Johns will take four months at the end of that time he expects to have atchieved two thousand miles mostly on Foot—George embarks for

*The Buns
*Somewhat he lisped for his Wantonnesse
To make his English Sweet upon his Tongue

[5] Sarah Jeffrey. [6] Doubtful reading. Lowell, II, 4, has "&ct."
[7] The War Office Army List for 1819, p. 469, describes Tonkin as a barrack master at Exeter. The *New Monthly Magazine*, October, 1818 (X, 281), lists the marriage at Exeter of "W. H. Tonquin, jun. esq. to Miss Mitchell, daughter of T. M. esq. of Teignmouth." Major Warwick Hele Tonkin was knighted on June 15, 1836 (W. A. Shaw, *The Knights of England* [1906], II, 337). Bartlett was a Teignmouth surgeon (see I, 246 n.).
[8] Torn out with the seal.

America—I shall either go by vessell to some port in the Adriatic or down the Rhine through Switzerland and the Alps into Italy most likely to the Town of Paiva [9]—there to remain untill I have acquired a stock of knowledge and strength which will better enable me to bustle through the world—I am persuaded this is the best way of killing time—now if I should go by vessel and the port of Plymouth has Communication ⟨to⟩ with that part I will take Teignmouth in my way thither and see you Once again—it will be some atonement for the abuse I have lav[i]shed on your Native Town till then I will bid you farewell—my Love to your mother and Sister—I insist upon the former's thinking for herself as well as for others—tell her selfishness is fashionable and she is not so much out of the world as to be able to do without it—

Believe me Your Sincere Friend

Thos Keats

P S—George has been busily occupied in preparing for his Journey they both [1] desire their Love—perhaps John will write [2]—he is also very much engaged with his Friends—I am the only idler—in regard of Idleness I fear you will say this letter out-Herods Herod [3] T. K.

Monday [4]—

John will write to you shortly—T—K—

· 83 ·

TO BENJAMIN BAILEY [1]

21, 25 May 1818

Address: Mr B. Bailey/ Magdalen Hall/ Oxford—
Postmarks: TwoPyPost Unpaid Hampstead; 7 o'Clock MY 25 NT; A MY 25 818

My dear Bailey, Hampstead Thursday—

I should have answered your letter on the moment—if I could have said yes to your invitation. What hinders me is insuperable; I will tell it at a little length. You know my Brother George has

[9] *For* Pavia. [1] George Keats and Georgiana Wylie.
[2] See No. 84. [3] *Hamlet*, III.ii.15. [4] May 18.
[1] *ALS:* Harvard. There is also a transcript in Woodhouse's letter-book, pp. 86–88. Bailey's invitation was written on or before May 20 (*KC*, I, 25 f.).

been out of employ for some time. it has weighed very much upon him, and driven him to scheme and turn over things in his Mind. the result has been his resolution to emigrate [2] to the back settlements of America, become farmer and work with his own hands after purchacing 1400 hundred Acres of the American Government. This for many reasons has met with my entire consent—and the chief one is this—he is of too independant and liberal a Mind to get on in trade in this Country—in which a generous Ma{n} with a scanty recourse must be ruined. I would sooner he should till the ground than bow to a Customer—there is no choice with him; he could not bring himself to the latter—I would not consent to his going alone—no; but that objection is done away with—he will marry before he sets sail a young Lady he has known some years —of a nature liberal and highspirited enough to follow him to the Banks of the Mississipi.[3] He will set off in a month or six weeks, and you will see how I should wish to pass that time with him— and then I must set out on a journey of my own—Brown and I are going a pedestrian tour through the north of England and Scotland as far a[s] John o Grots. I have this morning such a Lethargy that I cannot write—the reason of my delaying is oftentimes from this feeling—I wait for a proper temper—Now you ask for an immediate answer I do not like to wait even till tomorrow—However I am now so depressed that I have not an Idea to put to paper—my hand feels like lead—and yet it is and [4] unpleasant numbness it does not take away the pain of existence—I don't know what to write—Monday [5] —You see how I have delayed—and even now I have but a confused idea of what I should be about my intellect must be in a degen[er]ating state—it must be for when I should be writing about god knows what I am troubling you with Moods of my own Mind [6] or rather body—for Mind there is none. I am in that temper that if I were under Water I would scarcely kick to come to the top—I know very well 't is all nonsense. In a short time I hope I shall be in a temper to fell [7] sensibly your mention of my Book—in vain have I waited till Monday to have any interest in that or in any thing else. I feel no spur at my Brothers going to America and am almost stony-hearted about his wedding. All this will blow over—all I am

[2] *Written* resolutiom to emigiate.
[3] The Ohio would have been more appropriate.
[4] *For* an. [5] May 25. [6] See I, 263 n. [7] *For* feel.

sorry for is having to write to you in such a time—but I cannot force my letters in a hot bed—I could not feel comfortable in making sentences for you—I am your debtor—I must ever remain so—nor do I wish to be clear of my *r*ational [8] debt—There is a comfort in throwing oneself on the charity of ones friends—'t is like the albatros sleeping on its wings—I will be to you wine in the cellar and the more modestly or rather indolently I retire into the backward Bin, the more falerne [9] will I be at the drinking. There is one thing I must mention. My Brother talks of sailing in a fortnight [1] if so I will most probably be with you a week before I set out for Scotland. The middle of your first page should be suffic[i]ent to rouse me—what I said is true and I have dreamt of your mention of it and m{y} not a[n]swering it has weighed on me since—If I com{e,} I will bring your Letter and hear more fully your sentiments on one or two points. I will call about the Lectures at Taylors [2] and at Little Britain [3] tomorrow—Yesterday I dined with Hazlitt; Barnes, [4] and Wilkie at Haydon's. The topic was the Duke of Wellington very amusingly pro and con'd. Reynolds has been getting much better; and Rice may begin to crow for he got a little so so [5] at a Party of his and was none the worse for it the next morning. I hope I shall soon see you for we must have many new thoughts and feelings to analize, and to discover whether a little more knowledge has not made us more ignorant—

Your's affectionately John Keats—

[8] The italicized "r" marks a pun on "national."

[9] T. C. C., *NQ*, May 8, 1943, p. 288, asks: "Has he made an adjective for himself out of Horace's 'Interiore nota Falerni,' 'deep-stored cask of Falernian wine,' Odes ii, 3, 8?"

[1] Actually he left London on June 22.

[2] Taylor and Hessey had just published Hazlitt's *Lectures on the English Poets* (Howe, p. 232).

[3] That is, on the Reynoldses.

[4] Thomas Barnes (1785–1841), friend of Hazlitt, Hunt, and Lamb, contributor to the *Examiner*, editor of *The Times* (1817–1841). See Derek Hudson, *Thomas Barnes of The Times* (Cambridge, 1943).

[5] See I, 260 n.

· 84 ·

TO MARIAN AND SARAH JEFFREY [1]

4 June 1818

Address: For/ Misses M & S Jeffrey

My dear Girls, Hampstead June 4th

I will not pretend to string a list of excuses together for not having written before—but must at once confess the indolence of my disposition which makes a letter more formidable to me than a Pilgrimage—I am a fool in delay [2] for the idea of neglect is an everlasting knapsack which even now I have scarce power to hoist off —by the bye talking of everlasting knapsacks I intend to make my fortune by them in case of a War (which you must consequently pray for) by contracting with Government for said materials to the economy of one branch of the Revenue. At all events a Tax which is taken from the people and shoulder'd upon the Military ought not to be snubb'd at. I promised to send you all the News. Harkee! The whole city corporation with a deputation from the Fire Offices are now engaged at the London Coffee house [3] in secret conclave concerning saint Paul's Cathedral its being washed clean. Many interesting speeches have been demosthenized [4] in said Coffee house as to the Cause of the black appearance of the said Cathedral —One of the veal-thigh Aldermen actually brought up three witnesses to depose how they beheld the ci-devant fair Marble turn black on the tolling of the great Bell for the amiable and tea-table-lamented Princess [5]—adding moreover that this sort of sympathy in inanimate objects was by no means uncommon for said the Gentleman 'As we were once debating in the common Hall Mr Waith-

[1] *ALS:* Harvard (see the first note to No. 81).

[2] That is, delaying.

[3] See I, 206 n.

[4] Sieveking, *Fortnightly Review*, LX (1893), 732, calls this word "a vigorous neologism."

[5] See I, 190 n. The *Edinburgh Magazine, and Literary Miscellany*, December, 1817 (I, 483 f.), remarks that Princess Charlotte's funeral "was observed throughout every part of the kingdom, with all the devotion of national grief and humiliation. . . . Never, we are sure, was mourning more general or sincere."

man [6] in illustration of some case in point quoted Peter Pindar,[7] at which the head of George the third although in hard marble squinted over the Mayor's seat at the honerable speaker so oddly that he was obliged to sit down.' However I will not tire you about these Affairs for they must be in your news papers by this time. You see how badly I have written these last three lines so I will remain here and take a pinch of snuff every five Minutes until my head becomes fit and proper and legetimately inclined to scribble —Oh! there's nothing like a pinch of snuff except perhaps a few trifles almost beneath a philosophers dignity, such as a ripe Peach or a kiss that one takes on a lease of 91 moments,—on a b⟨u⟩il⟨d⟩ing lease. Talking of that is the Captn married yet, or rather married Miss Mitchel [8]—is she stony hearted enough to hold out this season. Has the Doctor given Miss Perryman [9] a little love powder—tell him to do so it really would not be unamusing to see her languish a little—Oh she must be quite melting this hot Weather. Are the little Robins w{eane}d yet? Do they walk alone? You have had a christening a top o' the tiles and a Hawk has stood God father and taken the little Brood under the Shadows of its Wings much in the way of Mother Church—a Cat too has very tender bowels in such pathetic Cases. They say we are all all (that is our set) mad at Hampstead. There's George took unto himself a Wife a Week ago [1] and will in a little time sail for America—and I with a friend am preparing for a four Months Walk all over the North and belike Tom will not stop [2] here—he has been getting much better—Lord what a Journey I had and what a relief at the end of it—I'm sure I could not have stood it many more days.[3] Hampstead is now in fine order I suppose Teignmouth and the *contagious* country [4] is now quite remarkable—you might praise it I dare say in the manner of a grammatical exercise—*The* trees *are* full—

[6] Robert Waithman (1764–1833), political reformer, M.P. for the City of London in 1818 and later, lord mayor in 1823. His statue, says Blunden, p. 498, "stands in a very sooty condition, interrupting the traffic, at Ludgate Circus."

[7] See I, 197.

[8] See I, 285 n.

[9] MBF says that her name was Periman.

[1] Lowell, II, 7, took this remark as meaning that George married on May 28. She is surely closer to the date than Kirk (Hampstead Keats, I, lxxxv) and MBF (*Connoisseur*, CXVI [1945], 8), who give it as June 4, the very day on which Keats was writing.

[2] Or perhaps "stope." See Tom's words at I, 285 f.

[3] See No. 81.

[4] From Sheridan's *Rivals*, I.ii.

the den [5] *is* crowded *the* boats *are* sailing—*the* musick *is* playi{ng.} I wish you were here a little while—but lauk we havent got any female friend in the house—Tom is taken for a Madman and I being somewhat stunted am taken for nothing—We lounge on the Walk opposite as you might on the Den—I hope the fine Season will keep up your Mother's Spirits—she was used to be too much down hearted. No Women ought to be born into the world for they may not touch the bottle for shame—now a Man may creep into a bung hole [6] however this is a tale of a tub—however I like to play upon a pipe sitting upon a puncheon and intend to be so drawn in the frontispeice to my next book of Pastorals—My Brothers respects and mine to your Mother and all our Loves to you

Yours very sincerely
John Keats

P.S. has many significations here it [7] signifies Post Script—on the corner of a Handkerchef Polly Saunders—Upon a Garter Pretty Secret—Upon a Band Box Pink Sattin—At the Theatre Princes Side [8]—on a Pulpit Parson's Snuffle and at a Country Ale House Pail Sider.

· 85 ·

TO JOSEPH SEVERN [1]

6 June 1818

My dear Severn,

The Doctor says I mustn't go out. I wish such a delicious fate would but [2] me in cue to entertain you with a Sonnet or a Pun.

I am
Yours ever
John Keats.

[5] Sieveking, p. 731 n., says, "The 'Den' was the fashionable promenade at Teignmouth." "This Den (=dune)," R. N. Worth, *A History of Devonshire* (1886), p. 313, remarks, "is now a public lawn adjoining the beach."

[6] A possible reminiscence of *Hamlet*, V.i.224–226.

[7] *Written* is.

[8] Sieveking, p. 732 n., says, " 'Prince's Side' would correspond in modern terms to Royal Box Side."

[1] Reprinted from P. J. and A. E. Dobell's catalog No. 273, August, 1918. It is also in Lowell, II, 7. MBF gives the name of the present owner of the *ALS* as Howard Eric, Severn's address as Islington Road, near the Angel Inn, 1 High Street. Lowell notes that the letter was postmarked at 2 o'clock on June 6, 1818. The original, of which I have seen a photostat, is endorsed, by some unidentified writer, "Addressed to Mr Consul Severn." The indisposition of which Keats speaks lasted past June 10 (see the next letter).

[2] *For* put.

·86·

TO BENJAMIN BAILEY [1]

10 June 1818

Address: M^r^ B— Bailey/ Magdalen Hall/ Oxford—
Postmark: C JU 10 818

My dear Bailey, London—

I have been very much gratified and very much hurt by your Letters in the Oxford Paper: because independant [2] of that unlawful and mortal feeling of pleasure at praise, there is a glory in enthusia[s]m; and because the world is malignant enough to chuckle at the most honorable Simplicity. Yes on my Soul my dear Bailey you are too simple for the World—and that Idea makes me sick of it—How is it that by extreme opposites we have as it were got disconted [3] nerves—you have all your Life (I think so) believed every Body—I have suspected every Body [4]—and although you have been so deceived you make a simple appeal—the world has something else to do, and I am glad of it—were it in my choice I would reject a petrarchal coronation—on accou[n]t of my dying day, and because women have Cancers.[5] I should not by rights speak in this tone to you—for it is an incendiary spirit that would do so. Yet I am not old enough or magnanimous enough to annihilate self—and it would perhaps be paying you an ill compliment. I was in hopes some little time back to be able to releive your dull-

[1] *ALS:* Harvard. Sending this letter to Taylor, above the address Bailey wrote: "There is so much amiable feeling & tenderness in this that I think it might be printed entire, or very copious extracts made from it. B B." There is a transcript of the letter in Woodhouse's letter-book, pp. 88–90.

[2] *Written* indepependant. Bailey's two articles on *Endymion* in the *Oxford University & City Herald, and Midland County Chronicle*, May 30, June 6, 1818, are reprinted in the Hampstead Keats, II, 237–243.

[3] *For* discontented.

[4] Bailey wrote to Milnes in 1849 (*KC*, II, 274): "In his letters he [Keats] talks of *suspecting* everybody. It appeared not in his conversation. On the contrary, he was uniformly the apologist for poor, frail human nature. . . . " Hunt, on the other hand, wrote in 1850 (*Autobiography*, II, 202 f.): "An irritable morbidity appears even to have driven his suspicions to excess. . . . [He] suspected both Shelley and myself of a wish to see him undervalued! . . . It appears . . . that all his friends dissatisfied him in the course of those trials of his temper."

[5] Compare I, 209.

ness by my spirits—to point out things in the world worth your enjoyment—and now I am never alone without rejoicing that there is such a thing as death—without placing my ultimate in the glory of dying for a great human purpose [6] Perphaps [7] if my affairs were in a different state I should not have written the above—you shall judge—I have two Brothers one is driven by the 'burden of Society' to America the other, with an exquisite love of Life, is in a lingering state—My Love for my Brothers from the early loss of our parents and even for earlier Misfortunes has grown into a affection 'passing the Love of Women' [8]—I have been ill temper'd with them, I have vex'd them [9]—but the thought of them has always stifled the impression that any woman might otherwise have made upon me—I have a Sister [1] too and may not follow them, either to America or to the Grave—Life must be undergone, and I certainly derive a consolation from the thought of writing one or two more Poems before it ceases—I have heard some hints of your retireing to scotland—I should like to know your feeling on it—it seems rather remote—perhaps Gleg [2] will have a duty near you. I am not certain whether I shall be able to go my Journey on account of my Brother Tom and a little indisposition of my own—If I do not you shall see me soon—if no [3] on my return—or I'll quarter myself upon you in Scotland next Winter. I had know[n] my sister in Law some time before she was my Sister and was very fond of her. I like her better and better—she is the most disinterrested [4] woman I ever knew—that is to say she goes beyond degree in it—To see an entirely [5] disinterrested Girl quite happy is the most pleasant and extraordinary thing in the world—it depends upon a thousand Circumstances—on my word 'tis extraordinary. Women must want Imagination and they may thank God for it—and so m[a]y we that a delicate being can feel happy without any sense of crime. It puzzles me and I have no sort of Logic to comfort me—I shall think it over. I am not at home [6] and your letter being there I cannot look it over to answer any particular—only I must say I

[6] Bailey called attention to the passage "I am never alone . . . purpose" by putting a brace in the margin. Compare Keats's words about "great Public good" at I, 267.

[7] *Sic.* [8] 2 Samuel i.26.

[9] See George Keats's words (1825) about "his nervous morbid temperament," his "pettishness," his jangling (*KC*, I, 284).

[1] Georgiana Keats. [2] Gleig (I, 170 n.). [3] *For* not.

[4] On this favorite word of Keats's see II, 79, 129, 279.

[5] *Written* entirelely. [6] Possibly he was staying with Taylor.

felt that passage of Dante—if I take any book with me it shall be those minute volumes of carey [7] for they will go into the aptest corner. Reynolds is getting I may say robust—his illness has been of service to him—like eny one just recoverd he is high-spirited. I hear also good accounts of Rice—With respect to domestic Literature—the Endinburgh Magasine in another blow up against Hunt calls me 'the amiable Mister Keats' [8] and I have more than a Laurel from the Quarterly Reviewers for they have *smothered* me in 'Foliage' [9] I want to read you my 'Pot of Basil' if you go to scotland I should much like to read it there to you among the Snows of next Winter. My Brothers' remembrances to you.

Your affectionate friend
John Keats—

· 87 ·

GEORGE KEATS TO JOHN TAYLOR [1]

About 18 June 1818

Address: ——Taylor Esqr/ Messrs Taylor & Hessey/ Fleet Street

28 Judd St—Brunswick Sq^r

My dear Sir

I am infinitely obliged for the perusal of these letters; [2] they raise my spirits (if it were possible for them to be higher), they certainly make my sanguine hopes appear somewhat more reasonable. In one respect however I must be disappointed; by what he says it appears clear I cannot be a very near neighbour, and since all his land is gone that he could recommend, it is hardly likely that he will make a fresh entry for my 640 acres; that not being done of course there will be no house to receive us: however the disappointment

[7] See I, 343 n.

[8] Lockhart, in a "Letter from Z. to Leigh Hunt," *Blackwood's*, May, 1818 (III, 197), called him an "amiable but infatuated bardling, Mister John Keats." Hunt's *Foliage* was reviewed in the *Quarterly*, January, 1818 (XVIII, 324–335).

[9] Keats is not definitely named in the review.

[1] *ALS:* Harvard. First printed in *KC*, I, 29 f. George and his bride, along with Keats and Brown, took the Liverpool coach on Monday, June 22. He wrote this letter before Saturday, June 20.

[2] Morris Birkbeck's *Letters from Illinois*, published by Taylor and Hessey in 1818.

is not immense; when I thought these things might be done the advantage seemed great, but when I consider the having to do them myself, I only feel an addition of pride to undertake and accomplish the whole task myself—You were so kind as to offer a letter to a Friend at Philadelphia [3] as well as another to Birkbeck I should be obliged if you would sent them to me before Monday; I will call on Saturday but perhaps you may not have time to write by that day noon. I start from lad lane at 11 1/2 Monday [4] Morning —Comp^s to Mr Hessey and beleive me

Your Friend (most obliged)

George Keats.

Reynolds will be with me this Evening can you come, I think John likewise, you must see Mrs Keats since you are physiognomist and discover if the lines of her face answer to her spirit.

ex scrawl

· 88 ·

TO JOHN TAYLOR [1]

21 June 1818

Address: John Taylor Esqre/ Taylor and Hessey's/ Booksellers &c/ Fleet Street—
Postmarks (imperfect): ... Hampstead; 7 o'Clock JU 22 1818 N^T

My dear Taylor, Sunday Evening

I am sorry I have not had time to call and wish you health till my return—Really I have been hard run these three last days.[2] However Au revoir! God keep us all well.—I start tomorrow morning. My Brother Tom will I am affraid be lonely—I can scarcely ask the loan of Books for him—since I still keep those you lent me

[3] Michael Drury, a merchant, who had married a cousin of Taylor's.
[4] According to *The Post Office London Directory* for 1819, stage coaches for Liverpool, 206 miles away, left from the Swan with Two Necks, Lad Lane, Milk Street, Cheapside, at 9 A.M., 6 P.M., 7:30 P.M.
[1] *ALS:* Harvard. There is also a transcript in Woodhouse's letter-book, p. 9.
[2] He had visited Abbey on the 19th and 20th, drawing £30 and £140 from his account there (William Dilke's notes, 1833, Keats Museum).

a year ago [3]—if I am overweening you will be I know will be indulgent—Therefore when he shall write do send him some you think will be most amusing—he will be careful in returning them. Let him have one of my Books bound.[4] I am ashamed to catalogue these Messages there is but one more which ought to go for nothing as there is a Lady concernd I promised Mrs Reynolds one of my Books bound. As I cannot write in it let the opposite be pasted in [5] prythee Remember me to Percy Street—Tell Hilton that one gratification on my return will bee to find him engaged in a History Piece to his content—and Tell Dewint I shall become a disputant on the Landscape—bow for me very genteelly to Mrs D [6] or she will not admit your diploma. Remember me to Hessey saying I hope he'll *Carey* his point [7]—I would not forget Woodhouse. Adieu Your sincere friend

John O'Grots [8]

Mrs Reynolds with J.K's respects

[3] See No. 163. Keats asked Taylor for other books in November, 1819 (II, 234 f.).

[4] See Tom's letter, No. 90.

[5] "The opposite," the only writing on page 3 (the address is on page 4), remains intact, although Keats intended it to be cut off and placed in Mrs. Reynolds' copy of *Endymion.* In his transcript Woodhouse annotates "the opposite": "a leaf with the name & 'from the author'." See also his note at I, 326.

[6] Peter De Wint (1784–1849), water-color painter, married Harriet, the sister of William Hilton (1786–1839), an equally celebrated historical painter. The three lived together at 10 Percy Street, Rathbone Place, from June 16, 1810, till Hilton married Justina Kent in February, 1828. Each painter contributed £10 to a fund for Keats's expenses in Italy, and Hilton made a well-known chalk drawing of Keats and, some years after the latter's death, painted the portrait which, it has been said (see the *Athenaeum,* November 16, 1895, p. 687), disgraces the National Portrait Gallery. Keats mentions "Percy Street" five times.

[7] "The allusion is probably to some point connected with the publication of Cary's Dante for which an agreement had been signed by the translator and Taylor and Hessey at Coleridge's Highgate home on the 11th of May 1818" (MBF).

[8] See I, 340 n.

·89·

TO THOMAS MONKHOUSE [1]

21 June 1818 [2]

Address: Monkhouse Esqre/ Queen Street West [3]

Hampstead Sunday Evening

My dear Sir,

I regret not being at home when you called the other day—the more because I shall set out tomorrow morning for the North. I was very much gratified in hearing from Haydon that you so great a Lover of Wordsworth should be pleased with any part of my Poem. In hopes of seeing you soon after my return, and Speaking of my visit to Rydal [4]—I remain

Your's very truly
John Keats—

·90·

TOM KEATS TO JOHN TAYLOR [1]

22 June 1818

Address: John Taylor Esqr/ Messrs Taylor and Hessey/ Fleet Street
Postmarks: TwoPyPost Unpaid SOHampstead; 12 o'Clock JU 2[2] 1818 N^{T}

Hampstead 22nd June 1818

Dear Sir—

My Brother [2] in the hurry of his Letter forgot to mention to you that he intended Mr Severn to have a copy of his Poem [3]—M^{r} S will call at your house for one

I am
Your humble Servt
Thos Keats

[1] *ALS:* Miss Joanna Hutchinson, Windsor, Berks. First printed by Ernest De Selincourt, *TLS*, October 23, 1937, p. 783. For Monkhouse (1783–1825), Mrs. Wordsworth's cousin, see I, 198 n., II, 120. [2] See the preceding letter.

[3] The address has been cut from its page and pasted at the foot of the letter. A badly blurred postmark is stamped over "Monkhouse." Keats was too indifferent to learn Monkhouse's first name, just as Brown was to learn Woodhouse's in December, 1818 (I, 409). [4] See I, 302 f., 306. [1] *ALS:* Harvard. First printed in *KC*, I, 30.

[2] He took the coach for Liverpool on the day this letter was written. [3] *Endymion.*

PS On consideration it strikes me that you will not be able to let me have books to read—your stock being as I should think mostly new—and modern Books—[4]

·91·

TO TOM KEATS[1]

25–27 June 1818

Here beginneth my journal, this Thursday, the 25th day of June, Anno Domini 1818.[2] This morning we arose at 4, and set off in a Scotch mist; put up once under a tree, and in fine, have walked wet and dry to this place, called in the vulgar tongue Endmoor, 17 miles; we have not been incommoded by our knapsacks; they serve capitally, and we shall go on very well.

June 26—I merely put *pro forma*, for there is no such thing as time and space, which by the way came forcibly upon me on seeing for the first hour the Lake and Mountains of Winander—I cannot describe them—they surpass my expectation—beautiful water—shores and islands green to the marge—mountains all round up to the clouds. We set out from Endmoor this morning, breakfasted at Kendal with a soldier who had been in all the wars for the last

[4] But on June 30 Tom thanked Taylor for having sent "the parcell of Books" (*KC*, I, 31).

[1] The original letter (which was mailed—see I, 303—at Ambleside) has disappeared. It was loaned by George Keats to James Freeman Clarke (1810–1888), who printed it in his Louisville, Kentucky, *Western Messenger*, June, 1836 (I, 772–777). Overlooked by the early editors of Keats's letters (though its importance was stressed in the American Art Association's sale catalog of Walter Thomas Wallace's library, March, 1920, lot 738, and though it was featured in the Boston Public Library Keats exhibition of February 21–March 14, 1921), it was first reprinted by R. L. Rusk in the *North American Review*, March, 1924 (CCXIX, 392–397).

[2] They left London on June 22, reached Liverpool the next afternoon, and early on the morning of June 24 took a coach for Lancaster, where they spent the night. Brown, who published part of his Journal of the tour twenty-two years later, says (see I, 422 ff.) that they arose on June 25 at 4 A.M., were detained three hours by rain, walked four miles to Bolton-le-Sands for breakfast, then to the King's Arms at Burton in Kendal for dinner, and on to Endmoor, where they spent the night at a public house kept by a Mrs. Black. See also Bushnell, pp. 19–28.

seventeen years—then we have walked to Bowne's [3] to dinner—said Bowne's situated on the Lake where we have just dined,[4] and I am writing at this present. I took an oar to one of the islands to take up some trout for dinner, which they keep in porous boxes.[5] I enquired of the waiter for Wordsworth—he said he knew him, and that he had been here a few days ago, canvassing for the Lowthers. What think you of that—Wordsworth versus Brougham!![6] Sad—sad—sad—and yet the family has been his friend always. What can we say? We are now about seven miles from Rydale,[7] and expect to see him to-morrow. You shall hear all about our visit.

There are many disfigurements to this Lake—not in the way of land or water. No; the two views we have had of it are of the most noble tenderness—they can never fade away—they make one forget the divisions of life; age, youth, poverty and riches; and refine one's sensual vision into a sort of north star which can never cease to be open lidded and stedfast over the wonders of the great Power.[8] The disfigurement I mean is the miasma of London. I do suppose it contaminated with bucks and soldiers, and women of fashion—and hat-band ignorance. The border inhabitants are quite out of keeping with the romance about them, from a continual intercourse with London rank and fashion. But why should I grumble? They let me have a prime glass of soda water—O they are as good as their neighbors. But Lord Wordsworth, instead of being in retirement, has himself and his house full in the thick of fashionable visitors quite convenient to be pointed at all the summer long. When we had gone about half this morning, we began to get among the hills and to see the mountains grow up before us—the other half brought us to Wynandermere,[9] 14 miles to dinner. The weather is capital for the views, but is now rather misty, and we are in doubt

[3] Bowness on Lake Windermere. For Keats's reaction to the scenery see Brown's words at I, 426.

[4] At the White Lion Inn, now the Royal Hotel (Bushnell, p. 29).

[5] Brown also went in the boat (see I, 426 f.).

[6] William Lowther (1787–1872), afterwards (1844) second Earl of Lonsdale, the Whig candidate, was elected M.P. for Westmorland after a bitter contest with Henry Brougham (1778–1868), later (1830) Baron Brougham and Vaux, the Tory whose cause Wordsworth was supporting. See also I, 423.

[7] Wordsworth lived at Rydal Mount, Westmorland, from 1817 till his death in 1850.

[8] Rusk (pp. 395 f.) comments on the apparent resemblance of this sentence to the opening lines of *Endymion* and to the thought and imagery of the "Bright Star" sonnet.

[9] Windermere was formerly called Winandermere.

whether to walk to Ambleside to tea—it is five miles along the borders of the Lake. Loughrigg will swell up before us all the way—I have an amazing partiality for mountains in the clouds. There is nothing in Devon like this, and Brown says there is nothing in Wales to be compared to it.[1] I must tell you, that in going through Cheshire and Lancashire, I saw the Welsh mountains at a distance. We have passed the two castles, Lancaster and Kendal. 27th—We walked here to Ambleside [2] yesterday along the border of Winandermere all beautiful with wooded shores and Islands—our road was a winding lane, wooded on each side, and green overhead, full of Foxgloves—every now and then a glimpse of the Lake, and all the while Kirkstone and other large hills nestled together in a sort of grey black mist. Ambleside is at the northern extremity of the Lake. We arose this morning at six, because we call it a day of rest, having to call on Wordsworth who lives only two miles hence—before breakfast we went to see the Ambleside water fall. The morning beautiful—the walk easy among the hills. We, I may say, fortunately, missed the direct path, and after wandering a little, found it out by the noise—for, mark you, it is buried in trees, in the bottom of the valley—the stream itself is interesting throughout with "mazy error over pendant shades." [3] Milton meant a smooth river—this is buffetting all the way on a rocky bed ever various—but the waterfall itself, which I came suddenly upon, gave me a pleasant twinge. First we stood a little below the head about half way down the first fall, buried deep in trees, and saw it streaming down two more descents to the depth of near fifty feet then we went on a jut of rock nearly level with the second [4] fall-head, where the first fall was above us, and the third below our feet still—at the same time we saw that the water was divided by a sort of cataract island on whose other side burst out a glorious stream—then the thunder and the freshness. At the same time the different falls have as different characters; the first darting down the slate-rock like an arrow; the second spreading out like a fan—the third dashed into a mist—and the one on the other side of the rock a sort of

[1] See Brown's comments at I, 427.

[2] They stayed at the Salutation Inn during the night of June 26 (Bushnell, p. 33).

[3] *Paradise Lost*, IV.239 (which has *under* for *over*).

[4] *Printed* tsecond.

mixture of all these. We afterwards moved away a space, and saw nearly the whole more mild, streaming silverly through the trees. What astonishes me more than any thing is the tone, the coloring, the slate, the stone, the moss, the rock-weed; or, if I may so say, the intellect, the countenance of such places. The space, the magnitude of mountains and waterfalls are well imagined before one sees them; but this countenance or intellectual tone must surpass every imagination and defy any remembrance. I shall learn poetry here and shall henceforth write more than ever, for the abstract endeavor of being able to add a mite to that mass of beauty which is harvested from these grand materials, by the finest spirits, and put into etherial existence for the relish of one's fellows. I cannot think with Hazlitt that these scenes make man appear little.[5] I never forgot my stature so completely—I live in the eye; and my imagination, surpassed, is at rest—We shall see another waterfall near Rydal[6] to which we shall proceed after having put these letters in the post office. I long to be at Carlisle, as I expect there a letter from George and one from you. Let any of my friends see my letters—they may not be interested in descriptions—descriptions are bad at all times[7]—I did not intend to give you any; but how can I help it? I am anxious you should taste a little of our pleasure; it may not be an unpleasant thing, as you have not the fatigue. I am well in health. Direct henceforth to Port[8] Patrick till the 12th July. Content that probably three or four pair of eyes whose owners I am rather partial to will run over these lines I remain; and moreover that I am your affectionate brother John.

[5] See his *Works*, XIX (1933), 23 f. So Charles Lamb wrote on September 24, 1802 (*The Works of Charles and Mary Lamb*, ed. E. V. Lucas, VI [1905], 244), that during a visit to the Lake District "I felt very *little*." Brown (see I, 427 f.) describes the waterfalls enthusiastically.

[6] *Printed* Kydal. [7] See II, 198. [8] *Printed* Post.

· 92 ·

TO GEORGE AND GEORGIANA KEATS [1]

27, 28 June 1818

Address: Mr George Keats/ Crown Inn/ Liverpool; *readdressed to* Messrs Frampton & Son [2]/ Leadenhall Street/ London
Postmarks: KESWICK . . . 88; LIVERPOOL 1 JY 1 1818 206

My dear George, Foot of Helvellyn June 27

We have passed from Lancaster ⟨from⟩ to Burton from Burton to Enmoor,[3] from Enmoor to Kendal from Kendal to Bownes on turning down to which place there burst upon us the most beautiful and rich view of Winander mere and the surrounding Mountains —we dined at Bownes on Trout which I took an oar to fetch from some Box preserves close on one of the little green Islands. After dinner we walked to Ambleside down a beautiful shady Lane along the Borders of the Lake with ample opportunity for Glimpses all the way—We slept at Ambleside not above two Miles from Rydal the Residence of Wordsworth We arose not very early on account of having marked this day for a day of rest—Before breakfast we visited the first waterfall I ever saw and certainly small as it is it surpassed my expectation, in what I have mentioned in my letter to Tom, in its tone and intellect its light shade slaty Rock, Moss and Rock weed—but you will see finer ones I will not describe by comparison a teapot spout—We ate a Monstrous Breakfast on our return (which by the way I do every morning) and after it proceeded to Wordsworths He was not at home nor was any Member of his family—I was much disappointed. I wrote a note [4] for him

[1] *ALS:* Harvard (first printed by Lowell, II, 26–29). Though it was endorsed by Tom "To be sent to George," the letter (see II, 195) was not sent.

[2] Haslam worked for Frampton and Sons (not Company), wholesale grocers, 34 Leadenhall Street.

[3] They went from Liverpool to Lancaster by coach on June 24 and "walked a Little zig zag" through the mountains (I, 310); on June 25 through Bolton-le-Sands and Burton in Kendal to Endmoor (I, 424 f.); on June 26 through Kendal and Bowness to Ambleside (see Bushnell, p. 301).

[4] Which unluckily has not been preserved. For Brown's comments on Wordsworth see I, 430 f. In his *Life of John Keats* (*KC*, II, 61), Brown, noting that Wordsworth was at Lowther Hall (see I, 299 n.), wrote and then deleted the sentence, "The young poet looked thoughtful at this exposure of his elder."

and stuck it up over what I knew must be Miss Wordsworth's Portrait and set forth again & we visited two Waterfalls in the neighbourhood, and then went along by Rydal Water and Grasmere through its beautiful Vale—then through a defile in the Mountains into Cumberland and So to the foot of Helvellyn whose summit is out of sight four Miles off rise above rise—I have seen Kirkstone, Loughrigg and Silver How—and discovered without a hint "that ancient woman seated on Helm Craig." [5] This is the summary of what I have written to Tom and dispatched from Ambleside—I have had a great confidence in your being well able to support the fatigue of your Journey since I have felt how much new Objects contribute to keep off a sense of Ennui and fatigue 14 Miles here is not so much as the 4 from Hampstead to London. You will have an enexhaustible astonishment; with that and such a Companion you will be cheered on from day to day—I hope you will not have sail'd before this Letter reaches you—yet I do not know for I will have my Series to Tom coppied and sent to you by the first Packet you have from England. God send you both as good Health as I have now. Ha! my dear Sister George, I wish I knew what humour you were in that I might accomodate myself [6] to any one of your Amiabilities—Shall it be a Sonnet or a Pun or an Acrostic, a Riddle or a Ballad—'perhaps it may turn out a Sang, and perhaps turn out a Sermon' [7] I'll write you on my word the first and most likely the last I ever shall do, because it has strucke me—what shall it be about?

> Give me your patience Sister while I frame
> Enitials [verse] [8]-wise of your golden name:
> Or sue the fair Apollo and he will
> Rouse from his Slumber heavy and instill
> Great Love in me for thee and Poesy—
> Imagine not that greatest Mastery
> And kingdom over all the realms of verse
> Nears more to heaven in aught than when we nurse

[5] Wordsworth, "Poems on the Naming of Places. II. To Joanna," line 56 (Colvin, p. 116 n.). See Brown's remarks at I, 430. "Craig" should be "Crag."

[6] Compare his remark to Reynolds at I, 324.

[7] Burns, "Epistle to a Young Friend" (Andrew Hunter Aiken), lines 7 f.

[8] The word apparently begins with "ves" and is followed after a space by "e." The version of this acrostic poem given in No. 199 has a considerable number of variants. De Selincourt, p. 557, calls it a "very weak composition."

And surety give to
⟨In its vast safety⟩ Love and Brotherhood.—

Anthropopagi in Othello's Mood,
Ulysses stormed, and his enchanted Belt
⟨By the sweet Muse are never never felt⟩
Glow with the Muse but they are never felt
Unbosom'd so, and so eternal made,
Such selfsame insence in their Laurel shade
To all the regent sisters of the Nine
As this poor offering to thee Sister mine.

Kind Sister! aye this third name says you are
Enhanced has it been the Lord knows where.
Ah! may it taste to you like good old wine—
Take you ⟨the⟩ to real happiness and give
Sons daughters and a Home like honied hive.

June 28th I have slept[9] and walked eight miles to Breakfast at Keswick on derwent water—We could not mount Helvellyn for the mist so gave it up with hopes of Skiddaw which we shall try tomorrow if it be fine—to day we shall walk round Derwent water, and in our Way see the Falls of Low-dore—The Approach to derwent water is rich and magnificent beyond any means of conception—the Mountains all round sublime and graceful and rich in colour —Woods and wooded Islands here and there—at the same time in the distance among Mountains of another aspect we see Bassenthwaite[1]—I {shall} drop like a Hawk on the Post Office at Carlisle {to ask for} some Letters from you and Tom—

Sweet sweet is the greeting of eyes,
And sweet is the voice in its greeting,
When Adieux have grown old and goodbyes
Fade away where old time is retreating—

Warm the nerve of a welcoming hand
And earnest a kiss on the Brow,
When we meet over sea and o'er Land
Where furrows are new to the Plough.[2]

[9] At the Nag's Head, Wythburn, where, says Brown (see I, 431), "many fleas were in the beds" (see Bushnell, pp. 50, 52). William Green, *The Tourist's New Guide* (Kendal, 1819), I, 421, however, calls the "Horse Head" "an excellent public house."

[1] See Brown's words at I, 433.

[2] No other copy of this poem is known.

This is all {. . .} in the m{. . .} please a{. . .} Letters as possi{bly . . .} [3] We will before many Years are over have written many folio volumes [4] which as a Matter of self-defence to one whom you understand intends to be immortal in the best points and let all his Sins and peccadillos die away—I mean to say that the Booksellers with [5] rather decline printing ten folio volumes of Correspondence printed as close as the Apostles creed in a Watch paper—I have been looking out my dear Georgy for a joke or a Pun for you—there is none but the Names of romantic Misses on the Inn window Panes. You will of course have given me directions brother George where to direct on the other side of the Water. I have not had time to write to Henry [6]—for I have a journal to keep for Tom nearly enough to employ all my leisure—I am a day behind hand with him—I scarcely know how I shall manage Fanny and two or three others I have promised—We expect to be in Scotland in at most three days so you must if this should catch you before you set sail give me a line to Port-Patrick—

God bless you my dear Brother and Sister.

John—

·93·

TO TOM KEATS [1]

29 June, 1, 2 July 1818 [2]

Keswick—June 29th 1818. [3]

My dear Tom

I cannot make my Journal as distinct & actual as I could wish, from having been engaged in writing to George. & therefore I must tell you without circumstance that we proceeded from Am-

[3] He wrote something like "This is all I did in the morning—please answer my Letters as possibly then We will before many Years. . . ."

[4] See his words to Fanny Keats at the end of No. 32.

[5] *For* will. For another joke about printing his letters see II, 282.

[6] Wylie.

[1] A transcript by Jeffrey, who heads it: "(Here follow 4 letters forming part of a Journal kept during John Keats visit to Scotland the rest of the Journal is lost—)." He copies only Nos. 93, 95, 100, 102, a fact proving that the originals of Nos. 91 and 92 were not in the possession of George Keats's family in 1845.

[2] Heretofore dated merely June 29.

[3] The last figure, apparently 8, is scratched out.

bleside to Rydal,[4] saw the Waterfalls there, & called on Wordsworth, who was not at home. nor was any one of his family. I wrote a note & left it on the Mantlepiece.[5] Thence on we came to the foot of Helvellyn, where we slept,[6] but could not ascend it for the mist. I must mention that from Rydal we passed Thirlswater,[7] & a fine pass in the Mountains from Helvellyn we came to Keswick on Derwent Water.[8] The approach to Derwent Water surpassed Winandermere—it is richly wooded & shut in with rich-toned Mountains. From Helvellyn to Keswick was eight miles to Breakfast, After which we took a complete circuit of the Lake going about ten miles, & seeing on our way the Fall of Low-dore. I had an easy climb among the streams, about the fragments of Rocks & should have got I think to the summit, but unfortunately I was damped by slipping one leg into a squashy hole. There is no great body of water, but the accompaniment is delightful; for it ooses out from a cleft in perpendicular Rocks, all fledged with Ash & other beautiful trees.[9] It is a strange thing how they got there. At the south end of the Lake, the Mountains of Bunowdale,[1] are perhaps as fine as any thing we have seen—On our return from this circuit, we ordered dinner, & set forth about a mile & a half on the Penrith road, to see the Druid temple.[2] We had a fag up hill, rather too near dinner time, which was rendered void, by the gratification of seeing those aged stones, on a gentle rise in the midst of Mountains, which at that time darkened all round, except at the fresh opening of the vale of St. John. We went to bed rather fatigued, but not so much so as to hinder us getting up this morning,[3] to mount Skiddaw It promised all along to be fair, & we had fagged & tugged nearly to the top, when at halfpast six there came a mist upon us & shut out the view; we did not however lose anything by it, we were high enough without mist, to see the coast of Scotland; the Irish sea; the hills beyond

[4] On June 27. [5] See I, 302 f. [6] At Wythburn (see I, 304 n.).

[7] Thirlmere, or Wythburn Water, five miles southeast of Keswick.

[8] On June 28. Bushnell (p. 50) thinks that they stayed at the Oak Inn (now the Royal Oak Hotel), Keswick.

[9] On Lodore see Brown's words at I, 432. Colvin, p. 115 n., compares the final words of Keats's sentence with the "Ode to Psyche," lines 54 f.

[1] Jeffrey's miscopying for "Borrowdale." The second word following he spelled "perpaps."

[2] The Druid Circle (or Druid Stones), two miles east of Keswick. Brown (see I, 432) describes it at length.

[3] At four o'clock, as usual, says Brown (see I, 432), who describes the ascent and descent at length.

Lancaster; & nearly all the large ones of Cumberland & Westmoreland, particularly Helvellyn & Scawfell: [4] It grew colder & colder as we ascended, & we were glad at about three parts of the way to
rum
taste a little ⟨wine⟩ which the Guide brought with him, mixed, mind ye with mountain water, I took two glasses going & one returning—It is about six miles from where I am writing to the top. so we have walked ten miles before Breakfast today. We went up with two others, very good sort of fellows, All felt on arising into the cold air, that same elevation, which a cold bath gives one—I felt as if I were going to a Tournament. Wordsworth's house is situated just on the rise of the foot of mount Rydall, his parlor window looks directly down Winandermere; I do not think I told you how fine the vale of Grassmere is, & how I discovered "the ancient woman seated on Helm Crag." [5]—We shall proceed immediately to Carlisle, intending to enter Scotland on the 1st of July via —— [6] July 1st —We are this morning at Carlisle—After Skiddow, we walked to Ireby the oldest market town in Cumberland—where we were greatly amused by a country dancing school, holden at the Tun,[7] it was indeed "no new cotillon fresh from France." [8] No they kickit & jumpit with mettle extraordinary, & whiskit, & fleckit, & toe'd it, & go'd it, & twirld it, & wheel'd it, & stampt it, & sweated it, tattooing the floor like mad; The differenc[e] between our country dances & these scotch figures, is about the same as leisurely stirring a cup o' Tea & heating [9] up a batter pudding. I was extremely gratified to think, that if I had pleasures they knew nothing of. they had also some into which I could not possibly enter I hope I shall not return without having got the Highland fling, there was as fine a row of boys & girls as you ever saw, some beautiful faces, & one exquisite mouth. I never felt so near the glory of Patriotism, the glory of making by any means a country happier.[1] This is what I like better than scenery. I fear our continued moving from place

[4] Scafell, the second highest summit in England. [5] See I, 303 n.

[6] After climbing Skiddaw on June 29, they walked past Bassenthwaite Water to Ireby; on June 30 (see I, 308) from Ireby through Wigton to Carlisle.

[7] Jeffrey's error for "Sun" (he wrote "nate Toone" for "nate Inn" at I, 319). Bushnell (p. 279) calls the Sun "the famous old inn."

[8] Burns, "Tam o' Shanter," line 116, "Nae cotillion, brent new frae France." Brown (see I, 434) gives more details.

[9] *For* beating.

[1] MBF compares the lines in No. 5 beginning "The Patriot shall feel. . . ."

to place, will prevent our becoming learned in village affairs; we are mere creatures of Rivers, Lakes, & mountains. Our yesterday's journey was from Ireby to Wigton, & from Wigton to Carlisle—The Cathedral does not appear very fine; The Castle is very Ancient, & of Brick [2] The City is very various, old white washed narrow streets; broad red brick ones more modern—I will tell you anon, whether the inside of the Cathedral is worth looking at. It is built of a sandy red stone or Brick. We have now walked 114 miles & are merely a little tired in the thighs, & a little blistered; We shall ride 38 miles to Dumfries,[3] where we shall linger a while, about Nithsdale & Galloway, I have written two letters [4] to Liverpool. I found a letter from sister George. very delightful indeed. I shall preserve it in the bottom of my knapsack for you.

—On visiting the Tomb of Burns—

The Town, the churchyard, & the setting sun,
The Clouds, the trees, the rounded hills all seem
Though beautiful, Cold—strange—as in a dream,
I dreamed long ago, now new begun
The shortlived, paly summer is but won
From winters ague, for one hours gleam;
Through [5] saphire warm, their stars do never beam,
All is cold Beauty; pain is never done.
For who has mind to relish Minos-wise,
The real of Beauty, free from that dead hue
Fickly [6] imagination & sick pride
* wan upon it! Burns! with honor due

Note. An illegible word [?Cast*] occurs here—

[2] *Leigh's New Picture of England and Wales* (1820), p. 94, dismisses both with the statement, "these edifices, or at least certain parts of them, being of considerable antiquity. . . ." See also Brown's comments at I, 434.

[3] They did so, via Gretna Green, on this day, July 1, reaching Dumfries in time to visit the tomb of Burns before dinner. Keats wrote the sonnet, as well as the portion of the letter from "I found a letter" to "Fairly about the Scotch" after dinner. Brown says (see I, 434 f.) that Gretna Green was "poverty-struck and barren," the ride to Dumfries dull. The churchyard, however, "might be called an enviable place to lie in, and I rejoice that Burns is buried there."

[4] Only one (No. 92) is known.

[5] Though *Garrod* (p. 488, who changes various spellings as well as punctuation and capitalization).

[6] Sickly *Garrod.* J. C. Maxwell, *K–SJ*, IV (1955), 78, thinks that Keats really intended "Fickly," a word found in the quarto of *King Lear*, II.iv.188.

I have oft honoured [7] thee. Great shadow; hide
Thy face, I sin against thy native skies.

You will see by this sonnet that I am at Dumfries, we have dined in Scotland. Burns' [8] tomb is in the Churchyard corner, not very much to my taste, though on a scale, large enough to show they wanted to honour him—Mrs Burns lives in this place, most likely we shall see her tomorrow—This Sonnet I have written in a strange mood, half asleep. I know not how it is, the Clouds, the sky, the Houses, all seem anti [9] Grecian & anti [9] Charlemagnish—I will endeavour to get rid of my prejudices, & tell you fairly about the Scotch [1]— July 2nd In Devonshire they say "Well where be yee going." [2] Here it is, "How is it all wi yoursel" [3]—A man on the Coach said the horses took a Hellish heap o' drivin—the same fellow pointed out Burns' [4] tomb with a deal of life, "There de ye see it, amang the trees; white, wi a roond tap." The first well dressed Scotchman we had any conversation with, to our surprise confessed himself a Deist. The careful manner of his delivering his opinions, not before he had received several encouraging hints from us, was very amusing—Yesterday was an immense Horse fair at Dumfries, so that we met numbers of men & women on the road, the women nearly all barefoot, with their shoes & clean stockings in hand, ready to put on & look smart in the Towns. There are plenty of wretched Cottages, where smoke has no outlet but by the door—We have now begun upon whiskey, called here *whuskey* very smart stuff it is—Mixed like our liquors with sugar & water tis called toddy, very pretty drink, & much praised by Burns. [5]
Mr Thomas Keats
Hampstead—

[7] I oft have honour'd *Garrod* (though only this letter text is known).
[8] Burn's *Jeffrey*. [9] ante *Jeffrey apparently*.
[1] He had not succeeded when Brown wrote to Dilke in July (*Papers*, I, 2 f.): "Keats has been these five hours abusing the Scotch and their country. He says that the women have large splay feet, which is too true to be controverted, and that he thanks Providence he is not related to a Scot, nor any way connected with them."
[2] HBF thinks that Keats took the Devonshire "you" for "ye."
[3] See I, 310. [4] Burn's *Jeffrey*.
[5] Nobody can tell how much Jeffrey omits here.

· 94 ·

TO FANNY KEATS [1]

2, 3, 5 July 1818

Address: Miss F. M. Keats/ Richd Abbey's Esqre/ Walthamstow/ Middx—/ Single
Postmarks: NEWTON STEWART; 10 o'Clock JY 8 1818 FN^{n}; *others illegible.*

My dear Fanny, Dumfries July 2nd

I intended to have written to you from Kirkudbright [2] the town I shall be in tomorrow—but I will write now bec[a]use my knapsack has worn my coat in the Seams, my coat has gone to the Taylors and I have but one Coat to my back in these parts. I must tell you how I went to Liverpool [3] with George and our new Sister and the Gentleman my fellow traveller through the Summer and Autumn —We had a tolerable journey to Liverpool—which I left the next morning [4] before George was up for Lancaster—Then we set off from Lancaster on foot with our knapsacks on, and have walked a Little zig zag through the mountains and Lakes of Cumberland and Westmoreland—We came from Carlisle yesterday [5] to this place—We are employed in going up Mountains, looking at Strange towns prying into old ruins and eating very hearty breakfasts. Here we are full in the Midst of broad Scotch 'How is it a' wi yoursel' [6]— the Girls are walking about bare footed and in the worst cottages the Smoke finds its way out of the door—I shall come home full of news for you and for fear I should choak you by too great a dose at once I must make you used to it by a letter or two—We have been taken for travelling Jewellers, Razor sellers and Spectacle venders because friend Brown wears a pair—The first place we stopped at with our knapsacks contained one Richard Bradshaw [7] a notorious

[1] *ALS:* Pierpont Morgan Library.
[2] His spelling throughout for "Kirkcudbright." So Brown's *Life of John Keats* (*KC*, II, 61).
[3] On June 22 and 23. [4] June 24 (see I, 298 n.).
[5] See I, 308. [6] See I, 309.
[7] At Endmoor, June 25. Brown (see I, 424 f.) calls him Richard Radshaw, and describes him at length.

tippler—He stood in the shape of a ℨ and ballanced himself as well as he could saying with his nose right in Mr Browns face 'Do— yo u sell Spect—ta—cles?' Mr Abbey says we are Don Quixotes—tell him we are more generally taken for Pedlars—All I hope is that we may not be taken for excisemen in this whiskey country—We are generally up about 5 walking before breakfast and we complete our 20 Miles before dinner—Yesterday [8] we visited Burns's Tomb and this morning the fine Ruins of Lincluden [9]—I had done thus far when my coat came back fortified at all points—so as we lose no time we set forth again through Galloway [1]—all very pleasant and pretty with no fatigue when one is used to it—We are in the midst of Meg Merrilies' country of whom I suppose—you have heard [2]—

Old Meg she was a Gipsey
  And liv'd upon the Moors
Her bed it was the brown heath turf
  And her house was out of doors

Her apples were swart blackberries
  Her currants pods o' broom
Her wine was dew o' [3] the wild white rose
  Her book a churchyard tomb

Her Brothers were the craggy hills
  Her Sisters larchen trees—
Alone ⟨wht⟩ with her great family
  She liv'd as she did please—

                                        morn
No breakfast has [4] she many a ⟨day⟩
  No dinner many a noon
And 'stead of supper she would stare
  Full hard against the Moon—

[8] July 1 (see I, 308 f.). [9] See Brown (I, 435) on Lincluden College.

[1] According to Brown (see I, 436 f.) they spent the night of July 2 at Dalbeattie, where a one-legged man named Murray, who kept a public house with a shop below it, provided food and lodging.

[2] See Brown (I, 438 f.) on this ballad. The text he prints (in four stanzas) has been generally overlooked, as have the texts of various other poems of Keats in the same paper.

[3] of *Garrod* (p. 489, who has other variants, though he is following the text in No. 94, not that in No. 95). Brown also has "of."

[4] had *Garrod and Brown* (see the text at I, 438).

But evey morn of woodbine fresh
She made her garlanding
And every night the dark glen Yew
She wove and she would sing—

And ⟨sometimes⟩ with her fingers old and brown
She plaited Mats o' Rushes
And gave them to the Cottagers
She met among the Bushes—

Old Meg was brave as Margaret Queen
And tall as Amazon:
An old red blanket cloak she wore;
A chip hat [5] had she on—
God rest her aged bones somewhere
She died full long agone!

If you like these sort of Ballads I will now and then scribble one for you—if I send any to Tom I'll tell him to send them to you—I [6] have so many interruptions that I cannot manage to fill a Letter in one day—since I scribbled the Song we have walked through a beautiful Country to Kirkudbright—at which place I will write you a song about myself—

There was a naughty Boy
A naughty boy was he
He would not stop at home
He could not quiet be—
He took
In his knapsack
A Book
Full of vowels
And a shirt
With some towels—
A slight cap
For night cap—
A hair brush
Comb ditto

[5] A hat made of wood fiber.

[6] It is now July 3. Keats gives no details about the walk through Auchencairn and Dundrennan to Kirkcudbright. But Brown (see I, 439) describes their walk to the ruins of Dundrennan Abbey and their entrance into Kirkcudbright. See Bushnell, pp. 83–86.

New Stockings
For old ones
Would split O!
This knapsack
Tight at 's back
He revetted [7] close
And followe'd his Nose
To the North
To the North
And follow'd his nose
To the North—

There was a naughty boy
And a naughty boy was he
For nothing would he do
But scribble poetry—
He took
An inkstand
In his hand
And a Pen
Big as ten
In the other
And away
In a Pother
He ran
To the mountains
And fountains
And ghostes
And Postes
And witches
And ditches
And wrote
In his coat
When the weather
Was ⟨warm⟩ cool
Fear of gout
And without

[7] "Revet" is an obsolete form of "rivet," but possibly Keats wrote "rivitted" and failed to dot the "i's."

When the w[e]ather
warm
Was ⟨cool⟩—
Och the cha[r]m
When we choose
To follow ones nose
To the north
To the north
To follow one's nose to the north!

There was a naughty boy
And a naughty boy we[8] he
He kept little fishes
In washing tubs three
In spite
Of the might
Of the Maid
Nor affraid
Of his Granny-good—
He often would
Hurly burly
Get up early
And go
By hook or crook
To the brook
And bring home
Miller's thumb
Tittle bat
Not over fat
Minnows small
As the stall
Of a glove
Not above
The size
Of a nice
Little Baby's
Little finger—

[8] *For* was.

O he made
'T was his trade
Of Fish a pretty kettle
A kettle—A kettle
Of Fish a pretty kettle
A kettle!

There was a naughty Boy
And a naughty Boy was he
He ran away to Scotland
The people for to see—
There he found
That the ground
Was as hard
That a yard
Was as long,
That a song
Was as merry,
That a cherry
Was as red—
That lead
Was as weighty
That fourscore
Was as eighty
That a door
Was as wooden
As in england—
So he stood in
His shoes
And he wonderd
He wonderd
He stood in his
Shoes and he wonder'd—

My dear Fanny I am ashamed of writing you such stuff, nor would I if it were not for being tired after my days walking,[9] and ready to tumble int{o bed} so fatigued that when I am asleep you might

[9] On July 4, Brown's Journal shows (see I, 440), they walked through Gatehouse-of-Fleet to Creetown, where apparently (see Bushnell, pp. 98, 301) they spent the night.

sew my nose to my great toe and trundle me round the town like a Hoop without waking me—Then I get so hungry—a Ham goes but a very little way and fowls are like Larks to me—A Batch of Bread I make no more ado with than a sheet of parliament; and I can eat a Bull's head as easily as I used to do Bull's eyes—I take a whole string of Pork Sausages down as easily as a Pen'orth of Lady's fingers [1]—Oh dear I must soon be contented with an acre or two of oaten cake a hogshead of Milk and a Cloaths basket of Eggs morning noon and night when I get among the Highlanders—Before we see them we shall pass into Ireland and have a chat with the Paddies, and look at the Giant's Cause-way which you must have heard of—I have not time to tell you particularly for I have to send a Journal to Tom of whom you shall hear all particulars or from me when I return—Since I began this we have walked sixty miles to newton

night [2]

stewart at which place I put in this Letter—to ⟨day⟩ we sleep at Glenluce—tomorrow at Portpatrick and the next day we shall cross in the passage boat to Ireland—I hope Miss Abbey has quite recovered—Present my Respects to her and to Mr And Mrs Abbey—God bless you—

Your affectionate Brother John—

Do write me a Letter directed to *Inverness*. Scotland—

[1] " 'Parliament' was a thin flat cake made of sticky ginger-bread; 'Lady's fingers' large white peppermints pink ringed" (Hewlett, p. 206).

[2] July 5: see the first postmark.

· 95 ·

TO TOM KEATS [1]

3, 5, 7, 9, July 1818

Address: Mr Thos. Keats/ Well Walk/ Hampstead/ Middx—/ Single
Postmarks: 10 o'Clock JY 13 18{18}; D 13 JY 13 1818; 1/2

My dear Tom, Auchencairn July 3rd

I have not been able to keep up my journal completely on accou[n]t of other letters [2] to George and one which I am writing to Fanny from which I have turned to loose no time whilst Brown is coppying a song about Meg Merrilies which I have just written for her—We are now in Meg Merrilies county and have this morning passed through some parts exactly suited to her—Kirkudbright County is very beautiful, very wild with craggy hills somewhat in the westmoreland fashion—we have come down from Dumfries to the sea coast part of it—The song I mention you would have from Dilke: but perhaps you would like it here—

Old Meg she was a Gipsey [3]
  And liv'd upon the Moors;
Her bed it was the brown heath turf,
  And her house was out of doors—
Her apples were swart blackberries,
  Her currants pods o' Broom,
Her wine was dew o' the wild white rose,
  Her book a churchyard tomb—
Her brothers were the craggy hills,
  Her sisters larchen trees—

[1] *ALS:* Harvard (formerly owned by James Freeman Clarke, Boston). Endorsed by Tom: "Received 13 July
"Answered—"—"
"No 3- from John"
Endorsed by Jeffrey: "Copied August 1845." The letter was written at a stop on the trip from Dalbeattie to Kirkcudbright. Passages in it are discussed at length by Georges A. Bonnard, *English Studies*, XXXII (1951), 72–76.

[2] None later than June 28 (No. 92) is known.

[3] Compare the text as given in No. 94.

Alone with her great family
  She liv'd as she did please.
No Breakfast had she many a morn,
  No dinner many a noon;
And 'stead of supper she would stare
  Full hard against the Moon—
But every Morn, of wood bine fresh
  She made her garlanding;
And every night the dark glen Yew
  She wove and she would sing—
And with her fingers old and brown
  She plaited Mats o' Rushes,
And gave them to the Cottagers
  She met among the Bushes—
Old Meg was brave as Margaret Queen
  And tall as Amazon:
And old red blanket cloak she wore
  A chip hat had she on—
God rest her aged bones somewhere
  She died full long agone!

Now I will return to Fanny [4]—it rains. I may have time to go on here presently. July 5—You see I have missed a day from fanny's Letter.[5] Yesterday was passed in Kircudbright [6]—the Country is very rich—very fine—and with a little of Devon—I am now writing at Newton Stuart six Miles into Wigton [7]—Our Landlady of yesterday [8] said very few Southrens passed these ways—The children jabber away as in a foreign Language—The barefooted Girls look very much in keeping—I mean with the Scenery about them—Brown praises their cleanliness and appearance of comfort—the neatness of their cottages &c It may be—they are very squat [9] among trees and fern and heaths and broom, on levels slopes and heights—They

[4] That is, to writing No. 94, I, 315 f.

[5] Bushnell, p. 282, explains, "Because he had written her on the evening of the third in Kirkcudbright [I, 312–315], and again on the morning of the fifth at Newton Stewart" (I, 316). Keats missed July 4 in both Nos. 94 and 95.

[6] He means "the Country" or shire. Apparently (Bushnell, pp. 92, 98, 301) he left the town of Kirkcudbright early on July 4, breakfasted at Gatehouse-of-Fleet, and slept at Creetown. On July 5 he walked from Creetown to Newton-Stewart for breakfast, and then to Glenluce for the night.

[7] Bushnell, p. 283, thinks Keats meant that he was about six miles *from* Wigtown.

[8] Presumably at Creetown.

[9] For "squat" compare I, 208, 321.

are very pleasant because they are very primitive—but I wish they were as snug as those up the Devonshire vallies—We are lodged and entertained in great varieties—we dined yesterday [1] on dirty bacon dirtier eggs and dirtiest [2] Potatoes with a slice of Salmon—we breakfast this morning [3] in a nice carpeted Room with Sofa hair bottomed chairs and green-baized mehogany—A spring by the road side is always welcome—we drink water for dinner diluted with a Gill of wiskey. July 7th Yesterday Morning we set out from Glenluce going some distance round to see some Ruins [4]—they were scarcely worth the while—we went on towards Stranrawier [5] in a burning sun and had gone about six Miles when the Mail overtook us—we got up—were at Portpatrick in a jiffy, and I am writing now in little Ireland [6]—The dialect on the neighbouring shores of Scotland [7] and Ireland is much the same—yet I can perceive a great difference in the nations from the Chambermaid at this nate Inn [8] kept by Mr Kelly—She is fair, kind and ready to laugh, because she is out of the horrible dominion of the Scotch kirk—A Scotch Girl stands in terrible awe of the Elders—poor little Susannas [9]—They will scarcely laugh—they are greatly to be pitied and the kirk is greatly to be damn'd. These kirkmen have done scotland good (Query?) they have made Men, Women, Old Men Young Men old Women, young women boys, girls and infants all careful—so that they are formed into regular Phalanges of savers and gainers—such a thrifty army cannot fail to enrich their Country and give it a greater apperance of comfort than that of their poor irish neighbours—These kirkmen have done Scotland harm—they have banished puns and laughing and kissing (except in cases where the very danger and crime must make it very fine and gustful.[1] I shall make a full stop at kissing for after that there should be a better paren*t*thesis: and go on to remind you of the fate of Burns. Poor unfor-

[1] At Newton-Stewart.

[2] Keats enjoyed this construction: compare "right . . . right . . . rightest," I, 173 f., "fuz . . . fuzziest," I, 324, and the play on "moreoverer," II, 69.

[3] At Glenluce.

[4] The ruins of Glenluce Abbey (1190), a mile and a half northwest on Luce Water.

[5] Stranraer.

[6] They sailed from Portpatrick on a mail-boat (discontinued in 1849) to Donaghadee, where Keats is now writing.

[7] Changed from "England."

[8] See I, 307 n.

[9] Keats had been reading the apocryphal book of Daniel.

[1] Brown is less severe on the kirk in his article (cited by MBF), "State of Religion in the Highlands," *New Monthly Magazine*, IV (1822), 329–333.

tunate fellow—his disposition was southern—how sad it is when a luxurious imagination is obliged in self defence to deaden its delicacy in vulgarity, and riot [2] in thing[s] attainable that it may not have leisure to go mad after thing[s] which are not. No Man in such matters will be content with the experience of others—It is true that out of suffrance there is no greatness, no dignity; that in the most abstracted Pleasure there is no lasting happiness: yet who would not like to discover over again that Cleopatra was a Gipsey, Helen a Rogue and Ruth a deep one? I have not sufficient reasoning faculty to settle the doctrine of thrift—as it is consistent with the dignity of human Society—with the happiness of Cottagers—All I can do is by plump contrasts—Were the fingers made to squeeze a guinea or a white hand? Were the Lips made to hold a pen or a kiss? And yet in Cities Man is shut out from his fellows if he is poor, the Cottager must be dirty and very wretched if she be not thrifty—The present state of society demands this and this convinces me that the world is very young and in a verry ignorant state—We live in a barbarous age. I would sooner be a wild deer than a Girl under the dominion of the kirk, and I would sooner be a wild hog than be the occasion of a Poor Creatures pennance before those execrable elders—It is not so far to the Giant's Cause way as we supposed—we thought it 70 and hear it is only 48 Miles—so we shall leave one of our knapsacks here at Donoghadee, take our immediate wants and be back in a week—when we shall proceed to the County of Ayr. In the Packet Yesterday we heard some Ballads from two old Men—one was a romance which seemed very poor—then there was the Battle of the Boyne [3]— then Robin Huid as they call him—'Before the king you shall go, go, go, before the king you shall go.' [4] There were no Letters for me at Port Patrick so I am behind hand with you I dare say in news from George. Direct to Glasgow till the 17th of this month. 9th We stopped very little in Ireland and that you may not have leisere to marvel at our speedy return to Portpatrick I will tell you that is it as dear living in Ireland as at the Hummums [5]—thrice the expence of Scotland—it would

[2] Colvin, p. 124, printed "rot" but noted "Reading doubtful."

[3] For ballads on the Boyne see Rollins, *The Pepys Ballads*, V (Harvard University Press, 1931), 186, 191, 195.

[4] "Robin Hood and the Bishop of Hereford," F. J. Child, *English and Scottish Popular Ballads* (Boston, 1882–1898), No. 144.

[5] C. and G. Harrison's "new" hotel at 13 Great Russell Street, Covent Garden.

£
have cost us 15 before our return—Moreover we found those 48 Miles to be irish ones which reach to 70 english—So having walked to Belfast one day and back to Donoghadee the next [6] we left Ireland with a fair breeze—We slept last night at Port patrick where I was gratified by a letter from you. On our walk in Ireland we had too much opportunity to see the worse than nakedness, the rags, the dirt and misery of the poor common Irish—A Scotch cottage, though in that some times the Smoke has no exit but at the door, is a pallace to an irish one—We could observe that impetiosity in Man {and b}oy and Woman—We had the pleasure of finding our way through a Peat-Bog—three miles long at least—dreary, black, dank, flat and spongy: here and there were poor dirty creatures and a few strong men cutting or carting peat. We heard on passing into Belfast through a most wretched suburb that most disgusting of all noises worse than the Bag pipe, the laugh of a Monkey, the chatter of women *solus* [7] the scream of [a] Macaw—I mean the sound of the Shuttle—What a tremendous difficulty is the improvement of the condition of such people—I cannot conceive how a mind 'with child' [8] of Philantrophy could gra[s]p at possibility—with me it is absolute despair. At a miserable house of entertainment half way between Donaghadee and Bellfast were two Men Sitting at Whiskey one a Laborer and the other I took to be a drunken Weaver—The Laborer took me for a Frenchman and the other hinted at Bounty Money saying he was ready to take it—On calling for the Letters at Port patrick the man snapp'd out 'what Regiment'? [9] On our return from Bellfast we met a Sadan [1]—the Duchess of Dunghill—It is no laughing matter tho—Imagine the worst dog kennel you ever saw placed upon two poles from a mouldy fencing—In such a wretched thing sat a squalid old Woman squat [2] like an ape half starved from a scarcity of Buiscuit in its passage from Madagascar to the cape,—with a pipe in her mouth and looking out with a round-eyed skinny lidded, inanity—with a sort of horizontal idiotic movement of her head—squab [3] and lean she sat and puff'd out the smoke while two ragged tattered Girls carried

[6] July 7 and 8. [7] Possibly he had in mind *Henry V*, II.i.47 ff.

[8] *The Faerie Queen*, I.v.1; Sidney, *Astrophel and Stella*, Sonnet 1, line 12.

[9] See I, 360. [1] On the sedan duchess see also I, 326. [2] See I, 208 n.

[3] "Squab" means short and stout. Probably Keats intended to repeat "squat" (see I, 318 n.), which Jeffrey has in his transcript of the letter.

her along—What a thing would be a history of her Life and sensations. I shall endeavour when I know more and have though[t] a little more, to give you my ideas of the difference between the scotch and irish [4]—The two Irishmen I mentioned were speaking of their treatment in England when the Weaver said—'Ah you were a civil Man but I was a drinker' Remember me to all—I intend writing to Haslam—but dont tell him for fear I should delay—We left a notice at Portpatrick that our Letters should be thence forwarded to Glasgow—Our quick return from Ireland will occasion our passing Glasgow sooner than we thought—so till further notice you must direct to Inverness

Your most affectionate Brother John—

Remember me to the Bentleys

·96·

TO J. H. REYNOLDS [1]

11, 13 July 1818

Maybole July 11. [2]

My Dear Reynolds.

I'll not run over the Ground we have passed. that would be merely [3] as bad as telling a dream—unless perhaps I do it in the manner of the Laputan printing press [4]—that is I put down Mountains, Rivers Lakes, dells, glens, Rocks, and Clouds,[5] With beautiful enchanting, gothic picturesque fine, delightful, enchancting, Grand, sublime—a few Blisters &c—and now you have our journey thus far: where I begin a letter to you because I am approaching Burns's Cottage very fast—We have made continual enquiries from the time we saw his Tomb at Dumfries [6]—his name of course is

plodding

known all about—his great reputation among the ⟨Plotting⟩ people

[4] He does so at I, 330 f.

[1] A transcript in Woodhouse's letter-book, pp. 70–73, by a clerk, with corrections by Woodhouse.

[2] Woodhouse adds "(1818)."

[3] Above "merely" Woodhouse wrote "so" (that is, the word should be "nearly"). Keats disliked descriptions (I, 301).

[4] *Gulliver's Travels*, part III, chapter 5.

[5] Written "blouds."

[6] On July 1 (see I, 308 f.).

is "that he wrote a good MONY [7] sensible things"—One of the pleasantest means of annulling self is approaching such a shrine as the Cottage of Burns—we need not think of his misery—that is all gone —bad luck to it—I shall look upon it hereafter with unmixed pleasure as I do upon my Stratford on ⟨and⟩ Avon day with Bailey [8]— I shall fill this sheet for you in the Bardies [9] Country, going no further than this till I get into the Town of Ayr which will be a 9 miles' walk to Tea—We [1] were talking on different and indifferent things, when on a sudden we turned a corner upon the immediate County of Air—the Sight was as rich as possible—I had no Conception that the native place of Burns was so beautiful—the Idea I had was more desolate, his rigs of Barley [2] seemed always to me but a few strips of Green on a cold hill—O prejudice! it was rich as Devon—I endeavour'd to drink in the Prospect, that I might spin it out to you as the silkworm makes silk from Mulbery leaves —I cannot recollect it—Besides all the Beauty, there were the Mountains of Annan [3] Isle, black and huge over the Sea—We came down upon every thing suddenly—there were in our way, the 'bonny Doon,' [4] with the Brig that Tam O' Shanter cross'ed—Kirk Alloway, Burns's Cottage and then the Brigs of Ayr—First we stood upon the Bridge across the Doon; surrounded by every Phantasy of Green in tree, Meadow, and Hill,—the Stream of the Doon, as a Farmer told us, is covered with trees from head to foot—you know those

[7] Woodhouse here (as at I, 283) underscores the word to show that it is correct.

[8] Bailey wrote to Milnes in May, 1849 (*KC*, II, 271): "Once we took a longer excursion of a day or two, to Stratford upon Avon, to visit the birthplace of Shakespeare. We . . . inscribed our names in addition to the 'numbers numberless' of those which literally blackened the walls: and if those walls have not been washed, or our names wiped out to find place for some others, they will still remain together upon that truly honored wall . . ." (see also I, 332). Similarly in an unpublished letter, July 8, 1814, Joanna Baillie told William Sotheby of visiting Stratford with her sister: "We went to the house & into the room where he [Shakespeare] was born, all written over with names of Princes & Peers & foreigners, who had been there to pay their devotions." According to the *Monthly Magazine*, February, 1818 (XLV, 2), a book for visitors "has latterly been kept at the tomb [of Shakespeare], which it would appear, from this record, is visited by nearly a thousand respectable devotees in every year." Colvin, 1920, p. 150, says that the date of Keats's visit "is fixed as October 2nd by his and Bailey's joint signatures in the visitors' book of Holy Trinity Church." That book seems now to be unknown.

[9] Burns's favorite diminutive of "bard."

[1] Keats is now writing at Kingswells (see I, 331) on July 13 of events in Ayr on July 11. For July 12 see I, 331 n.

[2] The refrain of Burns's song "It was upon a Lammas night."

[3] *For* Arran (see I, 329 n.).

[4] A reference to Burns's "The Banks o' Doon." The clerk wrote "do on," which Woodhouse corrected.

beautiful heaths so fresh against the weather of a summers evening —there was one stretching along behind the trees. I wish I knew always the humour my friends would be in at opening a letter of mine, to suit it to them nearly as possible [5] I could always find an egg shell for Melancholy [6]—and as for Merriment a Witty humour will turn any thing to Account—my head is sometimes in such a whirl in considering the million likings and antipathies of our Moments—that I can get into no settled strain in my Letters—My Wig! Burns and sentimentality coming across you and frank Floodgate [7] in the office—O scenery that thou shouldst be crush'd between two Puns—As for them I venture the rascalliest in the Scotch Region—I hope Brown does not put them punctually in his journal

-stool

—If he does I must sit on the cutty⟨school⟩ all next winter. We Went to Kirk allow'y "a Prophet is no Prophet in his own Country" [8]—We went to the Cottage and took some Whiskey—I wrote a sonnet for the mere sake of writing some lines under the roof—they are so bad I cannot transcribe them [9]—The Man at the Cottage was a great Bore with his Anecdotes—I hate the rascal—his Life consists in fuz, fuzzy,[1] fuzziest—He drinks glasses five for the Quarter and twelve for the hour,[2]—he is a mahogany faced old Jackass who knew Burns—He ought to be kicked for having spoken to him. He calls himself "a curious old Bitch" [3]—but he is a flat old Dog—I sho[d] like to employ Caliph Vatheck to kick him [4]—O the flum-

a

mery of ⟨the⟩ birth place! Cant! Cant! Cant! It is enough to give a spirit the guts-ache—Many a true word they say is spoken in jest

[5] Compare his remark to Georgiana Keats at I, 303.

[6] Compare *As You Like It*, II.v.12–14, "I can suck melancholy out of a song, as a weasel sucks eggs."

[7] Francis Fladgate, Jr. (1799–1892), a member of the Garrick Club and a friend of Horace Smith (see A. H. Beavan, *James and Horace Smith* [1899], pp. 238 f., and Thackeray's *Letters*, ed. G. N. Ray, 4 vols. [Harvard University Press, 1945–1946], *passim*). His father, Francis, of Fladgate, Young, and Jackson, 12 Essex Street, Strand, had at Rice's suggestion taken Reynolds as "an articled pupil" with Rice paying the fee. See I, 181 n.

[8] Mark vi.4, Luke iv.24, John iv.44.

[9] See I, 332 n. [1] Keats probably wrote "fuzzier" (see I, 319 n.).

[2] Coleridge, "Christabel," line 10, "Four for the quarters, and twelve for the hour."

[3] See Burns's "On a Noisy Polemic," line 3, "such a bleth'rin bitch." James Humphry, a Mauchline mason (died 1844), always introduced himself to strangers as "Burns's blethering bitch."

[4] In the novel *Vathek* by William Beckford (1759–1844).

—this may be because his gab hindered my sublimity.—The flat dog made me write a flat sonnet—My dear Reynolds—I cannot write about scenery and visitings [5]—Fancy is indeed less than a present palpable reality, but it is greater than rem⟨a⟩mbrance—(e) you would lift your eyes from Homer only to see close before you the real Isle of Tenedos.—you would rather read Homer afterwards than remember yourself—One song of Burns's is of more worth to you than all I could think for a whole year in his native country—His Misery is a dead weight upon the nimbleness of one's quill—I tried to forget it—to drink Toddy without any Care—to write a merry Sonnet—it wont do—he talked with Bitches—he drank with Blackguards, he was miserable—We can see horribly clear in the works of such a man his whole life, as if we were God's spies.[6]—What were his addresses to Jean in the latter part of his life—I should not speak so to you—yet why not—you are not in the same case—you are in the right path, and you shall not be deceived—I have spoken to you against Marriage, but it was general—the Prospect in those matters has been to me so blank, that I have not been unwilling to die—I would not now, for I have inducements to Life—I must see my little Nephews [7] in America, and I must see you marry your lovely Wife—My sensations are sometimes deadened for weeks together [8]—but believe me I have more than once yearne'd for the time of your happiness to come, as much as I could for myself after the lips of Juliet.—From the tenor of my occasional rhodomontade in chitchat,[9] you might have been deceived concerning me in these points—upon my soul, I have been getting more and more close to you every day, ever since I knew you, and now one of the first pleasures I look to is your happy Marriage [1]—the more, since I have felt the pleasure of loving a sister in Law. I did not think it possible to become so much attached in so short a time—Things like these, and they are real,[2] have made me resolve to have a care of my health—you must be as careful—The

[5] Compare his comments on description at I, 301.

[6] *King Lear*, V.iii.17.

[7] There were no nephews before John (1827) and Clarence (1830).

[8] MBF compares the remarks at I, 173, 186.

[9] Woodhouse in September, 1819 (No. 192), commented on "this sort of Keats-like rhodomontade."

[1] To Eliza Drewe, which was postponed till August 31, 1822.

[2] On this emphatic word see I, 282 n.

rain has stoppd us to day at the end of a dozen Miles,[3] yet we hope to see Loch-Lomond the day after to Morrow;—I will piddle out my information, as Rice says, next Winter at any time when a substitute is wanted for Vingt-un. We bear the fatigue very well.—20 Miles a day in general—A cloud [4] came over us in getting up Skiddaw—I hope to be more lucky in Ben Lomond—and more lucky still in Ben Nevis—what I think you wo^d^ enjoy is poking about Ruins—sometimes Abbey, sometimes Castle. The short stay we made in Ireland has left few remembrances—but an old woman in a dog-kennel Sedan [5] with a pipe in her Mouth, is what I can never forget—I wish I may be able to give you an idea of her—Remember me to your Mother and Sisters, and tell your Mother how I hope she will pardon me for having a scrap of paper pasted in the Book sent to her. I was driven on all sides and had not time to call on Taylor [6]—So Bailey is coming to Cumberland [7]—well, if you'll let me know⟨e⟩ where at Inverness, I [will] [8] call on my return and pass a little time with him—I am glad 'tis not scotland—Tell my friends I do all I can for them, that is drink their healths in Toddy—Perhaps I may have some lines by and by to send you fresh on your own Letter—Tom has a few to shew you.[9]

your affectionate friend
John Keats

Mr J. H. Reynolds
Little Britain
Christs Hospital
London

[3] That is, still at Kingswells, where part of No. 97 (I, 331 f.) was also written. But the rain stopped, and they walked into Glasgow that evening (Bushnell, pp. 287 f., and see I, 332).

[4] Written "Clould."

[5] Woodhouse changes from "Sadan" (see I, 321).

[6] See I, 296 f. Between "sent to her" and "I was driven" Woodhouse inserts: "('from the Author' was written by K. on a scrap of paper which he desired to be pasted into a Copy of Endymion & sent to Mrs Reynolds)."

[7] That is, to Carlisle: see the forwarding address on No. 99.

[8] Woodhouse supplies "(will)."

[9] Woodhouse inserts: "(The lines on Staffa)."

· 97 ·

TO TOM KEATS [1]

10, 11, 13, 14 July 1818

Address: Mr Thos Keats/ Well Walk/ Hampstead/ Middx—/ Single
Postmarks: GLASGOW 14 JUL{Y 14} 400; 10 o'Clock JY 17 1818 FN^n^; 1/2; D 17 JY 17 1818; Addl 1/2

Ah! ken ye what I met the day
  Out oure the Mountains
A coming down by craggis grey
  An mossie fountains
A [2] goud hair'd Marie yeve I pray
  Ane minute's guessing—
For that I met upon the way
  Is past expressing—
As I stood where a rocky brig
  A torrent crosses
I spied upon a misty rig
  A troup o Horses—
And as they trotted down the glen
  I sped to meet them
To see if I might know the Men
  To stop and greet them.
First Willie on his sleek mare came
  At canting gallop
His long hair rustled like a flame
  On board a shallop—
Then came his brother Rab and then
  Young Peggy's Mither
And Peggy too—adown the glen
  They went togither—

[1] *ALS:* British Museum. Endorsed by Tom: "Rec^d^ July 17th
"Ans^d^—D^o^—D^o^"
This letter, as well as No. 101, was loaned to Haydon, who kept it and fixed it in his Journal.

[2] Ah *Garrod* (p. 550, who has other slight variations from this unique text).

I saw her wrappit in her hood
  Fra wind and raining—
⟨There was a blush upon her⟩
Her cheek was flush wi timid blood
  Twixt [3] growth and waning—
She turn'd her dazed head full oft
  For thence her Brithers
Came riding with her Bridegroom [4] soft
  An mony ithers.
Young Tam came up an eyed me quick
  With reddened cheek
Braw Tam was daffed like a chick
  He coud na speak—
Ah Marie they are all 'gane hame
  Through blustring weather
                    full
An every heart is ⟨light on⟩ on flame
  An light as feather
Ah! Marie they are all gone hame
  Fra happy wedding,
Whilst I—Ah is it not a shame?
  Sad tears am shedding—

——— ——— ——— ———

My dear Tom, Belantree [5] July 10
The reason for my writing these lines was that Brown wanted to impose a galloway song upon dilke—but it wont do [6]—The subject I got from meeting a wedding just as we came down into this place—Where I am affraid we shall be emprisoned awhile by the weather—Yesterday we came 27 Miles from Stranraer—enterd Ayrshire a little beyond Cairn, and had our path th[r]ough a delightful Country.[7]

[3] *Written* Fwixt. [4] *Written* Bridegroon.

[5] Ballantrae, Ayrshire, where on July 9, says Brown (see I, 441), they stayed "at a dirty inn—the first of that description we had entered in Scotland."

[6] That is, Dilke will at a glance see that it is not a genuine folk-song. For the same phrase see I, 325, II, 9, 169.

[7] Presumably he means twenty-seven miles from Portpatrick, via Stranraer and Cairn Ryan to Ballantrae. Brown (see I, 440 f.) lyrically describes the enchanting scenery on their walk from Cairn Ryan and the overwhelming view of Ailsa Rock. His Journal suddenly ends here because the "pig-headed" proprietor of the *Plymouth and Devonport Weekly Journal* offended Brown, who wrote to Milnes (*KC*, II, 38): "To his astonishment, in spite of repentant entreaty, he finds he will have no more."

I shall endeavour that you may follow our steps in this walk—it would be uninteresting in a Book of Travels—it can not be interest{ing} but by my having gone through it—When we left Cairn our Road lay half way up the sides of a green mountainous shore, full of Clefts of verdure and eternally varying—sometimes up sometimes down, and over little Bridges going across green chasms of moss rock and trees—winding about every where. After two or three Miles of this we turned suddenly into a magnificent glen [8] finely wooded in Parts—seven Miles long—with a Mountain Stream winding down the Midst—full of cottages in the most happy Situations —the sides of the Hills coverd with sheep—the effect of cattle lowing I never had so finely—At the end we had a gradual ascent and got among the tops of the Mountains whence In a little time I descried in the Sea Ailsa Rock 940 feet hight [9]—it was 15 Miles distant and seemed close upon us—The effect of ailsa with the peculiar perspective of the Sea in connection with the ground we stood on, and the misty rain then falling gave me a complete Idea of a deluge—Ailsa struck me very suddenly—really I was a little alarmed—Thus far had I written before we set out this morning—Now we are at Girvan 13 Miles north of Belantree—Our Walk has been along a more grand shore to day than yesterday—Ailsa beside us all the way—From the heights we could see quite at home Cantire [1] and the large Mountains of ⟨Arran⟩ Annan one of the Hebrides [2]—We are in comfortable Quarters. The Rain we feared held up bravely and it has been 'fu fine this day" [3]—{To-}morrow we sh{all be} at Ayr—

To Ailsa Rock— [4]

Hearken thou craggy ocean pyramid,
  Give answer by [5] thy voice the Sea fowls screams!
  When were thy shoulders mantled in huge Streams?
When from the Sun was thy broad forehead hid?

[8] Glen App.

[9] *For* high *or* height. The height is actually 1114 feet. The next word is written "is."

[1] Kintyre, a hilly peninsula in southern Argyllshire.

[2] He meant the Isle of Arran in the Firth of Clyde (see I, 331).

[3] Adapted from the refrain of Burns's "The Holy Fair": cited by J. C. Maxwell, *NQ*, May 17, 1947, p. 215.

[4] They spent the night of July 10 at the King's Arms, Girvan (Bushnell, p. 142), where Keats wrote "Ailsa Rock" (*KC*, II, 62).

[5] from *Garrod* (p. 490, *q.v.* for details about other, non-autograph texts).

How long ist since the mighty Power bid
Thee heave to airy sleep from fathom dreams—
Sleep in the Lap of Thunder or Sunbeams,
Or when grey clouds are thy cold Coverlid—
Thou answerst not for thou art dead asleep
is but
Thy Life ⟨has been⟩ ⟨will be⟩ two dead eternities
The last in Air, the former in the deep—
First with the Whales, last with the eglle [6] skies—
Drown'd wast thou till an Earthquake made thee steep—
Another cannot wake thy giant Size!

This is the only Sonnet of any worth I have of late written—I hope you will like it.[7] 'T is now the 11th of July and we have come 8 Miles to Breakfast to to Kirkoswald—I hope the next Kirk will be Kirk-Alloway—I have nothing of consequence to say now concerning our Journey—so I will speak as far as I can judge on the irish and Scotch—I know nothing of the higher Classes. Yet I have a persuasion that there the Irish are victorious—As to the 'profanum vulgus' [8] I must incline to the scotch—They never laugh—but they are always comparitively neat and clean—Their constitutions are not so remote and puzzling as the irish—The Scotchman will never give a decision on any point—he will never commit himself in a sentence which may be refered to as a meridian [9] in his notions of things—so that you do not know him—and yet you may come in nigher neighbourhood to him than to the irishman who commits himself in so many places that it dazes your head—A Scotchman's motive is more easily discovered than an irishman's. A Scotchman will go wisely about to deceive you, an irishman cunningly—An Irishman would bluster out of any discovery to his disadvantage—
Scotchman
A⟨n Irishman⟩ would retire perhaps without much desire of revenge —An Irishman likes to be thought a gallous [1] fellow—A scotchman is contented with himself—It seems to me they are both sensible of the Character they hold in England and act accordingly to Eng-

[6] eagle- *Garrod.*

[7] *Blackwood's Edinburgh Magazine*, December, 1819 (VI, 239), however, ridiculed "Mister John Keates standing on the sea-shore at Dunbar, without a neckcloth, according to custom of Cockaigne, and cross-questioning the Craig of Ailsa!"

[8] Horace, *Odes*, III.i.1 (see I, 414).

[9] See this figure also at II, 167, 211, 227.

[1] Partridge defines "gallus" or "gallows" as "fine [fellow]."

TEIGNMOUTH, DEVON, AS IT LOOKED IN KEATS'S DAY

From a print in the Holman Collection,
Keats Room, Houghton Library

ST. STEPHEN'S, COLEMAN STREET, THE "KEATS CHURCH" (DESTROYED BY ENEMY ACTION)

From a photograph made by E. J. Goodwin in the Holman Collection, Keats Room, Houghton Library

lishmen—Thus the Scotchman will become over grave and over decent and the Irishman over-impetuous. I like a Scotchman best because he is less of a bore—I like the Irishman best because he ought to be more comfortable—The Scotchman has made up his Mind within himself in a sort of snail shell wisdom—The Irishman is full of strong headed instinct—The Scotchman is farther in Humanity than the Irishman—there his [2] will stick perhaps when the Irishman shall be refined beyond him—for the former thinks he cannot be improved the latter would grasp at it for ever, place but the good plain before him. Maybole—Since breakfast we have come only four Miles to dinner, not merely, for we have examined in the {way} t{wo} Ruins, one of them very fine called Crossragual Abbey.[3] there is a winding Staircase to the top of a little Watch Tower. July 13. *Kingswells*—I have been writing to Reynolds [4]—therefore any particulars since Kirkoswald have escaped me—from said kirk we went to Maybole to dinner—then we set forward to Burnes's town Ayr [5] —the Approach to it is extremely fine—quite outwent my expectations richly meadowed, wooded, heathed and rivuleted—with a grand Sea view terminated by the black Mountains of the isle of Annan.[6] As soon as I saw them so nearly I said to myself 'How is it they did not beckon Burns to some grand attempt at Epic'—The bonny Doon is the sweetest river I ever saw overhung [7] with fine trees as far as we could see—we stood some time on the Brig across it, over which Tam o' shanter fled—we took a pinch of snuff on the key stone—Then we proceeded to 'auld Kirk Alloway' [8]—As we were looking at it a Farmer pointed out the spots where Mungo's Mither hang'd hersel' [9] and 'drunken Charlie brake's neck's bane' [1] —Then we proceeded to the Cottage he was born in—there was a board to that effect by the door Side—it had the same effect as the

[2] *For* he.

[3] Founded in 1240, two miles southwest of Maybole. Robert Heron, *Observations Made in a Journey through the Western Counties of Scotland* (Perth, 1793), II, 326 f., says that the "ruinous castle of *Baltersan* . . . standing near, I should suppose to have been a palace for the abbots" of Crossraguel Abbey.

[4] See No. 96. Keats added nothing to Nos. 97 or 96 on July 12. On that day, Bushnell (p. 286) conjectures, he and Brown "covered only twelve miles, along the coast to Monkton and then inland to Kilmarnock, after a morning's sight-seeing in Ayr." They dined with a traveler, who talked about Kean (see I, 332).

[5] On July 11.

[6] *For* Arran (see I, 329 n.).

[7] *Written* ovelhung.

[8] "Tam o' Shanter," line 32. The kirk itself was a ruin.

[9] "Tam o' Shanter," line 96.

[1] "Tam o' Shanter," line 92.

same sort of memorial at Stradford on Avon [2]—We drank some Toddy to Burns's Memory with an old Man who knew Burns—damn him—and damn his Anecdotes—he was a great bore—it was impossible for a Southren to understand above 5 words in a hundred—There was something good in his description of Burns's melancholy the last time he saw him. I was determined to write a sonnet in the Cottage—I did—but it is so bad I cannot venture it here [3]—Next we walked into Ayr Town and before we went to Tea, saw the new Brig and the Auld Brig and wallace tower [4]—Yesterday [5] we dinned with a Traveller—We were talking about Kean—He said he had seen him at Glasgow [6] 'in Othello in the Jew, I me an er, er, er, the Jew in Shylock' He got bother'd completely in vague ideas of the Jew in Othello, Shylock in the Jew, Shylock in Othello, Othello in Shylock, the Jew in Othello &c &c &c he left himself in a mess at last—Still satisfied with himself he went to the Window and gave an abortive whistle of some tune or other—it might have been Handel. There is no end to these Mistakes—he'll go and tell people how he has seen 'Malvolio in the Countess' 'Twehth [7] night in 'Midsummer nights dream—Bottom in much ado about Nothing—Viola in Barrymore [8]—Antony in Cleopatra—Falstaff in the mouse Trap. [9]—July 14 We enterd Glasgow last Evening under the most oppressive Stare a body could feel—When we had crossed the Bridge Brown look'd back and said its whole pop{ulation} had turned to wonder at us—we came on till a drunken Man came up to me—I put him off with my Arm—he returned all up in Arms saying aloud that, 'he had seen all foreigners bu-u-u t he never saw the like o' me—I was obliged to mention the word Officer and Police before he would desist—The City of Glasgow I take to be a very fine one—I was astonished to hear it was twice the size of

[2] See I, 323.

[3] Bad as it is (see I, 324), Brown preserved a copy of "This mortal body of a thousand days," which was first printed by Milnes, I, 159. In his *Life of John Keats*, however (*KC*, II, 62), Brown says that the conversion of Burns's cottage "into a whiskey-shop, together with its drunken landlord, went far towards the annihilation of his [Keats's] poetic power."

[4] Of course Keats had in mind Burns's "The Brigs of Ayr." A new tower in honor of Wallace replaced the old High Street structure in 1835.

[5] July 12.

[6] According to Giles Playfair's *Kean* (New York, 1939), pp. 137, 152, Kean acted every night at Glasgow during Passion Week, 1815.

[7] So apparently.

[8] Blunden, p. 499, says the reference is to William Barrymore, who played Orsino.

[9] *Hamlet*, III.ii.247.

Edinburgh—It is built of Stone and has a much more solid appearance than London—We shall see the Cathedra{l} this morning—they have devilled it into a 'High Kirk [1]—I want very much to know the name of the Ship George is g{one} in—also what port he will land in [2]—I know ⟨k⟩nothing about it—I hope you are leading a quiet Life and gradually improving—Make a long lounge of the whole Summer—by the time the Leaves fall I shall be near you with plenty of confab—there are a thousand things I cannot write—Take care of yourself—I mean in not being vexed or bothered at any thing—God bless you!

John—

· 98 ·

TO TOM KEATS [1]

17, 18, 20, 21 July 1818

Address: Mr Thos Keats/ Well Walk/ Hampstead/ Middx—/ Single
Postmark: 10 o'Clock JY 30 1818 FN^n^; GL{ASGOW} 23 . . . 405; 1/2

My dear Tom, Cairn-something July 17th [2]—

Here's Brown going on so that I cannot bring to Mind how the two last days have vanished—for example he says 'The Lady of the Lake went to Rock herself to sleep on Arthur's seat and the Lord of the Isles coming to Press a Piece and seeing her Assleap remembered their last meeting at Corry stone Water so touching her with one hand on the Vallis Lucis while he [3] other un-Derwent her Whitehaven, Ireby stifled her clack man on, that he might her Anglesea

[1] The cathedral church of St. Mungo. [2] It was Philadelphia.

[1] *ALS:* Keats Museum. There is a facsimile in Williamson, plates XIII–XVI. Oddly enough this letter was in the possession of Severn, who on October 6, 1845 (*KC*, II, 131), offered to send it to Milnes. The latter accepted the offer, and had a copy made which is now in the Harvard Keats Collection.

[2] Bushnell, pp. 156 f., suggests that on July 14, after seeing the Glasgow cathedral church, Brown and Keats walked down the Clyde fourteen miles to Dumbarton and on July 15 up the Leven and along Loch Lomond twenty-one miles to Tarbet, and that on July 16 they rambled and rested at Tarbet, starting early on July 17 for Cairndow and Inverary.

[3] *For* the.

and give her a Buchanan and said.' I told you last how we were stared at in Glasgow—we are not out of the Crowd yet—Steam Boats on Loch Lomond and Barouches on its sides take a little from the Pleasure of such romantic chaps as Brown and I—The Banks of the Clyde are extremely beautiful—the north End of Loch Lomond grand in excess—the entrance at the lower end to the narrow part from a little distance is precious good—the Evening was beautiful nothing could surpass our fortune in the weather—yet was I worldly enough to wish for a fleet of chivalry Barges with Trumpets and Banners just to die away before me into that blue place among the mountains—I must give you an outline as well as I can [4] Not B— the Water was a fine Blue silverd and the Mountains a dark purple the Sun setting aslant behind them—meantime the head of ben Lomond was covered with a rich Pink Cloud—We did not ascend Ben Lomond—the price being very high and a half a day of rest being quite acceptable—We were up at 4 this morning and have walked to breakfast 15 Miles through two t[r]emendous Glens—at the end of the first there is a place called rest and be thankful which we took for an Inn—it was nothing but a Stone [5] and so we were cheated into 5 more Miles to Breakfast—I have just been bathing in Loch fine [6] a saltwater Lake opposite the Window—quite pat and fresh but for the cursed Gad flies—damn 'em they have been at me ever since I left the Swan and two necks [7]—

All gentle folks who owe a grudge
  To any living thing
Open your ears and stay your tudge [8]
  Whilst I in dudgeon sing—

The gad fly he hath stung me sore
  O may he ne'er sting you!
But we have many a horrid bore
  He may sting black and blue.

[4] A rough pen sketch is given here.

[5] At the top of Glen Croe, Argyllshire, is a stone bench with the inscription "Rest and be thankful." After passing through Glen Kinglas, Keats and Brown had breakfast at Cairndow Inn (Bushnell, p. 179), where the former began to write the present letter.

[6] Loch Fyne.

[7] William Kingford's coffeehouse and hotel, the Swan with Two Necks, Lad Lane, was a well-known coach station. See I, 295 n.

[8] *For* trudge.

Has any here an old grey Mare
  With three Legs all her store
O put it to her Buttocks bare
  And Straight she'll run on four

Has any here a Lawyer suit
  Of 17, 43
Take Lawyer's nose and put it to 't
  And you the end will see

Is there a Man in Parliament
  Dum founder'd in his speech
O let his neighbour make a rent
  And put one in his breech

O Lowther [9] how much better thou
  Hadst figur'd to'ther day
When to the folks thou madst a bow
  And hadst no more to say

If lucky gad fly had but ta'en
  His seat upon thine A—e
And put thee to a little pain
  To save thee from a worse.

Better than Southey it had been
  Better than Mr D——
Better than Wordsworth too I ween
  Better than Mr V—— [1]

Forgive me pray good people all
  For deviating so
In spirit sure I had a call—
  And now I on will go—

Has any here a daughter fair
  Too fond of reading novels

[9] See I, 299 n.

[1] MBF suggests that D. is Robert Saunders Dundas, second Viscount Melville (1771–1851), and that V. is Nicholas Vansittart, first Baron Bexley (1766–1851).

Too apt to fall in love with care
And charming Mister Lovels [2]

O put a gadfly to that thing
She keeps so white and pert
I mean the finger for the ring
And it will breed a Wert—

Has any here a pious spouse
Who seven times a day
Scolds as King David pray'd; [3] to chouse
And have her holy way—

O let a Gadfly's litt[l]e sting
Persuade her sacred tongue
That noises are a common thing
But that her bell has rung

And as this is the summum bo
Num of all conquering
I leave withouten wordes mo'
The Gadfly's little sting

Last [4] Evening we came round the End of Loch Fine to Inverary—the Duke of Argyle's Castle [5] is very modern magnificent and more so from the place it is in the woods seem old enough to remember to or three changes in the Crags about them—the Lake was beautiful and there was a Band at a distance by the Castle. I must say I enjoyed to or three common tunes—but nothing could stifle the horrors of a solo on the Bag-pipe—I thought the Beast would never have done—Yet was I doomed to hear another—On ente[r]ing Inverary we saw a Play Bill—Brown was knock'd up from new shoes—so I went to the Barn alone where I saw the Stranger accompanied by a Bag pipe—There they went on about 'interesting creaters' and 'human nater'—till the Curtain fell and then Came the

[2] As MBF notes, the hero of Scott's *Antiquary*.
[3] Psalms cxix.164.
[4] Keats is now writing on July 18 at Cladich.
[5] The castle of George William Campbell, sixth duke (1768–1839), was on Loch Shira near Inverary.

Bag pipe—When M[rs] Haller fainted down went the Curtain and out came the Bagpipe—at the heartrending, shoemending reconciliation the Piper blew amain—I never read or saw this play before; not the Bag pipe, nor the wretched players themselves were little in comparison with it—thank heaven it has been scoffed at lately almost to a fashion— [6]

Of late two dainties w⟨h⟩ere before me plac'd
  Sweet holy pure sacred and innocent
  From the ninth sphere to me benignly sent
That Gods might know my own particlar taste—
First the soft bag⟨e⟩ pipe mourn'd with zealous haste
  The Stranger next with head on bosom bent
  Sigh'd; rueful again the piteous bag-pipe went
                ings fresh did
Again the Stranger sigh⟨d in discontent⟩ waste
O Bag-pipe thou didst steal my heart away
  O Stranger thou my nerves from Pipe didst charm
O Bag pipe—thou did'st reassert thy sway
  Again thou Stranger gave'st me fresh alarm—
Alas! I could not choose. Ah! my poor heart
Mum chance art thou with both obliged to part.

I think we are the luckiest fellows in Christendom—Brown could not proced this morning on account of his feet and lo there is thunder and rain—July 20th [7] For these two days past we have been so badly accomodated more particularly in coarse food that I have not been at all in cue to write. Last night poor Brown with his feet blistered and scarcely able to walk, after a trudge of 20 Miles down the Side of Loch Awe had no supper but Eggs and Oat Cake—we

[6] A play by Augustus von Kotzebue which Benjamin Thompson (1776?–1816) included in his translation, *The German Theatre* (6 vols., 1801), vol. I. *The Stranger* was first acted at Drury Lane on March 24, 1798, with John Philip Kemble as the Stranger, Mrs. Siddons as the heroine. Mrs. Haller, the erring Countess Waldbourg, faints at the end of Act IV, is reconciled with her husband (the Stranger) in the final scene. Keats had probably read the parody by James Smith in *Rejected Addresses.* Mrs. Clement Parsons, *The Incomparable Siddons* (1909), pp. 156–158, says that Mrs. Siddons acted Mrs. Haller twenty-six times in 1798, and that the "British critics, to a man, fell upon the play." Reynolds, too, ran it down in the *Champion,* March 2, 1817, as "among the worst" specimens of German drama. The *European Magazine,* May, 1816 (LXIX, 445), however, praised Miss O'Neill and Mr. Young, who acted it on May 9 and 16, and in May, 1818 (LXXIII, 432), attacked it only on moral grounds—for its tenderness to a "fallen woman."

[7] Bushnell, pp. 289–291, shows that Keats is now writing at Ford.

have lost the sight of white bread entirely—Now we had eaten nothing but Eggs all day—about 10 a piece and they had become sickening—. To day we have fared rather better—but no oat Cake wanting—we had a small Chicken and even a good bottle of Port—but all together the fare is too coarse—I feel it a little—another week will break us in—I forgot to tell you that when we came through Glencroe it was early in the morning and we were pleased with the noise of Shepherds Sheep and dogs in the misty heights close above us—we saw none of them for some time, till two came in sight creeping among the Craggs like Emmets, yet their voices came quite plainly to us—The Approach to Loch Awe was very solemn towards nightfall—the first glance was a streak of water deep in the Bases of large black Mountains—We had come along a complete mountain road, where if one listened there was not a sound but that of Mountain Streams We walked 20 Miles by the side of Loch Awe—evey ten steps creating a new and beautiful picture—sometimes through little wood—there are two islands on the Lake each with a beautiful ruin—one of them rich in ivy [8]—We are detained this morning by the rain. I will tell you exactly where we are—We are between Loch Craignish and the Sea just opposite Long Island [9]—Yesterday our walk was of this description—the near Hills were not very lofty but many of their Steeps beautifully wooded—the distant Mountains in the Hebrides very grand the Saltwater Lakes coming up between Crags and Islands fulltided and scarcely ruffled—sometimes appearing as one large Lake, sometimes as th[r]ee distinct ones in different directions—At one point we saw afar off a rocky opening into the main Sea—We have also seen an Eagle or two. They move about without the least motion of Wings when in an indolent fit—I am for the first time in a country where a foreign Language is spoken—they gabble away Gælic at a vast rate—numbers of them speak English—There are not many Kilts in Argylshire—At Fort William they say a Man is not admitted into Society without one—the Ladies there have a horror at the indecency of Breeches. I cannot give you a better idea of Highland Life than by

[8] *Anderson's Tourist's Guide through Scotland* (Edinburgh, 1837), p. 118, says, "*Innishail,* one of the most conspicuous of the islands, contains the ruins of a convent; and on Innis-Chonnel are the remains of a castle, which belongs to the family of Argyle." With the next sentence, "We are detained . . . ," Keats is writing from Kilmelfort on the morning of July 21. See Colvin, p. 140 n., and Bushnell, p. 292.

[9] Luing Island.

describing the place we are in—The Inn or public is by far the best house in the immediate neighbourhood—It has a white front with tolerable windows—the table I am writing on suprises me as being a nice flapped Mehogany one; at the same time the place has no watercloset nor anything like it. You may if you peep see through the floor chinks into the ground rooms. The old Grandmother of the house seems intelligent though not over clean. N.B. No snuff being to be had in the village, she made us some. The Guid Man is a rough looking hardy stout Man who I think does not speak so much English as the Guid wife who is very obliging and sensible and moreover though stockingless, has a pair of old Shoes—Last night some Whisky Men sat up clattering Gælic till I am sure one o'Clock to our great annoyance—There is a Gælic testament on the Drawers in the next room—White and blue China ware has crept all about here—Yesterday there passed a Donkey laden with tin-pots—opposite the Window there are hills in a Mist—a few Ash trees and a mountain stream at a little distance—They possess a few head of Cattle—If you had gone round to the back of the House just now—you would have seen more hills in a Mist—some dozen wretched black Cottages scented of peat smoke which finds is [1] way by the door or a hole in the roof—a girl here and there barefoot There was one little thing driving Cows down a slope like a mad thing—there was another standing at the cowhouse door rather pretty fac'd all up to the ankles in dirt—We [2] have walk'd 15 Miles in a soaking rain to Oban opposite the Isle of Mull which is so near Staffa we had though[t] to pass to it—but the expense is 7 Guineas and those rather extorted—Staffa you see is a fashionable place and therefore every one concerned with it either in this town or the Island are what you call up [3]—'t is like paying sixpence for an apple at the playhouse—this irritated me and Brown was not best pleased—we have therefore resolved to set northward for fort William tomorrow morning—I feel [4] upon a bit of white Bread to day like a Sparrow—it was very fine—I cannot manage the cursed Oatcake—Remember me to all and let me hear a good account of you at Inverness—I am sorry Georgy had not those Lines.[5] Good bye.

Your affectionate Brother

John————

[1] *For* its.

[2] Keats is writing at Oban on the afternoon of July 21.

[3] That is, well-to-do.

[4] *For* fell.

[5] The "Lines" were No. 92, which was returned to Tom Keats.

· 99 ·

TO BENJAMIN BAILEY [1]

18, 22 July 1818

Address: Mr B. Bailey/ J. Bailey Esqre/ Thorney Abbey/ Peterborough—; *readdressed with* Revd *inserted before* Mr *to* Mr Fairbairn's/ Cant Square/ Carlisle
Postmarks: GLASGOW 31 JUL 1818 405; No 4; *and others unreadable*

My dear Bailey, Inverary July 18th

The only day I have had a chance of seeing you when you were last in London I took every advantage of—some devil led you out of the way—Now I have written to Reynolds to tell me where you will be in Cumberland—so that I cannot miss you—and when I see you the first thing I shall do will be to read that about Milton and Ceres and Proserpine [2]—for though I am not going after you to John o' Grotts [3] it will be but poetical to say so. And here Bailey I will say a few words written in a sane and sober Mind, a very scarce thing with me, for they may her{eaf}ter save you a great deal of trouble about me, which you do not deserve, and for which I ought to be ba[s]tinadoed. I carry all matters to an extreme—so that when I have any little vexation it grows in five Minutes into a theme for Sophocles—then and in that temper if I write to any friend I have so little selfpossession that I give him matter for grieving at the very time perhaps when I am laughing at a Pun. Your last Letter made me blush for the pain I had given you—I know my own disposition so well that I am certain of writing many times hereafter in the same strain to you—now you know how far to be-

[1] *ALS:* Harvard. Woodhouse copied this letter in his letter-book, pp. 90–95. John (the address really has "I") Bailey (died 1822) lived at Thornley Abbey, Cambridgeshire, seven miles northeast of Peterborough. It is no doubt his hand that forwarded this misaddressed letter (see Bailey's comments [*KC*, I, 33] to Taylor about its travels) to his newly reverend son. The latter was still at Mr. Fairbairn's when he wrote to John Taylor on August 29 and October 5, 1818 (*KC*, I, 31, 40). Another letter to Taylor of November 9, 1818 (the same, I, 60), has only the address "Carlisle."

[2] See *Paradise Lost*, IV.268–272.

[3] John o'Groat's, the northern extremity of Scotland's mainland (compare the signature to No. 88).

lieve in them—you must allow for imagination—I know I shall not be able to help it. I am sorry you are grieved at my not continuing my visits to little Britain [4]—yet I think I have as far as a Man can do who has Books to read to [5] subjects to think upon—for that reason I have been no where else except to Wentworth place so nigh at hand—moreover I have been too often in a state of health that made me think it prudent no[t] to hazard the night Air—Yet further I will confess to you that I cannot enjoy Society small or numerous—I am certain that our fair friends [6] are glad I should come for the mere sake of my coming; but I am certain I bring with me a Vexation they are better without—If I can possibly at any time feel my temper coming upon me I refrain even from a promised visit. I am certain I have not a right feeling towards Women—at this moment I am striving to be just to them but I cannot—Is it because they fall so far beneath my Boyish imagination? When I was a Schoolboy I though[t] a fair Woman a pure Goddess, my mind was a soft nest in which some one of them slept though she knew it not—I have no right to expect more than their reality. I thought them etherial above Men—I find then [7] perhaps equal—great by comparison is very small—Insult may be inflicted in more ways than by Word or action—one who is tender of being insulted does not like to think an insult against another—I do not like to think insults in a Lady's Company—I commit a Crime with her which absence would have not known—Is it not extraordinary? When among Men I have no evil thoughts, no malice, no spleen—I feel free to speak or to be silent—I can listen and from every one I can learn—my hands are in my pockets I am free from all suspicion and comfortable. When I am among Women I have evil thoughts, malice spleen—I cannot speak or be silent—I am full of Suspicions [8] and therefore listen to no thing—I am in a hurry to be gone—You must be charitable and put all this perversity to my being disappointed since Boyhood—Yet with such feelings I am happier alone among Crowds of men, by myself or with a friend or two—With all this trust me Bailey I have not the least idea that Men of different feelings and inclinations are more short sighted than myself —I never rejoiced more than at my Brother's Marriage and shall

[4] To the George Reynoldses' home. [5] *For* and.

[6] The Reynolds girls, whom Keats soon came to dislike: see I, 394, II, 187.

[7] *For* them. [8] Compare his remark at I, 292.

do so at that of any of my friends[9]—. I must absolutely get over this—but how? The only way is to find the root of evil, and so cure it "with backward mutters of dissevering Power"[1] That is a difficult thing; for an obstinate Prejudice can seldom be produced but from a gordian complication of feelings, which must take time to unravell⟨ed⟩ and care to keep unravelled—I could say a good deal about this but I will leave it in hopes of better and more worthy dispositions—and also content that I am wronging no one, for after all I do think better of Womankind than to suppose they care whether Mister John Keats five feet hight likes them or not. You appear to wish to avoid any words on this subject—don't think it a bore my dear fellow—it shall be my Amen—I should not have consented to myself these four Months[2] tramping in the highlands but that I thought it would give me more experience, rub off more Prejudice, use [me][3] to more hardship, identify finer scenes load me with grander Mountains, and strengthen more my reach in Poetry, than would stopping at home among Books even though I should reach Homer—By this time I am comparitively a a mountaineer—I have been among wilds and Mountains too much to break out much about the[i]r Grandeur. I have fed upon Oat cake—not long enough to be very much attached to it—The first Mountains I saw, though not so large as some I have since seen, weighed very solemnly upon me. The effect is wearing away—yet I like them mainely—We have come this evening[4] with a Guide, for without was impossible, into the middle of the Isle of Mull, pursuing our cheap journey to Iona and perhaps staffa—We would not follow the common and fashionable mode from the great imposition of expense. We have come over heath and rock and river and bog to what in England would be called a horrid place—yet it belongs to a Shepherd pretty well off perhaps—The family speak not a word but gælic and we have not yet seen their faces for the smoke which after visiting every cr{a}nny, (not excepting my eyes very much incommoded

[9] But see his remarks on Bailey's and Haslam's marriages at II, 66 f., 240.

[1] *Comus*, line 816 (HBF, 1895).

[2] The time he *planned* to take.

[3] Supplied by Woodhouse.

[4] July 22. On July 18, after writing the first part of this letter, Keats walked with Brown to Cladich on Loch Awe; on July 19 through Port-in-Sherrich to Ford; on July 20 to Kilmelfort; on July 21 to Oban; while on July 22 they ferried to the island of Kerrera and then to the island of Mull, where they spent the night at some cottage in Glen More. At that cottage Keats finished No. 99. See No. 100 and Bushnell, pp. 191 f., 302.

for writing), finds it [5] way out at the {door.} I am more com{f}ortable than I could have imagined in such a place, and so is Brown —The People are all very kind. We lost our way a little yesterday and enquiring at a Cottage, a yound [6] Woman without a word threw on her cloak and walked a Mile in a missling rain and splashy way to put us right again. I could not have had a greater pleasure in these parts than your mention of my Sister—She is very much prisoned from me—I am affraid it will be some time before I can take her to many places I wish [7]—I trust we shall see you ere long in Cumberland—at least I hope I shall before my visit to America more than once I intend to pass a whole year with George if I live to the completion of the three next—My sisters well-fare and the hopes of such a stay in America [8] will make me observe your advice—I shall be prudent and more careful of my health than I have beeen [9]—I hope you will be about paying your first visit to Town after settling when we come into Cumberland—Cumberland however will be no distance to me after my present journey—I shall spin to you [1] a minute—I begin to get rather a contempt for distances. I hope you will have a nice convenient room for a Library. Now you are so well in health do keep it up by never missing your dinner, by not reading hard and by taking proper exercise. You'll have a horse I suppose so you must make a point of sweating him. You say I must study Dante—well the only Books I have with me are those three little Volumes.[2] I read that fine passage you mention a few days ago. Your Letter followed me from Hampstead to Port Patrick and thence to Glasgow—you must think me by this time a very pretty fellow—One of the pleasantest bouts we have had was our walk to Burns's Cottage, over the Doon and past Kirk Alloway —I had determined to write a Sonnet in the Cottage. I did but lauk it was so wretched I destroyed it [3]—howev^{r} in a few days afterwards

[5] *For* its. [6] *For* young.

[7] Commenting on this passage, as printed by Milnes, I, 178, Bailey wrote in 1849 (*KC*, II, 279): "John always spoke very tenderly of his sister . . . ; but the guardians, I apprehend, had some feelings of repugnance to her being at that time under the protection of himself & his brothers."

[8] On his plans for travel see also I, 147, 172, 264, 268, 415, II, 111, 114, and the Index. [9] *Sic.* [1] Woodhouse and Milnes, I, 178, have "you [in]."

[2] See his comments about Cary at I, 294. Cary's complete translation of the *Divine Comedy* had been published in three 32mo volumes by Taylor and Hessey in 1814. The set that Keats took with him and afterwards gave to Fanny Brawne was owned by T. J. Wise, A. E. Newton, and F. W. Allsopp before passing into the hands of L. M. Rabinowitz, New York. [3] See I, 324, 332 n.

I wrote some lines cousin-german to the Circumstance which I will transcribe or rather cross scribe in the front of this—Reynolds's illness has made him a new Man—he will be stronger than ever—before I left London he was really getting a fat face—Brown keeps on writing volumes of adventures to Dilke—when we get in of an evening and I have perhaps taken my rest on a couple of Chairs he affronts my indolence and Luxury by pulling out of his knapsack 1st his paper—2ndy his pens and last his ink—Now I would not care [4] if he would change about a little—I say now, why not Bailey take out his pens first sometimes—But I might as well tell a hen to hold up her head before she drinks instead of afterwards—Your affectionate friend

John Keats—

There is a joy [5] in footing slow across a silent plain [6]
Where Patriot Battle has been fought when Glory had the gain;
There is a pleasure on the heath where Druids old have been,
Where Mantles grey have rustled by and swept the nettles green:
There is a joy in every spot, made known by times of old,
New to the feet, although the tale a hundred times be told:
There is a deeper joy than all, more solemn in the heart,
More parching to the tongue than all, of more divine a smart,
When weary feet forget themselves upon a pleasant turf,
Upon hot sand, or flinty road, or Sea shore iron scurf,
Toward the Castle or the Cot where long ago was born
One who was great through mortal days and died of fame unshorn.
Light Hether bells may tremble then, but they are far away;
Woodlark may sing from sandy fern,—the Sun may hear his Lay;
Runnels may kiss the grass on shelves and shallows clear
But their low voices are not heard though come on travels drear;
Bloodred the sun may set b[e]hind black mountain peaks;
Blue tides may sluice and drench their time in Caves and weedy creeks;
Eagles may seem to sleep wing wide upon the Air;
Ring doves may fly convuls'd across to some high cedar'd lair;

[4] *Written* cure.

[5] charm *Garrod* (*q.v.*, pp. 490–92, for variants in other texts), but the repetition in lines 5 and 7 shows that "joy" is the correct reading.

[6] Brown printed part of these verses in the *New Monthly Magazine*, IV (1822), 252, and Hunt printed them all in the *Examiner*, July 14, 1822, p. 445.

But the forgotten eye is still fast wedded to the ground—
As Palmer's that with weariness mid desert shrine hath found.
At such a time the Soul's a Child, in Childhood is the brain
Forgotten is the worldly heart—alone, it beats in vain—
Aye if a Madman could have leave to pass a healthful day,
To tell his forehead's swoon and faint when first began decay,
He might make tremble many a Man whose Spirit had gone forth
To find a Bard's low Cradle place about the silent north.
Scanty the hour and few the steps beyond the Bourn of Care,
Beyond the sweet and bitter world—beyond it unaware;
Scanty the hour and few the steps because a longer stay
Would bar return and make a Man forget his mortal way.
O horrible! to lose the sight of well remember'd face,
Of Brother's eyes, Of Sister's Brow, constant to every place;
Filling the Air as on we move with Portraiture intense
More warm than those heroic tints that fill a Painter's sense—
When Shapes of old come striding by and visages of old,
Locks shining black, hair scanty grey and passions manifold.
No, No that horror cannot be—for at the Cable's length
Man feels the gentle Anchor pull and gladdens in its strength—
One hour half ideot he stands by mossy waterfall,
But in the very next he reads his Soul's memorial:
He reads it on the Mountain's height where chance he may sit
down
Upon rough marble diadem, that Hills eternal crown.
Yet be the Anchor e'er so fast, room is there for a prayer
That Man may never loose his Mind {on} Mountains bleak and
bare;
That he may stray league after League some great Berthplace to
find,
And keep his vision clear from speck, his inward sight unblind— [7]

[7] It was just before receiving this letter that Bailey sent Keats an autographed copy of Livy dated "July, 1818," and now in the Keats Museum.

· 100 ·

TO TOM KEATS [1]

23, 26 July 1818

Address: Mr Thos Keats/ Well Walk/ Hampstead/ Middx— *Postmarks:* GLASGOW 31 JUL 1818 405; 10 o'Clock AU 3 18{18} FNn; 1/2; . . . 3 AU 3 1818

Dun an cullen [2]

My dear Tom,

Just after my last had gone to the Post in came one of the Men with whom we endeavoured to agree about going to Staffa—he said what a pitty it was we should turn aside and not see the Curiosities. So we had a little talk and finally agreed that he should be our guide across the Isle of Mull—We set out,[3] crossed two ferries, one to the isle of Kerrara of little distance, the other from Kerrara to Mull 9 Miles across—we did it in forty minutes with a fine Breeze—The road through the Island, or rather the track is the most dreary you can think of—betwe[e]n dreary Mountains—over bog and rock and river with our Breeches tucked up and our Stockings in hand—About eight o Clock we arrived at a shepherd's Hut [4] into w{h}ich we could scarcely get for the Smoke through a door lower than my shoulders—We found our way into a little compartment⟨s⟩ with the rafters and turf thatch blackened with smoke—the earth floor full of Hills and Dales—We had some white Bread with us, made a good Supper and slept in our Clothes in some Blankets, our Guide snored on another little bed about an Arm's length off—This morning we

[1] *ALS:* Harvard. Part of this letter also (see the first note to No. 91) was printed by James Freeman Clarke in the *Western Messenger*, July, 1836 (I, 820–823). The original is endorsed by Tom:
"Recd August 3rd
"Ansd Do Do"
Jeffrey likewise copied it with his usual changes and omissions and endorsed it: "Copied August 1845." Keats copied a good part of No. 100 into No. 199 (II, 196–200), making a few changes.

[2] The "mansion" of Derry-na-Cullen, at the foot of Glen More, where Keats and Brown breakfasted on July 23 before walking, presumably, to Bunessan (Bushnell, pp. 208, 302).

[3] On July 22.

[4] In Glen More (see I, 342 n.).

THE TWA BRIGS, AYR

From a nineteenth-century engraving in the Holman Collection,
Keats Room, Houghton Library

IONA, SCOTLAND

From an early nineteenth-century engraving in the Holman Collection, Keats Room, Houghton Library

IN FINGAL'S CAVE, STAFFA

From an early nineteenth-century engraving in the Holman Collection, Keats Room, Houghton Library

came about sax [5] Miles to Breakfast by rather a better path and we are now in by comparison a Mansion—Our Guide is I think a very obliging fellow—in the way this morning he sang us two Gælic songs—one made by a Mrs Brown on her husband's being drowned the other a jacobin one on Charles Stuart. For some days Brown has been enquiring out his Genealogy here—he thinks his Grandfather came from long Island [6]—he got a parcel of people about him at a Cottage door last Evening—chatted with ane who had been a Miss Brown and who I think from a likeness must have been a Relation—he jawed with the old Woman—flatterd a young one—kissed a child who was affraid of his Spectacles and finally drank a pint of Milk—They handle his Spectacles as we do a sensitive leaf —. July 26th Well [7]—we had a most wretched walk of 37 Miles across the Island of Mull and then we crossed to Iona or Icolmkill from Icolmkill we took a boat at a bargain to take us to Staffa and land us at the head of Loch Nakgal [8] whence we should only have to walk half the distance to Oban again and on a better road—All this is well pass'd and done with this singular piece of Luck that there was an intermission in the bad Weather just as we saw Staffa at which it is impossible to land but in a tolerable Calm Sea—But I will first mention Icolmkill—I know not whether you have heard much about this Island, I never did before I came nigh it. It is rich in the most interesting Antiqu[i]ties. Who would expect to find the ruins of a fine Cathedral Church, of Cloisters, Colleges, Mona[s]taries and Nunneries in so remote an Island? The Beginning of these things was in the sixth Century under the superstition of a would-be Bishop-saint who landed from Ireland and chose the spot from its Beauty—for at that time the now treeless place was covered with magnificent Woods. Columba in the Gaelic is Colm signifying Dove—Kill signifies church and I is as good as Island—so I-colmkill means the Island of Saint Columba's Church [9]—Now this Saint

[5] Burns gave him this word for *six*. Eight words later he wrote "parth" for "path." [6] Presumably the Island of Luing.

[7] They went from Derry-na-Cullen apparently to Bunessan on July 23; then on July 24 by boat to Iona, Staffa, and through Loch na Keal, and presumably passed the night at Salen; Bushnell (p. 302) thinks that on July 25 they went by ferry, via Kerrera, to Oban, where they may have remained through July 29.

[8] Loch na Keal.

[9] *Anderson's Tourist's Guide through Scotland* (Edinburgh, 1837), p. 151, says that St. Columba arrived here from Ireland in 565, and that "Icolmkill signifies the 'Island of Columba's Cell.' " F. N. Robinson tells me that *Colum(b)kill(e)* is the popular name of St. Columba, and that *Icolmkill* means "The Island of the Dove of the Church."

Columba became the Dominic of the barbarian Christians of the north and was famed also far south—but more especially was reverenced by the Scots the Picts the Norwegians the Irish. In a course of years perhaps the Iland was considered the most holy ground of the north, and the old kings of the afore mentioned nations chose it for their burial place—We were shown a spot in the Churchyard where they say 61 kings are buried 48 Scotch from Fergus 2nd to Mac⟨k⟩beth 8 Irish 4 Norwegian and 1 french [1]—they lie in rows compact—Then we were shown other matters of later date but still very ancient—many tombs of Highland Chieftains—their effigies in complete armour face upwards—black and moss covered—Abbots and Bishops of the island always of one of the chief Clans—There were plenty Macleans and Macdonnels, among these latter the famous Macdonel Lord of the Isles [2]—There have been 300 Crosses in the Island but the Presbyterains destroyed all but two,[3] one of which is a very fine one and completely covered with a shaggy coarse Moss—The old Schoolmaster an ignorant little man but reckoned very clever, showed us these things—He is a Macklean [4] and as much above 4 foot as he is under 4 foot 3 inches—he stops at one glass of wiskey unless you press another and at the second unless you press a third. I am puzzled how to give you an Idea of Staffa. It can only be represented by a first rate drawing—One may compare the surface of the Island to a roof—this roof is supported by grand pillars of basalt standing together as thick as honey combs The finest thing is Fingal's Cave—it is entirely a hollowing out of Basalt Pillars. Suppose now the Giants who rebelled against Jove had taken a whole Mass of black Columns and bound them together like bunches of matches—and then with immense Axes had made a cavern in the body of these columns—of course the roof and floor must be composed of the broken ends of the Columns—such is fin-
except that
gal's Cave ⟨expept the⟩ the Sea has done the work of excavations

[1] Many of Keats's details are explained or corrected in Lachlan Maclean's *Historical Account of Iona* (Edinburgh, 1833), pp. 88 f., 92–112, and Florence M. McNeill's *Iona* (1920). The latter says, p. 63, "Here were interred forty-eight crowned kings of Scotland, four of Ireland, and seven of Norway."

[2] Donald Macdonald (died 1420?), second Lord of the Isles. See Maclean, pp. 111 f.

[3] *Anderson's Tourist's Guide* (p. 152) speaks of "two elegant crosses formed of red granite, the one called St Martin's, and the other St John's cross." See also McNeill, p. 69.

[4] Allan Maclean, "the only religious instructor" on Iona, was the schoolmaster in 1790 and was still teaching, aged about 80, when Lachlan Maclean wrote his book (pp. 88 f.).

and is continually dashing there—so that we walk along the sides of the cave on the pillars which are left as if for convenient Stairs—the roof is arched somewhat gothic wise and the length of some of the
50
entire side pillars is ⟨80⟩ feet—About the island you might seat an army of Men each on a pillar—The length of the Cave is 120 feet and from its extremity the view into the sea through the large Arch at the entrance—the colour of the colums is a sort of black with a lurking gloom of purple therin—For solemnity and grandeur it far surpasses the finest Cathedrall—At the extremity of the Cave there is a small perforation [5] into another cave, at which the waters meeting and buffetting each other there is sometimes produced a report as of a cannon heard as far as Iona which must be 12 Miles—As we approached in the boat there was such a fine swell of the sea that the [6] pillars appeared rising imm{ed}iately out of the crystal—But it is impossible to describe it—

Not Aladin magian
Ever such a work began,
Not the Wizard of the dee
Ever such dream could see
Not St John in Patmos isle
In the passion of his toil
When he saw the churches seven
Golden aisled built up in heaven
Gazed at such a rugged wonder.
As I stood its roofing under
Lo! I saw one sleeping there
On the marble cold and bare
While the surges washed his feet
And his garments white did beat
Drench'd about the sombre rocks,
On his neck his well grown locks
Lifted dry above the Main
Were upon the curl again—
What is this and what art thou?
Whisper'd I and touch'd his brow.
What art thou and what is this?

[5] *Apparently* prerforation. [6] *Written* the the.

Whisper'd I and strove to kiss
his eyes.
The Spirits hand to wake ⟨him up⟩
Up he started in a thrice.[7]
I am Lycidas said he
Fam'd in funeral Minstrelsey—
This was architected thus
By the great Oceanus
Here his mighty waters play
Hollow Organs all the day
Here by turns his dolphins all
Finny palmer's great and small
Come to pay devotion due—
Each a mouth of pea[r]ls must strew[8]
⟨Many a Mortal comes to see
This Cathedrall of the S⟩
Many a Mortal of these days
Dares to pass our sacred ways
Dares to touch audaciously
This Cathedral of the Sea—
I have been the Pontif priest
Where the Waters never rest
Where a fledgy sea bird choir
Soars for ever—holy fire
I have hid from Mortal Man.
⟨Old⟩ Proteus is my Sacristan.
But the stupid eye of Mortal
Hath pass'd beyond the Rocky portal
So for ever will I leave
Such a taint and soon unweave
All the magic of the place—
'T is now free to stupid face
To cutters and to fashion boats
To cravats and to Petticoats.
The great Sea shall war it down
For its fame shall not be blow{n}

[7] trice *Garrod* (who has, pp. 492–494, various other slight changes in the text).
[8] The word is crowded and blurred and may be intended for "shew."

At every [9] farthing quadrille dance.
So saying with a Spirits glance
He dived— [1]

I am sorry I am so indolent as to write such stuff as this—it cant be help'd—The western coast of Scotland is a most strange place—it is composed of rocks Mountains, mountainous and rocky Islands intersected by Lochs—you can go but a small distance any where from salt water in the highlands
I have a slight sore throat and think it best to stay a day or two at {O}ban.[2] Then we shall proceed to Fort William and Inverness—Where I am anxious to be on account of [3] a Letter from you—Brown in his Letters puts down every little circumstance I should like to do the same but I {c}onfess myself too indolent and besides next winter {ever}y thing will come up in prime order as we verge on such and such things Have you heard in any way of George? I should think by this time he must have landed—I in my carelessness never thought of knowing where a letter would find him on the other side—I think Baltimore but I am affraid of directing to the wrong place—I shall begin some chequer work for him directly and it will be ripe for the post by the time I hear from you next after this—I assure you I often long for a seat and a Cup o' tea at well Walk—especially now that mountains, castles and Lakes are becoming common to me—yet I would rather summer it out for on the whole I am happier than when I have time to be glum—perhaps it may cure me—Immediately on my return I shall begin studying hard with a peep at the theatre now and then—and depend upon it I shall be very luxurious—With respect to Women I think I shall be able to conquer my passions hereafter better than I have yet done [4]—You will help me to talk of george next winter and we will go now and then to see Fanny—Let me hear a good account of your health and comfort telling me truly how you do alone—

Remember me to all including M^r^ and Mrs Bentley—

Your most affectionate Brother

Joh{n}—

[9] each *Garrod.* See also the partial version of the poem at II, 199 f.
[1] Brown wrote (*KC*, II, 63), "I never could induce him to finish" the poem.
[2] See I, 352 n. [3] *Written* if.
[4] In his transcript Jeffrey, perhaps naturally, omitted this sentence and others.

· 101 ·

TO TOM KEATS [1]

3, 6 August 1818 [2]

Address: Mr Thos Keats/ Well Walk/ Hampstead/ Middx—/ Single
Postmarks: INVERNESS 6 AUG 1818 637 E; TOO LATE; AUG B 9 A 1818; 10 o'Clock AU 12 1818 FNn; B 12 AU 12 1818; 1/2

My dear Tom, Ah mio Ben. Letter Findlay August 3rd

We have made but poor progress Lately, chiefly from bad weather for my throat is in a fair way of getting quite well, so I have had nothing of consequence to tell you till yesterday when we went up Ben Nevis, the highest Mountain in Great Britain—On that account I will never ascend another in this empire—Skiddaw is no thing to it either in height or in difficulty. It is above 4300 [3] feet from the Sea level and Fortwilliam stands at the head of a Salt water Lake,[4] consequently we took it completely from that level. I am heartily glad it is done—it is almost like a fly crawling up a wainscoat—Imagine the task of mounting 10 Saint Pauls without the convenience of Stair cases. We set out about five in the morning with a Guide in the Tartan and Cap and soon arrived at the foot of the first ascent which we immediately began upon—after much fag and tug and a rest and a glass of whiskey apiece we gained the top of the first rise and saw then a tremendous chap above us which the guide said was still far from the top—After the first Rise our way lay along a heath valley in which there was a Loch [5]—after about

[1] *ALS:* Harvard.

[2] Heretofore dated only August 3, but see I, 357 n. Keats and Brown's whereabouts after July 26 are not clear. Bushnell, pp. 296 f., 302, the most reliable guide, thinks they stayed in Oban, July 25–29, and then went on July 30 twelve miles to Portnacroish, on July 31 fourteen miles to Ballachulish, on August 1 twelve miles to Fort William, on August 2 twelve miles up and down Ben Nevis, on August 3 sixteen miles to Letterfinlay, on August 4 to Fort Augustus, on August 5 to Foyers, and on August 6 to Inverness. No. 101 was postmarked at Inverness on August 6, two days before Keats sailed from the nearby port of Cromarty, and it reached London only six days before him (see No. 104). It (like No. 97) was loaned to Haydon, who instead of returning it attached it to his Journal.

[3] Modern gazetteers say 4406. Skiddaw is 3054 feet.

[4] Loch Linnhe.

[5] Lochan Meall-an-t-Suidhe (or Meal-an-Tee): see Bushnell, p. 241.

a Mile in this Valley we began upon the next ascent more fo[r]midable by far than the last and kept mounting with short intervals of rest untill we got above all vegetation, among nothing but loose Stones which lasted us to the very top—the Guide said we had three Miles of a stony ascent—we gained the first tolerable level after the valley to the height of what in the Valley we had thought the top and saw still above us another huge crag which still the Guide said was not the top—to that we made with an obstinate fag and having gained it there came on a Mist, so that from that part to the verry top we walked in a Mist. The whole immense head of the Mountain is composed of large loose stones—thousands of acres—Before we had got half way up we passed large patches of snow and near the top there is a chasm some hundred feet deep completely glutted with it—Talking of chasms they are the finest wonder of the whole —the[y] appear great rents in the very heart of the mountain though they are not, being at the side of it, but other huge crags arising round it give the appearance to Nevis of a shattered heart or Core in itself—These Chasms are 1500 feet in depth and are the most tremendous places I have ever seen—they turn one giddy if you choose to give way to it—We tumbled in large stones and set the echoes at work in fine style. Sometimes these chasms are tolerably clear, sometimes there is a misty cloud which seems to steam up and sometimes they are entirely smothered with clouds—
After a little time the Mist cleared away but still there were large Clouds about attracted by old Ben to a certain distance so as to form as it appeard large dome curtains which kept sailing about, opening and shutting at intervals here and there and everrywhere; so that although we did not see one vast wide extent of prospect all round we saw something perhaps finer—these cloud-veils opening with a dissolving motion and showing us the mountainous region beneath as through a loop hole—these Mouldy[6] loop holes ever varrying and discovering fresh prospect east, west north and South—Then it was misty again and again it was fair—then puff came a cold breeze of wind and bared a craggy chap we had not yet seen though in close neighbourhood—Every now and then we had over head blue Sky clear and the sun pretty wa[r]m. I do not know whether I can give you an Idea of the prospect from a large Mountain top—You are on a stony plain which of course makes you forget you are on

[6] *Probably for* cloudy.

any but low ground—the horison [7] or rather edges of this plain being above 4000 feet above the Sea hide all the Country immediately beneath you, so that the next objects you see all round next to the edges of the flat top are the Summits of Mountains of some distance off—as you move about on all side[s] you see more or less of the near neighbour country according as the Mountain you stand upon is in different parts steep or rounded—but the most new thing of all is the sudden leap of the eye from the extremity of what appears a plain into so vast a distance On ⟨those⟩ one part of the top there is a handsome pile of stones done pointedly by some soldiers of artillery, I climed onto them and so got a little higher than old Ben himself. It was not so ⟨clo⟩ cold as I expected—yet cold enough for a glass of Wiskey now and then—There is not a more fickle thing than the top of a Mountain—what would a Lady give to change her head-dress as often and with as little trouble!—There are a good many red deer upon Ben Nevis we did not see one—the dog we had with us keep [8] a very sharp look out and really languished for a bit of a worry—I have said nothing yet of out [9] getting on among the loose stones large and small sometimes on⟨e⟩ two sometimes on three, sometimes four legs—sometimes two and stick, sometimes three and stick, then four again, then two{,} then a jump, so that we kept on ringing changes on foot, hand, Stick, jump boggl{e,} s[t]umble, foot, hand, foot, (very gingerly) stick again, and then again a game at all fours. After all there was one Mrs Cameron of 50 years of age and the fattest woman in all inverness shire who got up this Mountain some few years ago—true she had her servants but then she had her self—She ought to have hired Sysiphus—"Up the high hill he heaves a huge round [1]—Mrs Cameron" [2] 'T is said a little conversation took place between the mountain and the Lady—After taking a glass of Wiskey as she was tolerably seated at ease she thus begun

M^rs^ C—

Upon my Life Sir Nevis I am pique'd
That I have so far panted tugg'd and reek'd

[7] See I, 159 n. [8] *For* kept. [9] *For* our.

[1] MBF cites Pope's translation of Homer's *Odyssey*, XI.736 (which ends with "round stone").

[2] If Keats made up this yarn, perhaps the name was suggested by the "monument [on the bank of Loch Eil] to the memory of Colonel Cameron, who fell in the battle of Waterloo" (*Anderson's Tourist's Guide through Scotland* [Edinburgh, 1837], p. 129).

To do an honor to your old bald pate
And now am sitting on you just to bate,
Without your paying me one [3] compliment.
Alas 't is so with all, when our intent
Is plain, and in the eye of all Mankind
We fair one's show a preference, too blind!
tail—
You Gentleman immediatly turn ⟨tale⟩.
O let me then my hapless fate bewail!
Ungrateful Baldpate have I not disdaind
The pleasant Valleys—have I not mad braind
Deserrted all my Pickles and preserves
My China closet too—with wretched Nerves
To boot—say wretched ingrate have I not
Let [4] my soft cushion chair and caudle pot.
'T is true I had no corns—no! thank the fates
My Shoemaker was always Mr Bates.
And if not Mr Bates why I'm not old!
Still dumb ungrateful Nevis—still so cold!

(Here the Lady took some more wiskey [5] and was putting even more to her lips when she dashed to the Ground for the Mountain began to grumble which continued for a few Minutes before he thus began,)

Ben Nevis

What whining bit of tongue and Mouth thus dares
Distur'd [6] my Slumber of a thousand years—
Even so long my sleep has been secure
And to be so awaked I'll not endur{e.}
Oh pain—for since the Eagle's earliest scream
I've had a dam'd confounded ugly dream
you?
A Nightmare sure—What Madam was it ⟨true⟩
It cannot be! My old eyes are not true!
*Red-Crag, My Spectacles! Now let me see!
Good Heavens Lady how the gemini

**A domestic of Ben's*/

[3] *Or possibly* paying one one. [4] *For* Left.

[5] whiskey *Garrod* (who has, pp. 559–561, other slight variants). In the line above and once later Keats spelled "Nevis" as "Nevil."

[6] Disturb *Garrod*.

Did you get here? O I shall split my Sides!
I shall earthquake——

M^rs^ C—

Sweet Nevis do not quake, for though I love
You [7] honest Countenance all things above
Truly I should not like to be convey'd
So far into your Bosom—gentle Maid
Loves not too rough a treatment gentle sir
Pray thee be calm and do not quake nor stir
No not a Stone or I shall go in fits—

Ben Nevis

I must—I shall—I meet not such tit bits
I meet not such sweet creatures evey day [8]
By my old night cap night cap night and day
I must have one sweet Buss—I must and shall!
Red [9] Crag!—What Madam can you then repent
Of all the toil and vigour you have spent
To see Ben Nevis and to touch his nose?
Red Crag I say! O I must have you close!
Red crag, there lies beneath my farthest toe
A vein of Sulphur—go dear Red Crag go—
And rub your flinty back against it—budge!
Dear Madam I must kiss you, faith I must!
I must Embrace you with my dearest gust!
*Block-head, d'ye hear—Blockhead I'll make her feel
There lies beneath my east legs northern heel
A cave of young earth dragons—well my boy
Go thithers [1] quick and so complete my joy
Take you a bundle of the largest pines
And where the sun on fiercest Phosphor shines

turn to the beginning [2]

Fire them and ram them in the Dragons' nest
Then will the dragons fry and fizz their best
Until ten thousand now no bigger than

**another domestic of Ben's*

[7] Your *Garrod* (but see I, 121 n.). [8] *Written* evey/ —day.
[9] *Written* Reg. [1] thither *Garrod*.
[2] A direction to Tom to turn to the "crossing" on page 1 of the letter.

Poor Aligators poor things of one span
Will each one swell to twice ten times the size
Of northern whale—then for the tender prize—
The moment then—for then will red Crag rub
His flinty back and I shall kiss and snub
And press my dainty morsel to my breast
Blockhead make haste!
O Muses weep the rest—
The Lady fainted and he thought her dead
So pulled the clouds again about his head
And went to sleep again—soon she was rous'd
By her affrigh[t]ed Servants—next day hous'd
Safe on the lowly ground she bless'd her fate
That fainting fit was not delayed too late

But what surprises me above all is how this Lady got down again—I felt it horribly—'T was the most vile descent—shook me all to pieces [3]—Over leaf you will find a Sonnet I wrote on the top of Ben Nevis [4]—We have just entered Inverness. I have three Letters from you and one [from] Fanny—and one from Dilke I would set about crossing this all over for you but I will first write to Fanny and Mrs Wilie then I will begin another to you [5] and not before because I think it better you should have this as soon as possible—My Sore throat is not quite well and I intend stopping here a few days

Read me a Lesson muse, and speak it loud
Upon the top of Nevis blind in Mist!
I look into the Chasms and a Shroud
Vaprous [6] doth hide them; just so much I wist
Mankind do know of Hell: I look o'erhead
And there is sullen Mist; even so much
Mankind can tell of Heaven: Mist is spread
Before the Earth beneath me—even such
Even so vague is Man's sight of himself.

[3] What follows was written at Inverness on August 6.

[4] Written, that is, on August 2. Brown's *Life of John Keats* (*KC*, II, 63) says: "He sat on the stones, a few feet from the edge of that fearfull precipice, fifteen hundred feet perpendicular from the valley below, and wrote this sonnet."

[5] He did not write to Fanny (see No. 104) or Tom before he sailed on August 8.

[6] Vaporous *Garrod* (*q.v.*, p. 494, for other slight variations from this unique text).

Here are the craggy Stones beneath my feet;
Thus much I know, that a poor witless elf
I tread on them; that all my eye doth meet
Is mist and Crag—not only on this height
But in the World of thought and mental might—

Good bye till tomorrow

Your most affectionate Brother
John—

· 102 ·

TO MRS. JAMES WYLIE [1]

6 August 1818

My dear Madam— Inverness 6th August 1818 [2]

It was a great regret to me that I should leave all my friends, just at the moment when I might have helped to soften away the time for them. I wanted not to leave my Brother Tom, but more especially, beleive me, I should like to have remained near you, were it but for an atom of consolation, after parting with so dear a daughter; My brother George has ever been more than a brother to me, he has been my greatest friend,[3] & I can never forget the sacrifice you have made for his happiness. As I walk along the Mountains here, I am full of these things, & lay in wait, as it were, for the pleasure of seeing you, immediately on my return to town. I wish above all things, to say a word of Comfort to you, but I know not how. It is impossible to prove that black is white, It is impossible to make out, that sorrow is joy or joy is sorrow [4]———Tom tells me that you called on Mr Haslam with a Newspaper giving an account of a Gentleman in a Fur cap, falling over a precipice in Kirkudbrightshire.[5] If it was me, I did it in a dream, or in some magic interval between the first & second cup of tea; which is nothing extraordinary, when we hear that Mahomet, in getting out of

[1] A transcript by Jeffrey, who wrote at the end: "Note. the previous letter was addressed to the Mother of the lady just married to his Brother George—previous to George's departure for America— The following letters [Nos. 120, 137, 159, 199, 215] were written to George Keats & received in America—"

[2] The last figure is scratched out.

[3] See Keats's words at II, 113.

[4] See the Byron quotation at I, 279.

[5] Keats's usual spelling: see I, 310 n.

Bed, upset a jug of water, & whilst it was falling, took a fortnight's trip as it seemed to Heaven: yet was back in time to save one drop of water being spilt.[6] As for Fur caps I do not remember one beside my own, except at Carlisle—this was a very good Fur cap, I met in the High Street, & I daresay was the unfortunate one. I daresay that the fates seeing but two Fur caps in the North, thought it too extraordinary, & so threw the Dies which of them should be drowned. The lot fell upon Jonas—I daresay his name was Jonas. All I hope is, that the gaunt Ladies said not a word about hanging, if they did, I shall one day regret that I was not half drowned [7] in Kirkudbright. Stop! let me see!—being half drowned by falling from a precipice is a very romantic affair—Why should I not take it to myself? Keep my secret & I will. How glorious to be introduced in a drawing room to a Lady who reads Novels, with—"M^r^ so & so —Miss so & so—Miss so & so. this is M^r^ so & so. who fell off a precipice, & was half drowned Now I refer it to you whether I should loose so fine an opportunity of making my fortune—No romance lady could resist me—None—Being run under a Waggon; side lamed at a playhouse; Apoplectic, through Brandy; & a thousand other tolerably decent things for badness would be nothing; but being tumbled over a precipice into the sea—Oh it would make my fortune—especially if you could continue [8] to hint, from this bulletins authority, that I was not upset on my own account, but that I dashed into the waves after Jessy of Dumblane [9]—& pulled her out by the hair—But that, Alas! she was dead or she would have made me happy with her hand—however in this you may use your own discretion—But I must leave joking & seriously aver, that I have

[6] Jack Stillinger, *MLN*, LXXI (1956), 341, refers to what Addison, *Spectator*, No. 94, June 18, 1711 ("Harrison's Edition," II [1786], 187 f.), calls "a famous passage in the Alcoran": "It is there said, that the angel Gabriel took Mahomet out of his bed one morning to give him a sight of all things in the seven heavens, in paradise, and in hell, which the prophet took a distinct view of; and after having held ninety thousand conferences with God, was brought back again to this bed. All this, says the Alcoran, was transacted in so small a space of time, that Mahomet at his return found his bed still warm, and took up an earthen pitcher, which was thrown down at the very instant that the angel Gabriel carried him away, before the water was all spilt."

[7] Referring to the proverb, "He that is born to be hanged will never be drowned."

[8] So correctly printed by Milnes, I, 191, though Keats may have intended to write "contrive."

[9] A reference to "Jessie, The Flow'r o' Dumblane" by Robert Tannahill (1774–1810), in his *Poems & Songs* (1817), pp. 137 f., or more likely to R. A. Smith's "Jessie the Flow'r o' Dumblane, a favorite Scottish Song," which the *European Magazine*, January, 1816 (LXIX, 49 f.), reviewing its fourth edition, said "has obtained more popularity than any other [song] that has appeared for a considerable time."

been *werry* romantic indeed, among these Mountains & Lakes. I have got wet through day after day, eaten oat cake, & drank whiskey, walked up to my knees in Bog, got a sore throat, gone to see Icolmkill & Staffa, met with wholesome food, just here & there as it happened; went up Ben Nevis, & N.B. came down again; [1] Sometimes when I am rather tired, I lean rather languishingly on a Rock, & long for some famous Beauty to get down from her Palfrey in passing; approach me with—her saddle bags—& give me—a dozen or two capital roast beef sandwiches—When I come into a large town, you know there is no putting ones Knapsack into ones fob; so the people stare—We have been taken for Spectacle venders, Razor sellers, Jewellers, travelling linnen drapers, Spies, Excisemen, & many things else,[2] I have no idea of—When I asked for letters at the Post Office, Port Patrick; the man asked what Regiment? [3] I have had a peep also at little Ireland. Tell Henry I have not Camped quite on the bare Earth yet; but nearly as bad, in walking through Mull—for the Shepherds huts you can scarcely breathe in, for the smoke which they seem to endeavour to preserve for smoking on a large scale. Besides riding about 400, we have walked above 600 Miles, & may therefore reckon ourselves as set out. I wish my dear Madam, that one of the greatest pleasures I shall have on my return, will be seeing you & that I shall ever be

Yours with the greatest Respect & sincerity
(signed) John Keats—

Mrs Wylie
Henrietta Street [4] London

[1] He partly quotes the "King of France" nursery rime that goes back at least to James Howell's *Epistolae Ho-Elianae*, May 12, 1620 (ed. Joseph Jacobs [1890], I, 47).
[2] See I, 311. [3] See I, 321.
[4] If this address actually was on the original letter, Mrs. Wylie, whose house was at 3 Romney Street, was in her sister's, Mrs. Millar's, house on Henrietta Street. Mrs. Wylie and her sons entertained Keats at dinner there on September 12, 1819 (II, 186), when Mrs. Millar and her daughter were in the country.

· 103 ·

CHARLES BROWN TO C. W. DILKE, SR.[1]

7 August 1818

Inverness. 7th August 1818.

My dear Sir,

What shall I write about? I am resolved to send you a letter, but where is the subject? I have already stumped away on my ten toes 642 miles, and seen many fine sights, but I am puzzled to know what to make choice of. Suppose I begin with myself,—there must be a pleasure in that,—and, by way of variety, I must bring in Mr Keats. Then, be it known, in the first place, we are in as continued a bustle as an old Dowager at Home. Always moving—moving from one place to another, like Dante's inhabitants of the Sulphur Kingdom in search of cold ground,—prosing over the Map,—calculating distances,—packing up knapsacks,—and paying bills. There's so much for yourself, my dear. "Thank 'ye, Sir." How many miles to the next Town? "Seventeen lucky miles, Sir." That must be at least twenty; come along, Keats; here's your stick; why, we forgot the map!—now for it; seventeen lucky miles! I must have another hole taken up in the strap of my Knapsack. Oh, the misery of coming to the meeting of three roads without a finger post! There's an old woman coming,—God bless her! she'll tell us all about it. Eh! she can't speak English! Repeat the name of the town over in all ways, but the true spelling way, and possibly she may understand. No, we have not got the brogue. Then toss up heads or tails for right or left, and fortune send us the right road! Here's a soaking shower coming! ecod! it rolls between the mountains as if it would drown us. At last we come wet and weary to the long wished for Inn. What have you for Dinner? "Truly nothing." No Eggs? "We have two." Any loaf bread? "No, Sir, but we've nice oat-cakes." Any bacon? any dried fish? "No, no, no, Sir!" But you've plenty of Whiskey? "O yes, Sir, plenty of Whiskey!" This is melancholy.

[1] *ALS:* Keats Museum. There is a facsimile in Williamson, plates XVII, XVIII.

Why should so beautiful a Country be poor? Why can't craggy mountains, and ⟨crag⟩ granite rocks, bear corn, wine, and oil? These are our misfortunes,—these are what make me "an Eagle's talon in the waist." [2] But I am well repaid for my sufferings. We came out to endure, and to be gratified with scenery, and lo! we have not been disappointed either way. As for the Oat-cakes, I was once in despair about them. I was not only too dainty, but they absolutely made me sick. With a little gulping, I can manage them now.[3] Mr Keats however is too unwell for fatigue and privation. I am waiting here to see him off in the Smack for London.[4] He caught a violent cold in the Island of Mull, which far from leaving him, has become worse, and the Physician here thinks him too thin and fevered to proceed on our journey. It is a cruel disappointment. We have been as happy as possible together. Alas! I shall have to travel thro' Perthshire and all the Counties round in solitude! But my disappointment is nothing to his; he not only loses my company, (and that's a great loss,) but he loses the Country. Poor Charles Brown will have to trudge by himself,—an odd fellow, and moreover an odd figure;—imagine me with a thick stick in my hand, the knapsack on my back, "with spectacles on nose," [5] a white hat, a tartan coat and trowsers, and a Highland plaid thrown over my shoulders! Don't laugh at me, there's a good fellow,—altho' Mr Keats calls me the Red Cross Knight, and declares my own shadow is ready to split its sides as it follows me. This dress is the best possible dress, as Dr Pangloss [6] would say. It is light and not easily penetrated by the wet, and when it is, it is not cold,—it has little more than a kind of heavy smoky sensation about it. I must not think of the wind, and the sun, and the rain, after my journey thro' the island of Mull. There's a wild place! Thirty seven miles of jumping and flinging over great stones along no path at all, up the steep and down the steep, and wading thro' rivulets up to the knees, and crossing a bog, a mile long, up to the ancles. I should like to give you a whole and particular account of the many—many wonderful places I have visited,—but why should I ask a man to pay vigentiple [7] postage? In one word then,—that is to the end of the letter,

[2] *1 Henry IV*, II.iv.363 f. [3] On oat-cakes see I, 337 f.

[4] He sailed from Cromarty on the next day.

[5] *As You Like It*, II.vii.159. [6] In Voltaire's *Candide*.

[7] Coined word, meaning that the letter would be twenty times the normal size.

—let me tell you I have seen one half of the Lakes in Westmoreland & Cumberland,—I have travelled over the whole of the coast of Kirkcudbrightshire, and skudded over to Donaghadee. But I did not like Ireland,—at least that part,—and would go no farther than Belfast. So back came I in a whirligig,—that is in a hurry,—and trotted up to Ayr; where I had the happiness of drinking Whiskey in the very house that Robin Burns was born,—and I saw the banks of bonny Doon,—and the brigs of Ayr,—and Kirk Alloway,—I saw it all! After this we went to Glasgow, & then to Loch Lomond,—but you can read all about that place in one of the fashionable guide-books. Then to Loch Awe and down to the foot of it,—oh, what a glen we went thro' to get at it! At the top of the glen my Itinerary mentioned a place called "Rest and be thankful" nine miles off; now we had set out without breakfast, intending to take our meal there, when, horror and starvation! "Rest and be thankful" was not an Inn, but a stone seat! [8]

* * *

[8] See I, 334.

· 104 ·

TO FANNY KEATS [1]

19 August 1818 [2]

Address: Miss Keats/ Miss Tucker's [3]/ Walthamstow.
Postmarks: TwoPyPost Unpaid SOHampstead; 7 o'Clock AU 19 1819 N^T

My dear Fanny, Hampstead August 18th

I am affraid you will [think] *me* very negligent in not having answered your Letter—I see it is dated June 12—I did not arrive at Inverness till the 8th of this Month so I am very much concerned at your being disappointed so long a time. I did not intend to have returned to London so soon but have a bad sore throat from a cold I caught in the island of Mull: therefore I thought it best to get home as soon as possible and went on board the Smack from Cromarty—We had a nine days passage and were landed at London Bridge yesterday—I shall have a good deal to tell you about Scotland—I would begin here but I have a confounded tooth ache—Tom has not been getting better since I left London and for the last fortnight has been worse than ever—he has been getting a little better for these two or three days—I shall ask Mr Abbey to let me

[1] *ALS:* British Museum. On August 7 Brown (see Joanna Richardson, *TLS*, August 29, 1952, p. 565) wrote from Inverness to Dilke's nephew, Henry Snook at Eton: "Mr. Keats will leave me here, . . . he is not well enough to go on; a violent cold and an ulcerated throat make it a matter of prudence that he should go to London in the Packet; he has been unwell for some time, and the Physician here is of opinion he will not recover if he journeys on foot thro' all weathers, and under so many privations."

[2] Keats says that he reached Inverness on August 8 (a typical misdating for August 6), that he had "a nine days passage" from Cromarty, landing "at London Bridge yesterday." Bushnell, pp. 297–300, quotes the Inverness *Courier and General Advertiser*, which lists the smack *George* as having "cleared out" from Cromarty for London on August 8, "the only ship," he says, "clearing for London from any of the Inverness district ports during the entire week," August 1–8. "Nine days" (see also I, 393) would mean August 17 or 18. Though Keats dates this letter August 18, Mrs. C. W. Dilke is certainly a more reliable witness than he. She wrote (*Papers*, I, 5) on August 19: "John Keats arrived here last night." He could hardly have reached Wentworth Place on the night of August 18 "as brown and as shabby as you can imagine; scarcely any shoes left, his jacket all torn at the back, a fur cap, a great plaid, and his knapsack," and then have gone on to Well Walk to write this letter to Fanny. Besides, it was postmarked at 7 P.M. on August 19.

[3] An error for "Tuckey" (see also the following letter). See I, 153 n.

bring you to Hampstead. If Mr A should see this Letter tell him that he still must if he pleases forward the Post Bill to Perth as I have empowered my fellow traveller to receive it [4]—I have a few scotch pebbles for you from the Island of Icolmkill—I am affraid they are rather shabby—I did not go near the Mountain of Cairn Gorm—I do not know the Name of George's ship—the Name of the Port he has gone to is Philadelphia when[c]e he will travel to the Settlement [5] across the Country—I will tell you all about this when I see you—The Title of my last Book is 'Endymion' you shall have one soon—I would not advise you to play on the Flageolet however I will get you one if you please—I will speak to Mr Abbey on what you say concerning school [6]—I am sorry for your poor Canary. You shall have another volume of my first Book. My tooth Ache keeps on so that I cannot writ[e] with any pleasure—all I can say now is that you Letter is a very nice one without fault and that you will hear from or see in a few days if his [7] throat will let him,

Your affectionate Brother

John.

· 105 ·

TO FANNY KEATS [1]

25 August 1818

Address: Miss Keats/ Miss Tucker's [2]/ Walthamstow
Postmarks: TwoPyPost Unpaid Hampstead; 7 o'Clock AU 2{5} 1818 NT

Hampstead Tuesday

My dear Fanny,

I have just written to Mr Abbey to ask him to let you come and see poor Tom who has lately been much worse—He is better at present sends his Love to you and wishes much to see you—I hope

[4] Abbey's account shows that he had mailed Keats a draft for £30 on August 8 (William Dilke's notes, Keats Museum).

[5] Birkbeck's Albion, Illinois, colony.

[6] Abbey soon removed her from school in spite of Keats's efforts (II, 38).

[7] *Changed from* my.

[1] *ALS:* British Museum.

[2] For Miss Tuckey see I, 153 n.

he will shortly—I have not been able to come to Walthamstow on his account as well as a little Indisposition of my own—I have asked Mr A. to write me—if he does not mention any thing of it to you, I will tell you what reasons he has though I do not think he will make any objection—Write me what you what [3] with a Flageolet and I will get one ready for you by the time you come—

Your affectionate Brother
John—

· 106 ·

TO JANE REYNOLDS [1]

1 September 1818

Address: Miss Reynolds/ Little Britain—
Postmark: 7 o'Clock SP 1 1818 NT; *another illegible*

Well Walk Septr 1st

My dear Jane,

Certainly your kind note would rather refresh than [2] trouble me, and so much the more would your coming if as you say, It could be done without agitating my Brother too much—Receive on your Hearth our deepest thanks for your Solicitude concerning us.

I am glad John is not hurt, but gone save [3] into Devonshire [4]—I shall be in great expectation of his Letter—but the promise of it in so anxious and friendly a way I prize more than a hundred. I shall be in town to day on some business with my guardian 'as was' with scar[c]e a hope of being able to call on you.[5] For these two

[3] *For* want.

[1] *ALS:* Harvard. On the address fold is the autograph "F. Locker."

[2] *Written* than than.

[3] That is, safe.

[4] Hessey wrote to Taylor on August 29, 1818 (*KC*, II, 417 f.): "He [Reynolds] is gone off to Devonshire. . . . He went to Brighton a few nights since on Business and had the happiness to be overturned just opposite his friend Hunts old Residence [the jail] in Horsemonger Lane—no one was materially hurt."

[5] For Holman's ideas about this remark see I, 370 n.

last days Tom has been more cheerful; you shall hear again soon how he will be—

Remember us particularly to your Mother.

Your sincere friend
John Keats—

·107·

TO C. W. DILKE [1]

20, 21 September 1818

Address: C. W. Dilke Esqre/ —Snook's [2] Esqre/ Bedhampton/ near Havant—Hants
Postmarks: A SE 21 818; 7 o'Clock SP 21 1818 NT (*twice*)

My dear Dilke,

According to the Wentworth place Bulletin you have left Brighton much improved: therefore now a few lines will be more of a pleasure than a bore. I have a few things to say to you and would fain begin upon them in this forth [3] line: but I have a Mind too well regulated to proceed upon any thing without due preliminary remarks—you may perhaps have observed that in the simple process of eating radishes I never begin at the root but constantly dip the little green head in the salt—that in the Game of Whist if I have an ace I constantly play it first—So how can I with any face begin without a dissertation on letter writing—Yet when I consider that a sheet of paper contains room only for three pages, and a half how can I do justice to such a pregnant subject? however as you have seen the historry of the world stamped as it were by a diminishing

[1] *ALS:* Keats Museum (first printed in *Papers,* I, 6 f.). There is a facsimile in Williamson, plates XIX–XXI. The letter has heretofore been dated, from the postmark, only September 21. At I, 368, Keats says that "Reynolds by what I hear is almost over happy," and that he himself had intended to go to town with Mrs. Dilke "tomorrow" (September 21) but "this morning" (September 20) he has asked her to excuse him. That the last paragraph was written on September 21 is clear from the statements that Mrs. Dilke did go to town "This morning," that Keats "yesterday" had sent her "an unseal'd note of sham abuse," and that "I have just had a Letter from Reynolds." Until that letter came Keats had not heard directly from Reynolds for some time (see I, 366).

[2] John Snook, husband of Dilke's sister Letitia.

[3] *For* fourth.

glass in the form of a chronological Map, so will I 'with retractile claws' [4] draw this in to the form of a table—whereby it will occupy merely the remainder of this first page—

Folio——	Parsons, Lawyers, Statesmen, Physians [5] out of place—Ut—Eustace [6]—Thornton [7] out of practice or on their travels—
Fools cap—	1 superfine! rich or noble poets—ut Byron. 2 common ut egomet—
Quarto—	Projectors, Patentees, Presidents, Potatoe growers—
Bath [8]	Boarding schools, and suburbans in general
Gilt edge	Dandies in general, male female and literary—
Octavo or tears	All who make use of a lascivious seal—
Duodec—	May be found for the most part on Milliners and Dressmakers Parlour tables—
Strip	At the Playhouse doors, or any where—
Slip	Being but a variation—
Snip	So called from its size being disguised by a twist—

I suppose you will have heard that Hazlitt has on foot a prosecution against Blackwood [9]—I dined with him a few days sinc[e] at Hessey's—there was not a word said about [it], though I understand he is excessively vexed—Reynolds by what I hear is almost over happy [1] and Rice is in town. I have not seen him nor shall I for some time as my throat has become worse after getting well, and I am determined to stop at home till I am quite well—I was going to Town tomorrow with Mrs D. but I though [2] it best, to ask her excuse this morning—I wish I could say Tom was any better.

[4] Dante's *Inferno* (Cary's translation), XVII.101 (MBF). [5] *For* Physicians.

[6] J. C. Eustace (1762?–1815), *A Classical Tour through Italy*, 4th ed., 4 vols. (1817).

[7] Thomas Thornton (died 1814), *The Present State of Turkey* (1807).

[8] Many of the letters in these volumes are written on paper embossed at the top "Bath." *The Dictionary of Paper* (New York, 1940), p. 58, defines it as "A size of note paper, 8 x 14 inches (flat) or 8 x 7 inches (folded)."

[9] *Blackwood's Edinburgh Magazine*, August, 1818—the issue (III, 519–524) that demolished Keats in the "Cockney School of Poetry. No IV"—used extremely insulting language about Hazlitt in a letter called "Hazlitt Cross-Questioned" and an article "On Shakspeare's Sonnets" (III, 550–552, 585–588). *The Times*, September 21, announced Hazlitt's intention of bringing suit for libel against the publishers. The suit was dropped in February after Blackwood agreed to pay all expenses as well as "a certain sum as damages" to Hazlitt (Howe, pp. 241–246). Hessey wrote to Taylor on September 5 (*KC*, I, 37), "I have not seen Keats since the Mag. appeared, but Hazlitt has been here and he is very much moved."

[1] Apparently a reference to Reynolds' engagement to Miss Drewe (see I, 325 n.).

[2] *For* thought.

His identity presses upon me [3] so all day that I am obliged to go out—and although I intended to have given some time to study alone I am obliged to write, and plunge into abstract images [4] to ease myself of his countenance his voice and feebleness—so that I live now in a continual fever—it must be poisonous to life although I feel well. Imagine 'the hateful siege of contraries' [5]—if I think of fame of poetry it seems a crime to me, and yet I must do so or suffer —I am sorry to give you pain—I am almost resolv'd to burn this—but I really have not self possession and magninimity enough to manage the thing othe[r]wise—after all it may be a nervousness proceeding from the Mercury [6]—

Bailey I hear is gaining his Spirits and he will yet be what I once thought impossible a cheerful Man—I think he is not quite so much spoken of in Little Brittain.[7] I forgot to ask Mrs Dilke if she had any thing she wanted to say immediately to you—This morning look'd so unpromising that I did not think she would have gone—but I find she has on sending for some volumes of Gibbon—I was in a little funk yesterday, for I sent an unseal'd note of sham abuse, until I recollected from what I had heard Charles say, that {the ser}vant could neither read nor write—not even to her Mother as Charles observed. I have just had a Letter from Reynolds—he is going on gloriously. The following, is a translation of a Line of Ronsard—

'Love poured her Beauty into my warm veins'— [8]

You have passed your Romance and I never gave into it or else I think this line a feast for one of your Lovers—How goes it with Brown?

Your sincere friend
John Keats—

[3] On identity see I, 387, 392, II, 5, 77.
[4] Compare "abstractions," I, 370, "the abstract," I, 373, "abstract Idea," I, 403.
[5] *Paradise Lost*, IX.121 f. (HBF, 1895).
[6] See I, 171.
[7] Compare II, 66 f.
[8] Line 12 of the sonnet translated at I, 371.

· 108 ·

TO J. H. REYNOLDS [1]

22 (?) September 1818 [2]

My dear Reynolds,

Believe me I have rather rejoiced in your happiness than fretted at your silence.[3] Indeed I am grieved on your account that I am not at the same time happy—But I conjure you to think at Present of nothing but pleasure "Gather the rose &c" [4] Gorge the honey of life. I pity you as much that it cannot last for ever, as I do myself now drinking bitters.—Give yourself up to it—you cannot help it—and I have a Consolation in thinking so—I never was in love—Yet the voice and the shape of a woman [5] has haunted me these two days—at such a time when the relief, the feverous relief of Poetry seems a much less crime—This morning Poetry has conquered—I have relapsed into those abstractions which are my only life—I feel escaped from a new strange and threatening sorrow.—And I am thankful for it—There is an awful warmth about my heart like a load of Immortality.

Poor Tom—that woman—and Poetry were ringing changes in my senses—now I am in comparison happy—I am sensible this

[1] A transcript in Woodhouse's letter-book, pp. 18 f.

[2] Woodhouse notes: "No date, or place, or postmark." On September 21 Keats had "just had a Letter from Reynolds" (who was at the Drewes' in Devonshire), and was translating a sonnet of Ronsard. In No. 108 he replies to that letter and copies his translation. Whether he did it on September 22 or a few days later cannot be determined. Colvin, p. 165, dated the letter "about September 22," HBF, 1895, September [illegible] Holman, whose opinions are always worth consideration, notes that on October 14 (I, 394) Keats remarked, "On my return [from Scotland on August 18], the first day I called [on the Reynoldses]." He thought that, in spite of Keats's telling Jane Reynolds on September 1 (I, 366), "I shall be in town to day . . . with scar[c]e a hope of being able to call on you," Keats did call and met Jane Cox (see I, 394 f.), and hence that No. 108 was written two days later—on September 3. Jane Reynolds, he says, probably told Keats of her brother's "happiness" (see I, 368) on September 1. Furthermore, Holman argued, in No. 108 Keats is still suffering from the sore throat that had forced him to break up his Scottish trip.

[3] Which antedated September 1 (I, 366).

[4] As Keats owned copies of Herrick's and Spenser's poems, he may have had in mind the former's "Gather ye rosebuds while ye may" or the latter's "Gather therefore the rose of love, whilest yet is prime" (*The Faerie Queene*, II.xii.75). H. E. Briggs, *MLN*, LVIII (1943), 620–622, is almost certainly right in saying that by his "&c" Keats expected Reynolds to recognize and complete the quotation from Spenser.

[5] "Charmian," or Jane Cox. See I, 66 n., 394 f. Guy Murchie, *The Spirit of Place in Keats* (1955), pp. 129 f., however, thinks that Keats meant Fanny Brawne, since three weeks later he said that Charmian "kept me awake one Night."

will distress you—you must forgive me. Had I known you would have set out so soon I could have sent you the 'Pot of Basil' for I had copied it out ready.—Here is a free translation of a Sonnet of Ronsard, which I think will please you—I have the loan [6] of his works—they have great Beauties.

Nature withheld Cassandra in the skies &c &c

(here follow the 1st 12 lines of the Sonnet—Then 2 strokes are drawn for the last lines thus)

—— —— —— ——

—— —— ——

I had not the original by me when I wrote it, and did not recollect the purport of the last lines [7]—I should have seen Rice ere this—

Sawrey's

but I am confined by ⟨Saturday's⟩ mandate in the house now, and have as yet only gone out in fear of the damp night—You know what an undangerous matter it is. I shall soon be quite recovered —Your offer I shall remember as though it had even now taken place in fact—I think it can not be—Tom is not up yet—I can not say he is better. I have not heard from George.[8]

Yr affectte friend John Keats.

[6] Woodhouse notes: "N.B. In the middle of Septr 1818 I lent Keats Ronsard—on the 1st Decr his Brother Thomas died—The Sonnet & letter must have been written to R. during those periods. The Sonnet above translated in [*sic*] in the 1st Vol: of Ronsard p. R.W. 2 of my Copy: It begins as follows.

" 'Nature ornant Cassandre, qui devoit &c.' It will be found at length in my collection of his M.S. Poetry p 140." The sonnet is the second in *Les amours de Cassandre* (*Les amours de P. de Ronsard*, ed. Hugues Vaganay [Paris, 1910], pp. 7 f.), and runs thus:

"Nature ornant Cassandre, qui devoit
De sa douceur forcer les plus rebelles,
Luy fist present des beautez les plus belles
Que dès mille ans en espargne elle avoit.
De tous les biens qu' Amour-oiseau couvoit
Au plus beau Ciel cherement sous ses ailes,
Il enrichit les graces immortelles
De l'œil son Nyc, qui les Dieux esmouvoit.
Du Ciel à peine elle estoit descendue
Quand je la vy, quand mon ame esperdue
Perdit raison, et d'un si poignant trait
Le fier destin la poussa dans mes veines,
Qu' autres plaisirs je ne sens que mes peines,
Ny autre bien qu' adorer son pourtrait."

[7] Milnes, I, 241, translated them thus: "So that her image in my soul upgrew,/ The only thing adorable and true." After one copy Woodhouse noted (Finney, II, 454), "I believe I have the translation complete at home," but, if so, he did not supply the missing lines.

[8] See I, 378.

· 109 ·

FROM B. R. HAYDON [1]

25 September 1818

Address: John Keats Esq/ Well walk/ Hampstead/ London. *Postmarks (partly illegible)*: BRIDGEWATER 150; D 26 SE 26 1818; 10 o'Clock SP 26 1818 NT

Bridgwater Sepr 25th

My dear Keats

Here I am as Shakespeare says "Chewing the cud of sweet & bitter fancy," [2] solitary in the midst of society with no human being to exchange a notion with except my sister [3]—and she begins to be so occupied with her little brats that if I attempt to quote Shakespeare to her—I am ordered into silence—for fear I should wake the Children.—I came here for repose of mind—as I am now getting better I am again on the rack to be again in the midst of all the objects of my ambition.—I am getting about again my hero—and I hope to God I shall yet finish my picture [4] to the satisfaction of all of you.—I am longing to be among you—and hear your account of your last Tour—if it has done as much good to the *inside* as the outside of your head you will feel the effects of it as long as you live. —I shall leave this place tomorrow—or Monday [5] & hope to be in Town by Wednesday at furthest. I hope your brother Tom does not suffer much—poor fellow—I shall never forget his look when I saw him last.[6]—I can never say as much when I dictate a letter as when I write it myself—and this I hope will be a sufficient excuse for not writing a longer one to you—at any rate this is better treat-

[1] Only the signature and the postscript are in Haydon's hand. The letter is endorsed by Tom Keats "Haydon to John" and by another hand "From Haydon." First printed in the *Century Magazine*, October, 1895 (L, 953), when it was owned by W. H. Arnold (see his sale catalog, New York, May, 1901).

[2] *As You Like It*, IV.iii.102, "Chewing the food," etc.

[3] Mrs. James Haviland (see I, 145).

[4] See II, 284.

[5] September 28.

[6] Tom must have read these comments: see n. 1.

ment than you gave me when you went on your Tour.[7]—Believe me my dear Keats most affectionately & sincerely

Yours ever
B R Haydon

P.S. to give you an idea of the elegant taste of this place the other day, in company when I illustrated something by a quotation, one of the company said with great simplicity, "Lord Mr Haydon, you are full of *scraps!*"—adieu—my eyes will not permit me.

·110·

TO J. A. HESSEY [1]

8 October 1818 [2]

My dear Hessey.

You are very good in sending me the letter from the Chronicle —and I am very bad in not acknowledging such a kindness sooner. —pray forgive me—It has so chanced that I have had that paper every day—I have seen today's. I cannot but feel indebted to those Gentlemen who have taken my part—As for the rest, I begin to get a little acquainted with my own strength and weakness.—Praise or blame has but a momentary effect on the man whose love of beauty in the abstract makes him a severe critic on his own Works.

[7] No letters from Keats to Haydon are known between April 8 and December 22, 1818. Tom apparently sent all the Scotch letters to Reynolds (*KC*, I, 31, 40), from whom they may have passed to Haydon. The latter, at any rate (see I, 327 n.), had two (Nos. 97, 101) which he did not return.

[1] A transcript by Woodhouse in his letter-book, pp. 13 f.

[2] Woodhouse notes: "No date—Post Mark. Hampstead 9. Octr 1818—" Keats refers to a letter by J. S. in the London *Morning Chronicle*, October 3, and to another by R. B., October 8, each defending him against J. W. Croker's notorious onslaught on *Endymion* in the *Quarterly Review*, dated April but actually published in September (XIX, 204–208). Since he says, "I have seen today's," that is, the *Chronicle* with R. B.'s letter, he was writing on October 8. J. S. was probably John Scott (Colvin, p. 167 n., so identifies him without question), who even during his residence on the Continent kept up with current English literary controversies. Lowell, II, 89, remarked that Scott was abroad in October, 1818. Actually—so Elmer L. Brooks reminds me—his journal, partly printed in his *Sketches of Manners* (1821), shows, p. 166, that he first reached Calais on November 23. Woodhouse copied J. S.'s remarks in his letter-book, pp. 11 f., and noted, p. 13: "N. B. other Letters & Extracts from the work appeared in the Chronicle. The Sun—the Day or New Times. the Examiner & other papers. all speaking favorably of Endymion." R. B., who dates his letter from the Temple, must have been at least an acquaintance of Woodhouse.

My own domestic criticism has given me pain without comparison beyond what Blackwood or the ⟨Edinburgh⟩ Quarterly could possibly inflict. and also when I feel I am right, no external praise can give me such a glow as my own solitary reperception & ratification of what is fine. J.S. is perfectly right in regard to the slipshod Endymion.[3] That it is so is no fault of mine.—No!—though it may sound a little paradoxical. It is as good as I had power to make it—by myself—Had I been nervous about its being a perfect piece, & with that view asked advice, & trembled over every page, it would not have been written; for it is not in my nature to fumble—I will write independantly.—I have written independently *without Judgment*—I may write independently *& with judgment* hereafter.—The Genius of Poetry must work out its own salvation in a man: It cannot be matured by law & precept, but by sensation & watchfulness in itself—That which is creative must create itself—In Endymion, I leaped headlong into the Sea, and thereby have become better acquainted with the Soundings, the quicksands, & the rocks, than if I had ⟨stayed⟩ stayed upon the green shore, and piped a silly pipe, and took tea & comfortable advice.—I was never afraid of failure; for I would sooner fail than not be among the greatest [4]—But I am nigh getting into a rant. So, with remembrances to Taylor & Woodhouse &c I am

Yrs very sincerely
John Keats.

J.A.Hessey Esq[r]
Fleet S[t]

[3] J. S. found in it "very many passages indicating haste and carelessness" but also on nearly every page "beauties of the highest order."

[4] Compare his confident statement at I, 394.

· 111 ·

TO FANNY KEATS[1]

9 October 1818

Address: Miss Keats/ Miss Tuckey's/ Walthamstow—
Postmarks: TwoPyPost Unpaid SOHampstead; 12 o'Clock OC 9 1818 N^{n}; 4 o'Clock OC 9 1818 EV

My dear Fanny,

Poor Tom is about the same as when you saw him last; perhaps weaker—were it not for that I should have been over to pay you a visit these fine days I got to the Stage half an hour before it set out and counted the buns and tarts in a Pastrycooks window and was just beginning with the Jellies. There was no one in the Coach who had a Mind to eat me like Mr Sham-deaf. I shall be punctual in enqu[i]ring about next Thursday—[2]

Your affectionate Brother John

· 112 ·

TO THOMAS RICHARDS[1]

9 October 1818

My dear Richards,

I think the fortnight has passed in which I promised to call on you—I have not been able to come—My Brother Tom gets weaker every day and I am not able to leave him for more than a few hours —As I know you will be anxious about us, if I cannot come I will

[1] *ALS:* British Museum.

[2] October 15, but Keats (see No. 114) postponed Fanny's visit to Tom, and she never saw him again. See Adami, pp. 58 f.

[1] *ALS:* University of Virginia (Tracy W. McGregor Collection). The handwriting and the paper are like those of No. 111, and the letter is dated, apparently by Richards, "1818. J Keats 9 octr." For Richards see I, 121 n.

send you now and then a note of this nature that you may see how we are—Remeber [2] me to Mrs R—and to Vincent.[3]

Yours most sincerely
John Keats

· 113 ·

FROM J. H. REYNOLDS [1]

14 October 1818

Address: Mr John Keats/ No 1 Well Walk/ Hampstead
Postmarks: 2 o'Clock 14 OC 18{18} ANn; 4 o'Clock OC 14 18{18 E}V; TwoPyPost Unpaid EOStrand 210

My Dear Keats

I was most delighted at seeing you yesterday,[2]—for I hardly knew how I was to meet with you, situated as you are, and confined as I am. I wish I could have stayed longer with you. As to the Poem [3] I am of all things anxious that you should publish it, for its completeness will be a full answer to all the ignorant malevolence of cold lying Scotchmen and stupid Englishmen. The overweening struggle to oppress you only shews the world that so much of endeavour cannot be directed to nothing. Men do not set their muscles, and strain their sinews to break a straw. I am confident, Keats, that the Pot of Basil hath that simplicity and quiet pathos, which are of sure sovereignty over all hearts. I must say that it would delight me to have you prove yourself to the world, what we know you to be;—to have you annul the Quarterly Review, by the best of all answers. When I see you, I will give you the Poem, and

[2] Keats several times makes a similar error: see I, 252, II, 260.

[3] Grant Richards, *Author Hunting* (1934), p. 25, who first printed this letter, says, "No one knows with certainty who 'Vincent' was, but it seems likely that he was a member of the Novello family." But Holman is right in saying that Keats, who was chary about using first names, "would not be calling him [Vincent Novello] by his Christian name." Brown, writing to Richards in 1823 and 1825 (MBF, *Some Letters . . . of Charles Brown* [1937], pp. 25, 31, 54), sends his remembrances to "Mr. Vincent" (twice) and "Mrs. Vincent."

[1] *ALS:* Harvard. Endorsed by Tom Keats: "Reynolds to John."

[2] Reynolds had just returned from six weeks in Devonshire (I, 366).

[3] "Isabella."

pray look it over with that eye to the *littlenesses* which the world are so fond of excepting to (though I confess with that word altered which I mentioned, I see nothing that can be cavilled at)—And let us have the Tale [4] put forth, now that an interest is aroused. One or two of your Sonnets you might print, I am sure—And I know that I may suggest to you, which,—because you can decide as you like afte{rward. You} will remember that we were { . . . } [5] together—⟨but⟩ I give over all intention and you ought to be alone. I can never write anything now—my mind is taken the other way: —But I shall set my heart on having you, high, as you ought to be. Do *you* get Fame,—and I shall have it in being your affectionate and steady friend. There is no one I am more interested in—and there is no one that I have more pleasure in communicating my own happiness to. You will gratify me much by letting me have, whenever you have leisure, copies of what you write;—for *more than myself* [6] have a sincere interest in you. When shall I see you—& when shall I go with you to Severn's

Your ever affection{ate}

Wed[y] Morn[g] J.H.Reynolds

· 114 ·

TO FANNY KEATS [1]

16 October 1818

Address: Miss Keats/ Miss Tuckey's/ Walthamstow
Postmarks: HampsteadNO; 7 o'Clock OC 16 1818 N[T]

My dear Fanny, Hampstead Friday Morn

You must not condemn me for not being punctual to Thursday, for I really did not know whether it would not affect poor Tom too much to see you.[2] You know how it hurt him to part with you the

[4] Gittings, pp. 23, 61 f., thinks that Reynolds is referring to a prose tale of St. Agnes' Eve which Keats proposed to base on Boccaccio, and which he told George on October 16 (I, 401) he was about to begin. Murry, *Keats* (1955), pp. 139 f., rejects these ideas, and declares that Reynolds "was almost certainly referring to *Isabella*."

[5] Colvin, 1920, p. 313, has "we were to print," Lowell, II, 106, "we were [to] pu[t out]," the *Century Magazine*, October, 1895 (L, 953), where the letter—then owned by W. H. Arnold (see his sale catalog, New York, May, 1901)—was first printed, "[Nobody] will remember that we were [to write]." [6] A reference to his fiancée, Eliza Drewe.

[1] *ALS:* British Museum. [2] See I, 375 n.

last time. At all events you shall hear from me; and if Tom keeps pretty well tomorrow—I will see Mr Abbey the next day, and endeavour to settle that you shall be with us on Tuesday or Wednesday [3]—I have good news from George [4]—He has landed safely with our Sister—they are both in good health—their prospects are good—and they are by this time nighing to their journeys end—you shall hear the particulars soon—

Your affectionate Brother
John—

Tom's love to you.

· 115 ·

FROM RICHARD WOODHOUSE [1]

21 October 1818

My dear Keats,

Whilst in the country, from whence I am but ⟨just⟩ lately returned, I met with that malicious, but weak & silly article on Endymion in the last Quarterly Review.[2] God help the Critic, whoever he be! [3] He is as ignorant of the rudiments of his own ⟨his⟩ craft as of the Essentials of true Poetry* [4] I take it the precious article in question once formed a portion of the critique in the ⟨preceding⟩ former N^{o} upon L. Hunts foliage.[5]—That the reviewer, in a ⟨fit⟩ moment of compunction, changed his plan, & ⟨determined to⟩ reviewed ⟨L⟩ Hunts work by itself, intend^{g} to leave you alone;

[3] October 20 and 21.

[4] On October 18 Keats saw a letter that George Keats had written to Mrs. Wylie (I, 401). He had seen Henry Wylie on October 15 (I, 400).

[1] *ALS:* Harvard, a draft of the letter actually sent. First printed (in part) by Lowell, II, 97–99, and (in full) in *KC*, I, 46–52. Most of the canceled passages or words are given, but others cannot be read or else cannot be reproduced intelligibly.

[2] See I, 373 n.

[3] Copying J. S.'s *Morning Chronicle* letter of October 3, 1818 (I, 373 f.), into his letter-book, pp. 11 f., Woodhouse says that the reviewer (actually Croker) was "most probably" William Gifford. Keats (see II, 9) had the same notion.

[4] This sentence first ran: "He is as much to seek in the rudiments of his own craft, as he is ignorant of the essentials of true poetry.—" Then it was changed to "He is as ignorant of the rudiments of his criticism as of those of true poetry." By the asterisk Woodhouse calls attention to the remainder of the paragraph, which he wrote for insertion here at the bottom of the last—the fourth—page.

[5] January (XVIII, 324–335).

tho' the scissors with which this sentence ⟨operation⟩ of divorce was performed⟩ carr[d] into effect, left in the earlier article a few traces of the orig[l] union.—But that the Editor, finding himself at a loss for a few pages of matter to eke out his pres[t] N[o], bethought himself of the fragments of his former review, which he has cooked up afresh, ⟨& garnished out for⟩ as a side dish [6] for his readers.—

That his *very equitable* censures [7] may have the effect of scaring from the perusal of the Work some of the "Dandy" readers, male & female, who love to be spared the trouble of judging for themselves, is to be expected—But with men of sense, ⟨like⟩ (as the example of J.S. in the Chronicle, proves) the effect must be the reverse—The Criticism ⟨carries in it the sufficing cause of its own destruction⟩ is felo de se—It bears on its [8] front the sentence of its own condemn[g] ⟨on its front⟩: for the Reviewer in ⟨the sheerness of his⟩ his undiscriminating stupidity, has laid his finger of contempt upon passages of such beauty, that no one with a spark of poetic feeling can read them without a desire to know more of the poem.—"If"—said a friend of mine at Bath, who had ⟨read⟩ seen the critique, but not the work, "these are the worst passages, what must the best be."—To be praised in the same review that slabbers with its eulogy Barretts woman [9] would have been damnation Such a pestering insect may annoy ⟨one⟩ for a⟨n hour⟩ moment, but its impotent attacks can ⟨give⟩ cause no permanent uneasiness.—And I am happy to ⟨find from⟩ see by the daily papers,[1] that the crying injustice of the decision has roused ⟨the⟩ indignation ⟨of⟩ in a few who "do look with a jealous eye ⟨to⟩ on the honor of English literature." [2] But enough of such a ⟨bungling⟩ cobbling, carping, ⟨shallow⟩ decasyllabic, finger-scanning-criticaster.—His hour of ⟨bustling poking about, is nigh done⟩ "brief author[it][y]" [3] must be nigh over—His blindness will soon work its {own w}ay into the earth.—

The appearance of this "critical morsel," however, determines

[6] Here is canceled something like "as the finest banquet he would provide."

[7] First "That his unjust censures" and then "But his edifying censures."

[8] "own cond" is canceled here.

[9] Eaton Stannard Barrett (1786–1820), *Woman: A Poem* (1810; 2nd ed., revised, 1818). Reviewing the book in April (XIX, 246–250), the *Quarterly* said: "Mr. Barrett has evinced both talent and genius . . . and sustained a flight far above the common level." Shelley, as the preface to *Adonais* makes clear, had a far different opinion.

[1] Defenses of Keats in the *Alfred, West of England Journal*, October 6 (by Reynolds), and in the London *Morning Chronicle*, October 3 and 8 (I, 373 n.), may be read in HBF, 1883, III, 373–383.

[2] Preface to *Endymion.*

[3] *Measure for Measure*, II.ii.118.

me to address you on the subject of our late conversation at Hessey's,[4] ⟨to⟩ on which I have often since reflected, and never without ⟨some pa⟩ a degree of pain—I may have misconceived you,—but I ⟨then⟩ understood you to say, you thought there was now nothing original to be written in poetry; ⟨that⟩ that its riches ⟨were being⟩ were already exhausted,—& all its beauties forestalled—& That you should, consequently, write no more⟨: but continue increasing your knowledge, merely for your own gratification without any attempt to make use of your Stores⟩.—I cannot ⟨agree with you in⟩ assent to your premises, and I most earnestly deprecate your conclusion.—For my part I believe most sincerely, that the ⟨beauties riches⟩ wealth of poetry ⟨are⟩ is unexhausted & ⟨indeed⟩ inexhaustible—The ideas derivable to us from our senses singly & in their various combin^ns^ with each other store the mind with endless images of natural beauty & perfection—the Passions add life & motion—& reflection & the moral Sense give⟨s⟩ order relief unity & harmony to this mighty world of inanimate matter.[5]—It is in ⟨the⟩ the gleaning of the highest, the truest & the sweetest of these ideas, in the orderly grouping of them, & arraying them in the garb of exquisite Numbers, that Poetry may be said to consist.—It is then for the Poëta factus, the imitator of others, who sings only as has been sung, to say that our measure of poe⟨tr⟩sy is full, & that there is nothing new to be written, thus charging[6] upon "most innocent nature"[7] ⟨the faults arising out of his own dullness⟩ a dearth exist^g^ only in ⟨the [*word illegible*] of his⟩ his own dull brain—But the poëta natus, the true born Son of Genius ⟨& the Muse⟩, who creates for himself ⟨a⟩ the world in which his own ⟨Imagination⟩ fancy ranges ⟨wherein he may wander, &⟩ who culls from it fair ⟨samples⟩ forms of truth ⟨&⟩ beauty & purity & apparels them in hues ⟨of his own choosing⟩ chosen by himself, should hold a different language—⟨*He*⟩ he need ⟨be⟩ never fear that the treasury he draws on can

[4] Originally "Before the appearance of this critical morse[l]" and "I have several times lately reflected with some pain upon the Conversation we had together at Hessey's, the day before I left Town; and the appearance of this critical morsel determines me to address you on the subject."

[5] First written as "The ideas of beauty & perfection, natural as well as moral, derivable to us from our own senses only are most numerous—and those suggested by all our senses separately, & by them in combination one with another must be almost infinite in variety. Add the passions, and a world arises before you." (Revisions between this version and that printed above defy recording.)

[6] Changed from "to charge."

[7] *Comus*, line 761.

be exhausted, ⟨n⟩or nor despair of ⟨always⟩ being always able to ma{ke} an original selection.

It is true that in this age, the mass are not of soul to conceive ⟨of themselves,⟩ of themselves or even to apprehend when presented to them, the truly & simply beautiful ⟨in⟩ of poetry.—A taste vitiated by the sweetmeats & kickshaws of the ⟨last⟩ past century may be the reason ⟨of this⟩ of this. Still fewer of this generation are capable of properly embodying ⟨what⟩ the high conceptions they may have—and of the last ⟨few⟩ number few are the individuals [8] who do not allow their fire & originality to be damped by apprehensions of ⟨contemptible⟩ shallow censures from the groveling & the "coldhearted."

In these "evil days" however & amid these "Evil tonges" [9] (in the spirit of truth & sincerity & not of flattery I say it) I believe there has appeared *one* bard [1] who "preserves his vessel" in purity independance & honor—who judges of the beautiful for himself, careless [2] who thinks with him—who ⟨steers⟩ pursues his own self-appointed & selfapproved course right onward [3]—who stoops not from ⟨the height of⟩ his ⟨high⟩ flight to win sullied breath from the multitude—and who "leans away" for highest heaven, and sings,[4] pointing for his [*word illegible*]—to a standard of excellence dimly visible as yet even to himself & scarcely free from the shadows in which from unknown time it has been vested [5] and of which the meaner spirits of his day seem to be without even a conception [6]—And shall such a one, upon whom anxious eyes are fixed, at whose noble aspirings "unnumbered souls breathe out a *still* applause," [7] be dismayed at the yelpings of the tuneless, the envious, the malignant or the undiscerning? or shall he fall into the worse error of supposing that there is left no corner of the universal heaven of

[8] Originally "and of these ⟨not⟩ scarce are there two or three individuals."

[9] *Paradise Lost*, VII.25 f.

[1] Originally "If the spirit of truth & sincerity and not of flattery, (for I should despise myself If I flattered) I say, that I know but one bard." (Intermediate revisions are not recorded.)

[2] Changed to "reckless" and then back to "careless."

[3] Milton, Sonnet 22, lines 8 f., "still bear up and steer/ Right onward."

[4] *Endymion*, IV.568.

[5] This sentence has much revision of the original, " . . . multitude—and who appeals for justification in his [*word illegible*] to a standard of excellence set up by himself, & scarcely yet free from the shadows in which it has [*word illegible*] long rested, or discernible by the clearest eye."

[6] Something like "What conduct [*or* course?] should he pursue" is canceled.

[7] Keats's sonnet "Addressed to Haydon," line 13.

poesy unvisited by Wing?[8] Shall he subtract himself from the ⟨gaze⟩ expectations of his country; and leave its ⟨palled⟩ ear & its soul to be soothed only by the rhymers & the coupleteers? Shall he let "so fair a house fall to decay"[9]—and shall he give the land, which let Chatterton & K. White die of ⟨neglect &⟩ unkindness, & neglect—but which yet ⟨had⟩ retained the grace to weep over their ashes, no opportunity of redeeming its Character, & paying the ⟨great⟩ vast debt it ⟨yet⟩ owes to Genius?—Your conduct, my Dear Keats, must give these Questions an answer. . —

"Know thine own worth, and reverence the lyre"!—[1]

The world, I hope & trust, is not quite ⟨to⟩ so dead dull and ungrateful as you may have apprehended—or as a few malevolent spirits may have given you reason to imagine It contains, I know, many who have a warm "affection for the cause Of stedfast Genius toiling gallantly,"[2]—many who, tho' personally unknown to you, look with the eye of hope & anticipation ⟨at⟩ to your future course —but very few who in ⟨earnest⟩ sincere wishes for your welfare, & passion for your fame, exceed, Dear Keats,

Yours most truly,
Richd Woodhouse
Temple ⟨17⟩ ⟨21⟩ 21st Octr 1818.

[8] Compare *Paradise Lost*, III.13. [9] Shakespeare's Sonnet 13, line 9.

[1] Located by Jack Stillinger, *MLN*, LXXI (1956), 341, in James Beattie's *Minstrel*, I.59. Coleridge (*Unpublished Letters*, ed. E. L. Griggs [1933], I, 180) on August 11, 1801, misquoted "Know thy own self and reverence the Muse!"

[2] Keats's sonnet "Addressed to Haydon," line 10.

·116·

RICHARD WOODHOUSE TO MARY FROGLEY [1]

23 October 1818 [2]

My dear Mary,

I returned from Hounslow late last night, & your mother desired me to forward to you the enclosed letter. I brought Endymion back, thinking you might like to have it in Town whilst with your friends.

You were so flattering as to say the other day, you wished I had been in a company where you were, to defend Keats.—In all places, & at all times, & before all persons, I would express, and as far as I am able, support, my high opinion of his poetical merits—Such a genius, I verily believe, has not appeared since Shakspeare & Milton: and I may assert without fear of contradiction from any one competent to Judge, that if his Endymion be compared with Shakspeare's earliest work (his Venus & Adonis) written about the same age, Keats's poem will be found to contain more beauties, more poetry (and that of a higher order) less conceit & bad taste and in a word much more promise of excellence than are to be found in Shakspeare's work—This is a deliberate opinion; nor is it merely my own—The Justice of which, however, can only be demonstrated to another upon a full review of the parts & of the whole of each work. I sh[d] not shrink from the task of doing it to one whose candour I was acquainted with, and whose Judgment I respected..

But in our Common conversation upon his merits, we should always bear in mind that his fame may be more hurt by indiscriminate praise than by wholesale censure. I would at once admit that he has great faults—enough indeed to sink another writer. But they are more than counterbalanced by his beauties: And this is the proper mode of appretiating an original genius. His faults will wear

[1] *ALS:* Pierpont Morgan Library. First printed by Colvin, *TLS*, April 16, 1914, p. 182. On Miss Frogley, later Mrs. William Henry Neville, see I, 410 n.

[2] "Friday" at the end of the letter, and the references to "Gifford's" review of *Endymion*, which, though dated April, appeared in September, and to the "remonstrances" in "the daily papers," fix this date. A draft of this letter, varying from the present copy in trivial details and damaged by crumbling of the paper at the right-hand side of the pages, is also in the Pierpont Morgan Library.

away—his fire will be chastened—and then eyes will do homage to his brilliancy. But genius is wayward, trembling, easily daunted. And shall we not excuse the errors, the luxuriances of youth? are we to expect that poets are to be given to the world, as our first parents were, in a state of maturity? are they to have no season of Childhood? are they to have no room to try their wings before the steadiness & strength of their flight are to be finally judged of?—So says Mr Gifford of the Quarterly—But the world meted out a far different measure to his youthful Infirmities,—though he forgets it. —So said ⟨Horace Walpole of Chatterton—So said⟩ the Edinburgh Review⟨ers⟩ of Ld Byron—So said the Monthly [3] of Kirke White—So said Horace Walpole of Chatterton.[4] And how are such Critics now execrated ⟨by⟩ for their cruel injustice.—I see the daily papers [5] teem with remonstrances against Gifford's arbitrary decision. An appeal to the Country is lodged against it. Perhaps this age,—certainly posterity,—will judge rightly—However the decision be, the competence of a poet to write, and of a Critic to Judge of poetry are involved in the dispute, and *one* reputation must suffer deeply. Had I any literary reputation I would stake it on the result. You know the side I should espouse. As it is,—I can only prophesy. And now, while Keats is unknown unheeded, despised of one of our archcritics, neglected by the rest—in the teeth of the world, and in the face of "these curious days," [6] I express my conviction, that Keats, during his life (if it please God to spare him to the usual age of man, and the critics not to drive him from the free air of the poetic heaven before his Wings are fullfledged,) will rank on a level with the best of the last or of the present generation, and after his death will take his place at their head.—

But, while I think thus, I would make persons respect my judgment by the discrimination of my praise, and by the freedom of my censure where his writings are open to it. These are the Elements of true criticism—It is easy, like Momus, to find fault with the clattering of the slipper worn by the Goddess of b{e}auty: but "the serious Gods" [7] found better employment in admiration of her unapproachable loveliness.—A Poet ought to write for Posterity. But a critic should do so too.—Those of our times write for the day, or

[3] *Monthly Review*, February, 1804 (XLIII, 218).
[4] See J. H. Ingram, *The True Chatterton* (1910), pp. 162–178.
[5] See I, 373 f., 379. [6] Shakespeare's Sonnet 38, line 13. [7] *Endymion*, II.785.

rather the hour. Their thoughts & Judgments are fashionable garbs, such as they imagine a skin-wise world would like to array itself in at second hand.—How is the great Johnson

> "Fallen, fallen, fallen, fallen,
> "Fallen from his high Estate," [8]

by the malice, the Injustice, & envy of his criticisms in that "Monument of his Mortality the lives of the Poets," and by his deadness to the exalted & excellent in Poetry.

Adieu, my dear Mary;—I have mounted so far into the Clouds that I am, like Endymion,[9]

> ——"Become loth & fearful to alight
> "From such high soaring;"

but when he did, it was to pay his respects to a divinity. In this too I follow his example, kissing your poor *one* hand, and craving kind remembrances to the divine ones around you.

I am &c e[r] yours, Rich[d] Woodhouse
Friday Morn[g]

· 117 ·

TO FANNY KEATS [1]

26 October 1818

Address: Miss Keats/ Miss Tuckey's/ Walthamstow—
Postmarks: HampsteadNO; 7 o'Clock OC 26 1818 N[T]

My dear Fanny,

I called on M[r] Abbey in the beginning of last Week: [2] when he seemed averse to letting you come again from having heard that you had been to other places besides Well Walk—I do not mean to say you did wrongly in speaking of it, for there should rightly be no objection to such things: but you know with what People we are obliged in the course of Childhood to associate; whose conduct forces us into duplicity and fa[l]shood to them. To the worst of

[8] Dryden, "Alexander's Feast," lines 77 f. [9] I.583 f.
[1] *ALS:* British Museum. [2] Probably on October 19.

People we should be openhearted: but it is as well as things are to be prudent in making any communication to any one, that may [3] throw an impediment in the way of any of the little pleasures you may have. I do not recommend duplicity but prudence with such people. Perphaps [4] I am talking too deeply for you: if you do not now, you will understand what I mean in the course of a few years. I think poor Tom is a little Better: he sends his love to you—I shall call on Mr Abbey tomorrow: [5] when I hope to settle when to see you again. Mrs Dilke has been for some time at Brighton—she is expected home in a day or two. She will be pleased I am sure with your present. I will try for permission for you to remain here all Night should Mrs D. retu[r]n in time.[6]

Your affectionate Brother
John—

· 118 ·

TO RICHARD WOODHOUSE [1]

27 October 1818 [2]

Address: Richd Woodhouse Esqre/ Temple—
Postmarks: TwoPyPost Unpaid SOHampstead; 12 o'Clock OC 27 . . .

My dear Woodhouse,

Your Letter gave me a great satisfaction; more on account of its friendliness, than any relish of that matter in it which is accounted so acceptable in the 'genus irritabile' [3] The best answer I can give you is in a clerklike manner to make some observations on two principle points, which seem to point like indices into the midst of the whole pro and con, about genius, and views and atchievements and ambition and cœtera. 1st As to the poetical Character itself, (I mean that sort of which, if I am any thing, I am a Member;

[3] Changed from "make."
[4] Keats often had trouble with this word: see I, 172, II, 186, 235, 264.
[5] He did call, and he got £20 in cash (William Dilke's notes, Keats Museum).
[6] Fanny was not allowed to visit her brothers after the beginning of October. See I, 375 n.
[1] *ALS:* Harvard. There is also a transcript in Woodhouse's letter-book, pp. 15–17.
[2] Woodhouse adds "1818" to the blurred postmark on the original letter and dates the letter and his transcript October 27.
[3] Horace, *Epistles*, II.ii.102.

that sort distinguished from the wordsworthian or egotistical sublime; which is a thing per se and stands alone [4]) it is not itself—it has no self—it is every thing and nothing—It has no character—it enjoys light and shade; it lives in gusto, be it foul or fair, high or low, rich or poor, mean or elevated—It has as much delight in conceiving an Iago as an Imogen. What shocks the virtuous philosop[h]er, delights the camelion Poet. It does no harm from its relish of the dark side of things any more than from its taste for the bright one; because they both end in speculation. A Poet is the most unpoetical of any thing in existence; because he has no Identity—he is continually in for [5]—and filling some other Body—The Sun, the Moon, the Sea and Men and Women who are creatures of impulse are poetical and have about them an unchangeable attribute—the poet has none; no identity—he is certainly the most unpoetical of all God's Creatures. If then he has no self, and if I am a Poet, where is the Wonder that I should say I would ⟨right⟩ write no more? Might I not at that very instant [have] been cogitating on the Characters of saturn and Ops? [6] It is a wretched thing to confess; but is a very fact that not one word I ever utter can be taken for granted as an opinion growing out of my identical nature—how can it, when I have no nature? When I am in a room with People if I ever am free from speculating on creations of my own brain, then not myself goes home to myself: [7] but the identity of every one in the room begins to [8] to press upon me [9] that, I am in a very little time anhilated—not only among Men; it would be the same in a Nursery of children: I know not whether I make myself wholly understood: I hope enough so to let you see that no dependence is to be placed on what I said that day.

In the second place I will speak of my views, and of the life I purpose to myself—I am ambitious of doing the world some good: if I should be spared that may be the work of maturer years—in the interval I will assay to reach to as high a summit in Poetry as the nerve bestowed upon me will suffer. The faint conceptions I have

[4] *Troilus and Cressida*, I.ii.15 f., "he is a very man *per se*,/ And stands alone."

[5] Woodhouse copied "continually in for" and recognized no difficulty. George Beaumont, *TLS*, February 27, May 1, 1930, pp. 166, 370, emends to "informing."

[6] Characters in "Hyperion."

[7] Compare *Troilus and Cressida*, III.iii.105, 107, "the eye itself... Not going from itself."

[8] J. C. Maxwell, *NQ*, May 17, 1947, p. 215, emends to "so."

[9] With "identity... press upon me" compare I, 369 n.

of Poems to come brings the blood frequently into my forehead—All I hope is that I may not lose all interest in human affairs—that the solitary indifference I feel for applause even from the finest Spirits, will not blunt any acuteness of vision I may have.[1] I do not think it will—I feel assured I should write from the mere yearning and fondness I have for the Beautiful even if my night's labours should be burnt every morning and no eye ever shine upon them.[2] But even now I am perhaps not speaking from myself; but from some character in whose soul I now live. I am sure however that this next sentence is from myself. I feel your anxiety, good opinion and friendliness in the highest degree, and am

Your's most sincerely
John Keats [3]

·119·

RICHARD WOODHOUSE TO JOHN TAYLOR [1]

About 27 October 1818

I believe him to be right with regard to ⟨the⟩ his own Poetical Character—And I perceive clearly the distinction he draws between himself & those of the Wordsworth School.—There are gradations in Poetry & in Poets. One is purely descriptive ⟨&⟩ confining himself to external nature & visible objects—Another describes in add^{n} the effects of the thoughts of wh: he is conscious—⟨& the effects he has produced in others by such like [?] thoughts⟩ & wh: others are affected by—Another will soar so far into the regions of imagination

[1] Compare his comments to Hessey, I, 374.

[2] One wishes it were possible to prove that Keats knew Daniel's *Musophilus*, lines 567–578.

[3] Woodhouse adds: "N. B. The above letter was in answer to one which I addressed to Keats on 21 Oct^{r}—on occasion of the malicious & unjust article in the Quarterly Review—It gave me occasion to advert to what had fallen from him, about 6 weeks back, when we dined together at Mr Hessey's, respecting his continuing to write; which he seemed very doubtful of—but express^{d} at the same time, ⟨similar⟩ sentiments on the subject of acquisition of knowledge & of benefiting the wor[l]d by means of his studies similar ⟨to⟩ to those contained in his preceding letter⟨s⟩ of the 27. April to Mr J. Taylor [No. 78].—And I intimated in my letter a hope that he would not adhere to such a determination, or imagine that the Quarterly Review spoke the general opinion.—The answer was quite satisfactory upon the subject of his not intending to give over writing ⟨The answer was quite satisfactory on the subject of his not intending to write again and⟩."

[1] *Autograph:* Pierpont Morgan Library. A draft of a letter to John Taylor in which all the cancelations that I can read are included. First printed (in part) by Lowell, II, 102–104, and (in full) in *KC*, I, 57–60. Woodhouse here discusses No. 118 and Keats's view of the poetical character and negative capability.

as to conceive of beings & substances in situations different from what he has ever seen them but still such as either have actually occurred or may possibly occur—⟨Such is the tragedian⟩ Another will reason in poetry—another be witty.—Another will imagine things that never did nor probably ever will occur, or such as can not in nature occur & yet he will describe them so that you ⟨may⟩ recognize nothing very unnatural in the Descriptions when cert^{n} principles or powers or cond^{ns} are admitted—Another with [2] throw himself into various characters & make them speak as the passions wo^{d} naturally incite them to do The highest order of Poet will not only ⟨embrace⟩ possess all the above powers but will have as high an imag^{n} that he will be able to throw his own soul into ⟨the⟩ any object he sees or imagines, so as to see feel ⟨&⟩ be sensible of, & express, all that the object itself wo^{d} see feel ⟨&⟩ be sensible of or express—& he will speak out of that object—so that his own self will with the Exception of the Mechanical part be "annihilated."—and it is the excess of this power that I suppose Keats to speaks,[3] when he says he has no identity—As a poet, and when the fit is upon him, this is true—And it is a fact that he does ⟨creat⟩ by the power of his Imag^{n} create ideal personages substances & Powers—that he lives for a time in their souls or Essences or ideas—and that occasionally so intensely as to ⟨forget⟩ lose consciousness of what is round him. We all do the same in a degree, when we fall into a reverie—See below.[x]

---

[x] ⟨To instance⟩ The power of his Imagin^{n} ⟨It wo^{d} be enough to read his vol of poems⟩ is ⟨will be⟩ apparent in Ev^{y} page of his Endym$^{n\theta}$—& He has affirmed that he can conceive of a billiard Ball that it may have a sense of delight from its own roundness, smoothness ⟨& very⟩ volubility. & the rapidity of its motion.— [4]

[θ] Take p 69 [5]—only & look at the qualities with wh: in that one page ⟨69 End^{n}⟩ he Endues inan^{e} beings & even imagined ⟨beings⟩ ideas, as silence—⟨refreshment⟩.[6] a channel of a stream. a sallow by water side & the Sense of refreshm^{t}.

[2] *For* will.

[3] He first wrote "that Keats speaks" and when he added "I suppose" and "to" he failed to change "speaks" to "speak."

[4] In another note (*KC*, I, 275 n.) Woodhouse says: "He can conceive a billiard Ball to be soothed ⟨by a sense of its own smoothness⟩ & feel pleasure from a consciousness of its ⟨own⟩ own smoothness—& the rapid^{y} of its Motion."

[5] He refers to *Endymion*, II.340 ff.

[6] Another (illegible) canceled word follows.

If then his imag^{n} has such power: and he ⟨he⟩ is continually cultivating ⟨& exercising⟩ it, & giving it ⟨space to act⟩ play. It will acquire strength by the Indulgence & exercise ⟨And as⟩ This in excess is the Case ⟨with⟩ of mad persons. And this may be carried to that extent that he may lose sight of his identity so far ⟨that as generally to⟩ as to give him a habit of speak^{g} generally in an assumed character—so that What he says shall be tinged with the Sentiments proper to the Character which at the [7] time has possessed itself of his Imagination, ⟨and, thro' that, of his other faculties—⟩

This being his idea of the Poetical Character—he may well say that a poet has no identity [8]—as a man he must have Ident^{y}. But as a poet ⟨it is⟩ he need not ⟨necessary⟩—And in this Sense a poet is "the most unpoetical of Gods creatures." ⟨But⟩ for his soul has no distinctive characteristic—it can not be itself made the subj^{t} of Poetry that is another persons soul can not be thrown into the poet's —for there is no identity (separatedness) (distinctiveness) or personal impulse to be acted upon—

Shaksp^{r} was a poet of the kind above ment^{d}—and he was perhaps the only one besides Keats who possessed this power in an extr^{y} [?] degree, ⟨that⟩ so as to be a feature in his works. He gives a descr^{n} of his idea of a poet

The Poets eye &c [9]

Ld Byron does not come up to this Character. He can certainly conceive & describe a dark accomplished vilain in love—& a female tender & kind who loves him. Or a sated & palled [1] Sensualist Misanthrope & Deist—But here his power ends.—The true poet can not only conceive this—but can assume any Character Essence idea or Substance at pleasure. & He has this imaginative faculty not in a limited manner, but in full universality.

Let us pursue Speculation on these Matters: & we shall soon be bro^{t} to believe in the truth of every Syllable of Keats's letter, taken as a descript^{n} of himself & his own Ideas & feel^{gs}

* * *

[7] *Written* the the. [8] *Written* idenitity.

[9] *A Midsummer Night's Dream*, V.i.12. [1] *Originally* apalled.

· 120 ·

TO GEORGE AND GEORGIANA KEATS[1]

14, 16, 21, 24, 31 October 1818

My dear George; There was a part in your Letter which gave me a great deal of pain, that where you lament not receiving Letters from England—I intended to have written immediately on my return from Scotland (which was two Months earlier than I had intended on account of my own as well as Tom's health) but then I
Mrs W—[2]
was told by ⟨Haslam⟩ that you had said you would not wish any one to write till we had heard from you. This I thought odd and now I see that it could not have been so; yet at the time I suffered my unreflecting head to be satisfied and went on in that sort of abstract careless and restless Life with which you are well acquainted. This sentence should it give you any uneasiness do not let it last for before I finish it will be explained away to your satisfaction—

I am g[r]ieved to say that I am not sorry you had not Letters at Philadelphia; you could have had no good news of Tom and I have been withheld on his account from beginning these many days; I could not bring myself to say the truth, that he is no better, but much worse—However it must be told, and you must my dear Brother and Sister take example frome me and bear up against any Calamity for my sake as I do for your's. Our's are ties which independent of their own Sentiment are sent us by providence to prevent the deleterious effects of one great, solitary grief. I have Fanny and I have you—three people whose Happiness to me is sacred—and it does annul that selfish sorrow which I should otherwise fall into, living as I do with poor Tom who looks upon me as his only comfort—the tears will come into your Eyes—let them—and embrace each other—thank heaven for what happiness you have and after thinking a moment or two that you suffer in common with all

[1] *ALS:* Harvard. Part of this letter was first printed in the New York *World*, June 25, 1877, p. 2. It is endorsed by George, "John's of Feby—1819." Another hand has changed "1819" to "1829." Jeffrey made a transcript of the letter.
[2] Wylie.

Mankind hold it not a sin to regain your cheerfulness—I will relieve you of one uneasiness of overleaf: I retu[r]ned I said on account of my health—I am now well from a bad sore throat which came of bog trotting in the Island of Mull—of which you shall hear by the coppies I shall make from my Scotch Letters—Your content in each other is a delight to me which I cannot express—the Moon is now shining full and brilliant—she is the same to me in Matter, what you are to me in Spirit—If you were here my dear Sister I could not pronounce the words which I can write to you from a distance: I have a tenderness for you, and an admiration which I feel to be as great and more chaste than I can have for any woman in the world. You will mention Fanny—her character is not formed; her identity does not press upon me [3] as yours does. I hope from the bottom of my heart that I may one day feel as much for her as I do for you—I know not how it is, but I have never made any acquaintance of my own—nearly all through your medium my dear Brother—through you I know not only a Sister but a glorious human being—And now I am talking of those to whom you have made me known I cannot forbear mentioning Haslam as a most kind and obliging and constant friend—His behaviour to Tom during my absence and since my return has endeared him to me for ever—besides his anxiety about you. Tomorrow I shall call on your Mother and exchange information with her—On Tom's account I have not been able to pass so much time with her as I would otherwise have done—I have seen her but twice—on[c]e I dined with her and Charles. She was well, in good Spirits and I kept her laughing at my bad jokes—We went to tea at Mrs Millar's and in going were particularly struck with the light and shade through the Gate way at the Horse Guards. I intend to write you such Volumes that it will be impossible for me to keep any order or method in what I write: that will come first which is uppermost in my Mind, not that which is uppermost in my heart—besides I should wish to give you a picture of our Lives here whenever by a touch I can do it; even as you must see by the last sentence our walk past Whitehall all in good health and spirits—this I am certain of, because I felt so much pleasure from the simple idea of your playing a game at Cricket—At Mrs Millars I saw Henry quite well—there was Miss Keasle—

[3] On "identity" see I, 369 n.

and the goodnatured Miss Waldegrave [4]—Mrs Millar began a long story and you know it is her Daughter's way to help her on as though her tongue were ill of the gout—Mrs M. certainly tells a Story as though she had been taught her Alphabet in Crutched Friars. Dilke has been very unwell; I found him very ailing on my return—he was under Medical care for some time, and then went to the Sea Side whence he has returned well [5]—Poor little Mrs D— has had another gall-stone attack; she was well ere I returned —she is now at Brighton [6]—Dilke was greatly pleased to hear from you and will write a Letter for me to enclose—He seems greatly desirous of hearing from you of the Settlement itself—I came by ship from Inverness [7] and was nine days at Sea without being sick —a little Qualm now and then put me in mind of you—however as soon as you touch the thore [8] all the horrors of sick[n]ess are soon forgotten; as was the case with a Lady on board who could not hold her head up all the way. We had not been in the Thames an hour before her tongue began to some tune; paying off as it was fit she should all old scores. I was the only Englishman on board. There was a downright Scotchman who hearing that there had been a bad crop of Potatoes in England had brought some triumphant Specimens from Scotland—these he exhibited with national pride to all the Lightermen, and Watermen from the Nore to the Bridge. I fed upon beef all the way; not being able to eat the thick Porridge which the Ladies managed to manage with large awkward horn spoons into the bargain. Severn has had a narrow escape of his Life from a Typhous fever: he is now gaining strength—Reynolds has returned from a six weeks enjoyment in Devonshire, he is well and persuades me to publish my pot of Basil as an answer to the attacks made on me in Blackwood's Magazine and the Quarterly Review.[9] There have been two Letters in my defence in the Chronicle [1] and one in the Examiner, coppied from the Alfred Exeter paper, and written by Reynolds [2]—I do not know who wrote

[4] Henry Wylie appears to have lived with his aunt, Mrs. Millar. Apparently Miss Keasle and Miss Waldegrave were lodgers.

[5] He had left Brighton before September 20 (I, 367).

[6] She had been there "for some time" on October 26 (I, 386).

[7] Actually (see I, 364) from Cromarty, twenty miles northeast of Inverness.

[8] *For* shore.

[9] See No. 110.

[1] See I, 373 n.

[2] Reynolds' article in the *Alfred, West of England Journal*, October 6, was reprinted in the *Examiner*, October 12, pp. 648 f.

Chronicle
those in the ⟨Quarterly⟩—This is a mere matter of the moment—I think I shall be among the English Poets after my death.[3] ⟨The⟩ Even as a Matter of present interest the attempt to crush me in the ⟨Chro⟩ Quarterly has only brought me more into notice and it is a common expression among book men "I wonder the Quarterly should cut its own throat.'
It does me not the least harm in Society to make me appear little and rediculous: I know when a Man is superior to me and give him all due respect—he will be the last to laugh at me and as for the rest I feel that I make an impression upon them which insures me personal respect ⟨whic⟩ while I am in sight whatever they may say when my back is turned—Poor Haydon's eyes will not suffer him to proceed with his picture—he has been in the Country—I have seen him but once since my return [4]—I hurry matters together here because I do not know when the Mail sails—I shall enqu[i]re to-morrow and then shall know whether to be particular or general in my letter—you shall have at least two sheets a day till it does sail whether it be three days or a fortnight—and then I will begin a fresh one for the next Month. The Miss Reynoldses are very kind to me—but they have lately displeased me much and in this way —Now I am coming [5] the Richardson. On my return, the first day I called they were in a sort of taking or bustle about a Cousin of theirs [6] who having fallen out with her Grandpapa in a serious manner, was invited by Mrs R— [7] to take Asylum in her house—She is an east indian and ought to be her Grandfather's Heir. At the time I called Mrs R. was in conference with her up stairs and the young Ladies were warm in her praises down stairs calling her genteel, interresting and a thousand other pretty things to which I gave no heed, not being partial to 9 days wonders—Now all is com-

[3] Compare his words to Hessey at I, 374.

[4] Haydon returned from Bridgwater on or about September 28 (I, 372).

[5] W. J. Bate suggests "becoming," that is, coming to be like Samuel Richardson, who rakes and rummages (II, 221), makes mountains out of molehills (II, 196), and with self-satisfaction (II, 83) gives gossipy accounts of social and especially personal intrigue.

[6] MBF identifies her as Jane Cox, born in India, the daughter of Mrs. Reynolds' only brother, and says that she and her grandfather were "ultimately reconciled." Phyllis G. Mann, *K–SJ*, V (1956), 5–7, thinks that she was related to Captain William Beckford Cox, who served at Bencoolen and died at Fort Marlborough, Sumatra, in 1814. Holman (see I, 370) suggests that Keats called and saw her on September 1.

[7] Reynolds.

pletely changed—they hate her; and from what I hear she is not without faults—of a real kind: but she has othe[r]s which are more apt to make women of inferior charms hate her. She is not a Cleopatra; but she is at least a Charmian. She has a rich eastern look; she has fine eyes and fine manners. When she comes into a room she makes an impression the same as the Beauty of a Leopardess. She is too fine and too concious of her Self to repulse any Man who may address her—from habit she thinks that nothing *particular*.[8] I always find myself more at ease with such a woman; the picture before me always gives me a life and animation which I cannot possibly feel with any thing inferiour—I am at such times too much occupied in admiring to be awkward or on a tremble. I forget myself entirely because I live in her. You will by this time think I am in love with her; so before I go any further I will tell you I am not—she kept me awake one Night [9] as a tune of Mozart's might do—I speak of the thing as a passtime and an amuzement than which I can feel none deeper than a conversation with an imperial woman the very 'yes' and 'no' of whose Lips is to me a Banquet.[1] I dont cry to take the moon home with me in my Pocket not [2] do I fret to leave her behind me. I like her and her like because one has no *sensations*—what we both are is taken for granted—You will suppose I have by this had much talk with her—no such thing—there are the Miss Reynoldses on the look out—They think I dont admire her because I did not stare at her—They call her a flirt to me—What a want of knowledge? she walks across a room in such a manner that a Man is drawn towards her with a magnetic Power. This they call flirting! they do not know things. They do not know what a Woman is. I believe tho' she has faults—the same as Charmian and Cleopatra might have had—Yet she is a fine thing speaking in a worldly way: for there are two distinct tempers of mind in which we judge of things—the worldly, theatrical and pantomimical; and the unearthly, spiritual and etherial—in the former Buonaparte, Lord Byron and this Charmian hold the first place in our Minds; in the latter John Howard, Bishop

[8] "From Jane Austen's letters we know that 'being particular' was, in plain English, flirting" (Hewlett, p. 226).

[9] Her voice and shape "haunted me these two days," he wrote about September 22 (I, 370).

[1] Jack Stillinger cites *Much Ado about Nothing*, II.iii.21 f., "his words are a very fantastical banquet."

[2] *For* nor.

Hooker rocking his child's cradle [3] and you my dear Sister are the conquering feelings. As a Man in the world I love the rich talk of a Charmian; as an eternal Being I love the thought of you. I should like her to ruin me, and I should like you to save me. Do not think my dear Brother from this that my Passions are head long or likely to be ever of any pain to you—no

> "I am free from Men of Pleasure's cares
> By dint of feelings far more deep than theirs"

This is Lord Byron,[4] and is one of the finest things he has said—I have no town talk for you, as I have not been much among people —as for Politics they are in my opinion only sleepy because they will soon be too wide awake—Perhaps not—for the long and continued Peace of England itself has given us notions of personal safety which are likely to prevent the reestablishment of our national Honesty—There is of a truth nothing manly or sterling in any part of the Government. There are many Madmen In the Country, I have no doubt, who would like to be beheaded on tower Hill merely for the sake of eclat, there are many Men like Hunt who from a principle of taste would like to see things go on better, there are many like Sir F. Burdett [5] who like to sit at the head of political dinners—but there are none prepared to suffer in obscurity for their Country—the motives of our wo[r]st Men are interest and of our best Vanity—We have no Milton, no Algernon Sidney [6] —Governers in these days loose the title of Man in exchange for that of Diplomat and Minister—We breathe in a sort of Officinal Atmosphere—All the departments of Government have strayed far from Spimpicity [7] which is the greatest of Strength—there is as much difference in this respect between the present Government and oliver Cromwell's, as there is between the 12 Tables of Rome and the volumes of Civil Law which were digested by Justinian. A Man now entitlerd [7] Chancellor has the same honour paid to him whether he be a Hog or a Lord Bacon. No sensation is created by Greatness but by the number of orders a Man has at his Button holes Not-

[3] Howard (1726?–1790), famous philanthropist and reformer. Richard Hooker (1554?–1600) was not a bishop. Keats had been reading some such edition as Izaak Walton's *The Lives of Dr. John Donne, . . . Mr. Richard Hooker*, etc. (1805), I, 265 f.

[4] MBF identifies the lines in Hunt's *Story of Rimini*, III.121 f. (*Poetical Works*, ed. H. S. Milford [1923], p. 16, "And had been kept from men of pleasure's cares/ By dint of feelings still more warm than theirs").

[5] Sir Francis Burdett (1770–1844), politician.

[6] (1622–1683), republican. [7] *Sic.*

withstand [8] the part which the Liberals take in the Cause of Napoleon I cannot but think he has done more harm to the life of Liberty than any one else could have done: not that the divine right Gentlemen have done or intend to do any good—no they have taken a Lesson of him and will do all the further harm he would have done without any of the good—The worst thing he has done is, that he has taught them how to organize their monstrous armies—The Emperor Alexander [9] it is said intends to divide his Empire as did Diocletian—creating two Czars besides himself, and continuing the supreme Monarch of the whole—Should he do this and they for a series of Years keep peacable among themselves Russia may spread her conquest even to China—I think a very likely thing that China itself may fall Turkey certainly will—Meanwhile european north Russia will hold its horns against the rest of Europe, intrieguing constantly with France. Dilke, whom you know to be a Godwin perfectibil[it]y Man,[1] pleases himself with the idea that America will be the country to take up the human intellect where england leaves off—I differ there with him greatly—A country like the united states whose greatest Men are Franklins and Washingtons will never do that—They are great Men doubtless but how are they to be compared to those our countrey men Milton and the two Sidneys—The one is a philosophical Quaker full of mean and thrifty maxims the other sold the very Charger who had taken him through all his Battles [2]—Those American's are great but

[8] Keats evidently had seen this obsolete variant of "notwithstanding" somewhere; he uses it again at I, 403. Jeffrey has "notwithstanding." De Selincourt, p. xxxvi, remarks: "It is evident from this passage how the cheery Radicalism of Hunt has been tempered by the spirit of the *Sonnets dedicated to National Independence and Liberty*" of Wordsworth.

[9] Alexander I (1777–1825). *G.M.*, September, 1818 (LXXXVIII, ii, 268), reports a rumor "that Russia is to be divided into three parts, the North, West, and South; over which Alexander will place his three brothers, with the title of Kings; while he remains supreme head of the whole."

[1] Keats had read Godwin's *Political Justice* as well as at least three of his novels (II, 24 f., 153).

[2] Keats is probably repeating remarks made by Bailey, who in his *Discourse* upon the death of Princess Charlotte Augusta (1817), p. 24, speaks of "the eagle-eyes of our Alfreds, our Sidneys, our Miltons, and our long train of heroes and patriots." Readers who are distressed by Keats's "libel" on America's greatest hero may be comforted by Washington's adopted son's, G. W. P. Custis', *Recollections . . . of Washington* (New York, 1860), p. 249: "On the day of the [British] surrender, the commander-in-chief rode his favorite and splendid charger, named Nelson. . . . This famous charger died at Mount Vernon many years after the Revolution, at a very advanced age. After the chief had ceased to mount him, he was never ridden, but grazed in a paddock in summer, and was well cared for in winter; and as often as . . . [Washington visited the paddock] the old war-horse would run, neighing, to the fence, proud to be caressed by the great master's

they are not sublime Man—the humanity of the United States can never reach the sublime—Birkbeck's [3] mind is too much in the American Stryle [4]—you must endeavour to infuse a little Spirit of another sort into the Settlement, always with great caution, for thereby you may do your descendents more good than you may imagine. If I had a prayer to make for any great good, next to Tom's recovery, it should be that one of your Children should be the first American Poet.[5] I have a great mind to make a prophecy and they say prophecies work out their own fullfillment.

'Tis 'the witching time of night' [6]
Orbed is the Moon and bright
And the Stars they glisten, glisten
Seeming with bright eyes to listen
For what listen they?
For a song and for a cha[r]m
See they glisten in alarm
And the Moon is waxing warm
To hear what I shall say.
Moon keep wide thy golden ears
Hearken Stars, and hearken Spheres
Hearken thou eternal Sky
I sing an infant's lullaby,
A pretty Lullaby!
Listen, Listen, listen, listen
Glisten, glisten, glisten, glisten
And hear my lullaby?
Though the Rushes that will make
Its cradle still are in the lake:
Though the ⟨f⟩ linnen then [7] that will be

---

hands." See also P. L. Ford's *The True George Washington* (Philadelphia, 1896), p. 195, on Nelson and Blueskin.

[3] Morris Birkbeck (1764–1825) bought 16,000 acres of land in Illinois, where he founded the town of Albion. He wrote *Notes on a Journey through France* (1814, 1815), *Notes on a Journey in America* (1817), *Letters from Illinois* (1818). He was drowned while swimming his horse across the Wabash River.

[4] *For* style (Jeffrey).

[5] This phrase aroused the ire of John Howard Payne (see I, 3 n.): see *KC*, II, 224 f.

[6] *Hamlet*, III.ii.406. Since *Hamlet* has "time" and since this text is unique, it is odd that Garrod, p. 494, reads "hour" with Milnes, I, 233.

[7] Garrod omits.

Its swathe is on the cotton tree;
Though the wollen that will keep
It wa[r]m, is on the silly sheep;
Listen Stars light,[8] listen, listen
Glisten, Glisten, glisten, glisten
And hear my lullaby!
Child! I see thee! Child I've found thee
Midst of the quiet all ⟨the⟩ around thee!
Child I see thee! Ch[i]ld I spy thee
And thy mother sweet is nigh thee!
Child I know thee! Child no more
But a Poet *ever*more
See, See the Lyre, the Lyre
In a flame of fire
Upon the little cradle's top
Flaring, flaring, flaring.
Past the eyesight's bearing—
Awake it from its sleep
And see if it can keep
Its eyes upon the blaze.
Amaze, Amaze!
It stares, it stares, it stares
It dares what no one dares
It lifts its little hand into the flame
Unharm'd, and on the strings
sings
Paddles a little tune and ⟨signs⟩
With dumb endeavour sweetly!
Bard art thou completely!
Little Child
O' the [9] western wild
Bard art thou completely!—
Sweetly, with dumb endeavour.—
A Poet now or never!
Litt[l]e Child
O' the western wild
A Poet now or never!

[8] starlight *Garrod.* [9] th' *Garrod.*

This is friday, I know not what day of the Month [1]—I will enquire tomorrow for it is fit you should know the time I am writing. I went to Town yesterday, and calling at M[rs] Millar's was told that your Mother would not be found at home—I met Henry [2] as I turned the corner—I had no leisure to return, so I left the letters with him—He was looking very well—Poor Tom is no better to-night—I am affraid to ask him what Message I shall send from him —And here I could go on complaining of my Misery, but I will keep myself cheerful for your Sakes. With a great deal of trouble I have succeeded in getting Fanny to Hampstead—she has been several times [3]—M[r] Lewis [4] has been very kind to Tom all the Summer there has scar[c]e a day passed but he has visited him, and not one day without bringing or sending some fruit of the nicest kind. He has been very assiduous in his enquiries after you—It would give the old Gentleman a great pleasure if you would send him a Sheet enclosed in the next parcel to me, after you receive this—how long it will be first—Why did I not write to Philadelphia? Really I am sorry for that neglect—I wish to go on writing ad infinitum, to you—I wish for interresting matter, and a pen as swift as the wind—But the fact is I go so little into the Crowd now that I have nothing fresh and fresh every day to speculate upon, except my own Whims and Theroies—I have been but once to Haydon's, onece to Hunt's, once to Rices, once to Hessey's I have not seen Taylor, I have not been to the Theatre—Now if I had been many times to all these and was still in the habit of going I could on my return at night have each day something new to tell you of without any stop—But now I have such a dearth that when I get to the end of this sentence and to the bottom of this page I much [5] wait till I can find something interesting to you before I begin another.—[6] After all it is not much matter what it may be about; for the very words from such a distance penned by this hand will be grateful to

[1] October 16.

[2] As noted above (I, 393), Henry Wylie apparently lived with his aunt on Henrietta Street (see also II, 60).

[3] But certainly not after the first week in October: see I, 375 n.

[4] MBF has found "Mr. Israel Lewis" living at Well Walk (1815–1821) in a house rented at £80 yearly and "Mr. Lewis" living in the Vale of Health (1818–1820) in a house rented at £35 yearly. Keats mentions "M[r] David Lewis" at II, 253. Fanny Keats lived with a Mr. and Mrs. Lewis, Beaufort Row, Chelsea, in 1826 before her marriage (Adami, pp. 122 f.).

[5] *For* must.

[6] The page ends here.

you—even though I were to coppy out the tale of Mother Hubbard or Little Red Riding Hood—I have been over to Dilke's this evening—there with Brown we have been talking of different and indifferent Matters—of Euclid, of Metaphisics of the Bible, of Shakspeare of the horrid System and conseque[nce]s of the fagging at great Schools—I know not yet how large a parcel I can send—I mean by way of Letters—I hope there can be no objection to my dowling up [7] a qui[r]e made into a small compass—That is the manner in which I shall write. I shall send you more than Letters—I mean a tale—which I must begin on account of the activity of my Mind; of its inability to remain at rest—It must be prose and not very exciting.[8] I must do this because in the way I am at present situated I have too many interruptions to a train of feeling to be able to w[r]ite Poetry—So I shall write this Tale, and if I think it worth while get a duplicate made before I send it off to you—This is a fresh beginning the 21st October—Charles and Henry were with us on Sunday [9] and they brought me your Letter to your Mother—we agreed to get a Packet off to you as soon as possible. I shall dine with your Mother tomorrow, when they have promised to have their Letters ready. I shall send as soon as possible without thinking of the little you may have from me in the first parcel, as I intend as I said before to begin another Letter of more regular information. Here I want to communicate so largely in a little time that I am puzzled where to direct my attention. Haslam has promised to let me know from Capper and Hazlewood.[1] For want of something better I shall proceed to give you some extracts from my Scotch Letters—Yet now I think on it why not send you the letters themselves—I have three of them at present—I beli[e]ve Haydon has two which I will get in time.[2] I dined with your Mother & Henry at Mrs Millar's on thursday [3] when they gave me their Letters Charles's I have not yet he has promised to send it. The thought of sending my scotch Letters has determined me to enclose a few more which I have received and which will give you the best cue to how I am going on better than you could otherwise know—Your Mother

[7] Does he mean "dowel, to fasten with a pin"?
[8] See I, 377 n. [9] October 18.
[1] Stockbrokers of 15 Angel Court, Throgmorton Street.
[2] Actually Haydon never returned Nos. 97 and 101. Keats was writing on October 21. With the next sentence he resumed writing probably on October 24.
[3] October 22.

was well and I was sorry I could not stop later. I called on Hunt yesterday—it has been always my fate to meet Ollier there—On thursday I walked with Hazlitt as far as covent Garden: he was going to play Rackets—I think Tom has been rather better these few last days—he has been less nervous. I expect Reynolds tomorrow [4] Since I wrote thus far I have met with that same Lady again,[5] whom I saw at Hastings and whom I met when we were going to the English Opera.[6] It was in a street which goes from Bedford Row to Lamb's Conduit Street—I passed her and turrned back—she seemed glad of it; glad to see me and not offended at my passing her before We walked on towards Islington where we called on a friend of her's who keeps a Boarding School.[7] She has always been an enigma to me—she has ⟨new⟩ been in a Room with you and with Reynolds and wishes we should be acquainted without any of our common acquaintance knowing it. As we went along, some times through shabby, sometimes through decent Street[s] I had my guessing at work, not knowing what it would be and prepared to meet any surprise—First it ended at this Hou{s}e at Islington: on parting from which I pressed to attend her home. She consented and then again my thoughts were at work what it might lead to, tho' now they had received a sort of genteel hint from the Boarding School. Our Walk ended in 34 Gloucester Street Queen Square—not exactly so for we went up stairs into her sitting room—a very tasty sort of place with Books, Pictures a bronze statue of Buonaparte, Music, æolian Harp; a Parrot a Linnet—A Case of choice Liquers &c &c &c she behaved in the kindest manner—made me take home a Grouse for Tom's dinner—Asked for my address for

[4] Sunday, October 25.

[5] Keats was at Hastings at the end of May or the beginning of June, 1818 (No. 27). MBF plausibly suggests that he met "that same Lady again" in the afternoon of Saturday, October 24, and wrote this account of it that night. The lady from Hastings has been identified by Richardson, pp. 20, 172, and Gittings, pp. 30–36, 54–63, as Mrs. Isabella Jones. That beautiful, if enigmatic, woman, whose "protector" was an elderly Irishman, Donat O'Callaghan, was known to many members of the Keats circle, and, according to Woodhouse, suggested the subject of "The Eve of St. Agnes." See also *KC*, I, 260, II, 469.

[6] He refers to this visit to the English Opera, or Lyceum Theatre, in the Strand again at II, 8. It probably was made shortly before George's marriage in May, 1818.

[7] Gittings, pp. 32, 204, thinks that the friend was Mrs. Green, of Duncan Terrace, near the Angel, Islington, the wife of Lieutenant-Colonel Thomas Green, 6th Regiment of Native Infantry, Madras Presidency. Around the corner from Isabella Jones's at 2 Brunswick Row, Queen Square, he notes, there was a Miss Green's Boarding-School that had been connected with a Mary Green since 1815.

the purpose of sending more game—As I had warmed with her before and kissed her—I though[t] it would be living backwards not to do so again—she had a better taste: she perceived how much a thing of course it was and shrunk from it—not in a prudish way but in as I say a good taste—She cont[r]ived to disappoint me in a way which made me feel more pleasure than a simple kiss could do—she said I should please her much more if I would only press her hand and go away. Whether she was in a different disposition when I saw her before—or whether I have in fancy wrong'd her I cannot tell—I expect to pass some pleasant hours with her now and then: in which I feel I shall be of service to her in matters of knowledge and taste: if I can I will—I have no libidinous thought about her—she and your George are the only women à peu près de mon age whom I would be content to know for their mind and friendship alone—I shall in a short time write you as far as I know how I intend to pass my Life—I cannot think of those things now Tom is so unwell and weak. Notwithstand [8] your Happiness and your recommendation I hope I shall never marry. Though the most beautiful Creature were waiting for me at the end of a Journey or a Walk; though the carpet were of Silk, the Curtains of the morning Clouds; the chairs and Sofa stuffed with Cygnet's down; the food Manna, the Wine beyond Claret, the Window opening on Winander mere, I should not feel—or rather my Happiness would

s

not be so fine, a⟨nd⟩ my Solitude is sublime. Then instead of what I have described, there is a Sublimity to welcome me home—The roaring of the wind is my wife and the Stars through the window pane are my Children. The mighty abstract Idea I have of Beauty in all things stifles the more divided and minute domestic happiness —an amiable wife and sweet Children I contemplate as a part of that Bea{u}ty. but I must have a thousand of those beautiful particles to fill up my heart. I feel more and more every day, as my imagination strengthens, that I do not live in this world alone but in a thousand worlds—No sooner am I alone than shapes of epic greatness are stationed around me, and serve my Spirit the office ⟨of⟩ which is equivalent to a king's body guard—then 'Tragedy, with scepter'd pall, comes sweeping by" [9] According to my state of mind

[8] See I, 397 n.
[9] Adapted from Milton's "Il Penseroso," lines 97 f.

I am with Achilles shouting in the Trenches [1] or with Theocritus
w
in the Vales of Sicily. Or I thro⟨ugh⟩ my whole being into Triolus [2] and repeating those lines, 'I wander, like a lost soul upon the stygian Banks staying for waftage," [3] I melt into the air with a voluptuousness so delicate that I am content to be alone—These things combined with the opinion I have of the generallity of women—who appear to me as children to whom I would rather give a Sugar Plum than my time, form a barrier against Matrimony which I rejoice in. I have written this that you might see I have my share of the highest pleasures and that though I may choose to pass my days alone I shall be no Solitary. You see therre is nothing spleenical in all this. The only thing that can ever affect me personally for more than one short passing day, is any doubt about my powers for poetry—I seldom have any, and I look with hope to the nighing time when I shall have none. I am as happy as a Man can be—that is in myself I should be happy if Tom was well, and I knew you were passing pleasant days—Then I should be most enviable—with the yearning Passion I have for the beautiful,[4] connected and made one with the ambition of my intellect. Th[i]nk of my Pleasure in Solitude, in comparison of my commerce with the world—there I am a child—there they do not know me not even my most intimate acquaintance—I give into their feelings as though I were refraining from irritating {a} little child—Some think me middling, others silly, others foolish—every one thinks he sees my weak side against my will; when in truth it is with my will—I am content to be thought all this because I have in my own breast so great a resource. This is one great reason why they like me so; because they can all show to advantage in a room, and eclipese from a certain tact one who is reckoned to be a good Poet—I hope I am not here playing tricks 'to make the angels weep': [5] I think not: for

[1] See the *Iliad*, XVIII.228, which Pope translated "Thrice from the trench his dreadful voice he raised." Bailey told Milnes in 1849 (*KC*, II, 277): "Another object of his [Keats's] enthusiastic admiration was the Homeric character of Achilles—especially when he is described as 'shouting in the trenches'."

[2] So also Jeffrey for "Troilus."

[3] *Troilus and Cressida*, III.ii.9–11, "I stalk about her door,/ Like a strange soul upon the Stygian banks/ Staying for waftage."

[4] Keats often repeats this idea, as at I, 388, II, 126.

[5] *Measure for Measure*, II.ii.121 f., "Plays such fantastic tricks before high heaven/ As makes," etc.

I have not the least contempt for my species; and though it may sound paradoxical: my greatest elevations of soul leave⟨s⟩ me every time more humbled—Enough of this—though in your Love for me you will not think it enough.[6] Haslam has been here this morning, and has taken all the Letter's except this sheet, which I shall send him by the Twopenny, as he will put the Parcel in the Boston post Bag by the advice of Capper and Hazlewood, who assure him of the safety and expedition that way—the Parcel will be forwarded to Warder[7] and thence to you all the same. There will not be a Philadelphia Ship for these six weeks—by that time I shall have another Letter to you. Mind you I mark this Letter A.[8] By the time you will receive this you will have I trust passed through the greatest of your fatigues. As it was with your Sea sickness I shall not hear of them till they are past. Do not set to your occupation with too great an a[n]xiety—take it calmly—and let your health be the prime consideration. I hope you will have a Son, and it is one of my first wishes to have him in my Arms—which I will do please God before he cuts one double tooth. Tom is rather more easy than he has been: but is still so nervous that I can not speak to him of these Matters —indeed it is the care I have had to keep his Mind aloof from feelings too acute that has made this Letter so short a one—I did not like to write before him a Letter he knew was to reach your hands —I cannot even now ask him for any Message—his heart speaks to you—Be as happy as you can. Think of me and for my sake be cheerful. Believe me my dear Brother and sister

Your anxious and affectionate Brother

John—

This day is my Birth day—

All our friends have been anxious in their enquiries and all send their rembrances

[6] Some time elapsed between the writing of this sentence on October 24 and of the next. Perhaps Keats began with "Haslam has been" and finished the letter on "my Birth day," but unluckily he did not prevent controversy by telling whether the birthday was October 29 or 31.

[7] Who is mentioned again at II, 229.

[8] See how "B" begins No. 137.

· 121 ·

TO FANNY KEATS [1]

5 November 1818

Address: Miss Keats/ Miss Tuckey's/ Walthamstow—
Postmarks: HampsteadNO; 7 o'Clock NO 5 1818 Nt

My dear Fanny,

I have seen Mr [2] Abbey three times about you, and have not been able to get his consent—

He says that once more between this and the Holydays will be sufficient. What can I do? I should have been at Walthamstow several times, but I am not able to leave Tom for so long a time as that would take me. Poor Tom has been rather better these 4 last days in consequence of obtaining a little rest a nights. Write to me as often as you can, and believe that I would do any thing to give you any pleasure—we must as yet wait patiently—

Your affectionate Brother
John—

· 122 ·

TO JAMES RICE [1]

24 November 1818

Address: Mr James Rice/ Poland Street—
Postmarks: TwoPyPost Unpaid SOHampstead; 12 o'Clock NO 25 1818 Nn

My dear Rice, Well Walk—Novr 24—

Your amende honorable, I must call 'un surcroit d'amitié' for I am not at all sensible of any thing but that you were unfortunately engaged and I was unfortunately in a hurry. I completely understand your feeling in this mistake, and find in it that ballance

[1] *ALS:* British Museum. [2] *Written* Mrs.

[1] *ALS:* Harvard. Woodhouse copied this letter in his letter-book, pp. 113 f.

of comfort which remains after regretting your uneasiness—I have long made up my Mind to take for granted the genuine heartedness of my friends notwithstanding any temporery ambiguousness in their behaviour or their tongues; nothing of which how[ev]er I had the least scent of this morning. I say completely understand; for I am everlastingly getting my mind into such like painful trammels—and am even at this moment suffering under them in the case of a friend [2] of ours. I will tell you—Two most unfortunate and paralel slips—it seems downright preintention. A friend says to me 'Keats I shall go and see Severn this Week' 'Ah' says I 'You want him to take your Portrait' and again 'Keats' says a friend 'When will you come to town again' 'I will' says I 'let you have the Mss next week' In both these I appear to attribute and [3] interested motive to each of my friends' questions—the first made him flush; the second made him look angry—And yet I am innocent—in both cases my Mind leapt over every interval ⟨between⟩ to what I saw was per se a pleasant subject with him—You see I have no allowances to make—you see how far I am from supposing you could show me any neglect. I very much regret the long time I have been obliged to exile from you—for I have had one or two rather pleasant occasions to confer upon with you—What I have heard from George is [4] favorable—I expect soon a Letter from the Settlement itself—

Your sincere friend
John Keats

I cannot give any good news of Tom—

[2] Perhaps Reynolds. But if Keats refers to two friends, the second may have been Woodhouse.

[3] *For* an. [4] *Originally* have head . . . it.

· 123 ·

TO MRS. BURRIDGE DAVENPORT [1]

November 1818

Mr Keats's Compliments to Mrs Daventorp and is sorry to say that his Brother continues in the same state. He and his Brother are extremely sensible of Mrs Davenport's kindness—

· 124 ·

TO FANNY KEATS [1]

30 November 1818

Address: Miss Keats/ Miss Caley's [2] School—/ Walthamstow
Postmarks: TwoPyPost Unpaid SOHampstead; {12 o}'Clock DE 1 {1}818 N{n}; 4 o'Clock DE 1 {1818}

Tuesday Morn

My dear Fanny,

Poor Tom has been so bad that I have delayed your visit hither —as it would be so painful to you both. I cannot say he is any better this morning—he is in a very dangerous state—I have scar[c]e any hopes of him [3]—Keep up your spirits for me my dear Fanny—repose entirely in

Your affectionate Brother
John.

[1] *ALS:* British Museum. This note, with the lady's name once misspelled, was sent by messenger. It is endorsed in an unidentified hand "Nov 1818/ Jno Keats." Richardson, pp. 12 f., 156, observes that Mr. Davenport, whose Christian name has been given as Benjamin, Burrage, and Burridge, was in 1815 a merchant at 46 Lime Street and then at 2 (later 3) Dunster Court, Mincing Lane. He lived at 2 Church Row in one of the two finest Georgian buildings in Hampstead. Keats and later Fanny Brawne (see Edgcumbe, pp. 91–94) attended parties there, but Mrs. Davenport's name does not occur again in Keats's letters.

[1] *ALS:* British Museum.

[2] An error, no doubt caused by his agitation, for Miss Tuckey's. See I, 364 n.

[3] Tom died at 8 A.M., Tuesday, December 1 (see the next letter). In his *Life of John Keats* (*KC*, II, 64) Brown says: "Early one morning I was awakened in my bed by a pressure on my hand. It was Keats, who came to tell me his brother was no more." The present letter was postmarked at noon on December 1. Adami, p. 59 n., is evidently correct in saying that Keats wrote the letter during the night of November 30 to prepare

· 125 ·

CHARLES BROWN TO RICHARD WOODHOUSE [1]

1 December 1818

Address: ——Woodhouse Esqr

Hampstead
Tuesday 1st Dec^r^ [2]

Sir,

Mr Keats requests me to inform you his brother Thomas died this morning at 8 o'Clock quietly & without pain—Mr Keats is pretty well & desires to be remembered to you—

I am, Sir,
Your obed^t^ hum Servt
Chas Brown.

· 126 ·

FROM RICHARD WOODHOUSE [1]

10 December 1818

My dear Keats,

I have to thank you for a mark of kind consideration, shewn at a moment when an attention to such matters must have been peculiarly irksome.[2]—Accept this late acknowledgment—Believe me, I deeply sympathised with you, though I could not bring myself to interrupt the sacredness of recent affliction with common places

---

Fanny for the worst and posted it after Tom's death as he walked to or from Brown's. Tom was buried at St. Stephen's, Coleman Street, December 7 (Willard B. Pope, *TLS*, December 22, 1932, p. 977), a long interval corresponding to the seven days that elapsed between his father's death and burial, April 16–23, 1804. Early in January, 1819, Hunt wrote to Clarke (*Recollections of Writers* [1878], p. 201): "[Keats] has just lost his brother Tom after a most exemplary attendance on him. The close of such lingering illness, however, can hardly be lamented."

[1] *ALS:* Harvard. First printed by Lowell, II, 117. Woodhouse made a transcript of the letter in his letter-book, p. 25.

[2] "1818" is added in Woodhouse's hand. With the address compare that of No. 89.

[1] *ALS:* Harvard (first printed in *KC*, I, 70–72). Woodhouse's draft of this letter, differing in some details from that sent by messenger and here printed, is in the Pierpont Morgan Library.

[2] He refers to No. 125.

of condolence. Your brother is now, we trust, happier than we have ability to wish him; and it is our duty to turn eyes of gratitude around for the many blessings that yet remain to us.—It will please me to hear that you are well, and are recovering from the Shock of your loss.

I send enclosed a letter [3] which, when read, take the trouble to return to me. The history of its reaching me is this.—My cousin, Miss Frogley of Hounslow, borrowed my copy of Endymion for a specified time. Before she had time to look into it; her and my friend Mr Hy Neville of Esher,[4] Who was house⟨hold⟩ Surgeon to the late Princess Charlotte,[5] insisted upon having it to read for a day or two, & undertook to make my cousins peace with me on account of the extra delay.—Neville told me that one of the Misses Porter (of romance celcbrity) [6] had seen it on his table, dipped into it, & expressed a wish to read it. I desired he would keep it as long, and lend it to as many, as he pleased, provided it was not allowed to slumber upon any one's shelf. I learned subsequently from Miss Frogley that those ladies had requested of Mr Neville, if he was acquainted with the author, that they might have the pleasure of an Introduction.—About a week back the enclosed was transmitted by Mr Neville to my cousin, as a species of apology for keeping her so long without the book. And she sent it to me knowing it would give me pleasure.—I forward it to you, for somewhat the same reason, but principally because it gives me the opportunity of naming to you (which It would have been fruitless to do before) the opening [7] there is for an introduction to a Class of society, from which you may possibly derive advantage as well as gratification, if you think proper to avail yourself of it.—In such case I should be very happy to further your wishes—But do just as you please —If you decline the overture, rely upon it no Intimation from me shall ever reach the quarter in question, that the letter enclosed, or any thing that has transpired has come to your ear.—The whole

[3] See II, 9 f.

[4] Mary Frogley, "a member of the social circle of the Mathews, the cockney circle in which Keats and his brother George moved in 1814 and 1815" (Finney, I, 34 f.), gave Woodhouse copies of various poems by Keats which she had obtained from George Keats and Kirkman (see II, 7 n., 27). She married Neville on March 6, 1820.

[5] See I, 228 n.

[6] Jane (1776–1850), author of *Thaddeus of Warsaw* and *The Scottish Chiefs*, and Anna Maria (1780–1832), author of *The Barony*, *The Hungarian Brothers*, *Don Sebastian*, and so on.

[7] *Written* openening.

is entirely at present "inter nos."—I go out of town tomorrow for 3 or 4 days,—Do not therefore write to me till after Tuesday next.[8] —Believe me, my Dear Keats,

Most sincerely yours,
Rich[d] Woodhouse.
Temple 10 Dec[r] 1818.

P.S. I believe you are not at Hampstead,[9] I shall therefore beg Taylor to forward you this.

Jn[o] Keats Esq[r]

·127·

TO MRS. GEORGE REYNOLDS[1]

15 (?) December 1818

Address: M[rs] Reynolds/ Little Britain/ Christ's Hospital
Postmarks: TwoPyPost Unpaid SOHampstead; (*another blurred*) ... DE ... 1818 N[n]

My dear M[rs] Reynolds, Wentworth Place Tuesd—

When I left you yesterday, 't was with the conviction that you thought I had received no previous invitation for Christmas day: the truth is I had, and had accepted it[2] under the conviction that I should be in Hampshire[3] at the time: else believe me I should not have done so, but kept in Mind my old friends. I will not speak of the proportion of pleasure I may receive at different Houses—that never enters my head—you may take for a truth that I would have given up even what I did see to be a greater pleasure, for the

[8] The 15th. Keats waited till the 18th (No. 128).

[9] Keats had moved, or was about to move (II, 4), from Well Walk into Brown's Wentworth Place.

[1] *ALS:* Robert H. Taylor (formerly owned by A. S. W. Rosenbach). On Monday, December 21, Keats went to Walthamstow in the morning and dined with Haydon (I, 413 f.), and so the Tuesday on which he wrote this awkward note seems likely to have been December 15. On Monday, December 14, he had called on Mrs. Wylie, Mrs. Millar, Hazlitt, and presumably Mrs. Reynolds (II, 6, 8), and on December 22 (II, 15) he declared, "I seldom go to little Britain."

[2] From Mrs. Brawne. On December 13, 1821, Fanny Brawne (Edgcumbe, p. 55) told Fanny Keats that December 25, 1818, "was the happiest day I had ever then spent." See I, 67.

[3] At Bedhampton (II, 18, 32).

sake of old acquaintanceship—time is nothing—two years are as long as twenty—

Your's faithfully
John Keats

· 128 ·

TO RICHARD WOODHOUSE [1]

18 December 1818

Address: Richd Woodhouse Esqre/ Taylor and Hessey/ Fleet Street—
Postmarks: TwoPyPost Unpaid SOHampstead; 7 o'Clock DE 18 1818 N^{T}

My dear Woodhouse, Wentworth Place Friday Morn [2]—

I am greatly obliged to you. I must needs feel flattered by making an impression on a set of Ladies—I should be content to do so in meretricious romance verse if they alone and not Men were to judge. I should like very much to know those Ladies—tho' look here Woodhouse—I have a new leaf to turn over—I must work—I must read—I must write—I am unable to affrod [3] time for new acquaintances—I am scarcely able to do my duty to those I have—Leave the matter to chance—But do not forget to give my Remb^{rs} to you Cousin [4]

* * *

[1] *AL:* Harvard. Blunden, p. 500, thinks that this letter " 'puts Woodhouse in his place'—Keats seems to be deliberately keeping him at a distance." Probably Woodhouse thought otherwise, for he made a transcript in his letter-book, p. 27, noting: "N.B. I had sent Miss Porter's Note [which he copied on p. 26] to K. for perusal; with an Intimation that those ladies has [*sic*] asked Neville if he was known to them: as they sho^{d} be happy to be favored with an Introduction—& with an offer of aiding his wishes, if he desired to avail himself of the overture: & a promise of not noticing that he had seen the lady's letter or heard of her wishes, in case he declined it.—The above was the answer.—The modesty with which he speaks of his work is singular—the Sentiments ⟨of⟩ in his letter are in unison with those of the Note to M^{r} ⟨Hessey⟩ Taylor of 27 Ap^{l} respecting his studies." Woodhouse refers to No. 78, which is postmarked April 27, 1818.

[2] Friday was December 18.

[3] *For* afford.

[4] Mary Frogley (see I, 410 n.; H. W. Garrod, *TLS*, September 5, 1935, p. 552; and MBF, the same, September 19, 1935, p. 580). The signature is cut off.

· 129 ·

TO FANNY KEATS [1]

18 December 1818

Address: Miss Keats/ Miss Tuckey's/ Walthamstow—
Postmarks: {7 o'Clo}ck DE 21 1818 EV: *others blurred* [2]

My dear Fanny,

So much time has passed with me this last year, without my having had power to employ it—which is a[b]solutely necessary—that I am glad to take advantage of the present time to study and write a little—that is the reason I have not been to see you—However if on Monday [3] the frost continue I will endeavour to be up early and cut across the fields.

Your ever affectionate Brother
John—

· 130 ·

TO B. R. HAYDON [1]

20 December 1818 [2]

Wentworth Place

My dear Haydon,

I had an engagement to day—and it is so fine a morning that I cannot put it off—I will be with you tomorrow when we will thank the Gods though you have bad eyes and I am idle—

[1] *ALS:* Keats Museum. First printed by MBF, *TLS,* October 4, 1934, p. 670. It is written on the back of a letter from Mrs. Dilke to Fanny Keats (for which see MBF, 1952, p. 268). Dilatory as always, Mrs. Dilke failed to post the double letter promptly.

[2] A "TwoPyPost" stamp is imposed on a dated stamp with "181{8}." On the address page Dilke wrote what seems to have been intended for

"John
Keats }."

[3] December 21, the day on which the letter was postmarked. This promise (see also I, 414 n.) was carried out (II, 14).

[1] *ALS:* Formerly attached to Haydon's Journal, now at Harvard.

[2] Previously dated January 2, 1819, which (see *GM,* LXXXIX, i, 94) was not fine but a cold, foggy day. Keats had accepted an invitation to dine with Haydon on Sunday the 20th (II, 12), but in the present letter he broke it at the eleventh hour to dine instead with Haslam (II, 14).

I regret more than any thing the not being able to dine with you to day—I have had several movements that way—but then I should disappoint one who has been my true friend—I will be with you tomorrow mo[r]ning [3] and stop all day—we will hate the profane vulgar [4] & make us Wings—God bless you

J—Keats

· 131 ·

TO B. R. HAYDON [1]

22 December 1818

Address: R. B.[2] Haydon/ Lisson Grove North/ Paddington
Postmarks: TwoPyPost Unpaid SOHampstead; 12 o'Clock DE 23 1818 N^{n}; 4 o'Clock 23 DE 1818 EV

My dear Haydon, Tuesday Wentworth Place—

Upon my Soul I never felt your going out of the room at all [3] —and believe me I never rhodomontade any where but in your Company [4]—my general Life in Society is silence.[5] I feel in myself all the vices of a Poet, irritability, love of effect and admiration—and influenced by such devils I may at times say more rediculous things than I am aware of—but I will put a stop to that in a manner I have long⟨e⟩ resolved upon—I will buy a gold ring and put it on my finger—and from that time a Man of superior head shall never have occasion to pity me, or one of inferior Nunskull to chuckle at me—I am certainly more for greatness in a Shade than in the open day—I am speaking as a mortal—I should say I value more the Priviledge of seeing great things in loneliness—than the fame of a Prophet—Yet here I am sinning—so I will turn to a thing I have thought on more—I mean you means till your Picture [6] be

[3] Which meant any time before dinner. In the forenoon of December 21 Keats visited Fanny Keats at Walthamstow. He was back in time to dine with Haydon about three o'clock (II, 14), and for his discourteous "going out of the room" at that dinner Haydon the next morning sent an apology by his servant (No. 131).

[4] See I, 330 n.

[1] *ALS:* Formerly attached to Haydon's Journal, now at Harvard.

[2] *For* B. R.

[3] When Keats dined with him on the preceding day (No. 130).

[4] He might have added "and in Woodhouse's": see I, 325 n.

[5] Compare his comment to George at II, 12.

[6] "Christ's Entry."

finished: not only now but for this year and half have I thought of it. Believe me Haydon I have that sort of fire in my Heart that would sacrifice every thing I have to your service—I speak without any reserve—I know you would do so for me—I open my heart to you in a few words—I will do this sooner than you shall be distressed: but let me be the last stay—ask the rich lovers of art first —I'll tell you why—I have a little money which may enable me to study and to travel three or four years—I never expect to get any thing by my Books: and moreover I wish to avoid publishing—I admire Human Nature but I do not like *Men*—I should like to compose things honourable to Man—but not fingerable over by *Men*. So I am anxious to exist with [7] troubling the printer's devil or drawing upon Men's and Women's admiration—in which great solitude I hope God will give me strength to rejoice Try the long purses—but do not sell your drawing or I shall consider it a breach of friendship.[8] I am sorry I was not at home when Salmon* called—Do write and let me know all you present whys and wherefores—

Your's most faithfully
John Keats

*My Servant/ BRH [9]

· 132 ·

FROM B. R. HAYDON [1]

23 (?) December 1818

Keats! Upon my Soul I could have wept at your letter; to find one of real heart & feeling is to me a blessed solace; I have met with such heartless treatment from those to whom without ⟨men given⟩ reserve I had given my Friendship, that I expected no{t} what I wished in human Nature—th{ere} is only one besides yourself whoever offer{ed to}

[7] *For* without.

[8] Yet in September, 1819 (II, 206), Keats was angry because Haydon had not "sold his drawings to supply me."

[9] His name actually was Salmon, though Penrose (pp. 187, 241) has Haydon call him "Sammons, my model and corporal of the 2nd Life Guards," who was six feet three inches tall. After Mr. Lewis had called in the morning of December 22 (II, 15), Keats left the house, but returned to write this letter in time to have it postmarked at noon.

[1] *ALS:* An undated letter formerly attached to Haydon's Journal, now at Harvard. Haydon received No. 131 on December 23 and, overcome by the offer of a loan, answered it at once.

act & did act with such affection, he wa{s} of a different temperament from us; coo{ler} but not kinder, he did his best from *moral* feeling, and not from bursting impulse; but still he did it; you have behaved to me as I would have behaved to you my dear fellow, and if I am constrained to come to you at last; Your property shall only be a transfer for a limited time on such security as will ensure you repayment in case of my Death—that is whatever part of it you assist me with: but I will try every corner first—Ah my dear Keats my illness has been a severe touch!—I declare to God I do not feel alone i{n} the World now you have written me {th}at letter—If you go on writing as you {rep}eated the other night, you may wish to {live} in a sublime solitude, but you will {n}ot be allowed—I approve most completely {o}f your plan of travels and study, and {s}hould suffer torture if my wants {in}terrupted it—in short they shall not {m}y dear Keats—I believe you from my soul when you say you would sacrifice all for me; and when your means are gone, if God give me means my heart & house & home & every thing shall be shared with you—I mean this too—It has often occurred [2] to me but I have never spoken of it—My great object is the public encouragement of historical painting and the glory of England, in high Art, to ensure these I would lay my head on the block this instant—My illness the consequence of early excess in study, has fatigued most of my Friends—I have no reason to complain of the lovers of Art, I have been liberally assisted; but when a man comes again with a tale of his ill health; they dont believe him my dear Keats; can I bear the thousandth part of a dry hesitation, the searching scrutiny of an apprehensio{n} of insincerity; the musing hum of a *sounding* question; the prying, petty, paltry whining doubt, that is inferred from {a} wish *for a day to consider!*——Ah Kea{ts,} this is sad work for one of my soul, & Ambition. The truest thing you ever said of mortal was that I had a touch of Alexander in me! —I have, I know it, and the World shall know it, but this is the purgative drug I must first take,—Come so[o]n my dear fellow—Sunday [3] nobody is coming I believe—& I will lay [my] Soul bare before {you}—Your affectionate friend

B. R. Haydon

[2] *Written* orcurred.

[3] December 27. It was then that Haydon showed him the Ritchie letter (still in his Journal) that was postmarked "7 o'Clock 26 DE 1818 NT" (see II, 16).

·133·

TO JOHN TAYLOR[1]

24 December 1818

Address: John Taylor Esqre/ Taylor & Hessey's/ Fleet Street
Postmarks: HampsteadNO; 7 o'Clock DE 24 1818 N^{T}

My dear Taylor Wentworth Place

Can you lend me 30£ for a short time?—ten I want for myself —and twenty for a friend[2]—which will be repaid me by the middle of next Month—I shall go to Chichester on Wednesday[3] and perhaps stay a fortnight—I am affraid I shall not be able to dine with you before I return—Remember me to Woodhouse—

Your's sincerely
John Keats

·134·

TO FANNY KEATS[1]

30 December 1818

Address: Miss Keats/ R^{d} Abbey's Esqre/ Pancras Lane, Queen Street/ Cheapside
Postmarks: TwoPyPost Unpaid SOHampstead; 12 o'Clock DE 31 1818 N^{n}

My dear Fanny, Wentworth Place Wednesday—

I am confined at Hampstead with a sore throat; but I do not expect it will keep me above two or three days. I indended[2] to have been in Town yesterday but feel obliged to be careful a little while —I am in general so careless of these trifles, that they tease me for

[1] *ALS:* Harvard. Woodhouse made a transcript of this letter in his letter-book, p. 103.
[2] Presumably not Haydon.
[3] December 30, but a sore throat caused him to postpone the visit (II, 18). Instead he left London probably on January 18 or 19.
[1] *ALS:* British Museum. [2] *For* intended.

Months, when a few days care is all that is necessary—I shall not neglect any chance of an endeavour to let you return to School [3]—nor to procure you a Visit to Mrs Dilke's [4] which I have great fears about—Write me if you can find time—and also get a few lines ready for George as the Post sails next Wednesday.[5]

Your affectionate Brother
John—

[3] He failed: see II, 15, 38.
[4] "She never paid this visit" (Adami, p. 63 n.).
[5] January 6.

CHARLES BROWN'S
WALKS IN THE NORTH
1840

Charles Brown's Walks in the North (1840)

[Part of Charles Brown's Journal of his tour with Keats in Northern England and Scotland appeared in the *Plymouth and Devonport Weekly Journal*, October 1, 8, 15, 22, 1840. Not before reprinted (and because of the ravages of war now very rare), it is a valuable commentary on Keats's letters Nos. 91–97. I have corrected the most obvious typographical errors, while retaining some of Brown's odd spellings, and have omitted explanatory notes.]

WALKS IN THE NORTH,

During the Summer of 1818.

(WRITTEN EXCLUSIVELY FOR THIS PAPER.) [1]

CHAPTER I.

Lancaster to Bowness, 31 *Miles.*

The waies thorough which my weary steps I guyde,
In this delightfull Land * * *
Are so exceeding spacious and wyde,
And sprinckled with such sweet variety
Of all that pleasant is to eare and eye,
That I, nigh ravisht with rare thoughts delight,
My tedious travell do forget thereby,
And when I gin to feele decay of might,
It strength to me supplies, and chears my dulled spright.

Faery Queene.

Without preface—for the one I have written is more tedious than useful—imagine me setting out from Lancaster, accompanied by a dear and lamented friend, each with a knapsack on his back, to enjoy the scenery of Cumberland and Westmoreland, in our way to the Highlands of Scotland.

The early death of that dear friend is not lamented by me alone, but by his countrymen in general; for he was John Keats the poet.

[1] This title reappears at the head of the other three instalments.

Yet, before entirely taking leave of my rejected preface, it would not be amiss to extract one explanatory passage.

We were not bound on a journey of discovery into "the busy haunts of men." Not that cities, their rise, progress, and increasing prosperity, or the reverse, or their prevailing interests and politics, were objects of indifference; but attention to them, and a love of the beauty and sublimity of nature are so widely distinct in character as not to be harmonized together. Besides, large towns rarely lay in our route. On this account, my pains-taking journal, written at the conclusion of each several stage, though full twenty years old, may serve as an itinerary for a traveller on a similar excursion, equally well as if I had just taken off my knapsack at the end of my northern walks. A score of years will scarcely alter the appearance of a woodland scene; and a thousand years cannot affect the imperishable and unchangeable grandeur of mountain, rock, and torrent. It may be proper, also, to forewarn the reader that I did not go about with a hammer in my hand, to knock off a specimen of every rock in my way. I had no ambition to rival the geologists. Mine is literally a superficial view of nature; which has one recommendation at least —every body can understand it.

"Weather permitting," unless of the bad and excessive kind, was not of much force in our agreement. But, on the morning of our departure, ready to start at four, a heavy rain detained us till seven. The interim was occupied with Milton, and I particularly preached patience out of Samson Agonistes. When the rain had subsided into a Scotch mist, we chose to consider it as appropriate and complimentary, and we, therefore, felt a pleasure in encountering it. Just out of the town, we overheard a labourer rather sarcastically observe to his companion—"There go a couple of gentlemen!—having nothing to do, they are finding out hard work for themselves!"

True; and those who *must* work may be comforted still further by reflecting that all men, who lead happy lives, labour in some way or another, including the bodily fatigue of field sports and the mental exhaustion of study. Our fellow labourer was in the right. We all work for the means of enjoying life; some one way, some another; some for money, some for the pleasure of excitement, some for health.

Four miles brought us into Bolton to breakfast, when the rain came down heavily again. However, it is always a comfort to have actually begun a long intended journey; and we rejoiced to be out of that city, at the time of a general election, where "the aspiring blood of Lancaster" deprived us of all comfort. There we had to wait two hours for our promised dinner; and were then told—"Not a bed in the house, gentlemen!" Fortunately a private house received us—better than a public one on such roaring occasions.

At mid-day, contrary to the prophecies of country-folks, the clouds cleared off, and we had as pleasant a walk as the muddy state of the road would permit. Near the borders of Westmoreland, two miles from Bolton, there was a fine view, notwithstanding the mistiness of the horizon, and some impeding clouds that the wind had not strength to drive forward over the hills. On our arrival, quite ready for dinner, we turned into the first inn, the Green Dragon, and put up our petition with the usual phrase of—"what we could have?" A voice replied in an instant, and in the gruffest tone, "Nothing! you can have nothing here!" It was the Green Dragon himself, in the shape of a tall, corpulent figure, with the largest face that ever man was blessed with—a face like a target; and none that a starving traveller might be tempted to shoot at. This unfeeling lump went on to tell us his house was full of soldiers, and that he could neither give us food nor a room to sit in. Turning from him into the King's Arms, the landlady there uttered her spleen in a milder strain. She said—"Ah! gentlemen, the soldiers are upon us! The Lowthers had brought 'em here to be in readiness. There'll be sad work at Appleby! There's Mr. Brougham, a great speaker in the house, I understand, comes down to oppose the Lowthers. Dear me! dear me!—at this election time to have soldiers upon us, when we ought to be making a bit of money. Not to be able to entertain any body! There was yesterday—I was forced to turn away two parties in their own carriages; for I have not a room to offer, nor a bed for any one. You can't sleep here, gentlemen; but I can give you a dinner. Dear, dear me! It goes to my heart—my spirits are quite down—to be forced to turn away two such parties! Oh! it's the Lowthers as I suspect—but that's only one's own mind—that brought 'em in."

We truly sympathised with her grievance; for the turmoil of an election was a nuisance to the tranquilly disposed.

After dinner the rain returned. Though compelled to proceed, we gave up all idea of passing the night at Kendal. A little public-house on the road-side was a welcome sight. We entered, and beheld a most uninviting hostess, smoking her pipe in a most formidable style. She informed us her house was quite full, and sent us onward, under the protection of our oilskin capes, to a place called End Moor. There the landlady, eyeing the burthens on our backs, inquired if we provided our own eating; on being answered in the negative, she promised accommodation for the night; though, as she said, she was in a "*squeer*, as all her house was whitewashing." In the room, which served for parlour and kitchen, sat an old soldier—that is, no longer in the service, for he was not above forty. He was shrewd and good tempered—had served in America—in the Peninsula—indeed in the Continental war from the time of Sir John Moore to the battle of Waterloo. He had received but one bullet in his thigh, and a graze on the skull; and now, God bless him! he had a pension of fifteen pence a day. For some time it was difficult to change the conversation from the Appleby election. From a corner in the room came forth, still in a sort of puzzled doze, an old toper, one Richard Radshaw, drunk as a sponge. He staggered forward in an attitude something like a bear, half raising himself on his hind legs, and dangling his fore paws before him. Suddenly he thrust his face forward, made a grasp at my knapsack, and asked if we sold spectacles and razors. Being quietly discouraged he imagined me offended, protesting that nothing was further from his thoughts, and made his apology by assuring me he was always "foolish in his drink." He then whispered in my ear, "I never offend any man—not I!—so if you'll give me something to drink—why—I'll take it!" As this appeal was unavailing, he left the house in a maudlin fit of melancholy, hiccoughing out—"Ah, nobody trusts me with liquor! Well, I have seen all I ever loved to the grave, and I shall soon go there myself—and there'll be an end!"

While at tea, the attention of our hostess was attracted to our not using sugar, and called the unwilling notice of her loutish son to so economical a fact. Nay, on the following morning, she, the worthy Mrs. Black, almost made it a matter of conscience, on that score, to deduct a something from the reckoning.

During the evening I learnt more of poor Richard Radshaw. He had been once well to do, as a small farmer, with carts and horses, and all he wanted. His wife died; and then, in a short time, he lost both his sons, one in a fever, the other by an accident. No one was near him; for his two daughters were married to tradesmen in Lancaster. He endeavoured to drown his grief in liquor, became reckless, and neglected his farm till he was ruined. Now he was a day labourer, or he made bed mats, spending his money in drink as fast as he earned it.

Sorrow and solitariness may offer some excuse for the desperate remedy of intoxication; scarcely for its becoming an inveterate habit. Yet could not his daughters, by timely tokens of their affection and by their society, have saved him?

Without elevating him to the rank of a Lear in humble life, or degrading his daughters into a Regan and a Goneril, he may be commisserated, and, perhaps, they may be blamed.

One daughter, with a husband whose lordly will was not to be questioned, could not afford filial assistance, while he bluntly declared it was enough for him to support his own wife and family. The other daughter, indeed, ruled her husband; but she gave her father nothing, fearful it might add to his unhappy infirmity, often recurring, with many sighs and a few tears to his "distressing state," expatiating on her "hopelessness of his reformation," and protesting it was a subject which "cuts her heart in twain to dwell upon." And thus she had been known to drawlingly speak while taking her share of a pot of ale; but then, as she averred, her constitution was weak, and stood in need of a little help.

Richard Radshaw's case affords scope for a comparison between the evils of selfishness and drunkenness. Not having made up my mind as to which vice is worse than the other, for the present I leave gentlemen over their extra bottle to exclaim against selfishness, and the man who buttons up all the world in his own waistcoat to show no mercy towards the disgusting vice of drunkenness.

On the next morning, after reaching Kendal, we had our first really joyous walk of nine miles towards the lake of Windermere. The country was wild and romantic, the weather fine, though not sunny, while the fresh mountain air, and many larks about us, gave us unbounded delight. As we approached the lake, the scenery became more and more grand and beautiful; and from time to time we stayed our steps, gazing intently on it. Hitherto, Keats had witnessed nothing superior to Devonshire; but, beautiful as that is, he was now tempted to speak of it with indifference. At the first turn from the road, before descending to the hamlet of Bowness, we both simultaneously came to a full stop. The lake lay before us. His bright eyes darted on a mountain-peak, beneath which was gently floating on a silver cloud; thence to a very small island, adorned with the foliage of trees, that lay beneath us, and surrounded by water of a glorious hue, when he exclaimed—"How can I believe in that?—surely it cannot be!" He warmly asserted that no view in the world could equal this—that it must beat all Italy—yet, having moved onward but a hundred yards—catching the further extremity of the lake, he thought it "more and more wonderfully beautiful!" The trees far and near, the grass immediately around us, the fern and the furze in their most luxuriant growth, all added to the charm. Not a mist, but an imperceptible vapour bestowed a mellow, softened tint over the immense mountains on the opposite side and at the further end of the lake. To look on them, with their awful accompaniments, though with the eyes of the most stupid, must bring conviction that there is a God!—however he might half persuade himself to the contrary in a city. It is needless to argue that a single blade of grass—which, by the by, is difficult to be found within a city—its formation, its life, its growth—indicates and even displays the same incomprehensible power—that there can be no degrees in incomprehensibility—and much more that can be easily said. But these mountains stood before us,

"To elevate the more-than-reasoning mind;"

and the spirit was bowed in reverence.

(*To be continued.*) C. A. B.

CHAPTER II.

Bowness to Keswick, 22½ *Miles.*

Every thing at the inn of Bowness was within our beck and call. It was spacious, commodious, and flourishing under the patronage of tourists; for whom the whole conduct was as much after the London fashion as possible. Scarcely had we appeared, when a man was putting off a boat. As we were parties concerned in the operation, he being about to fish for a portion of our dinner, we went with him. Never can fishing be more expeditious, or reduced to a greater certainty. After rowing a short distance on the lake, we came among some pieces of floating cork; they were handles to different ropes; fixing on one, he hauled up a wooden cage, where were salmon trout all jumping alive. We returned; and by the time we had hastily refreshed ourselves with bathing, dinner was announced; experience having taught the landlord that the keen appetites of tourists are not to be trifled with by delay. Nothing could be better than our entertainment; no fault could be found; yet—as man is born never to be perfectly contented in this world—we thought the many luxuries, together with the cold, civil, professional formality attending them, but ill accorded with the view from the window; nay, the curtains, furnished by some gay upholsterer, about that very window, might almost be construed into something like an affront.

A walk or a jaunt by the side of Windermere lake to Ambleside has been so much celebrated, that it is difficult to add any thing in the way of description. Not heeding what others have said—why should I?—let me recur to the words of my journal, written at the close of the walk.

These mountains completely surpassed all our expectations. I had seen those of Wales; Keats had not seen any. Yet even he, with all his imagination, could not, until he beheld them, suggest to himself a true idea of their effect on the mind. You may hear people talk eloquently of these scenes; you may see them portrayed by the best painters—language and art are equally inefficient. The reality must be witnessed before it can be understood. What is it—while moving on, at times unconscious of feet, and incapable of uttering more than sudden tokens of wonder—that so presses on the brain, with such awe, with such intense delight? Can it be that the intellect is then susceptible of the sublimest poetry, is throbbing under its influence while bereaved of the power of clothing it in words? Differ as we may on the cause, all will acknowledge the effect. Our road rambled through a wood, or across open spaces, alternately; sometimes climbing on the hill, at other times close on the margin of the lake. There were a thousand enchanting peeps through the branches of the trees as we journied on. The wind had become fresh, waving the foliage and rippling the water—the sound of which, together with the singing of birds, was perfect. That craggy mountain at the head of Windermere increased in grandeur as we proceeded. We stopped; we strolled; we stopped again. At every third step, something new, some change came upon us. A chasm was more distinctly seen; the woods on the opposite side seemed, now and then, to separate as if to display the torrent they had concealed; a new effect of light and shade was shown by some travelling cloud, shrouding midway a mountain, while its head was dazzling in the sun. But how can a walk—so glorious a walk appear on paper? And what can be said of this romantic Ambleside? Here are the beautiful and the sublime in unison. I am inclined to suspect that this is not a fit place for a descriptive poet's residence—his faculty of ideality might ache in vain amidst these realities. Besides, as Rousseau says, who is good authority on this point—"Would I describe a lovely landscape, I must write within four blank walls." The distance from Bowness is no more than six miles; yet from the multiplicity of objects, of sensations, and, possibly, owing to our unavoidable, pleasant loitering on the way, more days than one, at first thought, must have passed since yesterday. Just before entering the inn, I looked up a richly wooded hill, saw a splendid crag rise high above it, around which—thanks to the viewless mists during the day, now congregated into a large thin cloud—the setting sun shot broad and defined rays of gold through the purple hue of the cloud.

As I rewrite this part of my journal, again is every thing brought before me; yet, those who have not enjoyed a visit to the scene, or who have no such artificial aid to memory, may not, by my description, have more than an indistinct notion of it.

If Ambleside is an unfit spot for the writing of a particular kind of poetry, it is far more so for the speaking of particular town-bred impertinence. A young tourist, habited for the occasion like ourselves, accosted us under pretence of conversation. For the sake of reciprocal information, concerning our common purpose, I was at first glad of the meeting. Not a word could be obtained from him on the subject. He was wholly intent on convincing us that he was a better personage than, according to his own suspicion, he appeared. If he did not mistake us for a brace of pedlers, and his uneasiness was a proof that he did not, why could he not rest satisfied in the belief that we did him equal justice? However, that was not enough; his ambition was to be regarded as an important gentleman in disguise. He complained of the awkwardness he felt in wearing an unaccustomed suit of clothes, and then regretting that he had not brought anything else than fashionable boots. Not giving me proper time to digest these miseries, he went on to talk of his uncle's carriage, of Almack's and of the opera, of the futile attempt at Bowness to ape a London hotel, and of the suppers he used to give at Oxford, interlarding this last account with sundry classic quotations, as evidence of his having been educated there. What could be said to this on the banks of Windermere, unless to ask—what route he had taken? "Oh! really I can hardly tell the names of the places!" Then, by an extraordinary process of digression, he inveighed against the silly pride of rank and birth, informing me that his lamented father was unhappily gifted with that failing, and that he left, among his papers, a genealogy traced from Edward the First; but he, at the same time, assured me, he thought nothing whatever of it. With his scholarship at Oxford or elsewhere, for certainly he had brought some away from some place, it is a pity he had not learnt how much obtrusive and unsupported attempts to gain distinction are liable to meet with the worst construction. He was very well as he first appeared; but, right or wrong, I soon harboured a suspicion he was a London sharper. Keats wisely walked off the moment he exposed his folly; and, afterwards, I became savage with myself for not having been savage towards him. Yet that was unreasonable; because no provocation ought to ruffle the temper at Ambleside.

Early the next morning, we sallied forth to see the waterfall about a mile off. Descending to a point of the rock, we beheld an almost perpendicular fall of about thirty feet, formed by two streams at the summit, which fell into a basin, from which another fall gushed forth, at the side, into a fan-like shape; after tumbling over huge fragments of rock, it leapt far, far beneath the spot where we stood. The immense chasm of rock in itself was a noble sight. The grove of trees above our heads, beneath our feet, overhanging every part, so that the branches were interwoven from one side of the torrent to the other, gave it the greatest richness. We went still lower down, till we were on a level with the bottom of the last fall; grasping the trees and edges of rock to prevent our tumbling headlong, when "one false step would be our ruin." Keats scrambled down lightly and quickly; but I never was a sure-footed beast. There we lost the topmost fall, which we had admired, but caught a brother torrent, that tumbled down from an equal height with the other, and they joined together where we stood. After climbing upwards, and at a little distance, we saw the whole in a milder view, from between the branches of the trees, when the water looked like molten silver.

When we returned, in accordance with Keats's desire to pay his respects to Mr. Wordsworth, we went to his house. Unfortunately he had just left Rydale for Lowther Hall. His house had a glorious situation. From the parlour window there was a view of chains of mountains, and of Windermere lake.

An old man escorted us into the park to see the waterfall. On the whole it was not so grand as that at Ambleside. The rocks were inferior; though the water struck us as falling in a more fanciful way. Perhaps it was better for a picture. It was as well wooded, but had not so great a variety of trees. Viewed from high ground, there was certainly a want of wood near the head fall; but that was not the proper place to look at it; and lower down that want was not discernible. The first, or head fall, was thirty feet perpendicular, so as to plunge without touching the rock. Then from the basin below it sprung forward in different ways, and formed, over rocks of various shapes and sizes, an elegant cascade, that almost appeared artificial. The striking merit in it was the contrast between the lower part and the headlong impetuosity of that above. Our old man then led us to another, which he called—"The beauty of the world!" It had nothing sublime about it, however beautiful it deserves to be called. The fall itself is a trifle. Its effect depends on being viewed through the window of a summer-house, and having a little bridge thrown over it. The date on the summer-house is 1617.

We proceeded by the side of Rydale water. It did not greatly please us; it is small; besides, there is not enough wood about it. A little onward, as we looked from a height, it came admirably into the view; and the number of reeds, which I disliked while passing, gave a shadowing in of the banks which had a good effect. Grasmere lake, adjoining it, is far preferable. The opposite shore is beautiful. Mr. Wordsworth formerly had a house there.

His line—

"That ancient woman seated on Helm Crag"

was brought to remembrance as the object itself came in sight. Some whimsically, though naturally disposed stones on the summit of the mountain certainly suggest the idea of a gigantic old woman sitting there. The finest landscape we enjoyed in this stage was when looking back on Grasmere. Thence to Wytheburn, a petty place, just within Cumberland, we had to walk through a defile of treeless mountains, probably the pass which in former times, served as a protection to either county. Here we were at the foot of Helvellyn, rising "far into the clear blue sky." Begging pardon of Mr. Wordsworth that was not the case just then as it was in the midst of large rolling clouds. It is four miles to the summit; whither we intended to ascend on the morrow, should the weather be favourable—if not, we hoped for better luck with Mount Skiddaw.

During the night there had fallen much rain; many fleas were in the beds; and in the morning, clouds and drizzling rain prevented us from ascending Helvellyn. We passed Hurles Water, a small lake, by no means well wooded; but the water itself was wonderfully transparent. For some little way the country was not interesting; and clouds rested on every mountain around us. As the weather became clearer, we observed that the character of the scenery was different from what we had seen in Westmoreland. The hills were rounder, stretched their bases further, and, in one sense, being less craggy, might be called more graceful. A traveller might be excused for calling the entrance into Keswick vale gorgeous and tremendous; it surpassed that of Windermere, though quite in a different style. A view up Derwent Water, with the nest of mountains there, was the finest part; though Bassenthwaite Water at the right hand, with mighty Skiddaw at its side, was scarcely inferior. It is a profusion of wood that gives Derwent water so much richness.

When wound up to enthusiasm for natural objects, it is like enduring a direct act of hostility to meet with something brought from the depths of sophistication. At the inn here, near mid-day, came a yawning dandy from his bed-room, and sat at his breakfast reading a bouncing novel!

(*To be continued.*) C. A. B.

CHAPTER III.

Keswick to Dalbeattie 82 *miles.*

Keswick is not a place to glance at, and then to be quitted, or to be afterwards visited with a mere nod of recognition. Our first jaunt was to walk entirely round Derwent Water, commencing with the east side. The fall of Lodore, however, disappointed us. Its situation is admirable—a mountain with an immense division, both sides nearly perpendicular, where ash trees grow in an inexplicable manner from top to bottom, without apparent nourishment from the earth. In no part is the fall itself of any height, though the water comes from an extraordinary one. That is, it tumbles, it jostles from rock to rock—it turns head over heels, but never once takes a leap. The nest of mountains, at the south end, which had so much attracted our admiration in the morning, still maintained its grandeur on a near view, and we could find none so fine. From the west side, on our return, is the best view of the scenery, though both are enchanting. A walk of only twelve miles completes the circuit.

In the evening we visited the Druidical remains. They are situated a mile and a half off, at the top of the first hill, rising out of the valley, on the road to Penrith, upon circular flat ground, now a field. There are many of them, in the form of a large circle, with others in an oval form touching one part of the inner circumference. Surrounded by a majestic panorama, the spot is suited to render the human mind awestruck, and, possibly, with the ignorant, superstitious.

Nothing was wanting in the town, at least by attempts, to please a London taste. It was full of lures to pass away the time—a circulating library, a fossil museum, an exhibition of Mr. Green's drawings, and a camera obscura. In the last we beheld our mountain scenery in miniature, and were made fully aware of the reason, why the best artist's representation must necessarily be inefficient. Simple magnitude possesses an effect of its own; deprive it of that quality, and, no longer being the same, it cannot possess the same effect. But this is not all: the character and accompaniments of a mountain are utterly destroyed when reduced to an undefinable—nay, an impercessible entity.

A promising morning authorized a guide to call us up at four o'clock, in order to ascend Skiddaw. The distance to the summit from the town is a little more than six miles. Its height, from the level of the sea, is 3,022 feet; but only 1,952 feet above Derwent water—so lofty is all this part of the country. Helvellyn and Skawfell are somewhat higher, but the view from Skiddaw is esteemed the best. In a short time the continued steep became fatiguing; and then, while looking upward to what I thought was no very great distance from the top, it sounded like cruelty to hear from our guide that we were exactly half way! Still, in a colder atmosphere, together with the extraordinary pure air, we climbed merrily; till the guide shook his head, prophesying of clouds and rain, as a cloud passed over the peak, gradually spreading downwards. We went on, till within three quarters of a mile to the summit, when we were enveloped in a hopeless cloud. Not able to see twenty yards around us, it was useless, unless for the sake of saying we had achieved the task, to proceed. It was fortunate we had opportunities of seeing every thing, from the winding road, before the mist came; and the guide confessed that the only advantage we lost was the not having it in our power to see every thing from the same point. After all, I was not much gratified by this sort of bird's-eye view. If you would be delighted with a garden, it is surely better to walk in it, than to stare down upon it from a garret-window. It must be acknowledged there is some thing grand in looking down on a country, as if it were a map; but the strangeness of the sight, more than any thing else, is its attraction. The mountains, which but yesterday I had gazed on with reverence, became comparatively insignificant. People talk of the extensive prospect—it may be too extensive. The hills on the other side of Lancaster appeared to us, and what of that? We had a discernment of Solway Firth, and the coast of Dumfries and Galloway; but any other Firth, and any other coast would have been the same. The rain came to cool my critical reflections. During the sultry weather below, the winter's snow had not melted; even now, at the end of June, on Helvellyn and Skawfell we saw patches of snow still remaining. It is a sad jolting trot down a mountain—a man's inside seems mixing together like a Scotch haggis. The views of the vale of Keswick, and of other places, from the lower part of Skiddaw, I thought preferable to the loftier ones.

We passed by Bassenthwaite Water, a lake of little repute; it possesses great simplicity of character, and, in some points, its clear and deeply shadowed water had a beautiful effect; it is five or six miles in length. As we approached its north end, we were astonished at the sudden change of scene before us—no mountains, but highly cultivated hills and dales, similar to most parts of Devon, only not so luxuriant.

Without a touch of regret we kept our backs towards the wonders of Cumberland and Westmoreland; for we chalked out a tour in another direction among them, on our return from the Highlands.

Ireby is said to be the oldest market town in the county—with not much of a market. It is a dull, beggarly looking place. Our inn was remarkably clean and neat, and the old host and hostess were very civil and preposessing—but, heyday! what were those obstreperous doings over head? It was a dancing school under the tuition of a travelling master! Folks here were as partial to dancing as their neighbours, the Scotch; and every little farmer sent his young ones to take lessons. We went up stairs to witness the skill of these rustic boys and girls—fine, healthy, clean-dressed, and withal, perfectly orderly, as well as serious in their endeavours. We noticed some among them quite handsome, but the attention of none was drawn aside to notice us. The instant the fiddles struck up, the slouch in the gait was lost, the feet moved, and gracefully, with complete conformity to the notes; and they wove the figure, sometimes extremely complicated to my inexperienced eyes, without an error, or the slightest pause. There was no sauntering, half-asleep country dance among them; all were inspired, yet by

> "Nae cotillion brent new frae France;
> "But hornpipes, jigs, strathspeys, and reels
> "Put life and mettle in their heels."

From time to time, on our way to Carlisle, old Skiddaw raised his head above the hills, as if to watch the progress of his late visitors. We were continually saluted on the road with—"a fine day!—a nice day!"—a voluntary and cheerful thanksgiving. "Merry Carlisle" did not, to our thinking, maintain its epithet—the whole art of yawning might have been learned there. The cathedral is better on the outside than within, where it is poor in size and in architecture; besides being spoiled by whitewash. The Castle, of which we had heard much, is very ancient—they call it 900 years old. It is a massy, ugly building; part is used as Barracks, part as a Magazine. We were displeased with the Court houses, modern buildings, though they give a grandeur to the entrance. They are exactly alike; each consisting of a square Gothic building, to which adjoins a very squab round tower; like a tea-caddy and low sugar-dish placed side by side.

Gretna Green is a sad, ominous place for a young couple—poverty-struck and barren! Aware there was nothing interesting in the country between Carlisle and Dumfries, and that, consequently, it would be toil without remuneration, we coached the distance. Till near the end of our ride, there was, indeed, little worth a traveller's regard. Certainly Dumfries stands in a delightful situation. Neither of us expected to remark much difference between English and Scotch towns, generally speaking; but it appeared as if we had stepped into a foreign country. It might be difficult to define in what the distinction lies; for perhaps it consists in numerous small particulars, each unimportant in itself. Without prejudice, however, it did not wear the air of comfort belonging to an English town; but that may have arisen from my not understanding what they possessed for those things which I, as a stranger, missed. The churchyard is the best site near the town for a view. It might be called an enviable place to lie in, and I rejoice that Burns is buried there; for though it may be truly argued that the situation of a grave matters nothing to the dead, yet it matters a great deal to the living —to his family, no doubt; and all Great Britain belongs to the family of a poet like Burns.

His mausoleum is a handsome structure, of red stone, but painted white; surrounded by iron rails, enclosing a flower and shrub garden, rather formally set out, but kept in great neatness. I have since seen a model for an appropriate basso-relievo to adorn this mausoleum. Such memorials to great men in the intellectual world, especially over their graves, should not be neglected. They may excite emulation; they must inspire reverence and gratitude, two feelings of which man is susceptible to the improvement of his nature.

Two miles off are the ruins of Lincluden College. The artist, according to my engraving has done them justice, giving an exact likeness. Praise for great beauty may be honestly bestowed on the Chapel. It was once admirable for much fine workmanship about the cornices and capitals, but it is now nearly effaced; the stone being rather soft, and the climate rather hard. There are several vaults beneath, very like the dungeons we read of, for the heretical, the refractory, or the frail.

To our minds the people we had seen and conversed with, both in and out of the town, were more serious and solidly inanimated than necessary. They had a quiet expression and manner, which might be construed into happiness! but why put strangers to the trouble of forming a favourable interpretation? They are, also, in their speech, tedious, slow, and drawling. Except two or three girls, who returned our "speerings"—alias, usual salutations—on the road, with a sort of grin, we did not perceive an approach to a laugh. If laughter, as it is said, proves our distinction from other animals, the line did not seem to be correctly drawn between them and these northerns.

We had been recommended to seek entertainment at the village of Dalbeattie from a Mr. Murray. Besides keeping a *Public*, he kept a shop below, supplying every one in the district with almost every article, from tea down to candles and brick dust, ironmongery of all sorts, whiskey, broad cloth, sheeting, printed cottons, pens, ink and paper. It was a day appointed by the Kirk for a fast in that parish; and, therefore, the shop was shut, and Mrs. Murray only at home. From some unexplained cause, she was at first unwilling to let us enter—she "didna ken what to say!" Such doubts sound cruelly in the ears of hungry travellers, and should be visited with a grievous penalty. A saunter through the village was pleasant, as the cottages were neat, clean, and snug-looking. Then the inhabitants whom we saw were very clean and healthy faced, and every one of the children was dressed tidily—possibly this was partly owing to its being a holiday, but, even then, it was a credit to the village. A chubby urchin stared in alarm at the strangers, and, when called a "fat pig," he cried and screamed till he brought out an "auld wific" upon us. She was "nae pleased to see bairns made game of." Atonement was made by a sixpence in the child's hand—his plump fingers closed over it with a true Scotch grasp, tight as the claw of a lobster; and off he went to take his place in a formal circle of children, who were amusing themselves by sitting down with their hands before them, in perfect silence—no wonder they grow up to be such staid men and women. Soon after this, a "sonsie lassie" put her head out of a cottage door. "There's a pretty girl!"—out came her shoulders. "A very pretty girl indeed!"—out she came on the threshold; and as we passed on, she stretched her neck out, like a goose in a coop, for more of the barley. But, all the time, she maintained an unbecoming gravity.

In the evening Mr. Murray informed us, to our sorrow that we had come by the wrong road for a beautiful country. Had we gone some eight or ten miles round, by what is perversely called the ruins of *New* Abbey, or Sweet-Heart Abbey, and the sea coast, we should have witnessed, he assured us, the finest scenery in the south of Scotland. His description was very enticing, but to return at the cost of forty miles was out of the question, and we rather hoped that he romanced. He gave us our route for the morrow, six miles astray, to Kirkcudbright, and promised we should be enchanted with it. He boasted of the trade of his shop; and told us he had a better retail trade than any man in Dumfries, and that he had taken as much as sixty three pounds in a day. "This village," said he, "did not exist thirty years ago; at that time it was a bog full of rocky stones. The gentleman who built it died the very day I had my leg cut off."

"I look down at his feet—but that is a fable,"

thought I with the philosophic Othello. Yet it was true, he had only five inches of thigh on his right side. I might have seen him a thousand times without guessing he had a wooden leg, so admirably was it made, so perfect in the joints—he scarcely walked lame, and was more active than most men with their two natural legs.

(*To be continued.*) C. A. B.

CHAPTER IV.

Dalbeattie to Ballantrae, 92 *miles.*

Thanks to Mr. Murray's directions, our first stage of eight miles to Auchencairn, a village, was delightful, with noble views on both sides, of wooded hills and craggy mountains to the right, and of a lovely landscape, wherein a lough of the sea appeared like a lake, to the left—a small bush-covered island near the shore added to the charm. For the most part, our track lay through corn-fields, or skirting small forests. I chatted half the way about Guy Mannering, for it happened that Keats had not then read that novel, and I enjoyed the recollection of the events as I described them in their own scenes. There was a little spot, close to our pathway, where, without a shadow of doubt, old Meg Merrilies had often boiled her kettle, and, haply, cooked a chicken. It was among fragments of rock, and brambles, and broom, and most tastefully ornamented with a profusion of honeysuckle, wild roses, and fox-glove, all in the very blush and fullness of blossom. While finishing breakfast, and both employed in writing, I could not avoid noticing that Keats's letter was not running in regular prose. He told me he was writing to his little sister, and giving a ballad on old Meg for her amusement. Though he called it too much a trifle to be copied, I soon inserted it in my Journal. It struck me as a good description of that mystic link between mortality and the weired sisters; and, at the same time, in appropriate language to the person addressed.

MEG MERRILIES.

Old Meg she was a gipsy,
  And lived upon the moors;
Her bed it was the brown heath-turf,
  And her house was out of doors.
Her apples were swart blackberries,
  Her currants, pods o' broom,
Her wine was dew of the wild white rose,
  Her book a church-yard tomb!

Her brothers were the craggy hills,
  Her sisters larchen trees;
Alone with her great family
  She lived as she did please.
No breakfast had she many a morn,
  No dinner many a noon,
And, 'stead of supper, she would stare
  Full hard against the moon!

But every morn, of woodbine fresh,
  She made her garlanding;
And every night, the dark glen yew
  She wove, and she would sing.
And with her fingers, old and brown,
  She plaited mats of rushes,
And gave them to the cottagers
  She met among the bushes.

Old Meg was brave as Margaret Queen,
  And tall as amazon,
An old red blanket cloak she wore,
  A chip-hat had she on;—
God rest her aged bones somewhere!
  She died full long agone.

The road to Kirkcudbright is ten miles; but we chose to add a couple more to them, in order to pass through Dundrennan, and see the Abbey. It is the ruin of a stately building, and must have bordered on the magnificent in its original state. Trees were not only growing about, but on the walls. There was, especially, a flourishing ash, that did not appear to derive any nourishment from earth; the root spreading itself down the wall, curving its branches between the stones, some forty feet from the ground, and feeding, as far as we could judge, on the mortar alone. Probably the mortar was in a nutritious state of decay. With the town not far before us, we were enchanted with the view; the winding bay—the wood-covered hills—the blue mountains beyond them—the island at the mouth of the bay—the sea on each side of it, and in the distance—the extraordinary fertility of the valley, and the surrounding country—all formed a scene that even Keats confessed to be equal and similar to the best parts of his favourite Devon. As we nearer approached the town, through the valley, every thing was in a most luxuriant state; the trees, the corn, the verdure, and even the hedges—nothing could surpass them. We visited the Castle, but were disappointed with those ruins. The date over the door is 1583; which sufficiently explains the ugliness of the architecture.

We began to like the natives much better. That cold, solemn Dumfries is a befitting place wherein to write a libel on the Scotch. For two days we had been admiring the people's neatness of attire, their civility, and their intelligence, both in feature and in speech—for I conversed with all I could. A comparison between them and our labouring classes would be, I am afraid, in these respects, not a little against us. That neatness of attire, however, in the women made me the more object to their not wearing shoes and stockings. Keats was of an opposite opinion, and expatiated on the beauty of a human foot, that had grown without an unnatural restraint, and on the beautiful effect of colour when a young lassie's foot was on the green grass. All this I freely acknowledged; but to see the same foot stumping through the dust of the road, or, what is worse, dabbling in the puddles of a town is the reverse of beautiful. It must be owned that, generally speaking, after trudging with bare feet on the road, to save the wear of shoes and stockings, they put them on just before entering a town.

To arrive at Gate House costs four miles to the top of a hill, and four more to the bottom. Fleet bay and its banks might be highly praised by those who have not seen the bay of Kirkcudbright. Taking the sea-side road to Cree Town, four miles longer than the usual road, we became acquainted with a custom which I wish were more general in all countries. We soon met, returning to Gate House, men, women and children, of all ages and descriptions. It looked like an emigration, and we inquired the reason; when "The salt water" was the reply; and truly the greater proportion of the population had taken the opportunity of high tide to wash and be clean, where a jutting rock on the coast separated the sexes; and, moreover, they told us it was their daily custom. There was nothing else remarkable in this stage except a deep glen, full of large trees, with a mountain stream running below—a spot that Meg Merrilies must have often frequented. Thence to Newton Stewart (quondam, Newton Douglas) Glenluce, Stranrawer, and Cairn, there was not scenery worth speaking of, though it was pleasant walking.

Our host at Stranrawer told us that, after leaving Cairn, there was a very bad road, either for horses or foot-passengers, being quite mountainous. From this account we promised ourselves a walk of twelve miles full of pleasure; nor were we disappointed. The first mile from Cairn was by the margin of the sea; then the road took a rise on the hill, that sloped, rather awfully, down to the coast. We there, after two miles of ascent, were about midway between the summit and the base. The view above us was grand, and that below both grand and beautiful. We stopped awhile. It was full tide, and the waves were dashing among the rocks, or telling their old tale in the hollow caverns. We proceeded; and, ever and anon, we crossed a little brig, that carried us over some deep, narrow, wooded glen. Yet all this was nothing to the vale of Glenap, through which we had to pass, and which, notwithstanding the length of our day's journey, we should have been sorry to find less than six miles in extent. The entrance to it was like an enchanted region:

the mountains so rich with trees, and so various in their shades of green, and the valley itself delightfully wooded, and the silent charm of little cottages at every turn—surely it was another world! For some days we had not met with any scenery fit to inspire raptures; but here our patience was rewarded. Onward as we moved, mountain beyond mountain, all clothed in the liveliest verdure, either of tree or herbage, together with the never ceasing change of prospect on all sides, they—"made us quite forget our labour and our toil." A little rain fell; but the clouds were still high, and there was not enough to obscure the atmosphere. At the end of the valley we had to climb a steep ascent, until we looked round on the tops of the neighbouring hills, and often did we cast our eyes beneath on that glen, from which we were loth to part. There, as we strode along, snuffing up the mountain air,—most exhilirating to those who have been long trudging on a plain—a sight of Ailsa rock came upon us like something supernatural. It was seventeen miles distant, rising perpendicularly from the sea nine hundred and forty feet. The strangeness of appearance was occasioned by its seeming to possess an invisible footing above the sea; as the horizon, the sea, was considerably lower than its apparent first rise—that is, the lowest part which, at that distance, could be perceived by us—an optical illusion. This rock is famous, like many others on the coast of Scotland, for sea-foul, and its rental was fifty pounds a year. There is a path-way to its summit; but, at that height, and standing so far off from the shore, there could not be a view from it to afford me much pleasure.

At nearly the close of our day's journey the rain fell in earnest, and we hastened down to Ballantrae, near the sea-shore, taking up our quarters in that little town, at a dirty inn—the first of that description we had entered in Scotland. We had been warned not to go to the Post-chaise-inn, as things might not be quite comfortable there, because the landlord was a little in trouble. A little in trouble!—he had been just taken up for being concerned in robbing the Paisley bank! Coming into the town, a lassie afforded some amusement by mistaking us, with our neat knapsacks, for jewellers, and by her eagerness to inspect the supposed finery.

I asked an old man, who spoke on several subjects with much intelligence, if he had ever seen his countryman Burns, or what he had heard of him. It was soon evident I had not pitched on one with the right intelligence. "I ha' ne'er seen that Burns," quoth he, "but I parfecly approve o' him; for he may ha' had, and so in fac I think, some guid sense; an', what I nae much ken o', he had a clever knack o' rhyming." Alas! a poet, no more than a prophet, is honoured in his own district!

A stormy night followed; "Dan Æolus, in great displeasure sent forth the winds"—

> "They breaking forth with rude unruliment
> "From all four parts of heaven do rage full sore,
> "And toss the deeps and tear the firmament";

and then at the end of every half hour—

> "All suddenly a stormy whirlwind blew
> "Throughout the house, that clapped every door";

so that, after our long walk, when watchfulness should not have been the order of the night, we met each other in the morning with mutual condolence on the want of sleep. Miserable accommodation! How provoking that the master of the good inn should have been so sillily improvident as to be taken up for a robbery, inflicting a bad lodging on us as well as on himself!

C. A. B.

(*To be Continued.*) [2]

[2] No further instalment was published (see I, 328 n.).

Lightning Source UK Ltd.
Milton Keynes UK
UKHW041021160822
407306UK00008B/323